Drugs and Popular Culture

Drugs and Popular Culture
Drugs, media and identity in contemporary society

edited by

Paul Manning

WILLAN
PUBLISHING

Published by

Willan Publishing
Culmcott House
Mill Street, Uffculme
Cullompton, Devon
EX15 3AT, UK
Tel: +44(0)1884 840337
Fax: +44(0)1884 840251
e-mail: info@willanpublishing.co.uk
website: www.willanpublishing.co.uk

Published simultaneously in the USA and Canada by

Willan Publishing
c/o ISBS, 920 NE 58th Ave, Suite 300,
Portland, Oregon 97213-3786, USA
Tel: +001(0)503 287 3093
Fax: +001(0)503 280 8832
e-mail: info@isbs.com
website: www.isbs.com

First published 2007

Hardback
ISBN-13: 978-1-84392-211-7

Paperback
ISBN-13: 978-1-84392-210-0

British Library Cataloguing-in-Publication Data

A catalogue record for this book is available from the British Library

Project managed by Deer Park Productions, Tavistock, Devon
Typeset by GCS, Leighton Buzzard, Bedfordshire, LU7 1AR
Printed and bound by T.J. International Ltd, Padstow, Cornwall

Contents

Notes on contributors

Judith Aldridge is Senior Lecturer in the School of Law at the University of Manchester. Her research is in the areas, drug use, the ethics of drug research, drug economies, and youth gangs. She is co-author of *Illegal Leisure* and *Dancing on Drugs* with Howard Parker and Fiona Measham. She was Research Fellow in SPARC at the University of Manchester.

Andrew Blake is Associate Head of Cultural Studies at the University of East London. An occasional saxophonist and composer, his writings include *The Music Business* (1992); *The Land without Music: Music, Culture and Society in Twentieth Century Britain* (1997); the edited collection *Living through Pop* (1999); and a contribution to *The Cambridge History of Twentieth Century Music* (2004). He is also the author or editor of books on sport, fiction, and consumer culture, including *The Irresistible Rise of Harry Potter* (2002), which has been translated into five languages.

Paul Carter is Programme Director for Media Production and Senior Lecturer in Media and Film Studies at the University of Winchester. His research interests include the relationship between broadcasting institutions and text, new media technologies and early cinema technologies. He has extensive experience as a broadcast journalist having worked for a variety of news organisations including the BBC.

Simon Cross is Senior Lecturer in Media and Communications at the University of Lincoln, UK. His research explores media representations of sensitive public policy issues including madness/mental distress and paedophiles released into the community. He is currently writing a book for Palgrave MacMillan entitled *Mediating Madness: Mental Distress and Cultural Representation*.

Oluyinka Esan is a Senior Lecturer in Media Studies at the University of Winchester. She is interested in the impact of the media on society. Much of her work has focused on the social relevance of media messages. This includes research into production practices and audience reception of media messages. Dr Esan's perspective is enriched by her lecturing experience at the Department of Mass Communication, University of Lagos, Nigeria, and an interesting portfolio of consultancy work on behaviour change communication, and advocacy for women, youth and children. She has worked with UNICEF, UNFPA, UNIFEM, other international bodies, and local NGOs in Nigeria. She holds a PhD in Sociology from the University of Glasgow.

Elizabeth Ettorre is Professor of Sociology at the University of Liverpool. She has interests in the sociology of health and illness as well as deviance including the sociology of substance use including both legal and illegal drugs; gender; sociology of the new genetics; new reproductive technologies; depression and mental health and autoethnography. She has published widely in these areas.

Sarah Dalal Goode is a medical sociologist and researcher. She is Director of the Research and Policy Centre for the Study of Faith and Wellbeing in Communities and she currently lectures on community development, health and social care at the University of Winchester. Her research interests are in non-mainstream behaviours and negotiating problematic identities. She has published in the areas of substance use and understanding adult sexual behaviour towards children.

Leighton Grist is Senior Lecturer in Film Studies, University of Winchester. A film specialist, he has published on a range of areas and issues, including work on classical and post-classical Hollywood, on film theory, on genre and on film authorship (and, especially, the filmmaker Martin Scorsese).

Vanessa Harbour is a research student at the University of Winchester. Her research interests include representation/representing problems in young adult fiction with particular reference to drugs and sex. Her first novel for children is to be published shortly.

Laura Hübner is a Senior Lecturer in Media and Film Studies at the University of Winchester. Most of her publications are in the area of European cinema, including *The Films of Ingmar Bergman: Illusions of Light and Darkness* (2007) and a chapter in *Studies in European Cinema* (2005). Her article on drugs and childbirth stems from long-standing research interests in cultural constructions of the female body.

Richard Huggins is the Assistant Dean of Social Sciences and Law, Oxford Brookes University. He has published widely on media, politics and democracy and globalisation, including the co-authored *Politics: An Introduction* (1997/2002, Routledge) and *New Media and Politics* (2001, Sage) together with a variety of chapters and articles on themes relating to criminal and social justice, public order issues, community and urban renewal and substance misuse. In recent years he has conducted a number of research projects in substance misuse issues. He is also a director and trustee of three UK-based drug charities.

Paul Manning is Head of Film and Media at the University of Winchester. His publications include *Spinning for Labour: Trade Unions and the New Media*

Environment (1998) and *News and News Sources* (2001). His research interests lie in the areas of the symbolic representation of drug consumption in popular culture, the mediated nature of crime, power relationships and news sources and the sociology of journalism.

Andrew Melrose is Professor of Children's Writing and Director of the MAs in Writing for Children and Creative and Critical Writing at the University of Winchester. He has over a hundred writing credits for films, books, songs, chapters and articles, including *The Story Keepers* animation series for ITV and international broadcast, *Write for Children* and chapters on various aspects of literature and creative and critical ideas. He is presently developing a book, an exhibition and a film on global warming; working on a project entitled *BoysDontRead* and writing a novel set in Brighton.

Tim Newburn is Professor of Criminology and Social Policy, Director of the Mannheim Centre for Criminology at the London School of Economics, and President of the British Society of Criminology. His main research interests lie in the areas of policing and security, young people and social exclusion, and comparative criminal justice and penal policy.

Howard Parker is Emeritus Professor in the School of Law at Manchester University. He has returned to consultancy, research and training with front-line Drug, Alcohol and Young People's Services.

Michael Shiner is a senior research officer in the Mannheim Centre for Criminology at the London School of Economics. His main research interests are young people, drugs and crime. He has published widely in these areas and has also helped to run a drugs agency in south London.

Lisa Williams is in the final stages of her PhD at the University of Manchester. Her current research focuses on risk and pleasure in both recreational and dependent drug taking, and she is analysing further data she has collected as part of North West England Longitudinal Study. She was Research Fellow at SPARC at the University of Manchester.

Part 1

Context, Theory and History

Introduction

Paul Manning

In an episode of the television drama *Shameless*, broadcast on Channel Four in February 2006, Lip, one of the main young characters seeks relief from his relationship troubles in the familiar pub of the series. Leaning wearily across the bar he orders a pint of lager, a whisky chaser and an 'E' from the barman who supplements his pub wages with a little local drug dealing. This is interesting for two reasons: firstly, because it portrays a picture of routine, normalised but illegal, recreational drug use which is not so very far removed from the everyday lived realities of many 'ordinary' young people in the UK today. Customers may not be able to order recreational drugs from the counter in pubs yet, but they are quite likely to be on sale somewhere near the bar. And secondly, it is interesting for the point that within the show this scene is presented as a fleeting, mundane moment of little consequence. Other, much more exciting things happen to Lip in this episode and his consumption of lager, whisky and ecstasy is represented as little more significant than what he had for lunch.

Here, then, is popular television drama offering us a picture of normalised poly-drug use as routine, everyday life. And, of course, this is hardly an isolated example of the representation of drug use in popular culture. From cinema, through television and popular fiction, to contemporary popular music (Blake (Chapter 5), Carter (Chapter 9) and Esan (Chapter 11) in this volume), the imagery of widespread drug consumption has, itself, become normalised. Even the moralising British daily red-top newspapers appear almost as frequently to condone as to condemn celebrity 'soft drug' use. In short, the media institutions that circulate and reproduce commodified forms of popular culture are very much more comfortable in dealing with themes of drug consumption than in previous decades. It is tempting to attribute this to important changes in 'real', lived popular culture: perhaps more films and television dramas feature drug consumption because more people see drug use as a normalised pattern of consumption. Measham and Brain (2005) point to a new 'culture of intoxication', suggesting that both alcohol and illegal drug use are now much more central elements in the dance and club cultures supported by the expanding commercial leisure industry of the late twentieth and early twenty-first centuries. Indeed, some critics point to the part played by the alcohol and club-based leisure industries in marketing, promoting and implicitly fostering this 'culture of intoxication' (Blake in Chapter 5 of this volume; Measham and Bain 2005). However, it is important to retain the distinction between *representations* of drug use through media and cultural institutions, and the cultural practices of those actually consuming drugs. In other words, an examination of the place of drug consumption in popular culture involves a consideration of both mainstream media representations and the 'real' cultural practices of ordinary people.

This volume brings together contributions from 15 different authors, who approach the relationship between drug use and popular culture from distinct disciplinary positions, including sociology, criminology, cultural studies, media studies and film studies. The approach is, thus, inter-disciplinary in bringing together contributions from these distinct disciplines, but it is hoped that this produces more than simply a collection of discrete papers. There is a coherence in that each discipline helps to illuminate the ways in which representations of drug consumption are mediated and the ways in which the cultural practices of drug consumption are reproduced through the micro-politics of daily life.

Licit and illicit drug consumption have always been lived elements of popular culture and, for that reason, have always provided subject matter for popular cultural texts. However, the approaches within this volume help us to explore the extent to which the popular cultural practices associated with drug consumption, and their mediated representations, have shifted from the sub-cultural to the mainstream. While there are some differences in approach and emphasis, the various contributions to this volume share a number of key assumptions. Firstly, there is, of course, the view that drug consumption is a popular cultural practice and that its mediations through society are of importance. For example, the very distinction between licit and illicit drugs is maintained through cultural definitions that are socially and politically administered. That, in some cases, these distinctions blur or erode, is itself, further confirmation of their cultural nature. Secondly, while by no means all explicitly embracing the vocabulary of this analysis, in practice, all the approaches within this volume tell us something about the symbolic frameworks within which patterns of drug consumption are framed or understood. These symbolic frameworks construct particular substances in particular ways, by associating such substances with certain social groups or identities rather than others, and by mobilising particular forms of language, and symbolism (Manning 2006 and Manning in this volume). Each of these chapters makes a contribution to understanding how and why these symbolic frameworks are reproduced and how they change, through processes of representation in television, cinema, newspapers and other media, or by examining the place of these symbolic frameworks in popular culture and everyday life. More work needs to be done, particularly of an ethnographic kind, in terms of exploring the ways in which media representations of drugs and the understandings of drug consumption, constructed at the micro-level in the course of everyday life, may intersect. But an approach that places the construction of symbolic frameworks, through mainstream media, and in the course of daily life at the micro level, has a lot of potential for future enquiry.

Another common assumption underpinning the approaches here is that the symbolic frameworks of drug consumption or substance misuse are historically specific and historically rooted. The language, symbols, imagery and associations with particular social identities that make up these symbolic frameworks, all have histories. They are a product, in part, of the exertion of power at specific historical moments, but also through the contests and skirmishes involving those 'at the bottom' as popular culture serves as a site of resistance to subordination. Andrew Blake in Chapter 2 provides an account of the imperialist pressures and colonial discourses at play in the construction of the discourses around opium and cannabis use in the late nineteenth and early twentieth centuries. This story is picked up and developed through the twentieth century as a backdrop to Simon Cross' analysis of confused public debate over cannabis classification (Chapter 7). As Andrew Blake underlines, in this imperial history, we find the roots of a number of powerful symbols and discourses, that are still at play and continue to contribute to contemporary symbolic frameworks. This chapter demonstrates very clearly the ways in which medical and political, as well as popular discourses generated symbolic frameworks that often racialised drug consumption and these frameworks surfaced, and re-surfaced, not only in official policy documents but in popular culture – nineteenth century novels and twentiety century cinema, the fiction of Dickens and Fleming, together with films about Fu Manchu. Significantly, this chapter also points to the cultural significance, during this historical period, of drug paraphernalia – the equipment or technology of consumption. The symbolism of the equipment, as well as the substances, is an important component of each symbolic framework of 'substance misuse'.

The first chapter in Part 1, however, provides a review of the main attempts to theorise the relationship between drug consumption and popular culture. It discusses the movement away from understanding drug consumption as a symptom of individual 'weakness', that characterised many of the most important approaches in the inter-war and immediate post-war years. Drug users at this time were often theorised as being in the grip 'forces' either located within the weak individual (moral weakness, psychological flaws, for example), or externally and signified by the inability of weak individuals to adjust to their social circumstances, if facing the 'blocked opportunities' typical of working class life. However, by the end of the twentieth century, there are very significant theoretical shifts that take account of the growing importance of consumption within popular culture, and of the centrality of media in contemporary social formations. If consumption and popular culture now occupy positions at the heart of late modern capitalism, then drug consumption is a further extension of the same cultural practices. If identity is invested in the things we consume, it is possible to see 'drug styles' (individual patterns of choice) in the context of the self-narratives individuals construct to make sense of themselves and their locations. These drug consumers are not necessarily either passive or weak. The constraints or possibilities of class, or gender, locality or ethnicity, have not disappeared. But contemporary social theory sees the development of 'drug styles' as part of the way in which individuals negotiate their experience of these structures to construct their own narratives. The remaining chapters in this book continue to prompt the intriguing questions: 'do the symbolic frameworks' mediated by mainstream or 'micro' media provide some of the resources whereby individuals use to think how they 'frame' different substances, who or what identities they associate those substances with, and how they choose to consume them.

References and suggested reading

Boyd, S. (2002) 'Media Constructions of Illegal Drugs, Users, and Sellers: A Closer Look at Traffic', *The International Journal of Drugs Policy*, 13: 397–407.

Manning, P. (2006) 'There's No Glamour in Glue: News and the Symbolic Framing of Substance Misuse', *Crime Media Culture*, 2 (1), April 2006.

Measham, F. and Brain, K. (2005): '"Binge" Drinking, British Alcohol Policy and the New Culture of Intoxication', *Crime Media Culture*, 1(3), December 2005.

Mignon, P. (1993) 'Drugs and Popular Music: The Democratisation of Bohemia', *Popular Cultural Studies*, 1: 175–191.

Shapiro, H. (2002) 'From Chaplin to Charlie – Cocaine, Hollywood and the Movies', *Drugs: Prevention Education and Policy*, 9 (2): 132–141.

Stevenson, J. (1999) *Addicted: The Myth and Menace of Drugs in Films*. New York: Creation Books.

1. An introduction to the theoretical approaches and research traditions

Paul Manning

Introduction

Early social and cultural theoretical approaches tended to focus either upon the 'real' social practices within drug consuming subcultures, or upon the ways in which drug consumption was represented or mis-represented in media coverage. Less attention was given to the, possibly quite subtle, relationships between each of these dimensions. Thus, for example, 'classical' moral panic theory has tended to begin with discussions of mainstream media representations, and to move from these to potential impacts upon policing, policy making or spectacular forms of deviancy amplification. But the rapidly changing media landscape of the twenty-first century seems too complex for unamended or 'classical' moral panic theory. Some critics question whether an overriding concern with 'mainstream media' is so relevant to an age in which many members of the public (including, of course, younger, potential drug consumers) gather so much of their information from 'less mainstream', media sources, such as fanzines, the music press, and electronic sources (McRobbie and Thornton 1995). And secondly, to offer models of 'media essentialism' which locate problems entirely in terms of media representation and not at all in terms of 'real' behaviours seems equally problematic (Murji 1998; Schlesinger 1990).

Significantly for the concerns of this book, the more recent criminological and sociological work on patterns of drug use has found it important to take account of the cultural and media contexts within which drug consumption occurs. Thus, for example, Measham, Aldridge and Parker (2001) locate contemporary recreational drug use within the context of dance culture and its antecedents in earlier youth subcultural forms, while Hammersley, Khan and Ditton (2002) include an extended discussion of perceptions held by their respondents of the media and symbolic representation of drugs, alongside data on patterns of use. The wider media effects debate is beyond the concerns of this volume. However, one of the assumptions underpinning the approaches in this book is that while media and symbolic representations of drug consumption and drug users should be distinguished from the *actual* social and cultural practices of drug use, it is important to acknowledge the possible interplays between the two. Such interplays are likely to be complex and certainly not mono-causal. For example, Hammersley, Khan and Ditton report that many of their ecstasy using respondents claimed to despise mainstream media representations of drug use and yet, 'a surprisingly large' number of these respondents indicated that they relied upon media rather than friends for their drug information (2002: 116). An equally complex picture is painted by Jenkins' study of 'designer drugs' in the US. Jenkins notes, on the one hand, growing public scepticism with regard to the more lurid drug scare stories circulated in the news media because an increasing proportion of the news audience has direct or indirect experience of drug use against which it can assess news media claims (1999: 18–19). And yet, Jenkins also thinks it possible that some patterns of media and popular cultural representation can have some impact in shaping fashions in drug use through the construction of symbolic frameworks that valorise particular drugs, or particular ways of consuming them (1999: 94). He cites the film treatments of heroin use in *Pulp Fiction*, *Trainspotting*, and *Killing Zoe*.

While subsequent chapters explore in more detail the various dimensions of 'normalisation' (see Part 2), we shall see in the development of social and cultural theory a shift in basic assumptions about the extent of drug use and the centrality of its place in popular culture. Early theories, whether pharmacological, psychological or sociological, assumed that drug use was exceptional, deviant and abnormal, located only amongst a small proportion of the population. Cultures associated with such drug use were equally seen as pathological and segregated from 'normal' everyday life. Contemporary theorising in this area has moved significantly from these assumptions. Informed by the empirical research on drug experiences amongst the 'normal' population over the last two decades, contemporary social and cultural theory is now much more likely to acknowledge the commonplace of drugs within popular cultures. Recent social and cultural theory has sought to describe the experiences of those living in a late modern or post-modern world, in which symbolic resources are routine prerequisites to ordinary life and the huge variety of media are central to our social experience (Jameson 1998; Lash 1994; Giddens 1991). While earlier theory largely maintained a demarcation between the social practices of drug consumption, on the one hand, and spheres of cultural production and media representation, on the other, contemporary theories of drug use within popular culture seem to pose interesting questions about the interplay between each, as popular culture is made and reproduced.

Beyond the bio-psychological

It may be helpful to begin by considering what kinds of explanation cultural and social theory can be distinguished from. A number of important explanations of illicit drug use to emerge in the post-war period were rooted in psychological or psycho-biological explanations of human behaviour. Such models seek to understand illicit drug use as 'caused' either by a genetically linked problem, a medical disease, individual moral weakness, as a product of 'inappropriate' conditioning and social learning processes, or as a combination of a plurality of these micro-level processes (Bean 2002: 16–19; Anderson 1995). In each instance, the primary concern lies with the individual illicit drug user as the site of analysis and a variety of individual treatments are offered, from detoxification and cognitive therapies, through to simple moral exhortation.

It would be foolish to entirely dismiss the psychological, or indeed, in certain circumstances, the biological or medical in seeking to 'explain' drug behaviour, particularly when considering the case of those users at the 'hard' end of the drug continuum, frequently the victims of multiple deprivations, including the emotional and familial, as well as the socio-economic. Nevertheless, the critics point to what such approaches do not address and for the purposes of considering the relationship between drug consumption and popular culture, these elements are important. In biological and psychological models we rarely find much attention given to the meanings or symbolic frameworks of drug consumption, shared amongst drug consumers, or indeed between these social groups and wider communities. In many of the social and cultural theories discussed below there is an emphasis upon the importance of the social, and in the shared symbolic universe, amongst drug users. It is hard to deny the social and cultural dimensions and the answers they suggest to questions that otherwise seem inexplicable. Why, for example, if drug use is best understood as a medical problem, do so many young people simply grow out of the 'disease' (Parker, Aldridge and Measham 1998: 20)? The great danger in adopting only psychological or psycho-biological models is that they 'individualise' patterns of drug consumption, in turn encouraging an understanding which is concerned only with individual pathology, rather than in terms of the play of social, symbolic and cultural energies (Anderson 1995). After all, it is difficult to explain the evidence of significantly widening drug use amongst those below the age of 35, discussed in Part 2 of this volume (the 'normalisation' of recreational drug use) strictly in terms of behavioural or disease models. That is, unless there has been an alarming recent increase in individual pathologies and behavioural problems in a number of late, modern Western societies.

The critique of pharmacological determinism

One element that all the social and cultural theoretical approaches considered here share, from the anthropological to sociological theories of late modernity, is a rejection of approaches that exclusively emphasise the potency of narcotics and chemicals, over the realms of culture and symbolism. In other words, all the theoretical approaches discussed below take the view that it is not the pharmacological power of particular drugs that provides the key to understanding the social and cultural practices associated with drug consumption but, rather, that it is the social and cultural practices that lend *meaning* to the perceived physiological effects of drugs. It is the cultural aspects that shape the use of drugs rather than the other way around.

An example from a recent ethnographic study of club culture illustrates the point. For Malbon, the use of drugs, such as ecstasy, were not the cause of the development of the vibrant 1990s dance club culture in the UK but, on the contrary, drugs contributed one element to the experiences and meanings – 'the emotional community' – shared by those involved (1998: 277). Indeed, rather than drugs determining social experience, clubbers carefully controlled and, indeed, timed the consumption of ecstasy to heighten the intensity of the climax to the evening (1998: 272). Certainly, some commentators have pointed to the impact shifts in drug fashions have had upon club culture – the switch from ecstasy to speed, for example, eroding the 'loved up' atmosphere of the early 1990s (Garrett 1998). But even here there are good reasons for supposing that wider social changes were in play shaping both the shift away from ecstasy and the alteration to cultural practices within the clubs of the mid to late 1990s (Measham, Aldridge and Parker 2001: 44).

The critique of pharmacological determinism has been firmly established for at least half a century. It was Howard Becker, who famously argued in his study of marihuana smoking jazz musicians, that the physiological effects and physical pleasures of such drug consumption had to be *socially learnt*. They were not immediately obvious to the novice but, rather, beginners learnt to recognise 'effects' of smoking marihuana as 'pleasures', just as they had to learn the techniques of rolling a joint, through social interaction with peers – by watching and listening (Becker 1963). According to Sterk-Ericson, Becker's argument holds equally true for drugs located towards the 'harder' end of the spectrum including cocaine (1996: 67). For Lindesmith (1968), it was not the chemical properties of heroin that determined the physical experiences of heroin addicts but, rather, the processes of social interaction through which the sensations of withdrawal were discussed amongst fellow 'addicts' and drugs workers. It was these that sensitised addicts to what they might recognise as 'withdrawal'.

The strongest card that is played in the cultural critique of pharmacological determinism is the comparative argument. There is an enormous amount of comparative cultural evidence charting wide variations in how the effects of consuming precisely the same chemicals are perceived in different cultures and societies. While cannabis has been widely regarded in the West as an agent of de-motivation and lethargy, in some cultures, including regions of India, it was regarded as a stimulant to combat fatigue (Grinspoon 1971). For cheerful and gentle Abipone Indians, dwelling in Paraquay, the consumption of alcohol was likely to induce aggression and belligerence; while for the habitually 'fierce and warlike' Yuruma Indians, a drop of alcohol was likely to stop them in their tracks, inducing an unusual passivity and introspection (Knipe 1995: 67). The same chemical compounds including cannabis, opium, cocaine, alcohol and tobacco, have been used for a bewildering variety of social purposes and activities, from the energised and elated to the plain immobile; in the contexts of the secular, the spiritual, the recreational and even war. Even patterns of recovery from apparent physiological addictions are understood to be rooted in particular cultural contexts: different cultures shaping quite markedly varied patterns of recovery from common patterns of substance misuse (Hazel and Mohatt 2001). From the social constructionist perspectives of cultural and social theory, if the same chemical compounds are associated with such widely varying social practices, it must be the cultural rather than the pharmacological that is determinant. Even the very distinctions between licit and illicit substances, legal and illegal modes of substance use are, from this perspective, rooted in cultural and normative concerns rather than pharmacological properties, and it is for this reason that such distinctions can sometimes shift or blur as social and historical changes unfold (Measham, Aldridge and Parker 2001; Young 1971).

Anthropological perspectives: drug consumption as cultural practice

This conclusion above leads logically to a consideration of the cultural norms and values associated with particular patterns of drug consumption and to the importance of social definition or meaning in its the interpretation. It is clear that cultural evaluations of different patterns of drug consumption are powerfully shaped by social context: the time, place and particular moment in history in which certain patterns of drug consumption are located; the social identities of those involved in consumption including their social class, gender and ethnicity, and the particular drugs paraphernalia or methods of ingestion (Blake (Chapter 2) and Manning in this volume; Knipe 1995; Kohn 1992). Societal reactions to drug consumption seem to be strongly influenced by matters such as, what particular social groups appear to be involved, the context in which they consume, and, indeed, their preferred technologies of consumption. Opium use by bourgeois women for medicinal purposes at the end of the nineteenth century prompted mild public concern; opium smoked by Chinese migrants in 'dens' a decade or so later provoked widespread moral outrage in both the US and Britain (Musto 1973). Cocaine snorted by white middle class 'achievers' in the early 1980s encouraged journalists to construct news stories around themes of 'recovery' and 'redemption'; the smoking of crack cocaine in black, working class communities in the late 1980s generated a full-blown moral panic in the US (Reeves and Campbell 1994).

The concern with drug consumption as a popular cultural practice follows from these perspectives. The assumption is that we can only really 'make sense' of increasing drug consumption if we understand it as being embedded in popular culture; inscribed within specific symbolic frameworks that lend meaning both to the substances, themselves, but also to the technologies of consumption, and to the social groups doing the consuming. It was the discipline of anthropology that first began to explore the insights offered by these ideas in a systematic way. Much of the comparative material demonstrating the varied cultural uses and means associated with drug use was produced by anthropologists studying a variety of societies from the simple to the industrial and post-industrial. Anthropologists have shown that the use of hallucinogens amongst the Yanomano of rain forest Venezuela actually functions to strengthen the existing social order by heightening the intensity of the experience in collective rituals; they have suggested that kava drinking on the West Polynesian Islands was bound up with the rituals securing existing power hierarchies, while khat chewing in the Yemen helped to reaffirm a gender segregation, and that to refuse an alcoholic drink in Andean village communities was to challenge in a profound way existing structures of authority (Knipe 1995: 185–190 and 340). In each case drug use was intimately bound up with meaning, cultural practice and power.

One of the most influential anthropological contributions in this area has been made by Mary Douglas. In *Purity and Danger* (1966), Douglas argued that in all societies, systems of cultural classification exist to demarcate the world in ways that help to bind communities together. Thus, she argued, the multitude of rules distinguishing the pure from the corrupt, the permissible from the prohibited, the sacred from the profane, to be found in the book of *Leviticus* in the Old Testament, actually served to consolidate social solidarity through fostering a collective or shared picture of the world in the Jewish communities of the middle eastern Iron Age. Such systems of classification laid down collectively shared rules about what could or could not be eaten, for example, or which animals were clean or unclean, in what condition the human body was either pure or impure, and in doing so consolidated a collectively shared social order. Behaviour and the objects associated with such behaviour, including food, were regarded as taboo, if they were 'out of place'. By classifying 'out of place' behaviour and objects as impure or taboo, society symbolically maintained the boundaries upon which the social order rested.

There are important implications here for an understanding of contemporary social responses to drug use. In contemporary societies, very strict rules usually function to narrowly proscribe the boundaries of licit drug use. Opiates including both heroin and morphine, for example, are used only 'legitimately' for pain relief in a medical context. When used 'out of place', on the street, they become taboo. Manderson extends this argument to the paraphernalia associated with drug use – the technologies of drug consumption. What is shocking for many about illicit intravenous drug use is that it involves the syringe – or 'metal out of place' (Knipe 1995: 801). Much the same could be said of pipes, bags and glue cans. All are everyday objects 'out of place' when used for the purposes of illicit drug consumption. All are, in these contexts, examples of symbolic boundary violation and it is, perhaps, this point that explains the power of the imagery in films, such as *Trainspotting*. Thus, we can use the insights provided by Mary Douglas to begin to explain the symbolic power of drug imagery reproduced through forms of popular culture.

Functionalism and drugs

This interest in the underlying social function of cultural practices was shared by sociology and, indeed, the two disciplines developed complementary intellectual frameworks for much of the early and mid-twentieth century. Within sociology, a functionalist approach encouraged researchers to explore not only the cultural classification of substance misuse but drug consumption, itself, in terms of its 'functions' for society. This is counter to conventional commonsense: illegal drug use is usually associated with dysfunctions, manifested in family or communal breakdown and the impairment of the individual's ability to fulfil social expectations. Nevertheless, as discussed above, anthropological research points to the ways in which drug consumption can 'function' to preserve structures of kinship or communal authority because the customs or cultural practices associated with drug consumption help to promote communal integration. Thus, for example, the social networks, and associated shared cultural practices, to be found in the opium dens of Laos served as an alternative source of social integration for those without families (Knipe 1995: 211). By extension it is not difficult to see how the, albeit less permanent, 'emotional communities' fostered around the experience of ecstasy in the dance clubs of Britain during the early 1990s 'functioned' to offer individuals the possibility to integrate within new communal structures (Measham, Aldridge and Parker 2001; Malbon 1998) in an era in which for many young people traditional sources of social integration, such as family or traditional workplace or career path, were being destabilised.

Durkheim assumed that deviancy was a 'normal' characteristic of society in that it was ever-present. Indeed, a 'moderate' amount of deviancy was a healthy indication that the consensus, or value system, was not so powerful as to stifle all forms of individual creativity (Durkheim 1964). A society with a value system that permitted individuals sufficient 'space' to think in original and creative ways, was also likely to include some individuals that would use that 'space' for less socially useful purposes. There is, then, even in the earliest functionalist writing an understanding of the relationship between social integration, the social space afforded to individuals to 'deviate' from mainstream values and the possibility that such deviations in certain circumstances might be at a latent level (that is at the level of unintentional consequences) socially functional. While some critics have likened ecstasy to soma, the drug used to keep populations 'happy' in Huxley's *Brave New World* (Cosgrove 1988), from a functionalist perspective it is perfectly possible to make a case for recreational drug use as a mechanism of social integration, permitting individuals to experience functional outcomes in terms of release from stress, excitement, and sense of belonging. A Durkheimian analysis might very well interpret the 'normalisation' of recreational drug use as a welcome adjustment of normative order to conditions determined by the social and economic structure.

However, slightly more recent social and cultural theory has tended to interpret the cultural practices of drug consumption in rather different ways, with much less emphasis upon their capacity to promote social cohesion and a much more pronounced interest in the ways in which such cultural practices represent an expression of conflict, difference, or as sites to be contested.

Drugs, criminology and sub-cultural theory

Subcultural theory has its roots in the Durkheimian preoccupation with the challenges to social consensus faced by industrial societies in the high modern era and the associated problem of anomie, or normlessness. Durkheim (1933) recognised that individual disenchantment with mainstream values was likely to grow more acute given the 'forced division labour' that characterised industrial capitalism. The American sociologist Robert Merton (1968) famously devised a typology to analyse possible individual responses to anomie.

The problem, he argued, facing American capitalism was that of structural 'strain', involving a disjunction between the normative order and the means of opportunity afforded by the social structure in terms of education and occupational mobility. Put simply America in the middle of the twentieth century was almost too successful in securing widespread commitment, across all social classes, to the goals of the American Dream – success measured in the material terms of money and wealth. The problem was that the social structure was characterised by massive inequalities that denied the means to achieve success, measured in these terms, for the vast majority of those located in the American working class. The condition of public schooling, the deadening weight of poverty upon family life, and the divisions of the workplace, all served to block legitimate opportunities for success. Paradoxically, the success American society enjoyed in fostering commitment to the values of material success, combined with such significant structural opportunity blockages, led to patterns of anomic behaviour including for a minority the option of professional crime (the use of illegitimate means to secure legitimate goals), or for an even smaller minority, 'retreatism', an abandoning of commitment to both goals and means via drug use and alcohol.

There is no recognition in Merton's analysis of the ways in which drug or alcohol consumption might be embedded in shared cultural practices and he had little appetite for exploring the lives of the 'psychotics, pariahs, outcasts, vagrants, vagabonds, and tramps' he lumped together with 'chronic drunkards and drug addicts' (1968). Merton saw drug use as an individual response to the experience of blocked opportunities and left it at that. It was for Cloward and Ohlin (1961), and other researchers interested in the new post-war concerns of 'juvenile delinquency' to combine Merton's insights with the concept of subculture, borrowed from the Chicago School, in ways that began to locate drug consumption as a shared cultural practice, though even here interest in the symbolic dimension is very limited. Cloward and Ohlin, drawing upon Merton, suggest that retreatist subcultures, arise 'from a continued failure to near the goal by legitimate measures and from an inability to use the illegitimate route [crime] because of internalised prohibitions or socially structured barriers ...' (1961: 181).

Cloward and Ohlin argued that 'retreatist' drug use was likely to occur amongst working class adolescent 'double failures'. The experience of structurally determined blocked opportunities might encourage some working class youngsters to join 'criminal subcultures', or in some cases to try to achieve status through street fighting in gangs or conflict subcultures. But retreatist subcultures offered an option for those who could neither achieve success through legitimate routes, or through criminal or fighting prowess (1961: 182–183). In short, drug or retreatist subcultures were for 'wimps', those who had failed not only in the eyes of mainstream society but in the eyes of their criminal or pugilistic peers.

Even four decades ago this strict demarcation between crime, fighting and drug consumption seemed a little too neat. But there were other reservations, too. David Downes, for example, in his work with working class mods in the East End of London in the 1960s, found little evidence of a 'retreatist subculture', though bizarrely given that this was the decade of the Krays, he found little evidence of a criminal opportunity structure, either. Nevertheless, he did believe that the language of jazz and the style or culture of the Afro-Caribbean immigrant communities emerging in London, was beginning to disseminate 'retreatist terminology, if not actually drug use' to young working class East Enders (1966: 135). Downes subtitles his book, 'a study in subcultural theory' and he retains a theory of blocked opportunity and social class to explain the development of delinquent gangs in the East End. Nevertheless, in the case of drug use his empirical evidence did not support the idea that drug cultures emerged at the bottom. Indeed, he believed that it was, on the contrary, those with rather more opportunities and cultural capital – students and 'hip' (sic) educated middle class youngsters – who were more likely to have contact with retreatist subcultures. However, importantly, he did recognise the importance of style and language in the consumption of drugs and implicitly he pointed to the need to explore the mechanisms that reproduce the symbolic frameworks that locate and describe drugs through their association with particular social groups.

Early subcultural theory was important because it invited researchers to think seriously about the relationship between drug consumption, cultural or symbolic practices, and the social structure but there is little attempt to explore these ideas in any fully developed way in the writing of Cloward and Ohlin, Downes, or other leading figures, such as Cohen (1956). Paradoxically, though post-war subcultural theory supplied several analytic concepts of great value in the analysis of drug cultures, it overlooked in its empirical research vibrant examples of popular cultures within which drug use was significantly embedded throughout the middle decades of the twentieth century, from the Mexican and Chinese migrant communities of the 1920s to the jazz clubs and bohemian movements of the 1940s and 1950s (Mignon 1993; Musto 1973). One reason for this, of course, was that these examples of drug embedded popular cultures were too complex to be read simply as products of working class blocked opportunity. Certainly, class structures shaped and constrained these examples but ideas of identity, ethnicity, gender, locality, and even creativity were also profoundly important. This illustrates one of the more familiar criticisms of post-war subcultural theory: that it exaggerated the extent to which behaviour could be understood as being 'determined' by class structures and underestimated the extent to which we all as social actors employ symbolic and cultural resources to actively create popular culture, including drug subcultures. The 'activity' in these examples of collective adaptation to structurally posed problems somehow got lost in the analysis.

In employing the concept of subculture, Cloward and Ohlin imply that drug consumption may be embedded within shared cultural practices that are in some ways set apart from the values and practices of mainstream society. Thus, a second line of criticism is that subcultural theory exaggerates the difference between the criminal and the law abiding, the deviant and the respectable. Certainly, Downes was sensitive to this criticism and was at pains to stress the 'ordinariness' of his East End gangs (Blackman 2004: 109). Nevertheless, there is a preoccupation with 'difference' in much of the subcultural research of this period and, perhaps, less attention to the 'fuzzy' overlap between the practices of 'ordinary' young people and their gang member friends. This is a weakness that has even greater significance in the first decade of the twenty-first century when the 'normalisation' of recreational drug use appears to be developing (see Part 2) and exposure to drug consumption, or at least 'offer situations' amongst quite 'ordinary' young people from varying class locations, seems common.

A final point follows from this. Ironically, the distribution of drugs has always offered young people facing blocked legitimate opportunities, a potentially lucrative alternative illegitimate opportunity structure (Bean 2002:21). In its concern to paint 'retreatists' as a category of marginalised, 'double failures', segregated from the mainstream by their individual weaknesses, subcultural theory overlooked the dynamic entrepreneurialism of the drug dealer. Thrasher may have studied 1,313 separate gangs in Chicago but he reports remarkably little evidence of drug distribution networks, merely some very localised and specialised 'dope peddling' (1927: 14). It was only in the much more recent British studies that drug distribution as a significant illegal opportunity structure began to be acknowledged, such as Howard Parker's study of Liverpool, *View from the Boys* (1974: 131).

Drugs, symbols and meaning

The functionalist leaning within the Chicago School can be credited with giving rise to the concept of subculture, but an equally important intellectual current within the school gave rise to a concern with cultural meaning and symbolism. This found full development in the writings of the symbolic interactionists and labelling theorists, most influential in the 1960s and 1970s. In the work of Becker (1973), for example, there is a much stronger interest in the 'interior world' of the deviant: the meanings they take from social interaction and the ways in which they construct their own identities. From the outset Becker is interested in the impact of the symbolic upon behaviour and cultural practices. He argues that the stereotyped constructions of deviancy, such as marihuana smoking, that society circulates in various ways, including through the mass media, act as mechanisms of moral regulation dissuading many from contemplating deviant behaviour. The novice marihuana smoker has to 'neutralise his sensitivity to the stereotype by accepting an alternative view of the practice' (1973: 73). In other words, the novice learns to challenge the dominant symbolic frameworks that are deployed in society to 'place' or 'make sense' of illicit drug consumption: the novice has to acquire the confidence to question the dominant beliefs that Mary Douglas suggests society uses to distinguish the appropriate from the taboo or polluted. A process whereby the beginner comes to see the dominant stereotypes of drug taking as uninformed or inaccurate, and through which they come to believe that they have a superior, 'insider's view' is necessary in order for them to become regular marihuana smokers (1973: 78).

Becker's argument rests upon the distinction between the novice and the experienced, rather than between the subcultural and the mainstream. He suggests that individual identity shifts in subtle ways as novices mix socially with experienced users. As we have seen, his radical challenge to the pharmacological model holds that the pleasures of marihuana have to be learnt through social interaction with more experienced smokers, in much the same way as the techniques of rolling and smoking (1973: 46–48). This is very much a cultural account of drug consumption: drug use is embedded within a set of cultural practices that lend the pharmacological processes meaning. As the beginner mixes more within the social group of regular smokers, not only their interpretation of drug use changes but the very understanding of their own motives. Becker insists that 'deviant motives actually develop in the course of experience with deviant activity' (1973: 42). Beginners learn to rationalise their behaviour as they get more experienced in interaction with other smokers. Thus, the meanings of marihuana smoking, the ability to question dominant framings of the drug, the techniques of ingestion, even its pleasures, and the very motivation for smoking, are learnt through social interaction and shared cultural practices. It is the language, symbolism and culture within which drug consumption is embedded that is of prime importance for the researcher.

The stress upon cultural practices sets Becker's approach apart from earlier subcultural theory but so does the theoretical opposition to the structural determinism of earlier approaches. Becker insists that there is not an inevitable or predictable 'end' to the 'deviant career'. In an argument directed particularly against contemporary models of addiction, Becker argued that just as the construction of meaning through social interaction and the exchange of symbols was always provisional and, to an extent, unpredictable, so also were patterns of marihuana smoking. Individuals might, depending upon who they met and how they interacted, become regular smokers but they might equally dabble a little before giving it up entirely for another kind of pleasure (1973: 44). The emphasis upon the capacity of the individual social actor to employ symbolic resources to construct or reinvent their own identities is a theme that is developed further in more recent contemporary social theory discussed at the end of the chapter.

Labelling and subcultures

Becker's work was extremely influential in the 1960s and early 1970s but in a period of radical and dissenting politics, critics searched for ways in which the questioning of dominant symbolic frameworks in Becker's work could be combined with a greater awareness of other sources of power. The National Deviancy Conference established in the late 1960s in Britain to provide a critique of orthodox criminology sought to do this. Thus, Young in *The Drugtakers* (1971), draws from both Becker and subcultural theory in providing an account of drug consumption, policing and the exercise of power. In Becker there is an emphasis upon self-identity, or how drug users saw themselves at each stage in their 'deviant careers'. This, of course, prompted the elaboration of labelling theory in the 1960s and a particular emphasis upon the repercussions for the individual of being publicly identified or labelled through arrest or exposure, as deviant. In turn, this pointed to questions about the power to label and in whose interests such labelling processes might work. Thus, interest moved from the meanings held by individual drug users to the societal reaction of control agencies and mass media and it is this that concerns Young in *The Drugtakers*. Young argues that the dominant labels or symbolic frameworks circulated in society can do a great deal of harm in shaping the ways in which individual drug users see themselves. In particular, 'absolutist' pharmacological models of addiction, circulated both by 'experts' and popular media, may label and, paradoxically, consolidate an identification with the role of addict on the part of the serious drug user (1971: 67). Thus, addicts come to see themselves as 'helpless' or 'sick' in ways that actually mystify the true, more complex nature of opiate addiction.

For Young drug subcultures may serve a positive purpose in helping to insulate drug users from the damage that such dominant images may cause. In that drug cultures provide a degree of moral regulation and help to integrate individual users, they are not necessarily part of the problem, and in that they provide a route for harm reduction strategies they might be part of the solution (1971: 42). However, in his study of hippy communities in Notting Hill Young argued that if delinquent subcultures emerge when young people are cut off from access to 'the material rewards which the system has to offer', bohemian drug cultures emerge amongst those who are, 'well capable of leading a materially successful life ... [but who in practice] find the rewards offered ... insufficient to warrant ... conformity to the work ethic' (1971: 147). In other words, drug consumption was part of a political and ideological resistance. Mass media stereotyping both entrenched values and oppositional cultural practices within the Notting Hill communities and encouraged more severe forms of policing which, in turn, further exacerbated the polarisation of perspectives. In short, a process of deviancy amplification was triggered (1971: 196).

In exploring the relationship between power, dominant symbolic frameworks and the actual cultural practices of those involved in the consumption of drugs, and in its insistence upon drug taking as an oppositional or resistive practice, *The Drugtakers* can be read as an important bridge between 1960s labelling theories and the revival of interest in subcultural theory to be found in cultural studies during the 1970s. However, in the debit column is, firstly, its inclination to reintroduce the reification of 'differences' between the normal and deviant, the ordinary young person and the drug user. Again, at a time when recreational drug use appears to be increasingly 'normalised', the picture of drug users in *The Drugtakers*, and the political meanings inscribed in their consumption seems rather distant. Secondly, the emphasis upon 'strong' media effects generated by a cohesive and centralised set of media institutions, reproducing dominant messages and labelling deviants needs at least some revision for a contemporary world. As we have seen, media consumption, particularly for young people with access to a variety of new media technologies, is very much more fragmentary.

Cultural studies: drug use, youth cultures, and resistance

The Centre for Contemporary Cultural Studies (CCCS), located at Birmingham

University, in the 1970s developed a heavily theoretical orientation to the study of popular culture that drew in its early work on insights provided by Symbolic Interactionism and the National Deviancy Conference, but applied these insights within a framework rooted primarily in the neo-Marxist writing of Althusser and Gramsci. Thus, patterns of deviant behaviour, such as illicit drug use, were located within the context of popular culture, and popular culture, itself, was read as a site of ideological struggle and resistance.

The 1976 CCCS 'classic', *Resistance Through Rituals: Youth Subcultures in Post-War Britain* (edited by Hall and Jefferson), includes a series of readings of the 'spectacular' youth subcultures of the early post-war years, as examples of symbolic resistance to dominant ideological formations. There is a strong rejection of pharmacological determinism in Willis' (1976) study of 'heads' or 'hippies'. Clearly influenced by Becker, he argues, '… the importance of drugs did not lie in their direct physical effects, but in the way they facilitated passing through a great symbolic barrier erected against "straight" society' (1976: 107). This very much echoes Becker's concern with the distinction between the novice and the experienced and the process of acquiring 'insider' knowledge. However, Willis puts much more emphasis upon ideological resistance. The 'meaning' of drugs was not pharmacologically determined but symbolic: drugs functioned as a 'trip switch' (1976: 107) demarcating the boundary between the hippy world of alternative values, critical of capitalism, and the straight world of conventional values. According to Willis, drugs 'symbolised a fundamental ontological change from the sense of feeling oneself as an autonomous determining agent, to feeling oneself, in part as a determining variable in the world' (1976: 109). Under the influence of acid, one 'head' (or hippy) comes to realise that, 'time is man-made, there is not such thing as "time", it's a load of cock, something that man has made to computerise himself' (1976: 111). Drugs offered the means to deconstruct a bourgeois ideology that mystified the real constraints of 'straight' society with an illusory promise of individual freedom. What is most valuable about Willis' contribution is his interest in the differing symbolic meanings of particular drugs: he explores in some detail the hippy understanding of what different kinds of substances 'meant' and how they were located in a symbolic hierarchy of taste. Opiates were regarded as most dangerous because those who used them were likely to permanently cross the symbolic barrier between 'straight' and 'alternative' worlds (1976: 117).

A frequent criticism of the CCCS researchers has been that the weight of the theoretical and political edifice they constructed could barely be supported by the relatively thin evidence provided by their subjects and Willis' work provided a case in point. A more prosaic interpretation of the 'hippie moment' might be that people took drugs to escape reality rather than grasp it. Even within the *Resistance Through Rituals* collection there were some dissenting voices, including Pearson and Twohig (1976) who drew the conclusion from their own ethnography that, counter to the views of both Willis and Becker, pharmacology and technologies of consumption made quite a difference to the nature of drug experiences. While the working class roots of other 'spectacular' youth subcultures lent themselves to the CCCS emphasis upon symbolic class resistance to dominant ideology, the middle class origins of so many hippies always posed something of a puzzle for the CCCS. Their ideological resistance could not be explained simply by their class origins: the 'hippy moment' was not only historically peculiar to the 1960s but peculiar as an anomaly within the CCCS theoretical framework.

In contrast, Hebdidge's early work included within *Resistance Through Rituals*, on mod subcultures, comes much closer to a view of drug consumption as an everyday cultural practice within a working class youth subculture. It also begins to explore the way in which drug consumption can be read as a further example of the symbolic appropriation of commodities, alongside the appropriation of Lambretta scooters and Parka jackets. 'Thus, pills, medically diagnosed for the treatment of neuroses, were appropriated and used as an end in themselves ...' (Hebdidge 1976: 93). At this stage in Hebdidge's work, his approach still fits broadly within the CCCS class framework: mods are 'read' as a subcultural problem-solving response to the experience of being young, urban and working class, with all the structural disadvantages that implies. However, even at this stage, there are some important nuances in his approach. To resist through mod was to struggle to open up both temporal and emotional space in the face of the constraints imposed by the work regimes of capitalism. The maximum enjoyment of leisure and the maximum demonstration of style had to be compacted into the nightlife of the club and weekend. Thus, 'speed was needed to keep mind and body synchronised perfectly' (1976: 89) and, for Hebdidge, bound up with the consumption of amphetamines was the appropriation, not only of clothes and physical commodities, but particular cultural archetypes – archetypes mods associated with 'coolness' but also criminality on the margins, including drug distribution. In particular, Hebdidge argues, mods favoured, or appropriated, styles of dress, language and manner associated with the Jamaican hustler or 'rudie', and the Italian-American 'Brooklyn sharp kid' because these styles spoke to the emotional inner-life of the mod, as well as signifying outwardly to the wider society (1976: 89).

Here we have, then, an approach which understood illicit drug consumption as being intimately bound up with the reproduction of particular symbolic frameworks; frameworks that consisted of images of ethnicity, gender, and place, and which offered meaning for the emotional interior, as well as the outwardly social or subcultural. Amphetamine use was part of the problem-solving strategy and, in this sense, there is a debt to earlier postwar subcultural theory. But in the approach of Hebdidge, there was a much greater awareness of the importance of style and symbolism as dimensions of resistance to authority. In contrast, to Cloward and Ohlin's passive 'retreatists', Hebdidge read these mods as energised and active subversive consumers, with illicit drug use as a key element in their oppositional strategies.

> Through the alchemy of 'speed', the mod achieved a magical omnipotence, whereby the dynamics of his movements were magnified, the possibilities of action multiplied, their purposes illuminated. Amphetamine made life tolerable, 'blocked' one's sensory channels so that action and risk and excitement were possible, kept one going on the endless round of consumption ... (Hebdidge 1976: 91).

Of course, within the CCCS framework, these 'magical solutions' were 'magical' precisely because they were not 'real' but, on the contrary, ultimately doomed. Mod styles would be inevitably incorporated within the commercial mainstream; amphetamines could not provide more than a temporary escape from the alienating experience of work and school. There is an interesting contrast to some of the more recent accounts of ecstasy use within the dance cultures of the last two decades where anxieties about 'false consciousness' have dissolved and 'E' fuelled clubbing seems to be regarded as much more of a reasonable strategy, a pattern of 'resistance on a micro-level, on the level of everyday life' (Malbon 1998: 280).

In preferring to study the 'spectacular' youth subculture to the more mundane realities of 'ordinary' young people's lives, the CCCS was sometimes criticised for permitting a Leavisite elitism to guide their work. Willis certainly tried to shift attention towards the lives of ordinary, working class youngsters in his subsequent work (Blackman 2004: 114), but neither he nor or Hebdidge devoted much more interest to the symbolic significance of drugs or the associated cultural practices. Researching *Common Culture* (1990) just before the explosion of dance cultures, Willis entirely misses the impact of dance drugs in the 1990s, while Hebdidge offers some suggestions about the homological relationship between drugs and other elements of subcultural style in his study of punk but does not expand (1979: 114). Nevertheless, while not fully grasping drug consumption as everyday cultural practice, their work significantly broke with the models of drug users as pathetic, weak, helpless, or oppressed. And, the insight that drug consumption has a symbolic power that may challenge hegemonic formations, is an important point that continues to be deployed in contemporary research (Anderson 1995; Reeves and Campbell 1994).

New drugs, new social theories and new social formations?

Teds, skinheads and mods have long departed the cultural landscape, other than as simulacra. Theories of subculture have been subjected to sustained critique by those who object to the reification of differences between those on the inside of subcultures, and those more 'ordinary' outsiders, to the privileging of social class over other social categories, the inappropriateness of such theories for grasping the more fluid and complex youth 'style tribes' of the contemporary scene, and their silence on the importance of mass mediated culture (Blackman 2004; Bennett 1999; McRobbie and Thornton 1995).

The contemporary social world is more complex compared to the immediate post-war world; there have been significant shifts in the structuring of global capitalism, mass media and cultural institutions have simultaneously fragmented and yet grown more embedded in peoples' lives; consumption of illicit drugs has become both easier with the globalisation of supply routes and more common as a cultural practice. The leisure industries and venues of the 'night time economy' are now more central to the lives of young people, making possible an intensified incorporation and commodification of leisure experiences. Within these structures, the cultural practices associated with the consumption of alcohol, food, sex and drugs are important elements (Measham, Aldridge and Parker 2001; Henderson 1997).

For several writers reflecting upon the contemporary scene in late modern/ postmodern societies, one of the distinctive features of these social formations is the new centrality of illicit drug consumption and, in some instances, the blurring of the distinction between the illicit and the licit (Pearson 1999; Parker, Aldridge and Measham 1998; Collinson 1996). For Parker, Aldridge and Measham, 'adolescence in postmodern times' (1998: 21) is different because it is longer and more complex in comparisons to earlier eras. The collapse of traditional apprenticeships, extension of further and higher education, the rising age for marriage and delays in beginning new families, all prolong a period of uncertainty, complexity and ambiguity for young adolescents or post-adolescents. In these social formations the perception of risk is intensified through a variety of agencies including media and government. According to Parker, Aldridge and Measham, for young people in these social formations there is a greater experience 'individualisation' because of the erosion of traditional sources of identity and integration associated with 'community', workplace, gender roles, and class (1998: 25). The disappearance of large scale, class based youth subcultures compounds the problem. This setting provides the context within which drug use becomes detached from particular youth subcultures, social groups or class locations, and begins to be understood, 'culturally', as a form of recreation available to 'consumers' from a plurality of social backgrounds.

In trying to make sense of illicit/licit drug consumption in the late modern/ postmodern era, two distinct kinds of approach can be identified in social and cultural theory. One draws explicitly upon the writing of Baudrillard and other theories of the postmodern, while the other draws upon the sociologies of late, modern social formations to be found in the writing of theorists, such as Giddens, Bauman, Beck and Lash. The former can be distinguished by a greater preoccupation with the centrality of media and a fascination with consumption and postmodern global culture (Redhead 1995). The latter is characterised by an interest in the strategies employed by individuals to address problems of ontological insecurity and identity crisis provoked by the conditions of late modernity (Collinson 1996).

(a) Postmodernism and rave culture

The eruptions of rave culture in the late 1980s and early 1990s prompted Steve Redhead to produce a manifesto for the study of politics, deviance and youth culture. For Redhead, earlier subcultural theory failed to grasp the complexities of youth cultures, the interconnections between contemporary youth cultures and earlier manifestations, and crucially, the important role played by mass media in mediating youth cultural practices (1995: 3–5). The media-saturated nature of contemporary, post-modern youth cultures, their depthlessness, and dislocation from structures such as social class, invited the application of ideas drawn from Baudrillard. According to Redhead, it was not only the centrality of the media, the globalised nature of commodified cultures, and the intersection of ethnicity and gender in the creation of styles, but the sheer quantity of available drugs that made the late 1980s and early 1990s qualitatively different to earlier periods in the history of youth culture. Famously, and drawing from Foucault, Redhead argued that it was the discourses on drugs that produced the framing of drugs as a problem, rather than the 'real' consequences drugs. Discourses of pathology should be challenged and, in their place, there needed to be a recognition that in the era of postmodernity, drugs were 'recreational' (1995: 7). For Redhead, '… ecstasy and rave culture go hand in glove' (1995: 13). In other words, to understand the consumption of ecstasy, one had to grasp the symbolic frameworks within which it was represented and the cultural practices associated with its use. What made rave culture a Baudrillardian phenomenon was the ever narrowing gap between original eruption of rave culture, and the cycle of media inspired revivals (1995: 24).

Undoubtedly, the widespread use of ecstasy in the late 1980s and 1980s, generated a huge level of news media interest reproducing, in turn, a powerful symbolic framework that constructed ecstasy as a particularly potent and threatening substance (Manning 2006). It was this construction that underpinned the series of moral panics over rave culture during the 1990s (Chritcher 2003; Wykes 2001; Palmer 2000). However, there are dangers in attributing too great a significance to the work of the news media in shaping the mediated culture of illicit drug use. As noted above, ecstasy users appear to have an ambivalent attitude towards news coverage of drugs, both directing a sceptical eye to the excesses of red-top newspaper hysteria, whilst also depending to a surprising extent upon news media for drug information (Hamersley, Khan and Ditton 2002: 145). Whilst correctly pointing to the mediated elements of contemporary popular drug cultures, paradoxically, one of the weaknesses of Redhead's postmodern analysis is precisely its media-centricity. There is very little material drawn from ethnographic sources in *Rave Off*; few explanations framed in terms of young people's own accounts of their engagement with popular drug cultures, or the symbolic frameworks that frame drug consumption, and little account taken of the way in which social class must still impact upon individual biographies, even in a world of 'classless', mediated consumer cultures.

(b) Drug styles and the conditions of late modernity

It would be a mistake to present the approaches below as one body of coherent social theory, or to ignore the extent to which concepts drawn from varieties of postmodern theory have influenced them. However, these approaches do share a debt to contemporary social theorists interested in the ways in which individual social actors negotiate the conditions of late modernity, including Giddens (1991), Beck (1992), Lash (1994) and Bauman (1992). These theorists share a common reading of late modernity; one that notes the impact of de-industrialisation, the restructuring of production, the dislocation of traditional class communities, and the growing importance of leisure industries and consumption for the economy. These processes occur alongside the spread of consumer cultures and values that promote highly individualised modes of being. Late modernity, or 'disorganised capitalism' encourages a greater degree of reflexivity in terms of self and more opportunities for individuals to re-invent their identities compared to an earlier era of 'simple modernity'. These opportunities arise from the dislocation of earlier sources of identity in class and locality, the diversification of regimes of femininity and masculinity, and the impact of the spread of a variety of diaspora through global patterns of migration. But these opportunities for reflexive work become powerfully inscribed with discourses of consumption. Individuals enjoy more 'cultural space' but there are powerful forces in play that encourage them to reinvent themselves primarily through consumption and the associated concepts of lifestyle and fashion.

Social theorists drawing upon these ideas focus strongly upon the tensions that are generated between the structural inequalities associated with late modernity – the creation of marginalised social groups, widening inequalities in access to resources, and localised areas of high unemployment – and the discourses of self and consumerism. Thus, there are 'reflexivity winners' and 'reflexivity losers' (Lash 1994: 127–130) because while consumer culture may appear 'classless', 'behind the ostensible equality of chances the market promotes and advertises, hides the practical inequality of consumers' (Bauman 1990: 211). And in the conditions of late modernity, or disorganised capitalism, individuals perceive themselves to be exposed to a greater variety of risk, as ever wider holes appear in social welfare nets, labour markets are deregulated, environmental hazards accumulate, and the very 'rational' strategies employed by public authorities to regain control, actually generate greater uncertainty (Beck 1994: 10). But even these risks and the means to address them are often unequally distributed.

This is the backdrop for two important studies of drug use in this late modern period (Foster 2000; Collinson 1996). Both seek to locate drug consumption within the context of the particular features of late modernity; both draw upon the concepts discussed above, or as Collinson puts it: 'these familiar and not so familiar themes in recent social theory and cultural studies' (1996: 429). Foster explores crime and drug behaviour as features of the *process* of exclusion in her study of a marginalised, 'hard to let' housing estate in the North East of England. Drawing upon Giddens, she argues that it is the experience of 'ontological insecurity' (2000: 323), a sense of helplessness or lack of control over life and events, that provides the context in which patterns of drug consumption and criminality are likely to develop. Collinson draws more deeply upon the 'biographical narratives' developed by the group of young, male offenders in his study. His starting point is the tension between the 'cult of the self' perpetuated by consumer culture and the structural inequalities experienced by these young offenders, located in excluded and marginalised positions at the bottom of the class structure. In these circumstances, 'one situational resolution' of this tension occurs through, 'male predatory street crime, excessive drug use, and normatively inappropriate leisure' (1996: 429). Often excluded from life style sectors (education, work, family) where others may embellish their 'narratives of self', these young men, develop their narratives and command respect through the chaotic and risk-laden trajectory associated with crime and drugs. In their life-style sectors, drugs are everyday commodities to be exchanged and consumed. Indeed, drug use helps to manage the anxieties associated with the experience of such risks and satisfies 'the need for action', the need to feel 'above everybody', the appetite for 'male excess' (1996: 433). In this context, risk was a source of pleasure as well as anxiety, associated with excitement and self-affirmation.

In short, Collinson suggests that for these young offenders, drugs are 'everyday commodities' that provide them with some means to consume other commodities (through the money generated via crime and drug distribution), but which also help them to manage the anxieties of risk, and importantly, also provide them with some of the symbolic resources used to construct their 'narratives of self'. The distribution and consumption of drugs conferred identity and status. If 'reflexivity winners' were able to script their 'self-narratives' through the adoption of consumer life styles, the poly drug use of these young men allowed them to script their 'drug-styles' from an early age (1996: 429). The symbols of drug consumption intersected with ideas of class and masculinity to create very particular identities.

Conclusion

Collinson and Foster are both concerned with the 'drugs-crime nexus' and, in that sense, are studying less 'normalised' patterns of drug use. However, the theoretical ideas associated with the analysis of late modernity are equally applicable to the non-criminal drug consumer, too. The features of 'adolescence in postmodern times' (Parker, Aldridge and Measham 1998: 21–25) are those of the social landscape described in theories of late modernity; the uncertain processes of 'individualisation' clearly those experienced by adolescents struggling to script 'self-narratives' in difficult times. While in the later *Dancing on Drugs*, Measham, Aldridge and Parker (2001) are keen to emphasise that the clubbers they study have higher than average rates of licit and illicit drug consumption, they explore the drug 'repertoires' involved within these patterns of *recreational* drug use in Britain at the turn of the twenty-first century (2001: 1). Repertoire is a significant word to use in this context, one which points to the idea of the purposeful 'drug-styles', as described by Collinson in the study of young male working class criminals. According to Measham, Aldridge and Parker, however, dance drug users can be both male and female, middle class as well as working class (2001: 9–12) and yet, they too develop drug styles, or repertoires, and engage in risk calculating 'cost-benefit assessments' in their consumption of drugs (2001: 12).

Whether studying ordinary 'post-modern adolescents', young criminals, young clubbers, or even young clubbing criminals, there are some important ideas that can be put together here. In the era of late modernity consumption occupies a central place within the 'de-industrialised economy' and in the lives of young people in a way that, perhaps, could not be anticipated by the researchers and theorists of the mid-twentieth century. The studies above seem to suggest that in the era of late modernity, the consumption of licit and illicit drugs is widely understood as having little difference in kind from other patterns of consumption. Social and cultural theory in addressing this, has moved away from models of drug users as a passive victims of their own inadequacies, psychological frailties, blocked opportunities or even oppressive policing. Rather drug consumption is understood as a cultural practice, just as other patterns of consumption have to be. Drugs are inscribed with meanings and understood within symbolic frameworks. It is these symbolic frameworks that, in part, provide the resources that drug users employ in developing their 'self narratives' or biographies. But these symbolic frameworks also provide a connection to wider processes of popular cultural reproduction. In this sense, the postmodern preoccupation with the mediation of culture and cultural practices is valuable. A number of the chapters in this volume explore the ways in which a variety of media reproduce images of drugs and particular symbolic frameworks that we are invited to use in making sense of them.

However, contemporary social theory and research also underlines the point that individuals are not free to construct 'self-narratives', including 'drug narratives or styles' in isolation or free from the constraining properties of structures of inequality, and other influences, including discourses associated with masculinities, femininities, and identities rooted in ethnicity. The process of developing a 'drug style' as a cultural practice still depends partly upon class location, and is still inflected by discourses of gender, for example. So the popular cultures within which drug consumption is located afford cultural space in which individuals can create the 'drug styles' as part of their 'self-narratives' but these cultural spaces are, at the same time, gendered, potentially racialised and constrained by the structures of social class that feature in the era of late-modern capitalism. And individual 'drug styles or narratives' are likely to be influenced by the symbolic frameworks within which particular substances are represented and 'understood' by particular communities, as well as by more material forces, such as street prices and the politics of supply. Part 3 of this volume provides plenty of evidence of the ways in which such symbolic frameworks are reproduced through particular media and institutions of cultural reproduction. But we also know that the reception of such symbolic frameworks is partly influenced by class and social identity. It is possible to speak of 'taste hierarchies', for example, in the consumption of drugs, with substances ranked according, not only to risk and pharmacological effects, but also in terms of the 'the kinds of users'. But these 'taste hierarchies' will vary to an extent according to class and social identity (Foster 2000; Collinson 1996; Sterk-Elifson 1996; Russell 1993). Part 4 explores some of the situations where the cultural practices associated with drug consumption are shaped in these ways.

References and suggested reading

Anderson, T.L. (1995) 'Toward a Preliminary Macro Theory of Drug Addiction', *Deviant Behaviour*, 16: 353–372.

Bauman, Z. (1990) *Thinking Sociologically*. Oxford: Blackwell Publishers.

Bauman, Z. (1992) *Intimations of Modernity*. London: Routledge.

Bean, P. (2002) *Drugs and Crime*. Cullompton: Willan Publishing.

Beck, U. (1992) *Risk Society: Towards a New Modernity*. London: Sage.

Becker, H. (1963) *The Outsiders*. New York: The Free Press.

Bennett, A. (1999) 'Subcultures or Neo-tribes? Rethinking the Relationship Between Youth, Style and Musical Taste', *Sociology*, 33 (3): 599–617.

Blackman, S. (2004) *Chilling Out: The Cultural Politics of Substance Consumption, Youth and Drugs Policy*. Maidenhead: Open University Press.

Boyd, S. (2002) 'Media Constructions of Illegal Drugs, Users, and Sellers: A Closer Look at Traffic', *The International Journal of Drugs Policy*, 13: 397–407.

Chritcher, C. (2003) *Moral Panics and the Media*. Buckingham: Open University Press.

Cloward, R.A. and Ohlin, L.E. (1961) *Delinquency and Opportunity. A Theory of Delinquent Gangs*. London: Routledge and Kegan Paul.

Cohen, A. (1956) *Delinquent Boys – the Subculture of the Gang*. London: Collier-Macmillan.

Collinson, M. (1996) 'In Search of the High Life: Drugs, Crime, Masculinities and Consumption', *British Journal of Criminology*, 36 (3): 428–444.

Cosgrove, S. (1988) 'Forbidden Fruits', *The New Statesman and Society*, 2 September 1998.

Douglas, M. (1966) *Purity and Danger*. London: Routledge and Kegan Paul.

Downes, D. (1966) *The Delinquent Solution. A Study in Subcultural Theory*. London: Routledge and Kegan Paul.

Durkheim, E. (1933) *The Division of Labour in Society*. London: Macmillan.

Durkheim, E. (1964) *The Rules of the Sociological Method*. New York: Free Press.

Foster, J. (2000) 'Social Exclusion, Crime and Drugs', *Drugs: Education, Prevention and Policy*, 7 (4): 317–330.

Garrett, S. (1998): *Adventures in Wonderland: A Decade of Club Culture*. London: Headline Books.

Giddens, A. (1991) *Modernity and Self-Identity*. Cambridge: Polity Press.

Grinspoon, L. (1971) *Marihuana Reconsidered*. Cambridge Mass: Harvard University Press.

Hall, S. and Jefferson, T. (eds) (1976) *Resistance through Rituals: Youth Subcultures in Post-war Britain*. London: Hutchinson.

Hammersley, R., Khan, F. and Ditton, J. (2002): *Ecstasy and the Rise of the Chemical Generation*. London: Routledge.

Hazel, K.L. and Mohatt, G.V. (2001) 'Cultural and Spiritual Coping in Sobriety: Informing Substance Abuse Prevention for Alaska Native Communities', *Journal of Community Psychology*, 29 (5): 541–562.

Hebdidge, D. (1976) 'The Meaning of Mod', in S. Hall and T. Jefferson (eds) (1976) *Resistance through Rituals: Youth Subcultures in Post-war Britain*. London: Hutchinson.

Hebdidge, D. (1979) *Subculture: The Meaning of Style*. London: Methuen.

Henderson, S. (1997) *Ecstasy: Case Unsolved*. London: Pandora.

Knipe, E. (1995) *Culture Society and Drugs*. Prospects Heights, Illinois: Waveland Press.

Kohn, M. (1992) *Dope Girls: The Birth of the British Drug Underground*. London: Lawrence and Wisehart.

Lash, S. (1994) 'Reflexivity and its Doubles: Structure, Aesthetics, Community', in U. Beck, A. Giddens and S. Lash (eds) *Reflexive Modernization*. Cambridge: Polity Press.

Lindesmith, A.R. (1968) 'A Sociological Theory of Addiction', *American Journal of Sociology*, 43: 593–613.

McRobbie, A. and Thornton, S. (1995) 'Rethinking "Moral Panic" for Multi-mediated Worlds', *British Journal of Sociology*, 46 (4): 559–574.

Malbon, B. (1998) 'Clubbing: Consumption, Identity and the Spatial Practices of Every-Night Life', in T. Skelton and G. Valentine (eds) *Cool Places: Geographies of Youth Cultures*. London: Routledge.

Manderson, D. (1995) 'Metamorphoses: Clashing Symbols in the Social Construction of Drugs', *Journal of Drug Issues*, 25 (4): 799–816.

Manning, P. (2006) 'There's No Glamour in Glue: News and the Symbolic Framing of Substance Misuse', *Crime Media Culture*, 2 (1): April 2006.

Measham, F. and Brain, K. (2005): '"Binge" Drinking, British Alcohol Policy and the New Culture of Intoxication', *Crime Media Culture*, 1 (3): December 2005.

Measham, F., Aldridge, J. and Parker, H. (2001) *Dancing on Drugs: Risk, Health and Hedonism in the British Club Scene*. London: Free Association Books.

Merton, R.K. (1968) *Social Theory and Social Structure*. New York: The Free Press.

Mignon, P. (1993) 'Drugs and Popular Music: The Democratisation of Bohemia', *Popular Cultural Studies*, 1: 175–191.

Murji, K. (1998): 'The Agony and the Ecstasy: Drugs Media and Morality', in R. Coomber (ed.) *The Control of Drugs and Drug Users: Reason or Reaction?* Amsterdam: Harwood Academic Publishers.

Musto, D. (1973) *The American Disease: Origins of Narcotic Control*. New Haven Connecticut: Yale University Press.

Palmer, J. (2000) *Spinning into Control*. Leicester: Leicester University Press.

Parker, H., Aldridge, J. and Measham, F. (1998) *Illegal Leisure: The Normalization of Adolescent Recreational Drug Use*. London: Routledge.

Pearson, G. (1999) 'Drugs at the End of the Century', *British Journal of Criminology*, 39 (4): 477–487.

Pearson, G. and Twohig, J. (1976) 'Ethnography Through the Looking Glass: The Case of Howard Becker', in S. Hall and T. Jefferson (eds) (1976) *Resistance Through Rituals: Youth Subcultures in Post-war Britain*. London: Hutchinson.

Redhead, S. (1993) 'The End of the Century Party', in S. Redhead (ed.) *Rave Off: Politics and Deviance in Contemporary Youth Culture*. Aldershot: Avebury.

Reeves, J. and Campbell, R. (1994) *Cracked Coverage: Television News, the Anti-Cocaine Crusade and the Regan Legacy*. London: Duke University.

Russell, K. (1993) 'Lysergia Suburbia', in S. Redhead (ed.) *Rave Off: Politics and Deviance in Contemporary Youth Culture*. Aldershot: Avebury.

Schlesinger, P. (1990): 'Re-thinking the Sociology of Journalism: Source Strategies and the Limits of Media-centrism', in M. Ferguson (ed) *Public Communication: The New Imperatives*. London: Sage.

Shapiro, H. (2002) 'From Chaplin to Charlie – Cocaine, Hollywood and the Movies', *Drugs: Prevention Education and Policy*, 9 (2): 132–141.

Sterk-Ericson, C. (1996) 'Just for Fun? Cocaine use Amongst Middle Class Women', *Journal of Drug Issues*, 26 (1): 63–76.

Stevenson, J. (ed.) (2000) *Addicted: The Myth and Menace of Drugs in Film*. New York: Creation Books.

Thrasher, F.M. (1927) *The Gang: A Study of 1,313 Gangs in Chicago*. Chicago: Chicago University Press.

Willis, P. (1976) 'The Cultural Meaning of Drug Use', in S. Hall, and T. Jefferson (eds) (1976) *Resistance Through Rituals: Youth Subcultures in Post-war Britain*. London: Hutchinson.

Willis, P. (1990) *Common Culture*. Buckingham: Open University.

Wykes, M. (2001) *News Crime and Culture*. London: Pluto Press.

2. Mental health and moral panic: drug discourses in history[1]

Andrew Blake

Introduction

The aim of this chapter is to provide a historical context for the study of the relationship between drug use, public policy and popular culture in the UK by comparing aspects of the contested nature of discourses concerning drugs, social identities and cultural practices in relation to the use of opium and cannabis.

A liberal regime in the 1890s, uneasily committed both to the maintenance of the Empire and to free trade, combated a puritanical popular culture which was hostile to narcotic drugs, seeing trade in them as both immoral and inimical to the spread of Christianity, and claiming that their use in Britain was the resort of evil foreigners liable to corrupt the native British. Meanwhile medical discourses insisted that drug use led almost inevitably to addiction, insanity, or both. One hundred and ten years later, while the official position is now (ambivalently) negative in its attempts to regulate both the personal use of and trade in drugs, those puritanical and medical discourses still thrive – but now alongside a libertarian popular culture which celebrates drug use. Using official and popular texts, this chapter suggests that both positive and normalised views of illegal substance use *and* opposition thereto are deeply ingrained in popular culture – which is precisely why no consistent and effective regulatory move in any direction is possible. In order to understand this complexity we need to examine the history of drugs in relation to the formation of British policy, and this means starting with the popular campaign against the opium trade.

Imperial opium

In the early eighteenth century the East India Company established a trading post at Canton, buying Chinese tea and silks, for which Indian calicoes were exchanged. Demand by the British consumer for tea increased faster than that of the Chinese for calicoes, but luckily for the British tea-drinking public a substitute was found which was produced in India: opium. The East India

Company, having established a monopoly of opium-growing in Bengal in 1773, began to supply it to China, smuggling the drug in against the wishes of the Chinese authorities. Successful companies founded by these activities included Jardine, Matheson and Co; David Jardine himself was convinced that opium was 'the safest and most gentlemanlike speculation I am aware of' (Greenberg 1951: 105).

Meanwhile the manufacturers of Great Britain, looking for new markets for their mass-produced textiles, put pressure on the British government to open the door to trade with 400 million Chinese. When Commissioner Lin confiscated imported opium at Canton, on 18 March 1839, the British government took his action as *casus belli* (an act or event that provokes or is used to justify war); the resulting conflict has become known as the 'First Opium War'. But in 1850 the value of British exports to China was only a little higher than in 1843. The 'Second Opium War' of 1856 to 1860 followed, at a point when the British regime was stretched by the Indian 'mutiny' – troops and warships originally despatched to China had to be rerouted to Calcutta, and as a result of the revolt the East India Company was disbanded, and direct British control over all aspects of Indian life, including the growing, preparation and sale of opium, increased (Sardesai 1977).

The 1860 Treaty of Tientsin legalised the India-Chinese trade in opium, which became an important part of the Chinese economy; rights of residence were granted to European merchants and missionaries, and toleration was granted to Chinese converts to Christianity. But missionary progress in winning converts was agonisingly slow. Reviled for trying to teach what they believed to be a message of love, the missionaries assumed that the Chinese associated them with the opium trade. Opium became the missionaries' symbol of Chinese resistance to Christianity (Legge 1905: 108; Harrison 1979: 103).

The Anglo-Oriental Society for the Suppression of the Opium Trade with China (hereafter 'the Society') was formed in response to this perception. Their campaign was among a series of interventions in which non-conformists opposed aspects of British foreign policy such as the Crimean War, while in relation to domestic policy the United Kingdom Alliance was pressing for temperance, and the Society for the Prevention of Cruelty to Animals had launched a test case which led to anti-vivisection legislation in 1876 (Johnson 1975; Hollis 1974; Harrison 1994; French 1975). 'Nothing which is morally wrong can be politically right ... we can put down the opium traffic as we put down slavery', announced Alderman McArthur, MP at the Society's first meeting in 1874.[2] Wealthy Quakers such as the Pease family set the Society on a firm financial footing, and paid its Secretary, the Rev. Frederick Storrs Turner, who edited the Society's magazine *Friend of China*, a publication whose motto, 'Righteousness before Revenue', encapsulated the moral knowledge of the nonconformist conscience.[3]

On 10 April 1891 the Society's lobbying paid off as Prime Minister Gladstone, fighting to keep his Cabinet together in order to pass Irish Home Rule, agreed to an investigation into the future of the Indian opium revenue. The resulting Royal Commission held its first meetings in London in September 1893. Peking medical missionary Dr Dudgeon summarised the Society's fundamental belief, stating baldly that 'Many drink, but few abuse; many smoke opium, but all abuse'.[4] This moral knowledge was strongly challenged.[5] Surgeon General Sir William Moore claimed that 'A moderate use would brighten the intellect and strengthen the system, render the people more able to go through fatigue'; he admitted having tried the drug himself, in a Bombay opium den.[6] Several witnesses noted that the two Indian groups to use opium most extensively, the Sikhs and Rajputs, were in the words of Sir John Strachey the 'finest physical specimens' of all the Indian ethnic and religious groups, and that their use of the drug was culturally important.[7] Others, with experience of China, also denied the Society's claims.[8]

The Commission moved to India, where the government made a big effort to combat the Society's moral knowledge by an 'official knowledge' of its own manufacture. Hand-picked witnesses all claimed both that opium could be taken in moderation, and that the opium revenue was irreplaceable to the Indian economy. Indian witnesses testified to the drug's cultural importance and harmlessness. Bhati Ragrunath Singh, a Rajput, said that he had taken a dose of some 60 grains per day for 16 years without ill effect; another Rajput, Thakur Budihana, admitted to taking eight grains per day, and stressed the importance of the drug at ceremonial and ritual occasions.[9] The Indian National Congress stressed the culturally sanctioned use of opium, claiming that prohibition would be tantamount to racial discrimination.[10] The anti-opiumists were shocked when the Anglican Bishop and clergy, and Catholic hierarchy, of Calcutta sent a letter to the Commission approving the use of opium.[11] Perhaps more shockingly, they failed to find in the Indian opium dens the wan, emaciated addicts their own propaganda had described: instead they saw healthy people puffing away quite happily. One of the Commission's anti-opium representatives, Arthur Pease, changed his mind and resigned from the Society. *The Final Report* of the Royal Commission, published on 25 April 1895, concluded that:

> ... whilst there are evils in the abuse of opium, they are not sufficiently great to justify us in restricting the liberty which all men should be permitted to exercise in such matters, medical testimony seeming to show that opium used in moderation is in this country [India] harmless, and, under certain conditions of life, extremely beneficial.[12]

It was, therefore, acceptable for the Indian Government to continue to export opium. It did so.

Imperial ganja

One of the constant reference points in the Royal Commission's investigations in India was ganja. There was no overseas trade in cannabis derivatives, and no public campaign to end its use either in India or the UK, but at the height of the anti-opium campaign, on 16 July 1891, one of the Society's leading Parliamentary campaigners, Sir Mark Stewart Bart, MP, asked the Secretary of State for India, Lord Kimberley, 'whether ganja is more harmful than opium, whether lunatic asylums in India are filled with ganja smokers, and whether he would prohibit its use in India'. He alleged that use of the drug encouraged criminality. Kimberley wrote to the Governor General, Lord Ripon 'I shall be glad to learn your views as to the effects of this drug, and whether you propose to take any further steps for restricting [its] consumption'.[13]

Almost a year later Ripon replied that the matter had been discussed extensively in 1872–3, and that he and his officials stood by the conclusions which had been reached after that investigation. Ganja had been outlawed in British-ruled Burma because its use was recent, but was still permitted in India, where it was traditional. Lord Ripon stressed the negative findings of the 1873 report, claiming that ganja was 'usually … noxious', and that 'its habitual use does tend to produce insanity'.[14] However, he was convinced both that it did not of itself produce crime, and that it would be impossible to enforce a prohibition.

The Governor General provided the entire documentation of the 1872–3 survey of the growth and use of ganja along with his own findings. These papers indicate an investigation which was by no means so negative as Ripon had suggested. As with the opium enquiry, official knowledge was produced by a racialised and bureaucratic power structure. The enquiry was delegated from the Governor General to the provincial Chief Commissioners, and thence downwards to Secretaries and Assistant Secretaries for smaller districts, who about a year after the original enquiry reported back to their superiors. They in turn had meanwhile consulted doctors, keepers of lunatic asylums, magistrates, revenue collectors and chiefs of police. The many missionaries in India were not involved in campaigning against ganja use. None of the reporting British officials referred to the Bible for moral doctrine.

By contrast to the fiercely contested knowledges at play in the Opium Commission, this was a purely official and secular knowledge, produced with the usual apparatus of categories and typologies, statistics and analyses, with an admixture of rumour and hearsay. Stewart's question about ganja and crime, for instance, was an aspect of the continuing British concern to identify and extirpate what they thought were hereditary Indian criminal tribes, castes, classes or religious sub-groups such as 'thugs' (van Woerkens 2003). This was a perception firmly rooted in their own biologist and racist stereotypes, beliefs which can be found in popular fictions of the time such as (opium user) Wilkie Collins's post-'Mutiny' text *The Moonstone* (1868) and the Sherlock Holmes story *The Sign of Four* (1890) and which remained virtually unchanged in twentieth-century representations such as the films *Help!* (directed by Dick Lester 1965) and *Indiana Jones and the Temple of Doom* (directed by Stephen Spielberg 1984). Local chiefs of police were enjoined to the task of finding these supposed criminal castes above all others, and the enquiry into cannabis use was partly based on these perceptions of associated criminality.

The investigation was not pursued only by white British people, however. Native Indians also spoke in these reports, as they did in the opium enquiry. This was usually from their subaltern positions on the periphery of the power structure, as assistant surgeons for example, but the report submitted to the Governor General include a detailed *Report on the Cultivation of, and Trade in Ganja in Bengal*, by Hem Chunder Kerr, which was the most sustained, scholarly and authoritative voice in this discursive set – an intervention whose influence can clearly be seen in the other scholarly article appended to the 1893–94 papers, 'Cannabis Sativa' by George Watt. Indian voices not only spoke, but were heard: many of the arguments against prohibition, put consistently by native officials, were confirmed both in the 1873 report and in the official response to Mark Stewart some 20 years later.

The 1873 and 1893 reports on ganja, with their delegated enquiries, sub-reports, abstracts and summaries, statistics, and appended medical and scientific articles on cannabis and its effects, provide an exemplary instance of the intellectual, critical and sociological apparatus of the Raj. Exemplary in their methodology and coverage, that is. The bureaucratic effort resulted in producing only a conditional and heterodox discourse, rather than univocal evidence-based opinion leading to new policy. In this discursive set, at least, the hegemony of the Raj has been acquired, and is reproduced, through compromise and negotiation between the interests of growers, sellers and traditional users, and those of revenue collectors, police, and legal and medical officials. There is no uniform set of responses, as the reports from local Commissioners to the Governor General make clear. Lepel Griffin, Secretary to the Commissioner of the Punjab, for example, wrote that 'the reports received are most contradictory, the civil and police officers differing greatly in opinion as to the influence of these preparations in exciting to crime, while the medical officers disagree as to their effect in inducing mania or mental derangement'.[15]

There was one point of agreement, over the medicalised typology of ganja. There were three common forms of drug produced by *cannabis indica* or Indian hemp (*cannabis sativa* is the similar European plant), which was widely available in the wild as well as cultivated as a cash crop in Bengal. Ganja, a preparation of dried flowers and leaves, and charas, the plant's resin, could be smoked. Bhang, also a decoction of the leaves, was made into a drink. That was the extent of the agreement. Some claimed that the Hindu middle class were the most frequent users, some that Moslems used it most heavily; some argued that its heaviest users were manual labourers, others that only the poorest, and especially faquirs and religious mendicants, took the drug. As with the evidence given to the Royal Commission on opium, there are some reports of cannabis in its various forms as uniquely harmful, degenerative and addictive – while others saw it as medically beneficial, or merely a harmless local custom.

Take the question of ganja-produced insanity, whose claimed incidence produced enquiries and reports in Egypt as well as India in the 1890s (Berridge and Edwards 1981: 213). The 1873 investigation's reports are typically contradictory: there were according to their medical officers lunatic asylums overflowing with victims of the weed, but also asylums in which surgeons reported that cannabis use and insanity could not be directly correlated at all; and some where it seems there was a fluctuating percentage, but constant presence, of reefer madness: between 10 and 20 per cent of those treated in Delhi asylums, according to Dr Penny, a Delhi civil surgeon.[16] One comparatively constant finding from the asylum keepers is that a large proportion of the reefer-mad can be treated successfully; according to Dr Ranking, of Mysore, 64 of 82 recent ganja admissions had been treated and released.[17] Elsewhere government representatives could only report the unsubstantiated beliefs of fellow British officials. A. MacKenzie, the Junior Secretary of Bengal, reported to his Commissioner that 'The medical officers in Chota Nagpore, though they can give no authenticated cases, are under the impression that ganja consumers often become insane'.[18]

If there was no agreement on the first point of Mark Stewart's enquiry, there was consensus that there was no direct relationship between ganja's use and crime. All local police chiefs argued that it did not produce criminals in any direct (physically or mentally determinist) way, though some argued that drug users stole to support their habit, and some claimed that bhang would often be taken before a crime to produce courage. Dr Alexander Thomas, writing from Kyat-Phoo in Burma, repeated a more powerful version of this rumour, opening once again that recent scar on the British psyche: 'this drug is said to have been brought into play at the time of the Sepoy rebellion to infuriate the men'.[19]

There were, on the other hand, dry comparisons with drugs taken by British criminals. The Secretary to the Commissioner for the Punjab, Lepel Griffin, claimed that:

> If people are prohibited the use of hemp and opium, they will in all probability take to some other form of stimulant, such as alcohol, the amount of crime resulting from which, as English statistics unmistakably prove, is more than that of all stimulants used in India put together'.[20]

H.S. Thomas reported to the Madras Board of Revenue that 'Ganja and the other preparations of hemp seem to be useful medicines, pleasant drinks and enjoyable smoking … the mischief done by their abuse can bear no comparison with the evil effects of alcohol'.[21]

In this he agreed with most of the native Indian contributors to the investigation. Here, too, the writers are not univocal, though there is agreement that the drug should not be prohibited. Magistrate, Iajoodeen Hoosain, reporting to the Commissioner for West Berar, agreed that bhang could be used for criminal courage-gathering, but emphasised that it was also an economically productive drug, imparting stamina: 'its users continue to work as long as they are under its influence … it is a means, I should say, of assisting them in gaining their livelihood'.[22] Babu Deno Nath Doss, sub-assistant surgeon of Akyab, agreed that 'some may be made to work much harder, without grumbling, than others who do not indulge in it. If a habitual indulger in ganja is also insane it is, I believe, a mere coincidence'.[23] Mr Balkristina, sub-assistant surgeon at the Sind lunatic asylum, claimed that most natives used it moderately without ill effects, though over-indulgence could cause temporary insanity[24]; Ram Naraim, District Superintendent, Pratabgarh, stressed the temporary nature of the insanity, and could find 'no instance' of permanent insanity caused by the drug,[25] a finding also confirmed by Mahomed Bulish, a doctor from Unao.[26] Assistant surgeon, Moodeen Sherif, reporting to the Indian Medical Department at Madras, argued that long-term ganja users were often sane, but in poor health, weakened by asthma in particular, though he claimed that bhang users 'are generally in robust health, and have a voracious appetite, with an equal increase in power of digestion'.[27] (By contrast, Dr Penny claimed that the drug's physical effects were like those attributed to opium by its opponents: 'Old bhang-drinkers, charas and ganja smokers are, as a rule, emaciated. They lose vital energy, become impotent, forgetful, weak-minded and melancholy'.)[28]

Hem Chunder Kerr's report on the growth of ganja in Bengal chronicled the place of the drug in Sanskrit literature and Hindu mythology, in Greek and Arabic literatures (noting the correspondence between the Arabic 'hashish' and 'assassin'), and in its use in the Arabic, Turkish and Persian cultures of his day. Like Moodeen Sherif, he claimed that charas and bhang do little harm to the constitution, but that long-term ganja use is harmful. His report describes the growth, packaging and sale of the ganja produced under official licence in 60,000 acres of the Rajshaye area of Bengal, concluding that it is a useful revenue raiser, and that as the poor use it, to tax it more heavily would be to increase smuggling, and/or make them use other drugs such as arrack or opium – thus reducing the revenue.[29] Chunder Kerr's findings were repeated by J Ware Edgar, the Secretary to the Commissioner for Bengal, who reported that revenue income had increased from 369,801 rupees in 1853–54, to 1,106,768 rupees in 1870.[30] The final resolution of the Indian Financial Department on 17 December 1873 was that 'On the whole, the general opinion seems to be that the evil effects of ganja have been exaggerated'.

Reviewing all this correspondence for his parliamentary reply to Mark Stewart, Secretary of State Lord Kimberley wrote to the Governor General:

> You are of the opinion that it would be impossible to enforce a general prohibition of the use of this stimulant, the more so as the practice of smoking ganja has existed from time immemorial to the present day. In this view I concur, as it would obviously be inexpedient to order a prohibition which could not be enforced, while there would be a continual danger lest the consumption should be merely diverted from recognised channels, the demand being met by an illicit trade.[32]

This liberal position on drug use and trade was, then, established by the British government as an official knowledge, and seemed an important aspect of the economic and cultural strategy for continued Imperial rule until the 1920s when, driven by the same enthusiastic American puritanism which had led to Prohibition in the USA, the international trade in narcotic drugs was proscribed by the League of Nations. The final resolution of the League's meetings on trade in opium, ratified in Britain in 1928 when the Dangerous Drugs Act 1925 came into force, also included, thanks to pressure from the Egyptian delegation, a ban on trade in cannabis (Mills 2003: 6–7 summarises these developments).

Imperial addictions

But opposition to drug use was not merely driven by American or Egyptian interests, or by the enthusiasm of the non-conformist conscience in the UK.

Despite the official position, British popular culture and medical discourses alike had become increasingly hostile to narcotics. At the beginning of the nineteenth century the taking of opium in the form of tablets or of the alcohol-based drink laudanum had been tolerated if not welcomed as a personal habit. Due both to changing medical opinion, and to the extension of non-conformist attitudes to alcohol use, the taking of drugs for pleasure came to be seen as an anti-social activity, and, increasingly as both a disease and a crime-controlled by isolation, treatment for addiction, or imprisonment. The medicalised and criminalised category of 'the addict' thus joined other emergent discursive categories – such as the insane; the unemployed man; the common prostitute; the homosexual man; and the hooligan – as a subject of surveillance and professional control (Berridge and Edwards 1981; Schwarz 1985; Mort 1987). Like the prostitute, the addict was seen as dangerous because of the possibility of contagion; the danger posed by the addict was further emphasised, at a time of concern over the future of the British 'race', by the category being itself racialised.

Though some medical opinion remained unconvinced by theories of addiction – several doctors gave pro-opium evidence to the Royal Commission – in general the arguments used to justify the increasing power over the body's diseases and desires exercised by the medical profession supported the anti-opium case. By the 1890s medical opinion had refined the concept of drug addiction. When it became clear in the aftermath of the American Civil War that the subcutaneous injection of morphine carried the risk of addiction the British medical profession turned against the 'self administration' of all opiates, even as pain-killers. Similarly the realisation that cocaine, proposed as a substitute for morphine in Vienna in the 1880s by Sigmund Freud (a user) was also potentially addictive, reinforced the arguments for professional medical control of drugs (Berridge and Edwards 1981: 135–172, 278–281; Parsinnen 1983: 68–114).

Another aspect to the issue was equally important in the British imaginary. At stake in the anti-opium campaign was a narrative of Empire which sought to reconcile the conflicting views of officials, merchants and missionaries into a moral, political and economic *apologia* for the entire Imperial project which placed the white English man as the hero of the story. And the villain? The Other. There is in these discourses of Empire a tendency for moral transposition, in which evil or degradation are ascribed to the victim rather than the perpetrator of imperial acts. This happens in much of the fiction of Empire – in Collins, Haggard, Henty, Buchan and indeed Conrad. The evil lies in the 'heart of darkness', and not in the hearts of the Europeans, unless (and this is a perpetual danger) they are corrupted by it – as, in these fictions as in the earlier dreams of De Quincey, is all too possible. The Protestant, succumbing to temptation, can lose both rationality and all chance of salvation; by analogy the white man can become, through contact with the Other or the Other's cultural products and practices, non-white. Thus while the Empire is morally justified as the assertion of cultural and racial superiority over the Other, discourses of One Empire are also constructed in response to a set of anxieties about the possibilities of racial failure which threaten the very existence of an Imperial heroism (Needham 1969; Kiernan 1969; Said 1994; Barrell 1992).

Many writings about drugs and their users, from De Quincey onwards, promote this narrative of race and infection. In discussing opium, James F. Johnston's *The Chemistry of Common Life*, published in 1855, notes 'this power of seduction even over the less delicate and susceptible organisation of our North European races',[33] while ranking Malays, Javanese and Africans alike as 'Orientals', and claiming that 'upon all of them [opium] produces those marked and striking effects which, among ourselves, we only see in rare instances, and in persons of uncommonly nervous disposition'.[34] A crucial transformation in the discourses around opium occurred when attention turned to Britain. Here the panic over infection was reinforced by growing fear of an enemy within, while the first post-Darwinian generation displayed anxieties about racial degeneration 'at home'. The implication, already present in De Quincey's fears of Orientalised subjectivity (which were amplified when a Malay sailor turned up on his own doorstep), is drawn out and emphasised to make opium use of itself a signal of irredeemable Otherness. The opening of China to missionaries in 1860, and the debates over the Pharmacy Bill later in the decade, constructed opium-as-problem within the general public imaginary. Where in *Hard Times* (1854) Dickens merely mentions the use of opium in passing, as an alcohol substitute, by the time of his last – unfinished – novel *Edwin Drood* (1870) a new rhetoric of disapproval is in play. Cathedral choirmaster Jasper leaves the cloisters for an East End opium den, dreams of murder while under the influence of opium, and then actually commits a murder. The East End of London, where the native British can meet foreign purveyors and users of opium, and thereby lose their Christian respectability, even their humanity, is the most potent symbol of internal Otherness. Indeed, the East End was itself a racialised, Orientalised Other, its creation as 'Darkest England' signalled by Jerrold and Doré's *A London Pilgrimage* (1872), from which this description of an East End opium den characterises the new structure of feeling: 'upon a mattress heaped with indescribable clothes, lay, sprawling, a Lascar, dead-drunk with opium … It was difficult to see any humanity in that face, as the enormous grey lips lapped about the rough pipe and drew in the poison'.[35] ('Lascars' were Indian sailors.)

The image of the London opium den involves a very specific transposition, around the figures of the Chinese owners of opium dens. Consider the opening of the Sherlock Holmes story 'The Man with the Twisted Lip': Watson's friend Whitney is found in an East End opium den. 'I can see him now', recalls the good Doctor, 'with yellow, pasty face, drooping lids, and pin-point pupils … the wreck and ruin of a noble man'.[36] Racial 'degeneration' is evident here: Whitney's use of opium has made him, yellow-faced and drooping-lidded, into a *para-Chinese*, corrupted by the evil foreigners who supply the drug into one of their own. The fictional apogee of this construction of the Chinese is Sax Rohmer's character Fu Manchu, who first appeared in 1913. Such works as Rohmer's *Yellow Claw* (1925) emphasise the drug's 'evil' nature, associating it with the seduction of innocent white women; fictionally driven fear of miscegenation was one reason for harassment of the East End Chinese community by the police (Parsinnen 1983: 119–121; in general, Kohn 1992). Fu Manchu is the epitome of many other characteristics ascribed to the Chinese: he has intelligence, sophistication and cruelty; his followers, slaves to his will, are dedicated workers. The stereotype remained in British culture well into the 1960s, through for example Ian Fleming's *Doctor No* (the book was published in 1958; the film, directed by Terence Young, appeared in 1962), and Hammer Studio's film reworkings of the Fu Manchu stories, starring Christopher Lee as Fu Manchu (the first of these, *The Face of Fu Manchu*, directed by Don Sharp, appeared in 1965; the last, *The Castle of Fu Manchu*, directed by Jess Franco, had a troubled production and release history – its original release was scheduled for 1968).

At stake, then, was the preservation of a distinctly British, white, Protestant identity which was highly masculinised, individualised and internalised, and which did not and could not rely on external chemical sustainers or stimulants. This identity was therefore unstable, in danger. A popular version of the threat is Stevenson's *Dr Jekyll and Mr Hyde* (1887), in which a professional man takes a drug and is transformed into a degenerate creature. The author's disapproval marries Darwinist and Christian concerns: 'Mr Hyde was pale and dwarfish; he gave an impression of deformity', which impresses one of his observers thus: 'God bless me, the man seems hardly human'.[37] Similarly, Oscar Wilde's *The Picture of Dorian Grey* (1891) uses the East End opium den, and is suffused with images of luxury and drug-induced ecstasy whose tendency, again, is degradation rather than mere decadence: 'Our limbs fail, our senses rot. We degenerate into senseless puppets'.[38] In the case of personal drug use this ascetic ideology remains hegemonic within official and some popular discourses. Far from being a simple pleasure-seeker, the drug user is seen as the devil within: whatever her or his ostensible social position, however innocent before using drugs, she or he became by the 1890s an outsider, an internal Other beyond the boundaries of respectability; a persona gleefully inhabited later by self-made outsiders such as Aleister Crowley – and by his sometime follower, Led Zeppelin guitarist Jimmy Page.

But not all drug users were simplistically represented, or represented themselves, as Mr Hyde. Conan Doyle, wishing to emphasise his hero Sherlock Holmes's relative separateness from the respectable world of late Victorian Britain which he observed and investigated, portrayed him as a bachelor, a violinist, and as an occasional user of both morphine and cocaine – to the disapproval of the quintessentially respectable Dr Watson.[39] And in doing so Conan Doyle made one of the most enduring literary heroes. Holmes is among the first of a number of characters and stereotypes who display the positive side of this Othering of Bohemianism. Holmes's scholarly bachelorhood and his knowledge of the underworld allow him to escape from the norms of masculine responsibility and family life, and to see, sometimes we must assume to partake in, its pleasures. He is therefore a forerunner of a number of types who revel in the possibilities of the city and its anonymity, of changes of identity (of which 'The Man with One Twisted Lip' makes much), of Orientalism as attraction to the body of the Other, and of gay and other non-marital sexual pleasures. However much he might himself use morphine, or masquerade, Holmes has no Hyde side.

Holmes's habit apart, most late-Victorian and Edwardian dreams or fears about drugs revolved around opium. Ganja did not inhabit the British imaginary in quite the same way as opium and its later derivatives. The same assumptions were often present in the literature on the drug. We return to Johnston's *Chemistry of Common Life*, which concludes its 18-page survey of *cannabis indica* with this piece of classic Orientalism: 'The drug seems, in fact, to be to the oriental a source of exquisite and peculiar enjoyment, which unfits him for the ordinary affairs of this rough life, and with which happily we are, in this part of the world, still altogether unacquainted',[40] while as with opium Johnston claimed that 'upon Europeans generally, at least in Europe, its effects have been found to be considerably less in degree than upon orientals'.[41]

However, ganja was in any case relatively harmless to that rectilinear white masculine figure, the hero at the centre of the British Empire, because there was so little evidence of cross-infection. Its effects were studied in Cairo or Delhi, not Limehouse or Wapping. Whatever may have been the practices of bored civil servants on summer evenings in Simla, the drug did not seem to make its way to Britain. Cannabis was experimented with by doctors from the 1840s on – in the treatment of insanity, interestingly enough – but it did not become a routine medicine. On the whole cannabis consumption in Britain is a mid to late-twentieth century phenomenon; the drug arrived in quantity via the incomers from the West Indian islands to which Indian contract labour took it during the second half of the nineteenth century. The increasing West Indian population, resident mainly in the inner cities of London, Birmingham, Bristol, Liverpool and Manchester, also brought with them musics such as calypso and reggae, which fitted seamlessly into the emerging multi-culture of post-colonial Britain.

It is a small step from the opium dens of late-Victorian London to the small-club jazz, blues, reggae and rock Othernesses and bohemianisms which punctuate the history of the early to mid-twentieth century city – whether that city be New York or Chicago, Paris or London – and a further small step from that small-club bohemianism to the hedonistic mass popular culture of stadium rock and the outdoor rock festival which characterised the second half of the century (McKay 2000). However hard he identified with Aleister Crowley, Jimmy Page remained a much-loved musician. Through this association of drugs with the pleasures conferred by twentieth century popular music, the negative fears of the puritans have been reversed, and as argued elsewhere in this volume, the compelling myths of narcotised pleasure, from the dance revolution of the 1920s to that of the late 1980s, have produced a popular culture of acceptable, and increasingly democratised, drug use which has popularised the pursuit of oblivion as a routine goal of any holiday, or indeed any night out (Garrett 1998; but cf. the less celebratory Thornton 1995). Drug-assisted hedonism has moved well beyond the Faustian stimulus for musicians, the upper-class bohemia of the West End club and the restricted illegal resorts of the East End opium den in the 1900s, the Anglo-West Indian 'shebeen' in the 1970s, or the warehouse 'rave' party in the 1980s. This culture is now part of the night clubs of every town, where – though the availability of narcotic drugs is hedged about by the problems of most drugs' illegality – thanks to the popularisation of the effects of drugs such as ecstasy, alcohol is currently *used as a narcotic* by large numbers of youngish people who find the regular purchase of illegal drugs tiresomely inconvenient. The use of cannabis, meanwhile, has become 'normal' in the sense debated in this volume, travelling well beyond that original community of West Indian users (see Part 2 in this volume).

A summary of cannabis use in Britain in the late 1990s and early 2000s might therefore read thus: mass use, not much harm, but, much public alarm. While the State, as usual, spent the minimum on rehabilitation and was content to criminalise large numbers of people who merely possessed the drug for personal use, there were constant (and often controversial) policing experiments, sometimes alongside other attempted supply and/or demand management programmes and campaigns for and against more liberal laws. As Simon Cross points out, in 1997, as a new and at first sight more liberal government settled into power, the *Independent on Sunday* newspaper mounted a campaign for legalisation which claimed that the drug was harmless to most users, and beneficial to some; meanwhile other campaigners against a hard line on the use of the drug invoked and supported medical debates on the possible benefit of cannabis use in the remission of pain for sufferers from the incurable wasting disease multiple sclerosis. In March 2002 the government's advisory group the Advisory Council on the Misuse of Drugs,[42] reviewing evidence which had accumulated since the Misuse of Drugs Act 1971, claimed that cannabis was significantly less harmful than other drugs in class B, and proposed that it should not be legalised but reclassified.[43] Home Secretary, David Blunkett, subsequently enacted the reclassification of the drug from class B to C, a change which came into effect on 29 January 2004, and which left the growing, preparation, sale and use of the drug illegal, but – somewhat confusingly – no longer led automatically to the criminalisation of those found in possession for personal use.

The response of the anti-drug community (including much of the popular press) was to invoke 'new research' which apparently proved that cannabis was becoming increasingly harmful, and that in particular it caused, yes, insanity among frequent users. Almost as soon as the Home Secretary's plans became public, these opponents of reclassification asked for their reconsideration on the basis of this 'new evidence' of the link between cannabis use and schizophrenia. In January 2003 there was a debate in the House of Lords, and thereafter further questions in the House of Commons, at which these arguments were rehearsed.[44] In July 2004, for example, Conservative MP, Ann Winterton, asked what assessment the government had made both of research linking the regular consumption of cannabis with schizophrenia and the effects of cannabis use on schizophrenia sufferers.[45] There followed a number of media-led moral panics about new forms of cannabis such as 'skunk' (grown indoors, hydroponically, under strong lights) which it was claimed contained far higher concentrations of the principal active constituent tetrahydrocarbinol.[46] People ingesting such materials regularly were, it was claimed, more likely to suffer from schizophrenia.

Eventually this pressure told. In December 2004 David Blunkett had been replaced as Home Secretary by the apparently less liberal Charles Clarke, and in March 2005 Clarke asked the Advisory Council on the Misuse of Drugs to evaluate the new evidence. It did so, and reported further in December 2005, repeating its position that cannabis was less harmful than class B drugs, acknowledging that the research into the relationship between cannabis and mental health was contradictory and inconclusive, and proposing – further research. These revived scares about the possible incidence of insanity from long-term cannabis use uncannily echo the debates of the 1870s; the more so as they were highly contentious. Like the 1873 and 1893 reports they contain an official knowledge which cannot be read off as containing, or justifying, a single policy outcome.

Home Secretary Clarke once again accepted the findings of this review, and announced in January 2006 that cannabis would remain classified under class C; he had also commissioned a new review of the entire classification schema. This was, then, not quite an *official* normalisation of the use of cannabis; but acceptance of the mass use of this drug seemed a lot more normal, even in official circles, than it had in the supposedly liberal 1960s. Meanwhile, however, British people were still constrained in their choice of narcotic in a way which had not applied to Indians under British rule in the 1890s.

In concluding this survey of continuities in drug discourses we turn to the *Times*, a newspaper close to the producers of official knowledge, and which has been commenting on these issues, usually from a libertarian point of view, since the heyday of the anti-opium campaign. In a leading article of 4 September 1893 denouncing the non-conformist conscience, 'the Thunderer' lived up to its Victorian nickname: 'The British Pharisee has already won for himself the hearty aversion of many races, white, black, and brown, upon this earth for his unsolicited anxiety for their moral welfare'. On 1 July 1967 a leading article asked plaintively of Mick Jagger's prosecution for personal drug use 'Who breaks a butterfly on a wheel?' On 7 January 2006, the day after Clarke's review announcement, a leading article debated the possibility of legalising the drug, brushing aside the renewed fears about mental health for adults while conceding that those whose brains had not fully developed – children – should receive protection, and arguing that everyone should be more fully informed about the potential effects of the drug. This article concluded that 'The logic is libertarian, but the leap is still a step too far. Alcohol remains our socially acceptable lubricant'.

As *The Times* implied, cannabis was perhaps knocking on the door of quasi-legality in the early twentieth century. Opiate use, on the other hand, was still totally unacceptable in official circles. Active efforts were being made to eradicate the growth of poppies as part of the neo-imperial intervention in Afghanistan, and official policy-makers were searching for other ways to 'intervene in the market' so as to reduce the supplies of heroin (and cocaine).[47] Though disappointed at their problem's persistence, the ghosts of those who had founded the Society for the Suppression of the Opium Trade would doubtless have nodded with approval.

Abbreviations used in Notes

FOC: Friend of China.
IH: Papers on Indian Hemp, in *Parliamentary Papers,* London, HMSO, 1893-94 vol. LXVI, pp 79–256.

PP: Parliamentary Papers.

RC: The Royal Commission on Opium. This was published in seven volumes, which are to be found within *Parliamentary Papers*, London, HMSO:

vol. 1: *PP 1894* vol. LX, pp 593–760;

vol. 2: *PP 1894* vol. LXI, pp 1–666;

vol. 3: *PP 1894* vol. LXI, pp 673–972;

vol. 4: *PP 1894* vol. LXII, pp 1–524;

vol. 5: *PP 1894* vol. LXII, pp 531–906.

vol. 6: *PP 1895* vol. XLII, pp. 31–220;

vol. 7: *PP 1895* vol. XLII, pp. 221-544.

SSOT: The Society for the Suppression of the Opium Trade with China.

Notes

1   This paper draws on two earlier publications of the author: (1996) 'Foreign Devils and Moral Panics: The Anglo-Indian Opium Trade with China', in B. Schwarz (ed.) *The Expansion of England. Essays in Postcolonial Cultural History*, London: Routledge, pp 232–259; and (2003) 'The Construction of a Liberal Response to Drug Use in India', in S. Caporale Bizzini (ed.) *We, the Other Victorians*, Alicante: University of Alicante Press, pp 53–70. While, therefore, it has been informed by the work of James H. Mills (2003) *Cannabis Britannica, Empire, Trade and Prohibition*, Oxford: Oxford University Press, and by Simon Cross's chapter in this volume, it should be stressed that the research on the late-Victorian opium and ganja investigations is the author's own.

2   (1875) *The Opium Trade*, p 3. London: SSOT.

3   *Ibid.*, pp 1, 12, 14–15.

4   *RC* vol. 1, p. 596.

5   *RC* vol. 1, pp 642–647 (evidence of Brigade Surgeon, R. Pringle); pp 651–660 (Sir John Strachey); pp 661–665 (Surgeon General. Sir William Moore) – all Indian officials; pp 676–689 (Sir Thomas Wade); and pp 671–676 (H.N. Lay), both Anglo-Chinese officials.

6   *RC* vol. 1, p. 661.

7   *RC* vol. 1, p. 672.

8   *RC* vol. 1, p. 673, evidence of H.N. Lay.

9   RC vol. IV, pp. 119, 150.

10   *Ibid.*, p. 130.

11   FOC vol. XIV no. 6, January 1894, pp. 190–192.

12   *RC* vol. VII p. 438.

13   *IH*, p. 81.

14   *IH*, p. 82.

15   *IH*, p. 91.

16   *IH*, p. 93.

17   *IH*, p. 89.

18   *IH*, p. 105.

19   *IH*, p. 114.

20   *IH*, p. 91.

21   *IH*, p. 163.

22   *IH*, p. 104.

23   *IH*, p. 115.

24   *IH*, p. 139.

25   *IH*, p. 123.

26 *IH*, p. 130.
27 *IH*, p. 160.
28 *IH*, p. 93.
29 The entire report is in *IH*, pp. 175–227.
30 *IH*, p. 147.
31 *IH*, p. 166.
32 *IH*, p. 171.
33 J.F. Johnston (1885) *The Chemistry of Common Life*, vol. II: 76. Edinburgh: Blackwood.
34 *Ibid.*, p 93.
35 G. Doré, and W. Jerrold (1872) *A London Pilgrimage*, pp. 147–148. London: Grant.
36 A. Conan Doyle (1891–93) 'The Man with the Twisted Lip', originally from *The Adventures of Sherlock Holmes*, in *The Strand Magazine*, London; here (1981) *The Penguin Complete Sherlock Holmes*, p. 229, London: Penguin.
37 R.L. Stevenson (1889) *Doctor Jekyll and Mr Hyde*. London; here Collins, n.d., p. 66.
38 O. Wilde (1891) *The Picture of Dorian Grey*. London: Ward Lock; here New York: The Modern Library, n.d., pp. 246–247.
39 Holmes's hypodermic appears in Conan Doyle (1890) *The Sign of Four*. London: Spencer Blackett.
40 Johnston *Chemistry*, vol. 2, p. 126.
41 *Ibid.*, p. 116.
42 The Advisory Council on the Misuse of Drugs had 39 named persons in 2005, of whom one was identified as being of a religious faith. Eight were charitable workers concerned with drug use, 23 were medical academics, administrators or practitioners, and the remaining 8 were police or lawyers.
43 Advisory Council on the Misuse of Drugs (2002) *The Classification of Cannabis Under the Misuse of Drugs Act 1971*. London: HMSO.
44 See *House of Lords Hansard*, 28 January 2003, columns 999–1002; *House of Commons Hansard*, 9 March 2004, column 1455W; *House of Commons Hansard*, 21 July 2004 columns 366-7W.
45 *Ibid.*
46 Media scare stories included Mark Henderson, 'One in Four at Risk of Cannabis Psychosis, *The Times* online, 12 April 2005; David McCandles, 'High Society: At up to £300 an Ounce, Exotic Strains of Designer Cannabis are Fuelling a Booming Market in Herbal Highs for Affluent Smokers', *The Independent* online, 5 September 2005.
47 No. 10 Downing Street Strategy Unit, 'SU Drugs Report. Phase 1: Understanding the Issues', 13 June 2005, London: Strategy Unit. The report, compiled by Lord Birt, onetime unpopular head of the BBC and then unpaid advisor to the Prime Minister, was put online after its leaked findings had been published by *The Observer* and *Guardian* newspapers: Alan Travis, 'Revealed: How Drugs War Failed', *Guardian* online, 5 July 2005. The second part of the report was similarly published after newspaper coverage. 'SU Drugs Report. Phase 2 Project: Diagnosis and Recommendations', 9 February 2006, London: Strategy Unit, and cf. Alan Travis, 'Prescribe More Free Heroin: Birt's Secret Advice to Ministers', *Guardian* online, 9 February 2006.

References and suggested reading

Barrell, J. (1992) *The Infection of Thomas de Quincey: A Psychopathology of Imperialism*. London: Yale University Press.

Berridge, V. and Edwards, G. (1987) *Opium and the People*. London: Allen Lane (1981), reprinted London: Yale University Press.

Chesneaux, J. *et al*. (1977) *China from the Opium Wars to the 1911 Revolution*. Hassocks: Harvester Press.

Collis, M. (1946) *Foreign Mud: Opium at Canton and the First Opium War*. London: Faber.

Doré, G. and Jerrold, W. (1872) *A London Pilgrimage*. London: Grant.

French, R.D. (1975) *Antivivisection and Medical Science in Victorian Society*. London: Yale University Press.

Garrett, S. (1998) *Adventures in Wonderland: A Decade of Club Culture*. London: Headline.

Graham, G.S. (1978) *The China Station: War and Diplomacy 1830–60*. London: Oxford University Press.

Greenberg, M. (1951) *British Trade and the Opening of China 1800–1842*. Cambridge: Cambridge University Press.

Hao, Y.P. (1986) *The Commercial Revolution in Nineteenth Century China*. Berkeley: University of California Press.

Harrison, B. (1979) *Waiting for China: The Anglo-Chinese College at Malacca 1818–1843*. Hong Kong: Hong Kong University Press.

Harrison, B. (1994) *Drink and the Victorians* (2nd edn). London: Faber.

Hollis, P. (ed.) (1974) *Pressure from Without*. London: Edward Arnold.

Johnson, B.D. (1975) 'Righteousness before Revenue: The Forgotten Moral Crusade against the Indo-Chinese Opium Trade', *Journal of Drug Issues*, 5 (4): 304–332.

Johnston, J.F. (1885) *The Chemistry of Common Life*. Edinburgh: Blackwood.

Kiernan, V. (1969) *The Lords of Human Kind*: London: Weidenfeld and Nicolson.

Kohn, M. (1992) *Dope Girls: The Birth of the British Drug Underground* (1st edn). London: Lawrence and Wishart.

Legge, H.E. (1905) *James Legge, Missionary and Scholar*. London: Constable.

McKay, G. (2000) *Glastonbury: A Very English Fair*. London: Victor Gollancz.

Mills, J. (2003) *Cannabis Britannica, Empire, Trade and Prohibition*. Oxford: Oxford University Press.

Morse, H.B. (1926) *The Chronicles of the East India Company Trading to China*. Oxford: Oxford University Press.

Mort, F. (1987) *Dangerous Sexualities*. London: Routledge.

Needham, J. (1969) *Within the Four Seas: The Dialogue of East and West*. London: Allen and Unwin.

Owen, D.E. (1934) *British Opium Policy in China and India*. New Haven: Yale University Press.

Parsinnen, T. (1983) *Secret Passions, Secret Remedies: Narcotic Drugs in British Society 1820–1930*. Manchester: Manchester University Press.

Pelcovits, N. (1948) *Old China Hands and the Foreign Office*. New York: King's Crown.

Said, E. (1994) *Orientalism* (2nd edn). Harmondsworth: Penguin.

Sardesai, B.R. (1977) *British Trade and Expansion in South-East Asia*. New Delhi: Allied Publishers.

Schwarz, B. (ed.) (1985) *Crises in the British State*. London: Hutchinson.

Spence, J. (1978) 'Opium Smoking in Ch'ing China', in F. Wakeman Jr. and C. Grant (eds) *Conflict and Control in Late Imperial China*. Cambridge: Cambridge University Press.

Thornton, S. (1995) *Club Cultures*. Cambridge: Polity Press.

Wakeman, F. Jr. (1978) 'The Canton Trade and the Opium War', in J.K. Fairbank (ed.) *The Cambridge History of China*. Cambridge: Cambridge University Press.

Wong, J.Y. (1976) 'The Building of an Informal British Empire in China in the Middle of the Nineteenth Century', *Bulletin of the John Rylands Library of Manchester*. 59: 472–485.

van Woerkens, M. (2003) *The Strangled Traveller: Colonial Imaginings and the Thugs of India*. Chicago: Chicago University Press.

Part 2

Considering the 'Normalisation Thesis'

Introduction: an overview of the normalisation debate

Paul Manning

Drug use was probably always more common than was publicly acknowledged though Downes, for example, found only very limited evidence drug use amongst London's East End youngsters in the early 1960s (1966: 135). However, even if confined to minority subcultures, the cultural practices associated with illicit drug use had an influence and significance that extended beyond sub-cultural networks, to reach wider audiences for jazz and popular music, beat poetry, new fiction, and to an extent, cinema.

Now, however, there is a strong case for viewing drug consumption and its cultural practices as occupying a more visible position within contemporary popular cultures. This view depends upon 'the normalisation thesis'; the argument that recreational drug use is now so familiar to those aged below 35 years that it should be regarded as 'normal', rather than an activity confined to minority subcultures. This part contains two important articles first published in the journal *Sociology* in 1997 and 2002 and they provide contrasting views of the 'normalisation thesis'. Howard Parker, Judith Aldridge and Fiona Measham, together with others, have undertaken extensive research on drug consumption amongst adolescents and young people in the North-west of England since 1991. Several major surveys and smaller scale studies have produced an important body of data tracking the drug choices of young people over nearly 15 years (The North West Longitudinal Survey, see suggested reading by Parker, Measham, Aldridge and colleagues below) and they draw upon this evidence to develop the most empirically grounded and theoretically informed version of the 'normalisation thesis'. However, Mike Shiner and Tim Newburn offer a fluent critique and their original article is included here (Chapter 3). A summary of Parker, Aldridge and Measham's original position is summarised in the remainder of this introduction, together with a brief review of some of the more recent evidence. Chapters 3 and 4 then follow, comprising of the Shiner and Newburn critique and a more recent article by Parker, Williams and Aldridge summarising follow up evidence from the North West Longitudinal Survey.

While newspapers, politicians and, occasionally, drugs workers have complained about the 'normalisation' of drug use in recent years (see Chapters 7 and 8), Parker, Aldridge and Measham (1998) offer a more sophisticated framework for interpreting the data they obtained from the first five years of their longitudinal study. By 'normalisation' they are describing change along two dimensions, behavioural and attitudinal. It involves the spread of 'drug activity and associated attitudes from the margins *towards* the centre of youth culture where it joins many other accommodated "deviant" activities such as excessive drinking, casual sexual encounters, and daily cigarette smoking' (1998: 152). So their analysis places the study of drug use firmly in the context of popular youth culture but they emphasise, 'normalisation need not be concerned with absolutes; we are not even considering the possibility that most young Britons will become illicit drug users' (1998: 153). It has been possible, they argue, for tobacco to have become 'normalised', and for most young people to have tried a cigarette, but for still only a minority to become regular smokers. This is an important point marking one of the matters of disagreement with Shiner and Newburn (1997). The latter suggest that the survey data still does not suggest that the minorities reporting regular soft drug use are sufficiently large to justify the term 'normalisation'. But for Parker, Aldridge and Measham, the 'normalisation' process is relational, not absolute, depending upon the extent to which drug use is regarded as usual or commonplace amongst both users and non-users. In other words, they are concerned with the extent to which illicit drug consumption is embedded within popular culture. They do make it clear, however, that their argument is based upon the use of 'soft' or recreational drugs, such as cannabis, amphetamines, ecstasy and LSD, while they believe the use of 'harder' drugs is still contained within 'opiate' and 'cocaine' subcultures.

In *Illegal Leisure* (1998), Parker, Aldridge and Measham identified six dimensions through which evidence of 'normalisation' could be detected. Firstly, they considered evidence of *drug availability*. Their longitudinal study tracked the experiences of young people over a five-year period from the age of 14 to 19. While almost 60 per cent of 14 year olds reported having been in 'offer situations', this figure rose to 91 per cent by year five of the study (1998: 83). The second dimension was concerned with the process of *trying a drug*. Again, the authors found significant evidence of greater involvement with age. At 14, 36.3 per cent reported trying at least one drug, but by 19 this figure had risen to 64.3 per cent with cannabis, amyl nitrate, amphetamines being mentioned most frequently (1998: 83–84). The authors argued that one of the most significant features of their data was 'the closure of the social class, gender and ethnicity differences' (1998: 153), as middle class as well as working class, girls as well as boys, white, Asian and black young people became more inclined to try recreational drugs.

Trying drugs may be one thing but becoming a more regular user is a distinct stage. The third dimension of evidence of 'normalisation' involved measuring *regular drug use*. This involved gathering data on the numbers using drugs in the 'last year' and 'last month', in addition to 'lifetime use'. At 14, 20.4 per cent reported drug taking in the last month and 30.9 per cent reported taking a drug in the previous year, but at 19 the figures had risen to 35.2 per cent and 52.9 per cent respectively (1998: 85). These were significant increases in use but asking respondents questions about their drug use in the 'last year' or 'last month' are still quite crude measures of complex cultural practices. Acknowledging this, Parker, Aldridge and Measham try to provide a more sensitive account of the meanings their respondents attached to their patterns of drug use. By tracking the 'pathways' of their respondents over five years, they were able to distinguish between 'abstainers', 'current users', 'ex-triers' and those in 'transition', and to explore in more depth, using attitude measures and qualitative in-depth interviewing, the ways in which individuals within each category understood their consumption practices, and those of others. For example, those who at nearly 18 years of age were in 'transition', frequently expressed ambivalent and complicated views, indicating that while they regarded the use of some drugs as inappropriate, they also recognised that as they grew into adulthood and left home for university or work, they would be tempted to use certain other drugs, particularly dance drugs, more (1998: 106). Within the group of 'abstainers' there were some who had very securely entrenched hostile attitudes to drugs, but there was a larger group who mixed in pubs and clubs as they grew older, and who while choosing to avoid the risks associated with drugs themselves, equally, did not condemn as immoral, those individuals who chose to run the risks (1998: 101).

The picture to emerge provides evidence to support the movement in theoretical approach (discussed in Chapter 1) away from the deterministic models presented by bio-psychological and early sub-cultural approaches. The respondents in the North West Longitudinal study were not weak or passive 'retreatists', but rational social actors, making their own assessments of risk and undertaking their own cost-benefit analyses of the pleasures or hazards of particular substances (1998: 119). This looks a lot like examples of the individual 'drug styles' or 'repertoires' that contemporary social theory would relate to the construction of self-narrative in the era of late modern capitalism (see Chapter 1). In *Illegal Leisure*, Parker, Aldridge and Measham found the process of 'normalisation' applied more strongly to cannabis than other 'soft' drugs, and that while significant numbers were moving into poly drug use as they gravitated towards dance cultures, these individuals remained a 'discrete minority'. However, they also recognised that one consequence of dance culture was 'that ecstasy has filtered into more "everyday" drug taking' (1998: 154). Ecstasy, and perhaps other 'soft' recreational drugs, might be on the way to a much wider 'normalisation'. In *Dancing with Drugs* (2001), they considered the case of post-adolescents or twenty-somethings in more detail and looked, particularly, at the unfolding impact of dance culture. In a review of a number of studies in the UK and Europe, their conclusion was that at the beginning of the new millennium, 'there were clear signs of an increase in recreational drug use', with between 20 and 25 per cent of young adults using cannabis regularly and 10 per cent ecstasy (Measham, Aldridge and Parker 2001: 8). They stressed that drug use within dance and club culture was higher than amongst the young adult population at large, but within the dance scene there was evidence of the development of sophisticated poly-drug styles emerging, based around alcohol, cannabis, and other 'time out' drugs, including ecstasy and amphetamines. It was not just the actual consumption of drugs that was important but that 'sensible drug use' was widely tolerated by non-users (2001: 7). In other words, it seemed as if contemporary popular cultures were accommodating 'sensible drug use'. In short, *Dancing with Drugs* provided some evidence to support the 'informed guesswork' of *Illegal Leisure*:

it did look as if significant minorities within the 'transitional' and 'current users' categories had developed more clearly defined 'journeys' towards poly dance drug use, and that the ambivalent liberalism of many 'abstainers', or non-users, was common within contemporary post-adolescent culture.

Turning to the fourth dimension of 'normalisation' set out in *Illegal Leisure*, *being drug wise*, the authors found that even amongst non-using abstainers, there was considerable knowledge of the recreational drug scene, simply because young people could not escape encounters with drugs and drug users through studying, training, working, being sociable, or going out at weekends (1998: 155). Drugs were no longer a distant phenomenon, located in a world of the 'other'; they were part of everyday life for users, triers, and abstainers, alike. It was this that informed the moral accommodation to drug use described above.

Finally, the fifth dimension of 'normalisation' discussed in *Illegal Pleasure*, concerned *future intentions*. Conventional wisdom, and quite a lot of academic research, understood adolescent drug consumption in terms of psycho-socio developmental processes; drug use was interpreted as part of the rule-testing, rebelliousness of youth with the implication being that young people would 'grow out of it'. However, the evidence from the North West Longitudinal Study pointed to a rather different prospect. Rather than giving up or growing out of drug use, many of these young people developed accelerated 'journeys' towards drug use as they approached post-adolescence; for 17 and 18 year olds over 33 per cent of former 'triers' returned to a transitional status and 37 per cent of those previously in 'transition' became 'current users'. These were the cultural currents that were to produce the post-adolescent clubbers regularly using alcohol, cannabis and 'time out' drugs described in *Dancing with Drugs* and later research (Measham and Brain 2005). In the 2002 article included in this part, despite some evidence of slightly less drug experience amongst the next cohort of young people arriving in their 20s, Parker, Williams and Aldridge conclude that between 10 and 15 per cent of late adolescents using cannabis grow to become between 20 and 25 per cent of young adults, while around 10 per cent of those aged between 18 and 25 regularly use ecstasy, amphetamines, and now cocaine, also, recreationally at weekends.

Is the case for the 'normalisation thesis' proven? Another source of evidence is provided by official government data including statistics on arrests and drug seizures, and the evidence provided by the British Crime Survey which uses a self-report survey to estimate experiences of crime and victimisation across the UK. We know, for example, that in 1967 196 kilos of cannabis plants were seized from more ambitious gardeners, but by 1997 this figure had grown to 149,996 kilos, while the number of LSD doses seized had increased from 7,720 to 164,000 (Corkery cited Bean 2002: 7). However, official data generated through seizures and arrests is not wholly reliable measure of the 'real' extent of drug production or drug use because annual figures are strongly influenced by variations in the strategies and priorities of police and customs. Partly for this reason, the British government has, for two decades, undertaken the British Crime Survey (BCS) to focus upon criminal experiences beyond those who are caught. A summary of recent BCS data is provided by the European Monitoring Centre for Drugs and Drug Addiction (EMCDDA). This suggests that in the early years of the new millennium, levels of drug consumption, overall, have remained stable but there has been an increase in the use of class A drugs; approximately one third of the adult population 'have tried' at least one illicit drug during their life times, and for those below the age of 30 this figure rises to a half; there has been a gradual decline in drug experiences of those aged between 16 and 24 over the last five years but that the age band of the drug experienced has widened as regular drug users grow into their 30s; and that there has been a doubling in the numbers of school children reporting at least one occasion of illicit drug use during the previous 10 years, from 10 per cent to nearly 20 per cent (Eaton *et al*. 2004: 22–23). So while the BCS offers some evidence of a 'slow down' in the rate of 'normalisation', it also points to a picture of extensive illicit drug use that extends well beyond adolescence.

Beyond the focus on criminal activity, the government also gathers data to inform health and education policies. Some of this material is discussed in the two articles that follow this introduction. A recent example of this is provided by the National Foundation for Educational Research which has conducted surveys relating to health and dietary issues amongst a sample of pupils aged between 11 and 15 in 225 schools in England and Wales. Questions relating to drug experiences have been included since 1998. From this there is evidence of high levels of 'drug awareness', with 36 per cent of respondents reporting being 'offered' drugs at least once. Cannabis was the most frequent substance (28 per cent), followed by stimulants (17 per cent) and heroin (6 per cent). Overall, 14 per cent reported using drugs during the last year but experience increased with age and at 15 years, 32 per cent reported using a drug at least once in their lifetimes, 29 per cent in the last year and 21 per cent in the last month. Just under 10 per cent of 15 year olds reported using class A drugs and 28 per cent using cannabis in the previous year (Boreham and Shaw 2001: 16).

In short, if we review much of the data from official and government sponsored sources, we find broad support for the picture that emerges from the North West Longitudinal Survey and summarised in *Illegal Leisure*. From the middle of adolescence onwards a significant minority of young people acquire drug experiences, these experiences grow more frequent through late adolescence and much of this activity is centred around cannabis. On the other hand, there is some evidence that the rate of increasing exposure to drug experiences is slowing down and if we look beyond cannabis to other slightly 'harder' recreational drugs it seems that only around 10 per cent of young people are regular consumers. Does this provide a picture of drug 'normalisation' or drug containment?

The Shiner and Newburn (1997) critique of the 'normalisation thesis' which follows this introduction rests upon two main arguments. Firstly, they question the interpretation of the survey data made by supporters of the 'normalisation thesis'. While they concede that much of the evidence points to increasing drug use, even in the case of cannabis consumption, it remains a minority pastime and for other 'soft drugs' the numbers regularly consuming appear to be much smaller. In the case of the North West Longitudinal Study, they wonder whether the inclusion of Manchester with its vibrant dance and club scene, makes the sample less representative of the wider population. In their view, the normalisation thesis overplays the internal coherence of youth culture and underplays the divisions and disagreements amongst young people in their approach to drug issues.

Secondly, Shiner and Newburn develop an argument around the meaning of drug consumption for young people. While Parker, Aldridge and Measham do gather qualitative data, Shiner and Newburn place rather more reliance upon qualitative methodologies and the 'thicker' data these provide. Shiner and Newburn argue that in their interviews with young people in East London what emerges is a set of complex responses to drug consumption but that frequency of use needs to be distinguished from 'normalcy'. In other words, young people may live in environments where drugs are quite common, but that does not necessarily imply a normative shift towards accepting them. They found a diversity of views the breadth of which they believe was not reflected in the 'normalisation thesis'. Even regular drug users shared many of the anxieties of non-users.

The 'normalisation thesis' has been criticised on other counts, too. For some critics it lacks an historical awareness of drug consumption in previous historical moments. The urge to seek intoxication is a feature of most societies going back to ancient and classical times prompting the question whether the use of drugs and alcohol has ever really been abnormal (Blackman 2004)? When one reads accounts of the gin shops of London in the eighteenth century or the cheerful reliance of workers upon beer rather than polluted water in the nineteenth century, it is clear that there have been other historical moments in which intoxication has been routine and common. However, the article by Parker, Williams and Aldridge (2002) included here develops an important response to the criticisms outlined above. In particular, it is worth noting the importance they attach to processes of 'cultural accommodation'. The point is not merely that a significant minority of younger adults and adolescents use drugs for recreational purposes. There is a much wider process of normative adjustment or 'cultural accommodation' occurring, as evidenced in the examples of films and television programmes that they mention. If 'normalisation' is occurring, this is happening within and through popular cultures. And these processes are also mediated through a diverse range of mass and 'micro' media, from films and television comedy to fanzines and internet blogs. So the 'normalisation thesis' has to be assessed against the landscape of contemporary popular cultures, the cultural practices associated with drug consumption, and the relationship of these to patterns of representation within the diverse range of contemporary media.

References and suggested reading

Bean, P. (2002) *Drugs and Crime*. Cullompton: Willan Publishing.

Blackman, S. (2004) *Chilling Out: The Cultural Politics of Substance Consumption, Youth and Drug Policy*. Maidenhead: Open University Press.

Boreham, R. and Shaw, A. (2001) *Smoking, Drinking, and Drug Use Among Young People in England*, National Centre for Social Research and National Federation for Educational Research.

Downes, D. (1966) *The Delinquent Solution: A Study in Subcultural Theory*. London: Routledge and Kegan Paul.

Eaton, G., Morleo, M., Lodwoick, A., Bellis, M. and McVeigh, J. (2004) *United Kingdom: New Developments, Trends and In-Depth Information on Selected Issues*. London: European Monitoring Centre for Drugs and Drug Addiction/Department of Health.

Measham, F. and Brain, K. (2005) '"Binge" Drinking, British Alcohol Policy and the New Culture of Intoxication', *Crime Media Culture*, 1 (3), December 2005.

Measham, F., Aldridge, J. and Parker, H. (2001) *Dancing on Drugs: Risk, Health, and Hedonism in the British Club Scene*. London: Free Association Books.

Parker, H., Measham, F. and Aldridge, J. (1995) *Drugs Futures: Changing Patterns of Drug Use Amongst English Youth*. London: ISDD.

Parker, H., Aldridge, J. Measham, F. (1998) *Illegal Leisure: The Normalization of Adolescent Recreational Drug Use*. London: Routledge.

Parker, H., Aldridge, J. and Egginton, R. (eds) (2001) *UK Drugs Unlimited: New Research and Policy Lessons on Illicit Drugs*. Basingstoke: Palgrave.

Parker, H. Williams, L. and Aldridge, J. (2002) 'The Normalization of "Sensible" Recreational Drug Use: Further Evidence from the North West England Longitudinal Study', *Sociology*, 36 (4): 941–964 (reprinted in this volume).

Shiner, M. and Newburn, T. (1997) 'Definitely, Maybe Not? The Normalisation of Recreational Drug Use Amongst Young People', *Sociology*, 31 (3): 511–529 (reprinted in this volume).

3. Definitely, maybe not? The normalisation of recreational drug use amongst young people*

Michael Shiner and Tim Newburn

It is only relatively recently that large-scale surveys have been successfully utilised to measure drug use among representative populations (*inter alia* Balding 1994; Mott and Mirrlees-Black 1993). Such surveys have shown that significant proportions of people – especially young people – use prohibited drugs at some stage in their lives (Ramsay and Percy 1996). As a consequence of this, the traditional image of drug use as a subterranean activity has been somewhat undermined. The change in the status of such activities by young people was reinforced by the emergence in the 1980s of a dance/rave culture in which certain specific forms of drug use were allegedly central. Indeed, some commentators have, on the basis of the emerging survey data, argued that drug use by young people is becoming so common that it is no longer regarded as a 'deviant' activity by them. Put another way, they claim that drug use among young people is becoming normalised. We wish to challenge this view – one we describe as the 'normalisation thesis' – and contend that far more has been read into the survey data than is warranted. Drug use among young people, we will argue, has some distance to travel before it assumes the status of a 'normalised' activity.

The normalisation thesis

What is meant by 'normalisation'? According to Becker (1963: 8) deviance is produced through 'the application by others of rules and sanctions to an "offender"'. Therefore, as Erikson (1964: 11) puts it: 'the critical variable in the study of deviance, then, is the social audience rather than the individual actor, since it is the audience which eventually determines whether or not any episode or behaviour or any class of episodes is labelled deviant.' This emphasis on the contingent nature of 'deviance' is clearly reflected in the process of normalisation. An audience can, by its reaction, alter the meaning of apparently 'deviant' activities so that 'certain kinds of deviancy may,

*Originally published in *Sociology* 31(3), 1997 (pp. 511–529) reproduced by permission of Sage Publications.

indeed, become so normalised that they are no longer managed as deviant' (Rock 1973: 84). The extent of this redefinition can vary. Cavan (1966: 18), for example, developed the term 'normal trouble' to refer to 'improper activities that are frequent enough to be simply shrugged off or ignored'. Rock (1973: 80) described a fuller process when he argued that, instead of simply 'assuming non-deviant forms', deviance may become 'the standard, taken-for-granted substance and form of acts within the setting'. In order, then, to argue that the status of a form of behaviour has moved from being 'deviant' to being 'normal', it is necessary to show that as well as being widespread, this form of behaviour has become accepted as normal by the relevant audience(s).

The 'normalisation thesis' was outlined in its most straightforward and authoritative form by Parker and colleagues (1995: 26) when they claimed that 'for many young people taking drugs has become the norm' and went on to predict that 'over the next few years, and certainly in urban areas, non drug-trying adolescents will be a minority group. In one sense they will be the deviants'. The explanation of contemporary drug use offered by these authors is underpinned by a subcultural perspective in which the liberal permissiveness of youth culture is contrasted with the conservative restrictiveness of the adult world. In this way, they have referred, for example; to 'the normalization of recreational drug use amongst English adolescents and the adult outrage it engenders' (1995: 310).

While Measham et al. (1994) and Parker et al. (1995) have concentrated on behaviour, the normalisation thesis has also been endorsed by social scientists adopting a more attitudinal focus. Coffield and Gofton, for example, having sought to 'enter the subjective world of young drug takers' (1994: 1) wrote of the 'ubiquity of drugs among the young' and claimed that 'drug taking is ... part and parcel of the process of growing up in contemporary Britain'. Reflecting the subcultural basis of the normalisation thesis, they went on to claim that while drug use is seen as being unproblematic by most young people it is seen as a problem by 'their uncomprehending parents, ... their largely uninformed teachers and ... the police' (1994: 3). Similarly, Hirst and McCamley-Finney argued that young people are 'constantly surprised at adults' perceptions of drugs as something dangerous or unusual as, for most of them, they are part of their life' and suggested that there is a need 'for a reappraisal of how adults react to young people's drug use, which recognises an unfolding process of normalisation' (1994: 42).

Social scientists are not the only commentators to claim that drug use is becoming normalised among the young. Janet Paraskeva, then Director of the National Youth Agency, speaking to the 1995 London Drug Policy Forum Conference argued that 'cannabis use by young people is not deviant behaviour. If drug education is to have a chance of success we must separate the soft drug culture embraced by so many young people from the hard drug culture which threatens us all' (quoted in Pike 1995). More contentiously, Colin Wiseley, a West Yorkshire based drugs worker, has argued that normalisation has extended beyond the 'soft drug culture' and that 'heroin has become fashionable and acceptable amongst the young' (quoted in Johnston 1996). Such opinions are increasingly typical of much media discourse surrounding drug use. Following the publication of Parker et al.'s (1995) most recent report, the *Guardian* noted the 'opening of a new generation gap' and claimed that 'drug taking has become an integral part of youth culture and a significant part of the lives even of schoolchildren' (Boseley 1995). Similarly, in relation to the death of Leah Betts, the same newspaper reported that 'an underground movement, which started in 1988 with the advent of house music to this country, has almost invisibly expanded into a giant culture. The secret is out; the adult world has had thrust upon it the attitudes and lifestyle of a generation it does not understand' (Hodgkinson 1995). Most recently the *Daily Telegraph* headlined a report about new research: 'Drug taking has become a "teenage rite of passage"' (Millward 1996).

Given the existence of large-scale surveys, we are in a much better position than previously to estimate levels of illicit drug use. It is not the data generated by these surveys, or the methods by which they were collected, that we find problematic, it is the manner of their interpretation. While we do not take issue with the view that there is much that young people do that adults find puzzling, we do wish to challenge the picture painted by some advocates of the normalisation thesis which stresses the uniformity and apparent ubiquitousness of youthful drug use, and underplays the tensions and divisions that continue to exist within youth culture(s).

The extent and frequency of young people's drug use

No discussion of the extent and frequency of young people's drug use can begin without the now familiar disclaimer that definitive answers are not available (ISDD 1994). Although the picture we have is incomplete, it is clear that drug use and age are linked. Although rare during the early teens, use of drugs increases sharply during the next couple of years so that the late teens are consistently found to be a peak period of illegal drug use (ISDD 1994). Research has also provided empirical support for the frequently-made claim that drug use by young people is on the increase. Mott and Mirrlees-Black (1993), for instance, note that the percentage of 16–19 year olds reporting cannabis use more than doubled between 1983 and 1991. Similarly, a 1992 survey of 15–24 year olds which replicated a 1989 survey, reported a virtual doubling of the percentage of respondents admitting drug use (Measham *et al.* 1993; Clements 1993).

As indicated earlier, it is the work of Howard Parker and colleagues (Parker *et al.* 1995; Measham *et al.* 1994) that has been most influential in this area. Beginning in 1991 their major study to date involved three surveys conducted annually which recorded the drug-related experiences of a group of 776 young people who were first contacted during the penultimate year of their compulsory education when most were 14 years old. These surveys were administered in the metropolitan North-west of England, an area which includes Manchester, the 'rave capital of Great Britain' (Coffield and Gofton 1994: 5), and the researchers have acknowledged the dangers of extrapolating from their data to the national situation. Referring to the area's higher than average levels of smoking, drinking and heroin use, they note that 'we must therefore anticipate that young people from this region are likely to report higher levels of illicit drug use during the 1990s than their peers elsewhere' (Parker *et al.* 1995: 21). Although the location of their research is therefore in this sense 'unusual', this is not the basis of our criticism of the conclusions they draw.

In order to reflect upon the national situation we have drawn, in some detail, upon the domestic element of the International Self-Report Delinquency Study (ISRD) which, focusing on the 14–21 age range, is the most recent survey of a representative sample of the nation's youth to consider drug use (Bowling *et al.* 1994; Graham and Bowling 1995). We will also consider, albeit more briefly, the evidence from the 1994 British Crime Survey, although it should be noted that this focuses on people aged 16 and above and is not a specialist youth survey (Ramsay and Percy 1996). Although Parker *et al.*'s (1995) survey, the ISRD and British Crime Survey vary in the details of their administration, they are similar in that the drugs components of these surveys are all based on a self-completion approach in which respondents are provided with a list of drugs or illicit substances and asked about their knowledge and use of them.

The data presented by Parker *et al.* (1995) and Graham and Bowling (1995) indicate that, for young people, having used a drug is a far from unusual experience. By the time that the majority of Parker *et al.*'s (1995) respondents were 15, 42 per cent of them indicated that they had, at some point in their lives, used at least one illicit drug. This increased to 51 per cent by the time they were 16. Turning to the national position, over a third (36 per cent) of the ISRD respondents (all of whom were aged 14–21) reported ever having used a drug (Graham and Bowling 1995).

Given that proponents of the normalisation thesis have tended to concentrate on measures of lifetime use (whether a respondent has used an illicit drug at some time in their life) it is worth noting that the extent to which such measures illuminate young people's drug using habits is limited. Arguments based on such measurements should be interpreted extremely cautiously. The inflexibility of lifetime measures means that they cannot capture the processual character of people's drug-use (Becker 1963). As a consequence, not only are they unable to distinguish one-off use from regular poly-drug use but they also fail to distinguish between current and ex-users. Given these problems it is reasonable to suggest that measures based on shorter time-frames – such as the previous year or month – are likely to provide somewhat more reliable estimates of the extent of current or regular use. Parker *et al.* (1995) included questions about drug use during the year and the month prior to each of their surveys, and the ISRD asked respondents about their drug use during the previous year (1992).

Inevitably, data concerning drug-related behaviour during the last year/ month give a more conservative picture than those based on lifetime measures. As Figure 3.1 shows, in Parker *et al.*'s second and third surveys, when the majority of the respondents were aged 15 and 16 respectively, drug use during the previous year was limited to approximately two fifths of the sample. During the month preceding the respective surveys, it was limited to about a quarter of them. Following their third survey, Parker *et al.* (1995: 19)

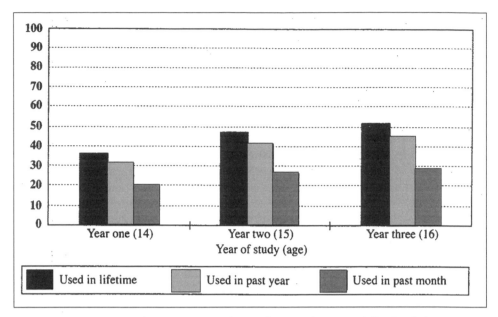

Figure 3.1 Drug use by young people in the North-west of England (percentage indicating use)
Source: Parker *et al.* (1995: 14).

estimated that 20 per cent of respondents (approximately three quarters of past month users) were 'regular users'.[1]

We have already mentioned the fact that Parker and colleagues recognise that their research is unlikely to be typical of the national picture. The situation relating to the nation as a whole is outlined in Figure 3.2. According to the ISRD slightly less than a third of males and less than a quarter of females aged 14–21 used drugs in 1992 and could, therefore, be thought of as 'current' users (Graham and Bowling 1995). While respondents aged 18–21 were, by some way, the most likely to have used a drug in 1992, less than half of the males and less than a quarter of the females in this age category had done so.

Although more illuminating than measures of lifetime use, those which focus on behaviour during the last year or month are of limited use if they fail to distinguish between different types of drug. Measures which aggregate a variety of different drugs simplify the decisions that young people make and fail to acknowledge the discerning approach many young people take towards drug use. That young people distinguish between different drugs is clearly reflected in their patterns of use. Both Parker *et al.* (1995) and the ISRD found that levels of use varied greatly by type of drug. Thus, reflecting its position as 'undoubtedly the most widely used drug in the UK' (ISDD 1994: 28), cannabis had been used by 45 per cent of respondents to Parker *et al.*'s (1995) third survey, when the majority of them were aged 16, and 33 per cent of ISRD respondents. At the other end of the popularity spectrum are heroin and cocaine. Lifetime use[2] of cocaine was limited to 4 and 3 per cent of Parker

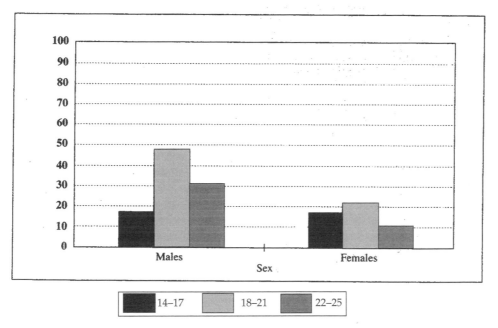

Figure 3.2 Drug use by young people in England and Wales during 1992 (percentage indicating use)
Source: Graham and Bowling (1995: 26).

et al.'s (1995) respondents when they were aged 15 and 16 respectively, and 2 per cent of ISRD respondents. Heroin use was even more unusual: 3 and 1 per cent respectively of Parker *et al.*'s respondents disclosed lifetime heroin use as did 1 per cent of ISRD respondents.

The rise of the dance/rave scene (Redhead 1993) and its associated drug use has a special position within the normalisation thesis (Coffield and Gofton 1994; Measham *et al.* 1993). The late 1980s and early 1990s did witness an apparently significant increase in the use of 'dance drugs', which became a relatively important part of the youth drug scene (Measham 1993; Clements 1993). In the case of ecstasy and LSD, however, this increase started from a very low baseline (Clements 1993) and, as Figures 3.3 and 3.4 show, the popularity of these drugs can easily be overstated.

Even though LSD was the most popular dance drug among Parker *et al.*'s (1995) respondents when they were aged 15 and 16 (and the second most widely used drug by them) it had only *ever* been used by approximately a quarter of them. In view of ecstasy's high media profile it is worth noting that only 1 in 20 respondents to Parker *et al.*'s (1995) third survey, when the majority of them were aged 16, had used this drug. Nationally, use of dance drugs appears to be limited to a small sub-section of the youthful population. Lifetime ecstasy-use was disclosed by 7 per cent of ISRD respondents and, although amphetamine and LSD were the second most widely used drugs within the sample, they had each only been used by 9 per cent of respondents (Graham and Bowling 1995).

When discussing general patterns of drug use we made the point that lifetime measures were too crude a tool for estimating levels of current or

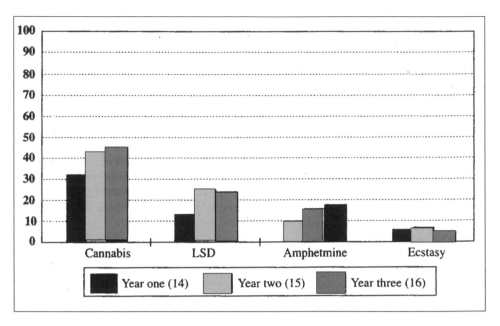

Figure 3.3 Lifetime use of cannabis and 'dance-drugs' in North-west England (percentage of users)
Source: Parker *et al.* (1995: 14).

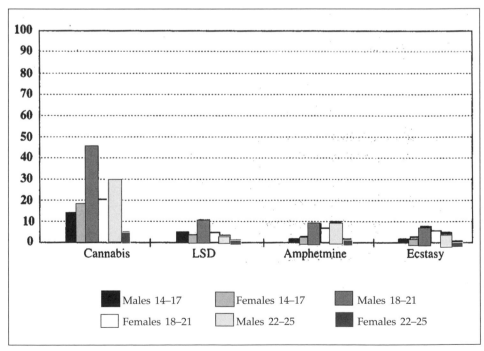

Figure 3.4 Use of cannabis and 'dance-drugs' in England and Wales during 1992 (percentage indicating use)
Source: Graham and Bowling (1995: 26).

regular drug use. This is equally applicable to discussions of the use of specific substances. Once again, predictably, shorter time-frame measures produce more conservative results. A third of the ISRD respondents who had ever used cannabis, and nearly half of the respondents who had ever used amphetamine, had not done so during the last year; the latter pattern also holds for use of LSD and ecstasy. Thus, while use of cannabis during the last year was limited to less than 1 in 4 of the ISRD respondents, use of each of the 'dance' drugs was limited to approximately 1 in 20 of them. Figure 3.4 shows that even among the 18–21 year olds (i.e. those respondents who revealed the highest levels of drug-taking) use of cannabis during the last year was limited to less than half the males and to a fifth of the females, and use of each of the 'dance' drugs hovered at around 1 in 10 for males and 1 in 15 for females.[3]

Furthermore, of those respondents who had used cannabis during the last year, a third of the males (32 per cent) and over a half the females (55 per cent) had done so only 'once or twice'. Of those who had used a controlled drug other than cannabis in the last year, more than half of them (56 per cent of males and 52 per cent of females) had done so only 'once or twice' (Graham and Bowling 1995: 19).

What are we to conclude from these data? First, even though there is clear evidence of increasing levels of drug use among young people, both the extent and frequency are easily exaggerated through over-reliance on lifetime measures. Second, when shorter time-frame measures are utilised, strong evidence for the normalisation thesis is even more elusive. Moreover, as we stated at the outset, convincing support for the normalisation thesis would not only require evidence that drug use is extremely widespread, but that usage is perceived to be normal. We turn now to ways in which drug use is understood by young people.

The meaning of drug use in the lives of young people

At the heart of the normalisation thesis, we would suggest, is a confusion between normalcy and frequency. There has been a tendency for self-reported behaviour to be taken at face value and for insufficient emphasis to be placed on the normative context of that behaviour. Normative behaviour is not necessarily the most frequently occurring pattern but is that which conforms to popular expectation. This distinction is, however, often ignored in discourse about youthful drug use. It is important to recognise that social norms, as prescriptions serving as common guidelines for social action, are grounded in values and attitudes rather than behaviour (Abercrombie et al. 1984). From this perspective what young people think is at least as important as what they do and, while we may expect an individual's behaviour to reflect their beliefs, this link is by no means always a clear one (Fishbein and Ajzen 1975; Charlton 1982; Eiser, Vander Pligt and Friend 1983; Nguyen-Van-Tam and Pearson 1986).

In considering the meanings that drug use has for young people we draw on qualitative data we collected as part of an evaluation of the peer approach to drug education for young people (Shiner and Newburn 1996). The study was conducted in the London borough of Newham, the most deprived local authority in the country according to the 1991 Census (Willmott 1994). A total of 52 young people were interviewed during the course of this study and, although the sample was a non-probability one, care was taken to ensure that people from a broad range of groups were well represented within it. Given the evidence that drug use increases fairly dramatically in the last few years of compulsory schooling (ISDD 1994), the study concentrated on 15–16 year olds, though nearly a quarter of the respondents were aged 11–14.

Thirty-seven of the respondents were interviewed in their schools and, of these, 22 were interviewed on two or three separate occasions. It is possible that the school setting may have encouraged respondents to give what they thought were socially desirable answers (de Vaus 1990), thus reducing the validity of the interview data. In order to minimise this possibility, however, guarantees of confidentiality were given and the interviews were conducted privately in rooms where only the interviewer and respondent were present. The interviews were, with respondents' permission, tape-recorded and subsequently transcribed. Eighteen of the school-based respondents had recently participated in a drugs workshop. At the outset of the study it was thought possible (although unlikely) that involvement in such a workshop would transform the drug related attitudes and behaviour of participants. Thus, people who had not attended such a workshop were included in the sample in order to generate a broader picture of the beliefs and norms which prevailed amongst young people in the area. There was, however, little evidence that participation in the workshops resulted in dramatic attitudinal or motivational changes. In general, participants felt that the workshops had reinforced, rather than changed, their views, and the attitudes and behaviour they reported did not differ systematically from those reported by respondents who had not attended a workshop (Shiner and Newburn 1996).

The school-based interviews were augmented by ethnographic work conducted in three youth clubs in the borough. Given that youth clubs, arguably, provide a more relaxed setting than schools and one in which young people feel more able to 'be themselves' this source of information was particularly useful. The school and youth club-based interviews were semi-structured. Although the interviewers had a series of questions they wanted to ask they did not ask them in any fixed order and, where appropriate, they probed areas as they were raised by respondents. This approach was favoured on the grounds that it minimised the extent to which respondents had to express themselves in terms defined by the interviewers and encouraged them to raise issues which were important to them. It was thus particularly well suited to the attempt to discover respondents' own meanings and interpretations (Bryman 1988; Cornwell 1984). Although the sample for this study cannot be viewed as being statistically representative of any population it was constructed in a way that was consistent with the aim of taking a 'tentative, hypothesis-generating, exploratory look at patterns' (de Vaus 1990: 77).

Before considering the drug-related attitudes of the young people included in our qualitative study it is worth outlining the extent of their drug-related experiences. For some, regular contact with drugs and drug users was part of their everyday lives. The nature of this contact varied greatly from seeing people use drugs to using them themselves. For some, their personal drug-related experiences extended beyond the everyday and embraced the dramatic: three had friends who had been hospitalised because of drug overdoses and four knew people (personal friends, family friends, local people) who had died as a result of drug use. More than a quarter (15) of the 52 respondents disclosed that they had taken illegal drugs or solvents at some time. The drug-using experience of 12 of them was limited to cannabis which, as well as being the most widely used drug, was also the most frequently used: levels of consumption ranged from one-off use to 'every other day'. Poly-drug use was disclosed by three respondents and, in addition to cannabis, involved solvents, amphetamines, LSD, ecstasy and cocaine.

The breadth of the views about drugs expressed by the young people in the study defied simple generalisation and challenged the monolithic implication of claims that drug use is becoming 'normalised'. Furthermore, while some of the respondents who had not used drugs did make positive connections between drug use and, for example, increased confidence with, and attractiveness to, members of the opposite sex, restrictive views, characteristic of the 'adult world' as described in the normalisation thesis, were widespread among non-users:

> If they haven't got a reason for taking drugs, then what's the point of taking them because it only affects your life and it ruins you, so I don't see what's the point in taking the drugs ... I reckon they [people who do drugs] are dumb because they know that well for themselves, they know if they buy it, and it does something to them they know they're going to be screwed up in their lives.

> If they [people] take drugs they're the ones that are going to suffer at the end, that's all I can say because they shouldn't have got into that mess in the first place, that's what I think.

That views such as these may be widely held by young people is suggested by Dowds and Redfern (1994) whose analysis of a nationally representative sample of over 1,000 12–15 year olds, concluded that high numbers of young people appear thoroughly convinced of the wrongness of taking cannabis. Two-thirds of their respondents thought taking cannabis was a very serious offence. Predictably, however, those who had tried drugs were far less censorious about taking cannabis than those who had not done so.

Returning to our qualitative study, underlying the anti-drugs views of the non-users were concerns about the health implications of drug use, a fear of addiction and losing control, the financial cost and the potential damage to relationships, particularly with parents, that drug use could entail. Of particular relevance to the normalisation thesis, however, was the negative association in the minds of many of the non-users between drug use and deviant activities such as crime and violence. Such was the strength of this association that some respondents felt drug use may lead them into crime:

> I wouldn't [try cannabis] because I don't want to get hooked into anything. I never even smoked so I don't want to get into anything like that, plus once you start hanging around with these gangs and then, if I try it, I think I probably might get addicted or something and then have problems later on. Then I have to borrow and steal the money to get the stuff. I hear about these things so, I mean it's best to keep away.

That drug use was far from being a normalised activity in some circles was evidenced by the folklore that surrounded it and by the lengths that some non-users went to in order to isolate themselves from others whose behaviour they considered inappropriate. Some of what respondents said about drugs took on the form of 'urban legends' and constitutes a form of modern (sub-cultural) folklore (Brunvand 1983). Folklore, according to Brunvand, is primarily an oral tradition which, made up of stories or legends, transmits accepted wisdoms, knowledge or modes of behaviour. Whether true or false these legends reflect some of the 'hopes, fears and anxieties of our time' (Brunvand 1983: 15). Scare stories which highlighted the potentially negative aspects of drug use were an important part of non-users' discourse around drug use. In explaining his non-use one respondent reflected:

> It's just because all the stories I've heard about it, like people getting messed up, people having hallucinations, think they're planes so they jump off buildings and stuff ... I heard [that] off a friend. I don't know whether it's true or not but I know some things have happened like that where people have had hallucinations and they thought that them things, I know somebody's jumped in front of a train, thought they were Superman and stuff ... My friend said like he heard from someone else, that this guy took trips [LSD] and he thought he was a hubcap and tried to jump on the side of a car and got squashed.

Stories such as this abounded in relation to the use of hallucinogens. The presence of the phrase, 'I don't know whether it's true or not', calls into question the veracity what it being said on this occasion. What may appear to be outlandish stories about tripping were, however, important in confirming and reinforcing norms within non-using circles. In this context, whether or not the 'bad trip' experiences really happened is of secondary importance. The story was believed and as such had an impact on behaviour, for as W.I. Thomas famously observed: 'If men [sic] define situations as real, they are real in their consequences' (quoted in Cuff *et al.* 1992: 152).

Despite their anti-drug views, non-users rarely confronted drug-using behaviour by their peers. Most felt that such a response was inappropriate and likely to be counter-productive. Much more common among non-users was the attempt to avoid meaningful relationships with drug users. Although the implied separation between drug users and non-users can be exaggerated (Shiner and Newburn 1996), we found considerable empirical support for the idea of peer selection – the idea that young people seek out and develop friendships with like-minded people (Coggans and McKellar 1994):

There's a couple of rough people around, they just take trips [LSD] and things like that but I don't really hang around with them kind of people because they're not worth hanging about with ... if one of my friends ... bring[s] someone new round, I just say 'is he alright or is he a bit of a div [idiot] doing stupid things?' If they say 'divi', I just say 'don't let him come round here, just keep him away'.

[My friend] just says 'if you want to do it then do it'. But I don't want to do it. He said do I want some before but I said 'no' and said 'if you ask me again I'm just going to go', like I don't like being with anybody who does it ... there's some kids round my way, about 16, 17 that take it. I just say 'hello' to them, I don't hang around with them or anything.

The process of peer selection was also alluded to by respondents who had used drugs. This did not, however, necessarily involve users gravitating towards each other as might be expected (Battjes 1985; Oetting and Beauvais 1987). Users' accounts were peppered with references to the rule-governed nature of drug use and indicated that, in the social milieu in which they operated, such behaviour was far from being a sanction-free activity. There were, for example, clear rules concerning why, where, what and how much it was considered legitimate to use, and those who broke these rules risked facing sanctions from, and even possible social exclusion by, other users:

Q: *So what do you think is alright, how often do you think it's ok to do dope (cannabis] say?*
No more than every couple of weeks I suppose, like every two weeks, like only a tenners (i.e. ten pound's] worth.

Q: *What would you think if someone did it a couple of times a week?*
I wouldn't say they were addicted, I wouldn't say they were doing it too much, but I mean you can't tell someone what to do and what not to do, it's the way it is these days. If you tell someone what to do and they're unable to deal with it and so you think well, I'll have to leave you to it and if he gets too out of it, then you have to stop hanging about with them, leave it to him to sort it out himself ... If one of my mates was doing drugs really bad, every night or coke [cocaine], you'd say to them 'sort it out because you're messing yourself up', like if you were out with your mate and you were pulling a girl, you were out with them and sometimes you see a nice couple of girls and you're really after them and your mates are out of it, he's just going to be laughing, and she's going 'what's wrong with him, he's a div [idiot]' and then she's going to think oh he's a div as well and they're just going to leave it and then you think, what I am hanging around with him for? Probably just bust up with your friend.

In seeking to understand the views of respondents who had used drugs, the work of Matza (1964) and Sykes and Matza (1957) is important. Of particular relevance is their rejection of the view that delinquents belong to some form of subcultural 'otherness'. Reflecting the claim that 'norms may be violated without surrendering allegiance to them' (Matza 1964: 60), they argued that 'delinquents' commonly support the same set of norms and values as everybody else and that they differ, primarily, in their use of techniques of neutralisation which temporarily render relevant social controls inoperative and allow them to engage in delinquent activities without feeling guilty or shameful. As Sykes and Matza (1957: 668) put it 'In this sense, the delinquent both has his cake and eats it too, for he remains committed to the dominant normative system and yet so qualifies its imperatives that violations are "acceptable" if not "right"'.

Although the respondents in our study who had used drugs tended to emphasise the 'safeness' of cannabis, this apparent liberalism was very limited. As was the case with the non-users, the views expressed by respondents who had used drugs – including multiple, repeat and one-off users – shared much with the restrictive views characteristic of the 'adult world':

> They [people who don't take drugs] are sensible aren't they, not doing it, if you're going round the streets takin drugs now, it's stupid.
>
> Q: *So what's sensible about not doing it?*
> Keep healthy, you can think better, you can sit there and you can think, puff a draw [cannabis] and you might forget things, put a pen down there and completely forget about it ... Like I don't want to destroy myself, ruining your lungs, damaging your brain cells, so it ain't worth it, it ain't worth damaging yourself just to have a laugh. You can easily have a laugh can't you, with your mates.

Further, they shared many of the concerns about drug use expressed by non-users, including a fear of addiction and of the damage that drug use could do to their relationships, particularly with their parents. In terms of their drug related attitudes, the principal difference between respondents who had used drugs and those who had not done so was the development, by the former, of techniques of neutralisation which allowed them to use drugs without feeling guilty about it. Some of them, for example, explained their use in terms of peer pressure:

> Nearly everyone does it [takes drugs]. You only get a handful that don't and there's more people doing it than there ain't so you sit there in a group of you and they go on, 'do it, do it', and you see them all happy and you feel right awkward and that, so then you just do it and then once you do it you keep doing it and you can't stop. [It makes you] ... feel a bit awkward because like you want to say 'no' but you know you've got to [keep doing it] ... [you couldn't say 'no'] ... because if you did; they just go on and on and they just go 'oh what's the matter, you're a chicken, you're a chicken' and make you feel like, well, like a right div in front of loads of people and it makes you feel small.

This is a classic neutralisation technique for, as Coggans and McKellar have noted, 'the assumption that drug use is caused by peer pressure places the blame on others and away from the drug user' (1994: 18). Other neutralisation techniques used by respondents included claims that the drugs they used were not harmful and were not really drugs and that they did not use enough to get addicted:

> I won't take no hard drugs ... because the side effects and all that, it takes quicker if you take the hard drugs, but it takes longer if you take the soft drugs ... I won't take hard drugs.

> Like ash and weed [cannabis], what I normally smoke and that, can't really harm you and that ... like I'm not addicted to like speed [amphetamine] or that, so I could give it up any time. The way I do it, I don't get addicted. Weed, I don't use it all that often, I don't get addicted to it. Sometimes like I smoke it like seven days in one week but then leave it for a couple of months ...

At the basis of these neutralisation techniques was the claim that there were no really serious consequences from the drug(s) being used, and, by implication, that the user was making responsible and rational choices:

> I don't mind people who take speed or like a joint [cannabis] now and again or something like that but I don't like the sort of people who take like coke and that ... because it's a bad drug and that and it could kill you ... [people who take cocaine] are putting their lives at risk and that going on coke, but people who smoke ash [cannabis] or take speed and that, they're not really putting their lives at risk because it takes a lot of speed to kill them ...
>
> Q: *Say you went round to your sister's tonight and say your sister offered you coke, what would you do?*
> I would tell her to fuck off ... the reason I'm so against that sort of drug and that, because my cousin, he was on it and that and he used to steal like off my auntie and that, like money and her TV and that to get his drugs.

The alignment by respondents who had used drugs with consensus values relating to drug use was strongly evident in their restrictive and censorious reactions to drug use, real or anticipated, by their siblings:

> I'd probably go mad. I'd probably tell him, 'Don't do it because it's not good', I'd say 'I've done it myself and it's not the best thing to do', he probably won't thank me for it but you have to tell him, probably say to me 'ah you do it so why can't I' and stuff like that, but you have to tell him, it's always an instinct with your brother.

Negative reactions were not reserved simply for younger siblings:

> Q: *Say you found out that the 18 year old brother was going drugs, maybe*
> *he is, what would you do?*
> It wouldn't bother me if I found out about John,[4] like I know he
> puffs a draw [cannabis] and I know he don't touch anything else,
> but if he did like, once he told me he tried a bit of coova [cocaine]
> and I didn't talk to him for ages because the way I look at it, it's
> disgusting.

Young people's reactions to drug use, it seems, are, in part, a function of their
relationship to the user and the roles that are available to them within the
context of that relationship. In explaining why they would challenge drug use
by their siblings but not their friends, respondents made a clear distinction.
Relationships with brothers and sisters were felt to be of a higher order than
those with friends and, in the case of younger siblings, respondents felt they
had a certain authority and responsibility which they lacked in relation to
their friends.

Conclusions

While recognising the increase in youthful drug use during recent years, we
have argued that the normalisation thesis exaggerates its extent and, more
importantly, oversimplifies the ways in which drug use is perceived by young
people. While it is not unusual for individuals to have experienced drug use
by their mid to late teens, this trend should not be treated uncritically. In part,
the exaggeration is a consequence of the measures used. Lifetime measures,
for example, do not reflect the dynamic nature of drug use and indicators
based on use during the last year and/or month show that regular drug use
(however this may be defined) remains a minority activity. Picking up on
our earlier work, the authors of the drugs report from the 1994 British Crime
Survey concluded that, while 'drug-taking may seem quite widespread if one
merely focuses on the ever/lifetime dimension', it is 'still apparently the case
that the majority of young people have not taken prohibited drugs; and more
importantly, that most drug users – even a clear majority of young ones – are
merely occasional, not showing up on a last month basis' (Ramsay and Percy
1996: 53–4).

Furthermore, the claim that drug-taking by young people has become
normalised simplifies the choices that young people make about drug use. It
does so primarily by using the term 'drugs' in an undifferentiated manner.
We have suggested that the global term 'drugs' has only a limited meaning
for young people. Trends in young people's use of specific substances give
the lie to the idea that 'illegal substances' somehow have some generic
property in the eyes of young people. Cannabis is, by some way, the most
widely and frequently used drug by young people and, although use of

dance/rave drugs has increased significantly in recent years, it still appears to be limited to a relatively small minority of young people. Reflecting their status as 'hard drugs', cocaine and heroin are very rarely used. Moreover, the attitudes displayed by young people towards these different drugs are not easily classifiable and are certainly not uniform.

Finally, we have suggested that the normalisation thesis pays inadequate attention to the normative context of behaviour. We have argued that, in general, young people do not view drug use as an 'unproblematic' activity. The young people who participated in our qualitative study and who had not used drugs commonly subscribed to a restrictive set of views, characteristic of the so-called 'adult world'. This was clear in the associations they made between drug use, crime and other forms of deviant behaviour. Surprisingly perhaps, the attitudes of those respondents who had used drugs were, in many respects, similar to those expressed by non-users. Users' accounts of drug use highlighted the rule-governed nature of such activities. Their affiliation with consensus values was also evident in their reactions to their siblings' drug use, whether this usage was real or hypothesised. The principal difference, we have argued, between users and non-users lies in the generation, by the former, of neutralisation techniques which allow them to engage in drug use while at the same time ascribing to consensus values.

Clearly, rising rates of drug use among young people must be taken seriously. The work done by all those agencies within and outside the criminal justice system in tackling drug use is not helped, however, by scaremongering about the seemingly inexorable disappearance from the social landscape of the drug-free teenager. As Plant wrote somewhat over a decade ago (1985: 350):

> Hardly a day now passes without either a radio or television documentary or the front page of a tabloid newspaper being devoted to the subject of drugs. This attention is reinforced by a veritable barrage of gloomy forecasts and sharply rising levels of recorded drug-related crimes. Some of this interest has been factual and considered. But sadly much of it has been couched in highly emotive terms.

It would be a shame if the academic community continues to ignore such warnings and inadvertently adds fuel to the fire.

Acknowledgement

The authors are grateful to Charlie Lloyd and Malcolm Ramsay for comments on an initial draft of this article.

Notes

1 What the authors meant by 'regular' use is not clearly defined.

2   Throughout this article the term 'lifetime use' has been used instead of 'ever use'. The figures relating to lifetime use indicate the percentage of respondents who reported having used an illicit drug (in this instance cocaine) at any point in their lives.
3   Data concerning the use of specific substances during the month and year before the surveys were not presented by Parker *et al.* (1995).
4   In the interests of confidentiality the names of people mentioned by respondents have been changed.

References and suggested reading

Abercrombie, N., Hill, S. and Turner, B. (1984) *The Penguin Dictionary of Sociology*. London: Penguin.

Balding, J. (1994) *Young People and Illegal Drugs*. Exeter: Health Education Unit, University of Exeter.

Battjes, R.J. (1985) 'Prevention of Adolescent Drug Abuse', *International Journal of the Addictions*, 20: 113–34.

Becker, H. (1963) *Outsiders: Studies in the Sociology of Deviance*. London: Macmillan.

Boseley, S. (1995) 'Drug culture opening new generation gap', *Guardian*, 25 July.

Brunvand, J-H. (1983) *The Vanishing Hitchhiker: Urban Legends and Their Meanings*. London: Picador.

Bryman, A. (1988) *Quantity and Quality in Social Research*. London: Routledge.

Cavan, S. (1966) *Liquor License*. Aldine: Chicago.

Charlton, A. (1982) 'Lung Cancer: The Ultimate Smoking Deterrent for Young People?', *Journal of the Institute of Health Education*, 20: 1.

Clements, I. (1993) 'Too Hot to Handle', *Druglink: The Journal on Drug Misuse in Britain* 8. London: Institute for the Study of Drug Dependence.

Coffield, F. and Gofton, L. (1994) *Drugs and Young People*. London: Institute for Public Policy Research.

Coggans, N. and McKellar, S. (1994) 'Peer Pressure: A Convenient Explanation', *Druglink: The Journal on Drug Misuse in Britain* 9.

Cornwell, J. (1984) *Hard Earned Lives: Accounts of Health and Illness from East London*. London: Tavistock.

Cuff, E.C., Sharrock, W.W. and Francis, D.W. (1992) *Perspectives in Sociology*. London: Routledge.

De Vaus, D.A. (1990) *Surveys in Social Research*, 2nd edn. London: Unwin Hyman.

Dowds, L. and Redfern, J. (1994) *Drug Education Amongst Teenagers: A 1992 British Crime Survey Analysis*. London: Home Office.

Eiser, R., Vander Pligt, J. and Friend, P. (1983) 'Adolescents' Arguments For and Against Smoking', *Journal of the Institute of Health Education*, 21: 3.

Erikson, K.T. (1964) 'Notes on the Sociology of Deviance', in H. Becker (ed.) *The Other Side: Perspectives on Deviance*. New York: Free Press.

Fishbein, M. and Ajzen, I. (1975) *Belief, Attitude, Intervention and Behaviour: An Introduction to Theory and Research*. Reading, Mass.: Addison-Wesley.

Hales, J. (1993) *British Crime Survey (England and Wales): Technical Report*. London: SCPR.

Hirst, J. and McCamley-Finney, A. (1994) *The Place and Meaning of Drugs in the Lives of Young People*. Sheffield: Health Research Institute, Sheffield Hallam University.

Hodgkinson, T. (1995) 'Who takes and eats?', *Guardian*, 17 November.

ISDD (1994) *Drug Misuse in Britain 1994*. London: Institute for the Study of Drug Dependence.

Johnston, I. (1996) 'Smack is back'. *The Big Issue*, January: 161.

Matza, D. (1964) *Delinquency and Drift*. New York: John Wiley & Sons.

Measham, F., Newcombe, R. and Parker, H. (1993) 'The Post-heroin Generation', *Druglink: The Journal on Drug Misuse in Britain*, 8.

Measham, F., Newcombe, R. and Parker, H. (1994) 'The Normalization of Recreational Drug Use Amongst Young People in North-West England', *British Journal of Sociology*, 45.

Millward, D. (1996) 'Drug taking has become "teenage rite of passage"', *Daily Telegraph*, 9 May.

Mott, J. and Mirrlees-Black, C. (1993) *Self-reported Drug Misuse in England and Wales from the 1992 British Crime Survey*. London: Home Office Research and Statistics Department.

Nguyen-Van-Tam, J. and Pearson, J. (1986) 'Teenagers and Motorcyles: Knowledge and Perception of Risks', *Journal of the Institute of Health and Education*, 24: 1.

Oetting, E.K. and Beauvais, F. (1987) 'Peer Cluster Theory: Socialisation Characteristics and Adolescent Drug Use', *Journal of the Institute of Health Education*, 24: 1.

Parker, H., Measham, F. and Aldridge, J. (1995) *Drugs Futures: Changing Patterns of Drug Use Amongst English Youth*. London: Institute for the Study of Drug Dependence.

Pike, R. (1995) 'Drugs advice chief urges legalisation of cannabis', *Daily Telegraph*, 25 March.

Ramsay, M. and Percy, A. (1996) *Drug Misuse Declared: Results of the 1994 British Crime Survey*. Home Office Research Study 151. London: Home Office.

Redhead, S. (1993) *Rave Off. Politics and Deviance in Contemporary Youth Culture*. Aldershot: Avebury.

Rock, P. (1973) *Deviant Behaviour*. London: Hutchinson.

Shiner, M. and Newburn, T. (1996) *The Youth Awareness Programme: An Evaluation of a Peer Education Drugs Project*. London: Central Drugs Prevention Unit, Home Office.

Sykes, G. and Matza, D. (1957) 'Techniques of Neutralization', *American Sociological Review*, 22.

Willmott, P. (1994) *Urban Trends 2: A Decade in Britain's Deprived Urban Areas*. London: Policy Studies Institute.

4. The normalisation of 'sensible' recreational drug use: further evidence from the North West Longitudinal Study*

Howard Parker, Lisa Williams and Judith Aldridge

Introduction

The concept of normalisation

The term normalisation was developed during the late 1950s in Denmark in respect of creating 'normal' living conditions for people with learning difficulties. The term has become increasingly influential in service development for disadvantaged groups and particularly people with disabilities (Emerson 1992). Its leading proponent has continuously revised the term and established it as both a principle and a theoretical perspective (Wolfensberger 1972, 1984).

Essentially normalisation is about stigmatised or deviant individuals or groups (and to some degree their social behaviour) becoming included in as many features of conventional everyday 'normal' life as possible, from life's rhythms and routines to economic and environmental 'standards' of life (Nirje 1980). Wolfensberger 'sociologised' normalisation by linking it to societal reaction or labelling theory yet, at the same time, arguing that difference (e.g. 'handicap') remained and could not be wished away by libertarian pronouncements of total equality or sameness (Wolfensberger 1980). The removal of cultural stereotypes about people with disabilities, which were often sustained and transmitted through conversation culture and mass media: could nevertheless be struggled for (Bogdan *et al.* 1982) whereby difference could become valued in a socially integrated world. Emerson notes that Wolfensberger's conceptualisations are 'purportedly applicable to any social group who are devalued or at risk of devaluation in any society' (Emerson 1992).

The application of the concept of normalisation as a way of exploring and explaining an unprecedented increase in the drug involvement of young Britons across the 1990s was introduced by the authors' research group in the mid 1990s. It was an attempt to make sense of the findings of a unique longitudinal study of several hundred 'ordinary' young people's experiences

*Originally published in *Sociology* 36(4), 2002, reproduced by permission of Sage Publications.

of growing up 'drugwise'. Having monitored this cohort annually from when they were 14 (1991) to 18 (1995), we had to explain why they increasingly knew so much about drugs, why they were highly likely to be drug triers and why drug involvement – an illegal activity – was as prevalent in young women as men and across all socio-economic profiles. In particular we were perplexed by the apparent social accommodation of 'sensible' recreational drug use by abstainers and more cautious young people. As they reached late adolescence they, too, even without personal drugs involvement, appeared fairly drugwise and increasingly willing to acknowledge that different types of drug use and drug user existed. Sensible, occasional, recreational drug users, particularly users of cannabis, were condoned rather than condemned (Measham *et al.* 1998; Parker *et al.* 1998).

From rather crude beginnings (Measham *et al.* 1994) we have attempted to better define and re-test the concept of normalisation and hopefully improve its utility in respect of understanding the growth of recreational drug use (Measham *et al.* 2000). One immediate problem with re-utilising the concept of normalisation, as operated in the disability and learning difficulty field, is that it is disabled people who have long been and continue to be stigmatised, more than their behaviour. Although problem drug users, whose physical appearance and social behaviour deteriorate, actually present as 'junkies' or 'smackheads' and thus become stigmatised by persona and behaviour, this is not really the case for young recreational drug users.

For societies which maintain and enforce blanket prohibition of all popular illicit drugs and refuse any review of their drugs laws, the notion of normalisation to explain the growth of recreational use is anathema because it highlights the loss of moral and social authority of the law and, by implication, the government and enforcement agencies. However, for societies which are committed to social inclusion and a pro-active approach to recognising that social policy and laws must adapt to social and cultural change, the concept is positively helpful.

Van Vliet (1990: 467) notes how the term was purposefully applied to Dutch drugs policy at the end of the 1980s:

> Normalisation essentially means the admission – as a government and as a society – that extensive drug abuse has obtained a firm footing in society, as already is the case with alcohol and tobacco … it proves to be an unrealistic option to eradicate drugs … It is far more realistic to try to contain the damage caused by drugs and abuse, to cope with the problems and manage them as well as possible … Normalisation also means setting limits to what society can and cannot tolerate as part of establishing clearness about obligations and rights of drug users as members of an organised society.

From our point of view normalisation is a multi-dimensional tool, a barometer of changes in social behaviour and cultural perspectives, in this case focusing on both illicit drug use and users. Normalisation is always a two-way street. So, for instance, cigarette smoking became normalised across the last century, yet there was only briefly a majority of regular smokers in the community. The smokers were tolerated by the non smokers. Smoking also became prevalent in all socio-economic sectors and involved both men and women. However in the new decade we see cohabitation and accommodation reducing. Smokers are no longer so easily tolerated, their social space is being restricted and their habit increasingly challenged, even stigmatised as anti-social. So, in trying to map and explain the increased accommodation of 'sensible' recreational drug taking utilising the normalisation perspective, the potential for limits being reached or processes reversing always remains.

The dimensions of this conceptualisation with which to measure the scale and limits of normalisation are: access and availability, drug trying rates, rates of drug use, attitudes to 'sensible' recreational drug use by adolescents and young adults, especially of non users, and the degree of cultural accommodation of illegal drug use.

Access and availability

The first dimension concerns the accessibility and availability of illicit drugs without which normalisation cannot develop. There have been substantial increases in the availability of a wider range of drugs over the past ten years which are being sustained. One measure of this is seizures. Seizures of all the main street drugs in the UK have climbed dramatically, probably tenfold in ten years (Cabinet Office 1999), although rates vary by particular drug through time, with heroin and cocaine currently showing the strongest seizure 'gains'; where ecstasy did so in the mid 1990s. With street prices stable or falling and purity levels maintained, the authoritative overview is that the supply of drugs has been growing rapidly and is being sustained (Corkery 2000; Independent Inquiry 2000). Moreover, the fall in the street price of drugs, for instance, cocaine, appears to generate increased use (Grossman and Chaloupka 1998).

Across the last decade school surveys have also documented rises in accessibility and availability and have consistently shown that nowadays a majority of respondents can from around 15 years old access drugs, particularly cannabis, quite easily. A recent national survey of England found 61 per cent of 15-year-olds had been offered at least one drug (Goddard and Higgins 1999). A large longitudinal study in Northern England is finding incremental rises in drugs offers and availability, with 80 per cent reporting being in offer situations by 16 years (Aldridge et al. 1999). Household surveys identify similar patterns with two thirds of 14–16-year-olds being in offer situations, rising with age, whereby nearly 90 per cent of 20–22-year-olds report these situations (HEA 1999).

The key to easy accessibility near the point of consumption is not primarily a product of aggressive drug-dealing. Most young people, even clubbers (Measham et al. 2000), obtain their drugs through social networks and friends-of-friends chains (Parker et al. 2001) connected to small dealers. Because most recreational drug users are otherwise fairly law-abiding, 'sorting' each other acts as a filter or social device which allows them to obtain drugs without venturing into the world of dodgy dealers and so risk apprehension or trouble. That probably half of young Britons have breached the Misuse of

Drugs Act in terms of possession and perhaps a quarter have acquired and distributed drugs in a way which makes them arrestable for 'intent to supply' is a key measure of normalisation. Passing on ecstasy tablets to friends and acquaintances for instance, if defined as supplying a Class A drug, can lead to a long prison sentence – yet this is exactly the way that most drugs are procured at the point of consumption (Parker *et al.* 2001). The routinisation of breaching the law in respect of 'recreational' drug use is a robust measure of normalisation to the point that authoritative sources are now recommending a change in the law to accommodate the realities of 'sorting' (Home Affairs Committee 2002; Independent Inquiry 2000).

Drug trying rates in adolescence and young adulthood

Because we must measure normalisation utilising long term indicators, the analysis becomes more complex in the new decade. We must investigate not only the drugs status of the children of the 1990s, now young adults, but also today's 'new' adolescents. There are complicating differences in consecutive birth cohorts.

It became clear by the late 1990s that adolescent drug trying in the UK had been rising steeply across the decade. Young Britons are the most drug-involved in Europe. In 1996 Scottish and English adolescents in particular had the highest rates of drug trying of 26 European countries (ESPAD 1997) and four years later the situation is basically the same (ESPAD 2001). For 'synthetic' dance drug use, the UK heads the league table by quite mammoth proportions (Griffiths *et al.* 1997). Indeed at the end of the decade rates of lifetime use of many drugs in the UK had matched those of American high school students (NHSDA 1999).

The highest rates of drug trying have been found in Scotland (Barnard *et al.* 1996; Meikle *et al.* 1996) and Northern England (Aldridge *et al.* 1999) where between 50 and 60 per cent of mid adolescents disclose drug trying, predominantly of cannabis, followed by amphetamines. Other studies have found lower rates down to about 30 per cent for lifetime prevalence (Goddard and Higgins 1999; Sutherland and Wilner 1998).

However there are now clear signs that, as this 'first wave' of drug experienced adolescents move into adulthood, their successors are slightly less drug experienced. Beginning evidence of this epidemiological shift comes from the large scale, on-going surveying of secondary school children by Exeter University (Balding 1999). Similarly, a national UK-wide survey of 15–16-year-olds in 1995 (Miller and Plant 1996), having discovered over 40 per cent reporting trying a drug, has recently (1999) found that today's 15–16-year-olds disclose significantly less, around 36 per cent, drug trying (Plant and Miller 2000). Despite identifying very early onset of drug trying, a longitudinal study in Northern England is also finding signs of plateauing in drugs experience in the 16–17 age band at a lower rate than a previous cohort three years older (Egginton *et al.* 2001).

All this said, two recent, large scale, national time series surveys have noted recent increases in young people's drug use (Flood-Page *et al.* 2000; Office of National Statistics 2000) and the tentative conclusion at this stage must therefore be that a plateau is being found whereby all those young people who wish to try drugs are doing so. This epidemiological process is to be expected whereby a levelling off of drug involvement is eventually found in each birth cohort.

The 'children of the 1990s', today's new young adults, are however still trailblazing and their rates of drug taking appear to be continuing to increase. We know far less about post-16s and must largely rely on what can be gleaned from household surveys and surveys of college students. The British Crime Survey 'system', despite under-estimating drug use (Gore 1999), has actually identified significant increases in drug trying amongst young adults. Whilst part of this will be a product of early 1990s adolescents retrospectively reporting earlier drug experience, there are signs of later onset. Thus for 20–24-year-olds lifetime prevalence has increased from 44 per cent (1994) to 49 per cent (1996) to 55 per cent (1998) over the past three bi-annual surveys with 58 per cent of males in this age group now disclosing drug experience. More unexpectedly we find a similar scale of rise for 25–29-year-olds (39% → 41% → 45%) (Ramsay and Partridge 1999) which suggests 'late' initiation into drug involvement occurred amongst twenty-somethings during the 1990s.

Universities provide one of the few arenas for the easy capture of young adults and a clutch of studies of undergraduates (Makhoul et al. 1998; Webb et al. 1996) and medical students (Ashton and Kamali 1995; Birch et al. 1999) has been generated. All these studies variously suggest that the majority of university students, up to 60 per cent, have some drug experience, a figure which has doubled over the past 15 years. Cannabis dominates this involvement, with only 13 to 18 per cent having ever used dance drugs. The application of personality and general health measurements and assessing views about drug use in some of these studies has led to the conclusion that drug experienced students are very little different from the 'normal population of students' and that drug taking has 'become part of the lifestyle of a significant and nondeviant proportion of students' (Makhoul et al. 1998).

Recent and regular drug use

Research suggests recent drug use rises with age from 15 into the early 20s. Larger school-based studies find around 20 per cent of mid adolescents nationally (e.g. Goddard and Higgins 1999) to higher rates of 28 per cent in northern England (Aldridge et al. 1999). The household surveys tend to replicate these rates, noting a peak either in the 16–19 age group (Ramsay and Partridge 1999) or the 20–22-year-olds. The HEA household survey of England found over a quarter of 20–22-year-olds were recent users (past three months). Interestingly when the sampling limitations of these surveys are reduced by pooling data, more significant increases are found, particularly in young adult 'stimulant' use (Gore 1999). The most persuasive evidence of increased drug use comes from the Youth Lifestyles Survey. The first sweep in 1992–93 found past year drug use for 14–25s was 22 per cent. In the second survey in 1998–99 it had risen to 32 per cent. In 1998–99 past month drug use was 26 per cent for 18–21-year-olds (Flood-Page et al. 2000), several per cent higher than reported in household surveys at the beginning of the decade.

The university student studies quoted earlier offer some help in measuring regular drug use. Between 20 and 25 per cent of the samples were deemed via self nomination to be regular drug users, primarily of cannabis, with only around 10 per cent reporting they use dance drugs 'often' (Makhoul *et al.* 1998; Webb *et al.* 1996).

Once we actually focus on drug-using populations and turn to the night club scene, drug involvement rates inevitably climb sharply. The cluster of studies undertaken during the last decade all paint very similar pictures. The clubbers are at the 'serious' end of recreational drug use. They are immensely drug experienced with lifetime rates of cannabis trying at nearly 100 per cent, rates for amphetamines, LSD and ecstasy in the 60–90 per cent range, with cocaine slightly lower but rising (Measham *et al.* 2000). For current use most are daily users of cannabis and regular weekend users of the dance drugs and they mix these drugs and alcohol as a matter of routine (Akram 1997; Forsyth 1998; Hammersley *et al.* 1999; McElrath and McEvoy 1999; Release 1997).

It is in this 'going out' sector that those who use drugs 'beyond' alcohol and cannabis are most often found. The clubbers, however, are a conundrum for the normalisation debate (Measham *et al.* 2000) because, as we shall discuss later, certainly outside club land, their poly-drug use and 'risky' nights out potentially clash with the notions of responsible, sensible recreational drug use which is at the core of our conceptualisation.

In summary, we cannot make robust estimates of the scale of regular drug use. On the measures we have and over-relying on too few studies, it appears that 10–15 per cent of late adolescents are recent, regular recreational drug users, with this proportion rising to 20–25 per cent amongst young adults. This drug use is dominated by cannabis taking but with perhaps around 10 per cent of the 18–25-year-old population using stimulant drugs, primarily amphetamines, ecstasy and cocaine recreationally, mainly at weekends. These rates have been rising for several years.

Social accommodation of sensible recreational drug use

An essential measure of the scale of normalisation is the extent to which recreational drug use is personally and socially accommodated by abstainers and 'ex' triers. We can only expect to find this potential accommodation in younger Britons, although, certainly in respect of cannabis, over thirties' attitudes are becoming more liberal (Independent Inquiry 2000) as they become 'educated' by their drugwise children.

Shiner and Newburn (1997) argued that young drug users feel guilty about illicit drug-taking and that abstainers are steadfastly against such behaviour. Unfortunately the empirical study they undertook to support this view was not really appropriate to test the normalisation thesis. The sample was very small, many interviewees were actually attending an anti-drugs workshop at which the researchers were present, the views of 11–13-year-olds were not distinguished from 15–16-year-olds, quotes relating to views about brothers' and sisters' drug-taking were mixed up with more general opinions and distinctions between different drugs were lost. However if Shiner and

Newburn are correct about drug use being strongly rejected by young non users and that users feel guilty and uncomfortable with their drug use, then the normalisation perspective has severe limitations.

Aside from one study which produced equivocal findings (Wibberley and Price 2000), all the remainder of a clutch of independently undertaken qualitative studies with young Britons note the presence of a rational, consumerist, decision-making process which distinguishes between drugs, their effects and dangers and identifies a style of recreational drug use which can be accepted or at least tolerated by non users or cautious drug triers. These investigations in southern England (Hart and Hunt 1997), around Merseyside (Young and Jones 1997) in S.E. England (Boys et al. 2001), Sheffield (Hirst and McCameley-Finney 1994) and nationally (Perri 6 et al. 1997) all reach conclusions broadly consistent with the notion of increasing accommodation of 'sensible' drug use into the perspectives of young people. This does not mean the risks of drug use to health, performance or 'getting caught' are ignored or dismissed. Dependent or over-frequent drug use, and heroin and crack cocaine taking, for instance, were condemned by users and abstainers alike. This accommodation was strongest for cannabis and more equivocal for ecstasy (Boys et al. 2000).

Despite all these studies generally supporting the normalisation thesis in respect of young people's knowledge, decision-making processes and attitudes to 'sensible' recreational drug use, we must continue to take the attitudinal dimension very seriously. The whole area is very complex because young people change their minds about so many issues through time and can anyway hold negative attitudes about a social habit even though they continue to indulge in it, for instance as with smoking, 'excessive' drinking and unprotected sex. Indeed, given the persuasive evidence of normalisation in respect of the increasing availability, trying rates and regular recreational drug use, it is with this dimension – the attitudes and social behaviour of non drug-using young people – that much rests. The hypothesis which has emerged from the authors' longitudinal studies is that, whilst abstentious early teenagers often display strong anti-drugs attitudes, these attitudes 'mellow' with age and life experience amongst the majority (Parker et al. 1998). Student surveys support this in finding that abstainers (18–22 years) respect the rights of others to take drugs 'sensibly' and that most have current drug-using friends (e.g. Pirie and Worcester 1999).

Cultural accommodation

Assessments of the extent to which the realities of recreational drug use are being accommodated in cultural understandings of normality are very difficult to make. Our view is that there are multiple indicative signs of recreational drug use being accepted as a 'liveable with' reality by the wider society. The blurring of the licit (e.g. alcohol) with the illicit (e.g. cannabis and cocaine) in 'going out' social worlds and as part of weekend relaxation is now routinely referred to in television dramas and serials (e.g. This Life, BBC2). Drug-taking adventures are a key source of inspiration in stand up comedy (e.g. Ali G, Channel 4) and youth movies (e.g. Human Traffic 1999). Drugs realities are nowadays discussed in youth magazines in a wholly practical 'how to' way.

The drug-taking of film and popular music 'stars' are increasingly described in neutral rather than condemnatory terms. For cannabis, in particular, we find public opinion surveys showing a majority of Britons in favour of some decriminalisation (Independent Inquiry 2000). Even senior politicians can now admit to drug experience. And, with influential broadsheet newspapers articulating the same views and official government strategy reluctantly moving towards the decriminalisation of cannabis use and sidestepping the ecstasy phenomenon, whilst concentrating on heroin and cocaine as drugs which 'do the most harm', we see the same hierarchy of dangerousness first articulated by drugwise youth now being reflected in official thinking and even parental attitudes. In other words the conclusions reached by 1990s youth from their social experience about different drugs and their benefits and risks during the 1990s are now beginning to be understood and acknowledged in more cautious and conservative cultural and institutional arrangements and by adult worlds. All this is consistent with the move towards normalisation.

Methods

The North West Longitudinal Study began in 1991 (Year 1) when over 700 14-year-olds formed the original cohort. This sample was tracked, annually, utilising self report questionnaires, initially for five years until, in Year 5, they were 18 (1995). The initial aim of the investigation was to explore how 'ordinary' English adolescents were growing up in respect of their introduction to and subsequent consumption of alcohol and illicit drugs. The study was also concerned with lifestyles and leisure and how illicit drugs related to these (Parker *et al.* 1998).

The cohort was initially representative of young people in two mixed metropolitan boroughs in North West England. The subjects attended eight secondary 'high' and grammar schools which were picked to represent evenly middle class and working class catchments. However there was substantial attrition at 16 (Year 3) when, fairly predictably, a proportion of primarily working class respondents, most of whom were male, were lost. A small number of respondents from Asian and Muslim backgrounds also withdrew. There was little further attrition at Years 4 and 5 (see Table 4.1).

The cohort was successfully recaptured as part of a follow up during 1999 when 465 successfully completed and returned a new questionnaire. With gap Years 6–8 this follow up occurred at Year 9 (see Table 4.1). The follow up initially involved sending a humorous Christmas-type card to over 700 potential respondents who had variously been attached to the study primarily at Years 4 and 5. The card also had a return slip to help establish a current residential or contact address, given that up to half of this sample had been away to college/university and were anyway at an age where leaving the parental home becomes likely. Several months later, after a further postal/ telephone contacting exercise, 711 questionnaires were sent out although over 200 addresses had been 'unconfirmed' since 1995–6. A £10 music token was promised upon the satisfactory completion and return of the questionnaire.

Accounting for decliners and questionnaires returned by the postal service, the response was 71 per cent.

The 465 returners proved fairly representative of the cohort at Year 5 (n = 529) with the small attrition leaving the gender and social class composition largely unaffected. In this article we particularly compare Years 4/5 data with the new Year 9 results and have complete returns for these three surveys for 354 respondents with the remainder having one or more missing annual returns (see Table 4.1).

The normalisation thesis which developed around this cohort study also involved utilising qualitative data. Back in 1994–95 when they were 17 years old, 86 panel members had been interviewed in-depth (Parker *et al.* 1998). During 2000 and by coincidence, exactly 86 subjects were interviewed in depth as part of the follow up. Every effort was made to make this interview sample representative of the recaptured, surveyed cohort. Quota sampling was used in respect of gender, ethnic origin, income and different drugs status. The sample included 29 per cent abstainers who had never tried an illicit drug, and 29 per cent ex-triers who declared they had no intention of re-taking an illicit drug. The other 42 per cent were opportunistic drug users (occasional drug users) and regular current users.

Given the need to gather information on the gap years and take into account the cohort's new adult status, we redesigned and piloted the questionnaire. Its basic structure remained the same, as did that of the interview schedule, but numerous minor changes were required. As well as a revised section to disclose any drugs involvement across the gap years, new questions focused on feelings of security/insecurity in respect of personal, occupational, financial and domestic situations, given the transitional life-course phase the cohort was negotiating.

Table 4.1 Total returns from Year 3 to Year 9 follow up

	Total
Year 3, 4, 5 & 9	301
Year 4, 5 & 9	53
Year 3, 4 & 9	16
Year 3, 5 & 9	21
Year 3 & 9	15
Year 4 & 9	9
Year 5 & 9	20
Year 9*	30
	465

*25 of these respondents completed returns for either Year 1, 2 or 1 & 2
5 returners at Year 9 had clearly made earlier returns but could not be matched via their ID codes.

Longitudinal studies offer quite different challenges in terms of reliability than the usual one-off or time series surveys. Whilst there was some inconsistent reporting by a small minority of subjects in the early years, both internal and inter-year consistency became very high. In short, what subjects checked one year they accurately repeated in subsequent years. One inconsistency, however, was noticeable in respect of reporting lifetime prevalence of solvents which fell, independently of any attrition. The interviewees confirmed this was a product of re-definition. At 14 sniffing solvents was seen as a drugs experience; at 17 and far more drugwise, it was thought a childish act. This process of biographical reconstruction is well known to panel studies (e.g. Plant *et al.* 1985). In the recapture we have also seen occasional examples of this process, primarily around whether an earlier incident, such as taking a puff on a cannabis spliff being passed around, is, for an abstainer, a `real' drugs experience (especially if no effect was experienced), thereby changing their lifetime status. Through time the tendency is to deny this episode particularly, if one's social identity is presented as abstentious.

Finally, in respect of reliability, we asked all those in the interview sample who had taken a drug how accurately they felt they could recall a drug-taking event and its timing by 'gap' year. The vast majority (84 per cent), given a scale of one to 10, scored their recall as seven or more – an encouraging result.

In Table 4.2 the demographic characteristics of the sample at Year 5 and the Year 9 follow up are presented. The new attrition has done little to disturb the picture. The sample remains fairly balanced by socio-economic status but continues to under-represent males. Given that the males still in the study are now more likely to be drug users (males ever had drug 79.2 per cent, females also 73.3 per cent) this should be borne in mind when interpreting the results.

Results

'Offer' situations provide the established measure of drugs availability. However longitudinal surveys inadvertently also capture changes in availability of all or particular substances as, despite being asked to utilise an 'ever' lifetime measure, young respondents routinely use shorter recall periods. Table 4.3 nevertheless clearly demonstrates how drug offers have increased with age for any drug. There are incremental increases for all but one of the main drugs. Cannabis is the most available with cocaine powder showing a rapid recent presence in this cohort's social worlds. Only LSD shows a fall in availability.

Interviewees generally supported the notion that drugs had a greater availability and presence in their everyday lives and that there had been changes in the accessibility of different substances:

It (access to drugs) has sort of changed quite a lot. You seem to be able to get it (drugs) anywhere nowadays.

(63497, female current drug taker)

Table 4.2 Demographic characteristics of sample at 18 (Year 5) and 22 (Year 9)

| | Year 5 | | Year 9 | |
	n size	%	n size	%
Sample size	**529**		**465**	
Male	224	(42.3)	197	(42.4)
Female	305	(57.7)	268	(57.6)
Protestant		51.8		53.1
Catholic		15.3		13.8
Muslim		3.8		3.2
Other Religion		4.7		5.4
Atheist/Agnostic/None		15.1		18.1
Don't know		8.9		6.3
Black		2.7		1.3
Asian		4.9		3.7
White		92.0		93.8
Other		0.4		1.3
Middle class		69.1		68.8
Working class		30.9		31.2
Still living in parental home		64.6		56.6
Became a parent		–		7.2
In higher education		39.3		26.4

Table 4.3 Drugs offers age 14–22 years inclusive (in hierarchical order at Year 9)

| | Year 1 | Year 2 | Year 3 | Year 4 | Year 5 | Year 9 |
| n size | 776 | 752 | 523 | 536 | 529 | 465 |
Column percentage	%	%	%	%	%	%
Cannabis	54.6	61.6	72.7	77.4	83.9	89.0
Amphetamines	29.6	40.6	47.9	60.0	67.0	76.1
Amyl nitrites	24.1	37.3	41.7	51.4	58.9	63.9
Ecstasy	21.4	32.9	36.3	49.7	62.3	62.1
LSD	40.4	55.0	56.1	65.3	65.6	56.3
Cocaine powder	8.0	12.7	12.4	18.3	22.9	46.5
Magic mushrooms	24.5	32.5	29.2	26.9	26.2	32.4
Solvents	25.6	27.2	23.1	33.7	27.3	21.8
Tranquilisers	4.3	11.4	7.1	12.8	14.4	15.2
Crack cocaine	–	–	–	5.6	5.7	11.6
Heroin	5.4	8.2	5.4	6.6	5.4	8.9
At least one drug	59.1	70.9	76.5	87.5	91.1	93.1

When I was at University all I used to do was to take acid, and now I can't get it for love nor money at all. So it's very much like an ecstasy kind of generation and that is dead easy to get hold of and now I'm getting into a circle where like you can bump into a coke dealer whenever you want as well.

(83X40, female current drug taker)

Now in young adulthood men (93.9 per cent) are slightly more likely to be in offer situations than women (92.5 per cent) with a significant difference found in respect of cocaine (55.5 per cent against 40.0 per cent). However, because of the shortcomings in the established 'offer' questions, in terms of ambiguous meaning and recall difficulties, the sample was asked in the recapture how easy, difficult or impossible it would be for them to obtain illicit drugs if they had the time, motivation and money. Table 4.4 thus provides a more accurate, contemporary picture of drugs access and availability. This said, the picture is similar to the offers measurement with cannabis, by far the most accessible drug, followed by the stimulant dance drugs – amphetamines, ecstasy, nitrites and cocaine powder. The reduced availability of LSD is well illustrated by the high 'difficult' assessment. Overall nine in 10 respondents felt it was easy to get at least one illicit drug.

During the Year 9 survey respondents were asked how they usually obtained their drugs. For the majority (65.1 per cent) friends or 'friends-of-friends' were nominated as the sourcing contact. Drug 'dealers' (14.5 per cent) are not, as popular discourse would have it, the key retail outlet although this cohort's definitions are largely socially constructed whereby a *de jure* supply offence is re-defined as 'sorting' and a small time opportunistic dealer becomes 'like a friend' (13079, male). This acquaintance network is also believed to ensure better quality drugs 'well I trust my mates and they trust the people they get it off' (63515, male).

Turning to lifetime trying rates for the samples since Year 1, trying rates for any drug have climbed incrementally from 36.3 per cent at 14 years to 75.8 per cent at 22 years (see Table 4.5). The gender symmetry in early adolescence continues to fall away with the emergent differences at 17–18 years continuing with 79.2 per cent of men but only 73.2 per cent of women now having tried a drug. At recapture we can see how ecstasy, as a later onset drug associated with access to bars and night clubs, and cocaine, as an increasingly available popular 'recreational' drug, have increased significance. This said, the dominance of cannabis (69.9 per cent) stands out again. The same small gender differences are present for each individual drug.

Turning to recency measures Table 4.6 describes past year drug use right across the study but with Years 6–8 based on recall at recapture. The increases in past year use, noted in mid adolescence, appear to have peaked at 20 (Year 7) and essentially having plateaued, look set to fall. Past year use of some drugs, notably amphetamines and LSD, has declined whereas the millennial cocaine phenomenon again stands out.

Table 4.7 describes very recent 'past month' use. It was felt that any attempt to obtain accurate past month use in the gap years was unrealistic. At Year 9, however, nearly a third of the sample (31.2 per cent) disclosed a recent drug experience but, as high as this is, it is a reduction from rates in late adolescence. Although the small attrition of male respondents at recapture will partly explain this fall, we are at the very least seeing a plateau and perhaps

Table 4.4 Ease of access reported for individual drugs by 22-year-olds (in hierarchical order)

	Easy	Difficult	Impossible	Don't know
n size	465	465	465	465
Column per centage	%	%	%	%
Cannabis	84.3	2.8	1.1	11.8
Solvents	60.3	3.7	1.7	34.3
Amphetamines	57.8	13.5	2.2	26.3
Ecstasy	49.5	15.2	2.6	32.7
Amyl nitrite	48.8	6.9	3.9	40.4
Cocaine powder	39.1	15.6	5.1	40.0
LSD	24.9	21.9	4.7	48.4
Magic mushrooms	16.6	20.3	7.3	55.7
Tranquilisers	14.7	12.6	6.1	66.0
Crack cocaine	11.7	12.3	8.7	66.9
Heroin	9.1	18.0	10.2	62.8
GHB	5.0	9.5	8.2	76.6
At least one drug	90.9	–	–	–

Table 4.5 Lifetime prevalence of illicit drug taking (age 14–22 years inclusive) by individual drug

	Year 1	Year 2	Year 3	Year 4	Year 5	Year 9
n size	776	752	523	536	529	465
Column percentage	%	%	%	%	%	%
Amphetamines	9.5	16.1	18.4	25.2	32.9	41.8
Amyl nitrites	14.2	22.1	23.5	31.3	35.3	45.2
Cannabis	31.7	41.5	45.3	53.7	59.0	69.9
Cocaine powder	1.4	4.0	2.5	4.3	5.7	24.6
Crack cocaine	–	–	–	0.6	0.8	2.4
Ecstasy	5.8	7.4	5.4	12.9	19.8	28.5
Heroin	0.4	2.5	0.6	0.6	0.6	0.9
LSD	13.3	25.3	24.5	26.7	28.0	28.8
Magic mushrooms	9.9	12.4	9.8	9.5	8.5	12.6
Solvents	11.9	13.2	9.9	10.3	9.5	10.3
Tranquilisers	1.2	4.7	1.5	3.9	4.5	5.8
At least one drug	36.3	47.3	50.7	57.3	63.1	75.8

the beginnings of a fall in recent drug use. The dominance of cannabis is even more apparent on this measure with only the stimulants and dance drugs used by the partying, clubbing minority (less than one in ten of the sample), showing any real increase. The developing gender gap is particularly apparent on this measure. For instance, at 17 years (Year 4) 35 per cent of men reported past month cannabis use, compared to 28.5 per cent of young women, a 6.5 per cent difference which at 22 years has increased to 12 per cent.

Utilising Year 9 data to assess the frequency of past month cannabis use we find the mean rate of use was three episodes. Five per cent of these past

Table 4.6 Past year prevalence of illicit drug taking (age 14–22 years inclusive) by individual drug

	Year 1 776 %	Year 2 752 %	Year 3 523 %	Year 4 536 %	Year 5 529 %	Year 6* 465 %	Year 7* 465 %	Year 8* 465 %	Year 9 465 %
n size									
Column per centage									
Amphetamines	4.1	6.8	8.8	16.6	24.0	25.6	20.9	17.1	11.0
Amyl nitrites	5.3	9.8	10.3	17.4	20.4	23.1	17.2	13.9	10.3
Cannabis	9.2	12.3	11.3	44.0	47.8	45.7	47.3	46.9	46.8
Cocaine powder	0.4	1.5	1.1	2.6	4.0	5.2	8.2	14.2	16.2
Crack cocaine	–	–	–	0.0	0.4	0.2	0.6	0.6	0.9
Ecstasy	2.3	2.7	1.9	9.5	17.4	14.0	15.1	14.9	14.5
Heroin	0.2	0.8	0.6	0.4	0.2	0.0	0.2	0.0	0.2
LSD	6.3	8.7	9.4	13.2	15.2	15.1	10.3	4.3	2.8
Magic mushrooms	3.2	4.8	4.2	4.0	4.2	4.9	4.2	1.1	1.7
Solvents	4.1	4.0	1.5	2.2	1.1	3.9	0.5	0.0	0.0
Tranquilisers	0.7	2.3	0.8	1.9	1.5	2.2	1.9	1.1	1.1
At least one drug	30.9	40.6	40.5	46.1	52.9	56.3	58.2	56.8	52.1

*Based on longer term recall disclosed at Year 9 survey

Table 4.7 Past month prevalence of illicit drug taking (age 14–22 years inclusive) by individual drug

	Year 1	Year 2	Year 3	Year 4	Year 5	Year 9
n size	776	752	523	536	529	465
Column percentage	%	%	%	%	%	%
Amphetamines	3.8	5.4	4.8	7.4	9.6	3.7
Amyl nitrites	4.9	6.5	5.6	6.6	7.8	4.1
Cannabis	17.7	22.1	25.3	31.4	31.6	25.8
Cocaine powder	0.8	0.9	0.2	1.1	1.5	7.0
Crack cocaine	-	-	-	0.0	0.0	0.0
Ecstasy	2.6	3.2	1.4	6.4	7.8	8.3
Heroin	0.3	0.4	0.0	0.2	0.2	0.0
LSD	5.2	12.8	4.7	4.1	1.1	0.0
Magic mushrooms	3.5	3.4	0.8	1.4	0.8	0.9
Solvents	4.5	2.9	0.6	1.2	0.6	0.0
Tranquilisers	0.4	1.5	0.2	0.6	0.2	0.2
At least one drug	20.4	26.2	27.7	34.1	35.2	31.2

month users are daily (i.e. 30 times+) users. Males were heavier users (8.2 per cent male daily users; 2.6 per cent females). For all the other drugs used in the past month frequency was essentially 'once', suggesting that stimulants are used for special occasions or occasional clubbing weekends. We describe elsewhere the articulate and positive accounts these current drug users give for their recreational drug use. These users, whilst concerned about 'getting caught', actually hold measurable positive or pro drugs attitudes and nominate positive reasons for their use (Williams and Parker 2001). Personal guilt was neither nominated nor detected, except amongst some ex-triers.

Turning to the scale of social accommodation of 'sensible' recreational drug use, particularly amongst abstainers and ex-drug triers, the recaptured sample was asked how many of their three closest friends had taken illicit drugs. Based on a far more sophisticated assessment of drugs status utilising attitudinal scales, self-nominated status, recency and frequency of use and future intentions (see Parker *et al.* 1998), Table 4.8 describes the results by these four dominant drugs status groups in respect of at least one friendship.

As expected, cannabis is the key drug, with the majority of respondents (85.5 per cent) having friends who have taken this drug. Remarkably half the abstainers (50.5 per cent) and almost all the ex-triers (96.2 per cent) indicated at least one (and often more) friends have tried cannabis. Unsurprisingly, current users (99.2 per cent) and occasional opportunistic users (86.3 per cent) also have very high rates.

In relation to dance drugs such as amphetamines (65.9 per cent) and ecstasy (56.3 per cent) over half of the sample have at least one close friend who has tried these drugs. As would be expected, current drug takers reported the highest friendship rate; however, over a quarter of abstainers have close friends who are drug experienced in relation to amphetamines and ecstasy. In all cases, with the exception of heroin, ex-drug takers are more likely to have close friends who are drug experienced compared to opportunistic drug takers.

Table 4.8 Percentage of 22-year-olds by drug status who have a least 1 close friend who has tried individual drugs

	Current drug taker	Opportunistic drug taker	Ex-drug taker	Abstainer	Total
n size	130	73	159	101	463*
Column per centage	%	%	%	%	%
Amphetamines	91.5	60.3	71.0	28.0	65.9
Amyl nitrites	84.4	52.2	65.0	16.0	57.7
Cannabis	99.2	86.3	96.2	50.5	85.5
Cocaine powder	77.4	33.8	46.8	16.0	46.4
Crack cocaine	23.4	5.6	13.9	5.0	13.1
Ecstasy	85.6	47.1	56.9	25.0	56.3
GHB	9.5	1.4	5.1	2.0	5.1
Heroin	11.2	9.7	5.6	3.0	7.2
LSD	83.0	38.5	52.2	17.9	51.3
Magic Mushrooms	67.2	19.7	35.6	12.0	36.8
Solvents	30.3	9.8	15.9	5.0	16.7
Tranquilisers	29.0	5.6	14.6	2.0	14.5
At least one drug	100.0	100.0	97.3	72.9	93.9

*2 respondents were unclassifiable in terms of drug status

The data suggest that, whilst abstainers are not personally drug experienced, they do associate with close friends who have tried drugs. The vast majority (93.9 per cent any drug) have at least one friend with some drug experience.

During interviews subjects were asked how they felt about others who take drugs. Nearly two thirds of abstainers (61.5 per cent) held approving attitudes. Ex-drug takers (53.8 per cent) were similar in their tolerant attitudes. Repeatedly, abstainers and ex-drug takers commented: 'it's up to them'. Two ex-drug takers summarise how many felt about people taking drugs:

> I mean they know about the hazards or the benefits of whatever. So I mean it's up to them, they know the risks, so if they want to … it's up to them. If they benefit from taking drugs then that's their decision and if something happens to them because of the drug, I mean the decision is solely up to them. So if someone is a drug user I won't hold it against them and if somone doesn't use drugs, you know, I won't like judge that person as well.
>
> (53409, male, ex-drug taker)

The second interviewee, a non smoker, non drinker, actually lived in a 'cannabis house'. He'd only ever smoked cannabis once yet:

> If you're in this house a lot you'll notice what I'm talking about. I mean there are no dangers, no negative things, against it. It's just that it isn't my thing … It doesn't bother me at all … it's their business and like I say I'm not on drugs and it makes no odds to me.
>
> (73748, male, ex-trier)

To explore these attitudes further abstainers were asked if they held different views about different types of drug taking. The results are evenly balanced with 45.8 per cent reporting they hold different views about different types of drug-taking behaviour. Cannabis was the drug which received most tolerance or accommodation.

> Only a few weeks ago we went to a car show in Doncaster and when we were all finished we stopped and just sat in this field. It was the brothers of one of Johnny's friends and they were sat there quite happily all smoking cannabis and everything. And that wasn't like a really odd situation.
>
> (43341, female, abstainer)

> If they're just smoking cannabis I don't have any problems with somebody doing that, I've been in, sort of a room and people have been, and that doesn't bother me as long as it's not, as I say, right in my face. I mean any harder drugs I do object and I would leave the company.
>
> (33661, female, abstainer)

This said, some steadfast abstainers still classify all illicit drugs together and negatively, and decline to make distinctions.

> ... don't (accept differences) ... I wouldn't say that I'm more sort of against one than the other because I just wouldn't tolerate any of it.
>
> (43341, female)

> All drugs are drugs to me.
>
> (83X52, female)

Finally, whilst this panel study cannot easily measure macro social accommodation, one key feature of this dimension is the way the licit (alcohol and tobacco) and illicit (illegal drugs, solvents, nitrites) are 'blurred' by consumption patterns. This combining of substances was evident at 18 years but is now remarkably prevalent. No less than three quarters of the sample who disclosed drug taking (n = 327) drank alcohol (75.5 per cent) and just under two thirds (62.3 per cent) smoked tobacco the last time they took illicit drugs. Men (82.8 per cent) were more likely than female peers (69.1 per cent) to have been drinking but conversely women (66.3 per cent) were more likely than men (57.6 per cent) to have smoked tobacco. A key reason for this blurring is found in weekend time out adventures whereby drug use is prevalent in licensed bars and clubs and at, ostensibly, drinking parties.

Conclusions

The normalisation thesis in respect of sensible recreational drug use can only be comprehensively assessed using long term epidemiological and social trends data. The new evidence from this longitudinal study supports the notion that 'sensible' recreational drug use is continuing to be gradually further accommodated into the lifestyles of ordinary young Britons. In line with the national picture the availability and accessibility of illicit drugs continues to increase in the new decade, with a wider range of substances, particularly cocaine, becoming easily available. For the half of this sample who are drug involved, access to their drugs of choice is straightforward. Moreover, because demand is so high amongst educated and employed, otherwise conforming, young adults, an informal drugs distribution system at the point of consumption has developed (Parker *et al.* 2001) whereby friends and friends of friends 'sort' each other, thereby putting physical and symbolic distance between the user and 'real' dealers. That so many otherwise law-abiding citizens have collectively socially reconstructed an illegal act, the supplying of controlled drugs, which carries severe penalties, is a good example of the interplay of the dimensions of normalisation; availability and access of drugs continues to grow but is only made possible by socio-cultural accommodation of 'sorting' by youth populations.

Whilst adolescent drug trying has found its level and at the highest rate in Europe, drug taking amongst young adults continues to increase on the main established survey measures. The same has occurred with this cohort with significant late onset over the 18–21 life stage. Lifetime prevalence for this cohort is now up to 76 per cent. In terms of current on-going drug involvement, half of this sample, based on past year disclosures, remains drug active. Only with past month measures can we see any beginning signs of moderation. Traditionally we have invariably recorded the impact of maturation and settling down processes and pressures in reducing drugs consumption amongst their predecessors for this age group. However, thus far, their drug involvement is only plateauing and at a high rate. It is only with their increasing tendency to become cannabis only users despite previous, more florid drugs repertoires, that these users are showing signs of moderation. There were 81 'past year' cannabis only users at recapture, of whom 80 had previously taken other drugs as well.

Overall all this strongly suggests that in post modern times, with longer, more uncertain and risky journeys to full adult citizenship, 'settling down' will be delayed or deferred (Williams and Parker 2001). The continuing use of psycho-active substances for recreational 'time out' purposes and beyond traditional markers, thus seems very likely and will certainly be the case for this cohort. Their consumption decisions are increasingly framed by new responsibilities and weekday work demands, well illustrated by the increasing focus on substances which do not impact negatively on getting up for work. LSD and amphetamines are being left behind whereas cocaine powder, with its role in energising for socialising but with, for most, a short life in terms of after-effects, is becoming increasingly popular.

All this said, however, rates of regular stimulant use are low and the stimulants-dance drugs are consumed sparingly. This suggests that such 'serious' recreational drug use will remain a small minority activity for this cohort, as it is nationally. The limits of 'sensible' are thus being defined both by drug users and, as importantly, abstainers who are overall far less comfortable with friends who take Class A drugs. We argued in the mid 1990s that it would be with cannabis that normalisation would proceed and we were equivocal about the dance/stimulant drugs (Parker *et al.* 1998). This remains our position. Indeed, depending on the scale of uptake and accommodation of cocaine use over the next few years, we are increasingly of the view that, whilst cannabis has already met the normalisation criteria of availability, trying and use rates and cultural accommodation, there is little prospect of other drugs being viewed similarly. Clearly the partying–clubbing scene is the main setting for extensive recreational poly-drug use and whilst the clubbers offer much support for the normalisation thesis (Measham *et al.* 2000), their excesses are not as acceptable outside this semi-private setting. Moreover, because the dance drug users report so many negative effects from their long weekends (Measham *et al.* 2000; Winstock 2000), even though they suffer these willingly, these costs represent the very reasons why more cautious peers remain uncomfortable with such consumption. Stimulant drug use has clearly, on each dimension, moved towards normalisation but compared with cannabis the case is not proven and we must simply wait and see. What the Class A stimulant drug users have done, however, is pose a very knotty political dilemma. As primarily educated, employed young citizens with otherwise conforming profiles, they challenge the war on drugs discourse which prefers to link drug use with crime and personal tragedy and utilises this discourse as a reason for not calling a truce.

Unsurprisingly the children of the 90s constantly stir the drugs debate with their 'defiance'. As something of a vanguard generation, they appear to have 'educated' the rest of society about cannabis and, by expounding a clear hierarchy of dangerousness in respect of illegal drugs, have actually encouraged official and respected sources to follow their lead. The softening of attitudes to cannabis reported in public opinion surveys are now showing up in middle aged populations. At 22 our interviewees reported their parents as far more 'realistic' and tolerant of cannabis use than they were a few years ago.

This loosening of public attitudes, plus ever stronger demands for some review of the drugs laws in respect of cannabis possession and the informal supplying ('sorting') of recreational drugs (Independent Inquiry 2000), poses a challenge for drugs policy and strategy in the UK. Whilst cannibis is currently being declassified so that personal possession is no longer an arrestable offence, the scale of normalisation of sensible drug use suggests further demands will not go away.

Whilst the UK drugs strategy (Cabinet Office 1999) has much integrity it neither fully sanctions nor overtly encourages secondary prevention approaches. Yet, once again, the scale of drug involvement amongst UK adolescents and young adults begs for such a public health/harm reduction component to be bolted on. The rise in cocaine use was predicted several years ago, yet there is very little official and impartial information being transmitted to warn new users that, for a minority, cocaine will in due course generate health and dependency problems. Instead, we will see cocaine users learning from experience and mishap transmitted through informal drugs stories until collective drugs wisdom has been updated.

The normalisation debate will no doubt continue, not least because the term itself has been acquisitioned by official and academic drugs discourses. The further evidence from this longitudinal study is that it is only with the recreational use of cannabis that the normalisation criteria have been adequately satisfied. Whether the 'sensible' use of stimulant drugs like ecstasy or cocaine will come to be so fully accommodated remains to be seen.

Acknowledgement

The recapture of the North West Longitudinal cohort was funded by the Economic and Social Research Council, Grant 8000237912. We are extremely grateful to the Council for continuing to support this study.

References and suggested reading

Akram, G. (1997) *Patterns of Use and Safety Awareness Amongst Users of Dance Drugs in Nottingham*. Master of Public Health, Nottingham: University of Nottingham.

Aldridge, J., Parker, H. and Measham, F. (1999) *Drug Trying and Drug Use Across Adolescence*. DPAS Paper 1, London: Home Office.

Ashton, C. and Kamali, F. (1995) 'Personality, Lifestyles, Alcohol and Drug Consumption in a Sample of British Medical Students', *Medical Education*, 29: 187–192.

Balding, J. (1999) *Young People in 1998*. Exeter: Exeter University.

Barnard, M., Forsyth, A. and McKeganey, N. (1996) 'Levels of Drug Use Among a Sample of Scottish School Children', *Drugs: Education, Prevention and Policy*, 3 (1): 81–89.

Birch, D., White, M. and Kamali, F. (1999) *Factors Influencing Alcohol and Illicit Drug Use Amongst Medical Students*. Newcastle upon Tyne: University of Newcastle.

Bogdan, R., Biklen, D., Shapiro, A. and Spelkerman, D. (1962) 'The Disabled: Media's Monster', *Social Policy*, 12: 32–35.

Boys, A.J., Fountain, J., Griffiths, P., Marsden, J., Stillwell, G. and Strang, J. (2000) *Making Decisions: A Qualitative Study of Young People, Drugs and Alcohol*. London: Health Education Authority.

Cabinet Office (1999) *First Annual Report and National Plan*. London: United Kingdom Anti-Drugs Co-ordination Unit.

Corkery, J. (2000) 'Snowed Under – Is it the Real Thing?' *Druglink*, 15 (3): 12–16.

Egginton, R., Aldridge, J. and Parker, H. (2001) 'Unconventional? Adolescent Drug Triers and Users in England', Chapter 3 in H. Parker, J. Aldridge and R. Egginton *UK Drugs Unlimited: New Research and Policy Lessons on Illicit Drug Use*. Basingstoke: Palgrave.

Emerson, E. (1992) 'What is Normalisation?', in H. Brown and H. Smith (eds) *Normalisation: A Reader for the Nineties*. London: Routledge.

ESPAD (1997) *Alcohol and Other Drug Use Among Students in 26 European Countries*. Stockholm: Swedish Council on Alcohol and Other Drugs.

ESPAD (2001) *Alcohol and Other Drug Use Among Students in 30 European Countries*. Stockholm: Swedish Council on Alcohol and Other Drugs.

Flood-Page, C., Campbell, S., Harrington, V. and Miller, M. (2000) *Youth Crime: Findings from the 1998/99 Youth Lifestyles Survey*. London: Home Office Research Study 209.

Forsyth, A. (1998) A Quantitative Study of Dance Drug Use. PhD Glasgow University.

Goddard, E. and Higgins, V. (1999) *Smoking, Drinking and Drug Use Among Young Teenagers in 1998*. London: Office of National Statistics.

Gore, S. (1999) 'Effective Monitoring of Young People's Use of Illegal Drugs', *British Journal of Criminology*, 39 (4): 575–603.

Griffiths, P., Vingoe, L., Jansen, K., Sherval, J., Lewis, R. and Hartnoll, R. (1997) *New Trends in Synthetic Drugs in the European Union*. Lisbon: EMCDDA.

Grossman, M. and Chaloupka, F. (1998) 'The Demand for Cocaine by Young Adults: A Rational Addiction Approach', *Journal of Health Economics*, 17: 427–474.

Hammersley, R., Ditton, J., Smith, I. and Short, E. (1999) 'Patterns of Ecstasy Use by Drug Users', *British Journal of Criminology*, 39 (4): 625–647.

Hart, L. and Hunt, N. (1997) *Choosers not Losers?* Invecta Community Care, NHS.

HEA (1999) *Drugs Realities: A Summary of the 1996 National Drugs Campaign Survey*. London: Health Education Authority.

Hirst, J. and McCameley-Finney, A. (1994) *The Place and Meaning of Drugs in the Lives of Young People*. Sheffield: Sheffield Hallam University.

Home Affairs Committee (2002) *The Government's Drugs Policy: Is It Working?* London: House of Commons.

Independent Inquiry (2000) *Drugs and the Law*. Report of the Independent Inquiry into the Misuse of Drugs Act (1971). London: Police Foundation.

McElrath, K. and McEvoy, K. (1999) *Ecstasy Use in Northern Ireland*. Belfast: Queens University.

Makhoul, M., Yates, F. and Wolfson, S. (1998) 'A Survey of Substance Use at a UK University: Prevalence of Use and Views of Students', *Journal of Substance Misuse*, 3: 119–124.

Measham, F., Aldridge, J. and Parker, H. (2000) *Dancing on Drugs: Risk Health and Hedonism in the British Club Scene*. London: Free Association Books.

Measham, F., Newcombe, R. and Parker, H. (1994) 'The Normalisation of Recreational Drug Use Amongst Young People in North West England', *British Journal of Sociology*, 45 (2): 287–312.

Measham, F., Parker, H. and Aldridge, J. (1998) 'The Teenage Transition: From Adolescent Recreational Drug Use to The Young Adult Dance Culture in Britain in the mid-1990s', in R. Power (ed.) *Journal of Drug Issues*, Special Edition, Contemporary Issues Concerning Illicit Drug Use in the British Isles, 28 (1): 9–32.

Meikle, A., McCallum, C., Marshall, A. and Coster, G. (1996) *Drugs Survey on a Selection of Secondary School Pupils in the Glasgow Area Aged 13–16*. Glasgow: Glasgow Drugs Prevention Team.

Miller, P. and Plant, M. (1996) 'Drinking, Smoking and Illicit Drug Use Among 15 and 16 Year Olds in the United Kingdom', *British Medical Journal*, 313: 394–397.

NHSDA (1999) *The 1998 National Household Survey on Drug Abuse*. Department of Health and Human Services.

Nirje, B. (1980) 'The Normalisation Principle', in R. Flynn and K. Nitsch (eds) *Normalisation, Social Integration and Community Services*. Baltimore: University Park Press.

Office of National Statistics (2000) *Drug Use, Smoking and Drinking Among Young Teenagers in 1999*. London: Office of National Statistics.

Parker, H., Aldridge, J. and Egginton, R. (2001) *UK Drugs Unlimited: New Research and Policy Lessons on Illicit Drug Use*. Basingstoke: Palgrave.

Parker, H., Aldridge, J. and Measham, F. (1998) *Illegal Leisure: The Normalisation of Adolescent Recreational Drug Use*. London: Routledge.

Perri 6., Jupp, B., Perry, H. and Laskey, K. (1997) *The Substance of Youth*. York: Joseph Rowntree Foundation.

Pirie, M. and Worcester, R. (1999) *The Next Leaders?* London: Adam Smith Institute.

Plant, M., Peck, D. and Samuel, E. (1985) *Alcohol, Drugs and School Leavers*. London: Tavistock.

Plant, M. and Miller, P. (2000) 'Drug Use Has Declined Among Teenagers in the United Kingdom', *British Medical Journal*, 320: 1536 (3 June).

Ramsay, M. and Partridge, S. (1999) *Drug Misuse Declared in 1998: Results from the British Crime Survey*. Home Office Research Study 197, London: Home Office.

Release (1997) *Release Drugs and Dance Survey*. London: Release.

Shiner, M. and Newburn, T. (1997) 'Definitely, Maybe Not? The Normalisation of Recreational Drug Use Amongst Young People', *Sociology*, 31: 511–529.

Sutherland, I. and Wilner, P. (1998) 'Patterns of Alcohol, Cigarette and Illicit Drug Use in English Adolescents', *Addiction*, 93 (8): 1199–1208.

Van Vliet, H. (1990) 'Separation of Drug Markets and the Normalisation of Drug Problems in the Netherlands: An Example for Other Nations', *Journal of Drug Issues*, 20 (3): 463–471.

Webb, E., Ashton, C., Kelly, D. and Kamali, F. (1996) 'Alcohol and Drug Use in UK University Students', *Lancet*, 348: 922–925.

Wibberley, C. and Price, J. (2000) 'Young People's Ideas on Drugs and Drug Use Implications for the Normalisation Debate', *Drugs: Education, Prevention and Policy*, 147–162.

Williams, L. and Parker, H. (2001) 'Alcohol, Cannabis, Ecstasy and Cocaine: Drugs of Reasoned Choice amongst Young Adult Recreational Drug Users in England', *International Journal of Drug Policy*, 12 (5/6): 397–413.

Winstock, A. (2000) 'Risky Behaviour and Harm Reduction Amongst 1151 Clubbers', Paper for 11th International Conference on the Reduction of Drug Related Harm. Jersey.

Wolfensberger, W. (1972) *The Principle of Normalisation in Human Services*. Toronto: National Institute on Mental Retardation.

Wolfensberger, W. (1980) 'The Definition of Normalisation. Updates, Problems Disagreements and Misunderstandings', in R. Flynn and K. Nitsch (eds) *Normalisation, Social Integration and Community Services*. Baltimore University Park Press.

Wolfensberger, W. (1984) 'A Reconceptualistion of Normalisation as Social Role Valorization', *Mental Retardation*, 34: 22–25.

Young, L. and Jones, R. (1997) *Young People and Drugs*. Liverpool: SHADO.

Part 3

Representing Drugs in and as Popular Culture

Introduction

Paul Manning

The chapters in Part 2 explore empirical evidence of the extent of illicit and licit drug use amongst young people in recent years within the UK. It is clear that recreational 'drug use', particularly as part of club and pub night time leisure, has increased, although there is some evidence to suggest that alcohol is now becoming the routine 'drug of choice' for many young people. As we have seen, while the self-report survey data confirms that recreational drug experiences are now more common than a decade ago, the question as to whether this represents a 'normalisation' of recreational drug use depends upon the interpretation of the data and, crucially, how the concept of 'normalisation' is understood. As all participants in the debate agree, those enthusiastic, recreational poly-drug users that characterise dance culture are still only a minority of young people, and even regular cannabis use is probably restricted to around 25–30 per cent of those under 30 years. If only one third of the young population are regular users of even the 'softest' soft drug, this must mean that around two thirds of the young are not regular users. How, then, can we speak of 'normalisation'?

As the chapters in Part 2 make clear, patterns in popular culture are crucial to the debate. For the supporters of the 'normalisation thesis', the argument is not simply about the absolute numbers reporting drug experiences at any particular moment. Rather, normalisation is understood as a dynamic concept with several dimensions, one of the most important being the possibility of cultural accommodation. In other words, is there evidence within particular cultural arenas or through specific media forms, of a new accommodation to the 'reality' of widespread and routine recreational drug use?

The idea that popular culture should be understood as a contested terrain is one of the central ideas underpinning cultural studies as a discipline, opening up possibilities for the application of neo-Gramscian hegemony theory, Foucauldian analysis, notions of tactical resistance through everyday life as in the work of De Certeau, and several other theoretical frameworks. In the past, a great deal of moral and economic effort was invested in the demonisation of drug use through mainstream media (Stevenson 1999a; Reeves and Campbell 1994; Cohen and Young 1973), though popular culture always opened up spaces within which dominant moral and political definitions were contested. Thus, for example, while mainstream Hollywood frequently understood illicit drug use as a threat, particularly to the stability of the family (Grist in Chapter 6), independent and underground cinema offered a variety of different perspectives, sometimes subverting and parodying these dominant frames on drug use, sometimes simply parading the more grotesque aspects of 'hard drug' use (Stevenson 1999b).

The chapters in this part all examine aspects of the representation of drug consumption in mainstream media, from news, television situation comedy, Hollywood cinema, popular music, and teenage literature. They, therefore, provide a means of gauging the extent to which the process of cultural accommodation, central to the 'normalisation thesis' is actually occurring. The evidence they contain illustrates the tensions, ambivalences and patterns of resistance that one might anticipate; a cultural accommodation to recreational drug use was unlikely ever to be smooth or coherent. Each media form discussed here provides a distinct cultural terrain, with very specific moral, political and economic forces at play. The symbolic frameworks for 'understanding' drug consumption generated across these different media territories are, therefore, distinct in terms of the imagery, symbolism and construction of particular substances and in the representation of the identities of social groups consuming these drugs. In Chapter 6, Leighton Grist contrasts earlier Hollywood approaches to drug use with recent mainstream movies, such as *Traffic*, *Blow*, and *Narc*. In these recent films, drugs are now acknowledged as plot concerns and yet, as the chapter demonstrates, the symbolic constructions of drug consumption continues to draw upon some of the powerful images of drug demonisation. In constructing routine drug use in opposition to, and as a threat to the family, Hollywood seems here to be acknowledging normalisation but only as a 'cautionary tale'. On the face of things, the most promising evidence for the 'normalisation thesis' in this part is provided in Chapter 9. While reference to the use of drugs has crept in to an increasing number of television dramas, soaps, and belatedly, some television comedy in recent years, the BBC Three series *Ideal* would seem to represent a first in offering to the audience not a drug user but a drug dealer as the main sympathetic character. This is, on the face of things, a powerful example of cultural accommodation; an acknowledgment of the routine realities for many young people who know someone to 'sort them out' for the weekend. And yet, as Paul Carter suggests, there is also a moral equivocation in *Ideal*. Here is a cuddly drug dealer who only distributes cannabis, the 'softest' of drugs; even BBC Three which is targeted at the young, appears to have baulked at the idea of a cuddly ecstasy dealer. Crack rocks may have made an appearance in the *Archers* on BBC Radio Four, but those who deal them still cannot be constructed sympathetically.

Popular music probably offered the widest cultural space within which drug experiences and drug pleasures could be represented. As Andrew Blake suggests in Chapter 5, the energies and opportunities for experimentation in musical form found a parallel in the willingness of popular musicians to experiment with drugs. Perhaps, more than other forms of popular culture, pop music at certain times has appeared to offer audiences the possibility, real or imagined, of sharing experiences and knowledge, with the cultural producers. The pleasures and experiences of drug use were, at certain moments, secrets shared between performers and fans. And yet, as Andrew Blake concludes, pop music has played a central part in the construction and wider circulation of the symbolic frameworks available for 'making sense' of drugs and drug consumption. These frequently challenged frameworks that stressed only the dangers or risks and suppressed the pleasures. Amongst communities of musicians, from jazz to trance, 'normalisation' set in a long time ago, and inevitably many of the symbolic representations of drug use to be found in music reflect this.

In contrast, mainstream news media have, until recently, offered much less space within which to contest dominant definitions of drug use. As Simon Cross demonstrates in Chapter 7, all the political and moral ambivalences that characterise government policy in the regulation of drug consumption are to be found in news coverage of the debate over the de-classification or re-classification of drugs, particularly cannabis. This is hardly surprising given the reluctance of many news organisations to move beyond the parameters of political debate that underpin mainstream party politics at Westminster. And yet, newspapers find themselves in a quandary because, whilst their instincts are often to clutch the status quo prescription, as circulation struggles intensify, the imperative may be to 'move with the times' in order to keep up with readers. The 'normalisation' of recreational, soft drug use is at the heart of this quandary and may explain why even some historically conservative papers have begun to contemplate the 'unthinkable' of de-criminalisation. However, Chapter 8 explores the symbolic frameworks that are employed by newspapers to organise news about ecstasy and volatile substance abuse (VSA). What emerges here is that very different symbolic frameworks may be deployed in the reporting of different substances. An acknowledgement of 'normalisation' is very much contingent upon what substances are being discussed and what kinds of people are assumed to be involved.

Chapter 10 considers the significance of the emergence of writing about teenage drug use in fiction aimed at the young. There are some powerful sources of symbolism and framing that might encourage the construction of drug use primarily in terms of danger and threat. The legacy of Victorian discourses at play in the construction of 'childhood' as a quite separate status, to be segregated from the adult world and vigilantly policed, might be expected to exert a powerful influence here. But, as Melrose and Harbour discuss in Chapter 10, there are actually many more possibilities offered in teenage fiction. Despite the anxieties about children and teenagers, frequently voiced by politicians and commentators, only a 'light' regulatory regime operates in the field of children's and teenage fiction compared with, for example, children's broadcasting. The 'normalisation thesis' suggests that while only a minority of teenagers may regularly use recreational drugs, a rather larger majority operate in social networks where such drug use is commonplace. Writers of children's and teenage fiction explicitly construct symbolic frameworks for making sense of young people's experience but attempts to represent 'the reality' of normalisation amongst teenagers will inevitably provoke controversy and criticism. Fiction for teenagers, just as much as popular television, represents a media terrain in which symbolic frameworks of drug use are constructed and contested.

References and suggested reading

Cohen, S. and Young, J. (1973) *The Manufacture of News*. London: Constable.

Reeves, J. and Campbell, R. (1994) *Cracked Coverage: Television News, the Anti-Cocaine Crusade and the Regan Legacy*. London: Duke University.

Stevenson, J. (1999a) 'Highway to Hell', in J. Stevenson (ed.) *Addicted: The Myth and Menace of Drugs in Film*. New York: Creation Books.

Stevenson, J. (1999b) 'Underground Cinema', in J. Stevenson (ed.) *Addicted: The Myth and Menace of Drugs in Film*. New York: Creation Books.

5. Drugs and popular music in the modern age

Andrew Blake

Intro

If the 'normalisation' referred to in the opening section of this book has happened, it has come about, in part, because of popular music. If it hasn't … well, in popular music cultures it *has,* and that's that. From the role of the 'reefer' in early twentieth century jazz and blues, to the centrality of amphetamines and hallucinogens for dance music at the close of the century and beyond, there has been an intimate relationship between drug consumption and music. The relationship has been expressed through journalism, biography and fiction, the lyrics of songs, the cultural practices of popular musicians and audiences, and through musical forms and performance styles.

No confessional or hagiographic biography of a rock star, appreciation of a popular music genre, or attempt to put music into its broad cultural and historical context, is complete without extensive reference to the use of drugs by the major participants and/or the author. Take for example John Harris's *The Last Party: Britpop, Blair and the Demise of English Rock* (Harris 2003). This is, as the title implies, an analysis of a particular moment in both pop and politics in mid-1990s Britain. The book is at the same time a searing critique of the New Labour ideologists who tried to use popular music's eternal hedonism for their own (deeply puritanical) purposes, and, simultaneously, a resume of the use of drugs by musicians in mid-1990s Britain, and of the often very deleterious effects this had on their music.

'Britpop' had been born in the early 1990s as a music-business ploy to counter the re-Americanisation of popular music sales in Britain (led by Nirvana's 'grunge', an aggressively shabby guitar-band rock). A clever mixture of youngish performers with a rock 'attitude', playing guitar-band pop rock with witty lyrics, Britpop bands such as Blur, Pulp, and Oasis formed a sonic nostalgia replete with references to the British music of the 1960s and 1970s (Harris 2003; Cavanagh 2001). Thanks to the resulting multi-generational appeal of the music, Britpop dominated UK tabloid celebrity culture in the mid-1990s, and was picked up and celebrated as a sign of an emerging, and successful, 'cool Britannia' by the 'New Labour' party which came to political power at the 1997 general election. A couple of months into the new administration, however, the relationship had already soured, at least in part because many of the musicians had already drowned their mid-90s successes in a sea of, in Pulp singer Jarvis Cocker's words, 'self-congratulatory cocaine' (*Live Forever* 2003), and their music had lost its zest. Pulp's album *This is Hardcore* (1998) represented this feeling of achieved loss most thoughtfully, while as Noel Gallagher said about the third Oasis album, *Be Here Now* (1997) 'It's the sound of a bunch of guys on coke in the studio not giving a fuck' (*Live Forever* 2003).

'twas ever thus ...

First verse: jazz and blues

In 1922 Aleister Crowley published his first novel, *The Diary of a Drug Fiend*. The central characters, Sir Peter Pendragon and his wife Lou, meet and fall for each other at a night club where some of the aristocratic patrons are passing cocaine around to the accompaniment of a jazz band. 'A wave of almost insane excitement swept through the club ... The band struck up a madder jazz. The dancers raved with more tumultuous and breathless fury' (Crowley 2000: 22). A few minutes later 'I drew the little heap of powder through my nostrils with one long breath' (Crowley 2000: 25) as Sir Peter takes cocaine at the start of a drug-fuelled romp round Europe. Even in the early 1920s, jazz, drugs and the bohemian lifestyle are irretrievably mixed in the popular imagination.

Why? The jazz musician is, in mythology at least, the ultimate Other to a rectilinear white masculinity whose musicianship is based on the puritanical values of hard work, the disciplined learning of instrumental or vocal technique, the obscurities of music notation, and obedience to the will of the composer and/or conductor. The travelling bluesman or jazz band represented an invasive and improvisatory oral culture, supported by a musicianship based on 'natural' ability rather than learned skill, which was apparently hastening the decline of the Western tradition of classical concert music. At the turn of the nineteenth–twentieth centuries, this tradition was indeed implosively decadent. All too often new concert music was the site of public protests – there were riots at performances of music by Schoenberg and Stravinsky – from an audience which did not like what it heard. In this climate a vigorous and danceable new music from the New World was all the more welcome to a general public (and to many musicians) mystified and angered by contemporary composers' complexities (Lambert 1934).

A defining symbol of the early influence of African-American music on European culture is the opera *Jonny Spielt Auf* (Jonny Strikes Up the Band), by Austrian composer Ernst Krenek, which was premiered in Leipzig on 10 February 1927. The production was strikingly modern, featuring innovative Expressionist and Bauhaus influenced stage sets, and incorporating modern technologies such as telephones, radios, and cars into the scenario. Equally symbolic of its daring modernity was the music: Krenek's opera uses jazz-infused orchestration, harmonies, and rhythmic syncopation. Several months before the premiere of *Jonny Spielt Auf* Krenek had attended an American revue featuring the music, songs, and arrangements of a then up-and-coming young

African-American composer named Duke Ellington, in Frankfurt (though it's also likely that he was following the example of an earlier European response to the arrival of jazz, Stravinsky's 1916 piece *The Soldier's Tale*, which uses a New Orleans-style ensemble to accompany its narrator). The opera has an inter-racial and intercultural storyline: its African-American jazz-musician hero, Jonny, becomes involved with opera singer Anita; as Jonny hides a classical violinist's instrument (an Amati, no less) in a banjo case, the storyline also symbolically represents the new jazz replacing the old concert music.

Operating throughout the history of twentieth-century music from this point onwards are narratives of the decline of the Western classical tradition, and of its replacement by music of black American origin, processes which are simultaneously feared and welcomed within the West. Lurking behind these feelings – though less often welcomed – are similarly recurrent fears of the seduction of white women by black men, and fears that the syncopated dance musics of ragtime, jazz, r'n'b, rock'n'roll and so on, and the illegal drugs associated with the music, are the primary instruments of that seduction. The music, the drugs, and the alleged sexual potency of the black male, formed a mythopoeisis of intoxication, illegality and, especially, 'cool', which informed the attitudes of musicians and audiences, black and white alike (Pountain and Robbins 2000).

The alterity of blackness is part of the legacy of slavery and racism; but the Otherness of jazz is also due to the music's association with illegal drugs, and therefore with organised crime. American organised crime supplied wants which adherents of the puritanical heritage which had founded the USA found difficult to conceive of as legitimate desires, whether they are for sex, gambling or intoxication. Prohibition – the prohibition of the sale of alcohol – was an experiment tried in the USA in the 1920s, the same decade which saw USA-led stringent international controls on the heretofore legal trade in opiates, cocaine and cannabis. While the re-legalisation of alcohol in the USA took place in 1933, in the interim the demand for intoxicants of all sorts had empowered organised crime. The social experiment of Prohibition, in other words, led to the trade in other intoxicating drugs such as cannabis and heroin becoming not just illegal but crime-controlled. Jazz, as music to dance or listen to, was from the start an accompaniment of organised crime and its narratives, jazz musicians providing the entertainment at bordellos in New Orleans, speakeasies in Chicago, or the Cotton Club in Harlem where Duke Ellington's 'jungle music' sold blackness as seductively dangerous exotica to a whites-only audience.

For the musicians, however, there was more at stake than the pleasures of listening: musicians were among organised crime's best customers, because narcotics were often seen as necessary chemical performance aids. Arguably the founding moment in this musical version of the Faust legend, associating black Americans with the myth of the performer prepared to die for his art, is the story of bluesman Robert Johnson meeting the Devil at a quiet Mississippi crossroads one night in the mid-1930s; the two apparently struck a deal. This was, the myth goes, followed by a massive upswing in the level of Johnson's live performances, and opportunities for him to record a legacy of some 18 songs which are widely regarded as among the most important documents of the music. However these songs, such as 'Crossroads Blues', 'Me and the Devil Blues' and 'Hell-hound on my Trail', tended to register Johnson's fear that he might have the wrong end of the bargain. Sure enough within a couple of years of the alleged meeting the Devil had claimed his own: Johnson died at the age of 27. It was often suggested that Robert Johnson had been poisoned through drinking whisky handed to him by a rival, jealous not of his new musicality but of his sexual successes.

As a repeated trope, however, the Faustian musical myth typically revolves around the use of illegal narcotics. Alto saxophone virtuoso Charlie Parker set new standards in performance with a number of recordings and live performances from the late 1930s onwards which helped to invent a new style in jazz, 'be-bop'. Parker could quite simply play faster and louder than anyone else in the music. He was a heavy drinker, and also, very publicly, a heroin addict, who occasionally withdrew from public performance in order to attempt to de-tox (Russell 1972; *Bird* 1998: Shipton 1999). He died, aged 35, in 1955. Many jazz musicians then proceeded to take heroin – usually becoming addicts – in the belief that it would allow them to reproduce Parker's level of performance: this applies, for example, to most of the next generation of leading American musicians, such as trumpeter Miles Davis, who played with Parker in the early 1950s, and in turn saxophonist John Coltrane, who was a member of Davis's bands from the later 1950s (Szwed 2002; Thomas 1975).

It applies equally to the growing number of British followers of Parker and Coltrane and the musical genres they invented and/or dominated. The use of heroin in the UK was pioneered partly by musicians who genuinely believed that its use would improve their performance whatever its other effects on their lives. Heroin would, they believed, make white Brits play like black Americans: the use of illegal drugs for performance enhancement was a dangerous form of masquerade. Heroin use affected the careers of players such as saxophonists Tubby Hayes (who died, in his 30s, in 1973) and Dick Heckstall-Smith, whose autobiography is illuminating (Heckstall-Smith 1988). For pianist Stan Tracey, 'there was sort of a junkie brotherhood' among London jazz musicians in the early 1960s (*Jazz Britannia* 2006), though its actions did not always display brotherly love; saxophonist Bobby Wellins, who became a regular drug user during a visit to the USA, used to wear a waistcoat which was 'full of phials of cocaine and bottles of heroin tablets' – and remembers Tubby Hayes helping himself to the contents when he was incapacitated (*Jazz Britannia* 2006).

First chorus: jazz effects

Despite, or perhaps because of, the Faustian way in which jazz musicians seemed to use their narcotics, there remained an association of drugs, blackness and 'cool', and music (and people) to one side of the social norm.

In the grouping known as 'beats' we find the expression of an alienated white masculinity which took black coolness and the cultural superiority of jazz and blues-related music for granted. As a *textual* object, the key year for this new whiteness is 1957, the year of Jack Kerouac's autobiographical novel *On the Road* and Norman Mailer's essay 'The White Negro: Superficial Reflections on the Hipster'. Echoed in the UK in Colin MacInnes' novels *City of Spades* (1957) and *Absolute Beginners* (1959), these texts propose a masculinity which is relentlessly, and politically, narcissistic and hedonistic. Seeking the pleasures of sex, drugs and music, and uninterested in settled familial-domestic heterosexuality, the white 'beat' or 'hipster' constructed an identity in relation to his reading of blackness: this meant engaging with music and drugs. Mailer's piece opens with a quotation from journalist Caroline Bird which is arguably a more important document of the time than his essay itself:

> The hipster is an *enfant terrible* turned inside out. In character with his time, he is trying to get back at the conformists by lying low ... You can't interview a hipster because his main goal is to keep out of a society which, he thinks, is trying to make everyone over in its own image. He takes marijuana because it supplies him with experiences that can't be shared with "squares." He may affect a broad-brimmed hat or a zoot suit, but usually he prefers to skulk unmarked. The hipster may be a jazz musician; he is rarely an artist, almost never a writer. He may earn his living as a petty criminal, a hobo, a carnival roustabout or a freelance moving man in Greenwich Village, but some hipsters have found a safe refuge in the upper income brackets as television comics or movie actors. (The late James Dean, for one, was a hipster hero.)
>
> (Mailer 1957/1967: 1)

The landmark *musical* symbol in this catalogue of cool appeared in the same year. Miles Davis's *The Birth of the Cool*, an album which had been recorded 1950, was only released, by the Capitol label, in 1957. This album was – unusually for the time, in a racist America which preferred all-white or all-black jazz bands – made with an ethnically mixed band. The arrangers included white composer and bandleader Gil Evans (subsequently a regular Davis collaborator), while the session's musicians included white baritone saxophonist (and heroin user) Gerry Mulligan, who had followed up the Birth of the Cool recordings by forming, in the early 1950s, a pathbreaking quartet with white trumpeter and vocalist Chet Baker (whose own career was massively affected by heroin addiction). 'Cool jazz' had indeed been born; based on the West Coast rather than the older industrial cities of the USA, it was among the sub-genres of jazz which seemed particularly open to white musical innovation. Reefer in hand, and cool sounds in head, the hipster walked the earth.

This was, however, while emulated by a few in the capital cities of Europe, at this moment a specifically American masculinity. Popular music in the UK, for example, was still trying to find a way of evolving beyond music hall's singalong democracy. Similarly, drugs were just not prominent in mainstream British popular culture after World War II – there is not much evidence of the use of heroin, cocaine or cannabis, or anything else for that matter outside the bohemianism of the very wealthy, and little or no direct connection between drugs and popular music beyond those repeated, sometimes feared, connections with and mimickings of the Other which was cool America by the would-be Charlie Parkers. The one very strong symbolic connection between drugs and cool, non-familial masculinity does not belong directly to the musical world. The very cool Mr James Bond first used an amphetamine in the 1955 novel *Moonraker:*

> 'Benzedrine,' said James Bond. 'It's what I shall need if I'm going to keep my wits about me tonight. It's apt to make one a bit overconfident, but that'll help too.' He stirred the champagne so that the white powder whirled among the bubbles. Then he drank the mixture down with one long swallow. 'It doesn't taste,' said Bond, 'and the champagne is quite excellent'.
>
> (Fleming 1955: 107)

In imbibing thus, Bond was of course following that archetypal non-familial outsider, the pre-cool-cool masculinity of cocaine user (and violinist) Sherlock Holmes. Bond's drug-taking is a long way from, and yet coeval with, the enthusiasm of the early stirrings of teenage youth culture, which arrived in the UK as much via 'trad' and modern jazz – the latter giving us 'mods' and in the end also the 'acid jazz' of the early 1990s – as through rock-n'roll itself.

Second verse: rock and pop

Nonetheless, as we know, rock'n'roll arrived, and spearheaded a new form of commercial music aimed at teenagers: pop. While the tiny British jazz elite was Americanising itself, and all too often destroying itself, through the use of heroin, James Bond's little helper, amphetamines or 'speed', was the drug of choice of those in and around the early-60s pop scene in the USA and UK; and indeed it was the drug of choice of mid-1970s punk and northern soul and of their various living relatives. However, as rock'n'roll turned to pop, and as the first wave of immigrants from the Indian subcontinent and the Caribbean settled in the UK from the mid-1950s onwards, cannabis use increased exponentially, as did calls for its legalisation. While not directly associated in the public imaginary with jazz, pop and rock, cannabis was associated with the musics of the new Anglo West Indians, who brought ganja with them. In the 1950s and 1960s calypso, bluebeat, ska and reggae made their mark in UK popular music; by the 1970s reggae had mutated in various ways, one of which was the spaced-out sonic lexicon of dub, whose inventive use of the mixing desk spatialised the music in ways which seemed to many hearers to reflect the experiential effects of heavy cannabis use.

Something similar happened through the development of 'rock'. During the mid-1960s Californian experiments with LSD or 'acid' produced a new counter-culture which had almost as a by-product a new music, sometimes bluntly referred to as acid rock, developed from pop and rhythm'n'blues. The music was album-based rather than driven by chart singles; live or on record, tracks tended to be longer than chart pop, encouraging singers and instrumentalists into more virtuoso display, and often experimenting with non-Western scales and modes. The Grateful Dead were among the longer-lasting relics of this moment of comparative musical freedom. One of the UK's variants was 'progressive rock', whose subgenres in turn included 'Canterbury Rock', perhaps the least Americanised of British rock musics outside folk-rock. The music of Canterbury Rock bands such as Camel, Caravan, Soft Machine, and Hatfield and the North used compositional techniques which had clearly been learned from school music lessons as much as from listening to records, in what could be interpreted as a denial of the African-American roots of popular music. Unlike the UK popular music of the early 1950s, however, this politely experimental music was by no means drug-free. The use by musicians of synthetic chemicals such as LSD (developed originally from ergot, a fungal growth found on rye), rather the 'natural highs' of material made directly from the opium poppy, the coca leaf or the cannabis plant, can be seen as a direct parallel to progressive rock's engagement with the highly synthetic, lengthy and relatively complex Western tradition of classical music composition.

Long compositions, emphasising virtuosity in performance rather than the creative use of the mixing desk, by the Canterbury bands and also by more commercially successfully by bands such as Pink Floyd, Genesis, Emerson Lake and Palmer (ELP) and Yes, seemed to reflect the lengthy timescale of the 'acid trip' rather than the shorter hit of cocaine or speed, or dub reggae's metonymous relationship with ganja mediated through the recording studio. When popular music attempts to represent or reproduce the effects of particular drugs (dub with cannabis, certain psychedelic songs with acid), this must be a clear sign that drugs are becoming a central part of a popular culture because these attempts at musical replication of drug experience must rest on the assumption that the audience will recognise them for what they are – that there is a common experience shared by artist and audience. In other words, in the terms of this book, they signify a certain mode of 'normalisation'.

Much of the music of Pink Floyd up to and including *Atom Heart Mother*, (1970) can be seen as a metonym of the acid-trip experience – and certainly the concert performances represented in the films *Tonite Let's All Make Love in London* (directed by Peter Whitehead 1967, including inventive real-time light shows and Syd Barrett's strange theatricals) and *Pink Floyd Live at Pompeii* (directed by Adrian Maben 1973) seem to be synaesthetic synonyms for tripping, even if the band weren't. If so, there was an apparent reaction, in the gloomy mid-tempo songs from the two most financially successful Pink Floyd albums *The Dark Side of the Moon* (1973) and *Wish You Were Here* (1975), which signal withdrawal from such psychotropic indulgences; *Wish You Were Here* directly acknowledges the dark side of former band member Syd Barrett's experiences with mind-altering drugs such as LSD. Normal or not, the drugs' dark side was acknowledged.

Indeed, a number of variations on the Faustian theme emerged during and after the 1960s. Drug use was, of course, still seen to contribute to the deaths of star performers well before their time, much along the lines tragically pioneered by Charlie Parker: there were the deaths of stars such as Jimi Hendrix, Janis Joplin, Jim Morrison, Brian Jones, and Keith Moon, and perhaps we should include on this list not the death but the decline of Syd

Barrett. One variation was what could be called an inverted *Picture of Dorian Grey* model, in which the public observe through the tabloid celebrity column what lies behind the airbrushed and made-up stage personae: the gradually crumbling faces and mental capacities of those who did not lose all their marbles or die before they got old, such as Pete Townshend himself, Keith Richard, Iggy Pop, Jimmy Page, the recently rehabilitated Brian Wilson – and perhaps most horribly Gary Glitter, middle-aged, unflatteringly bald and a convicted paedophile. For all of them the Devil seems to have postponed the day of reckoning in order to expose these particular bargainers to the ridicule of those who think of rock and its lifestyles as a mere phase, an aspect of teenage rebellion, and are as appalled by the survival of the physically slowly crumbling Rolling Stones as they and/or their parents or grandparents were by the Stones' first moment of fame in the early 1960s. This narrative of revealed decline is among the ways in which popular music contributes to the construction of the symbolic frameworks of substance misuse that are circulated and reproduced through society.

Another variation on this theme came from the repeated attempts to represent a pop music world apparently without sex or drugs. Boy-next-door or boy- or girl-group pop was aimed from the late 1950s at teenagers (as the emerging consumer category with money to spend), and similar products were from the mid-1990s also made for what marketing consultants call 'tweenagers', the 10–13 age group whose enthusiasm and pester-power control over their parents' money created the global success of the Spice Girls in the summer of 1996. Solo singer or boy-girl-group pop was not sold as rebellious or alternative but as mainstream mass-market entertainment, and was therefore seen to be 'clean'. When it appears that performers have broken this rule – as did Brian Harvey of boy-band East 17, who boasted in early 1997 of taking 12 doses of MDMA (ecstasy) and then driving home – the band ceases to exist. However, in the post-career narratives of singers or bands which did not apparently have a drug use problem, whether Frankie Lymon in the 1960s or Take That in the 1990s, we often learn retrospectively that they did. Even in the narratives associated with apparently clean-living pop, then, we usually return to the assumption that a pop/rock lifestyle, creativity and performance, is irretrievably mixed with drug use, and that this often leads to its performers' downfall; which again reinforces the common perception that drug use is always destructive.

The flood of media self-righteousness along these lines which greeted Harvey's confessions replicated prurient mass-media responses to drug use by figures such as the Rolling Stones' Mick Jagger in the 1960s (though it is worth remembering that the leading broadsheet newspaper of the day, the *Times*, actually defended Jagger in a 1 July 1967 editorial headlined 'Who Breaks a Butterfly on a Wheel?'). Such responses should remind us that all this activity remained illegal, and that the 1960s, far from being a decade of liberation on this issue, confirmed the puritanical legal verdict that chemicals taken for pleasure were and should remain taboo. While there were relatively open debates about the use and status of cannabis, despite a positive 1969 report by a committee chaired by Baroness Wootton, its use was not legalised. Media hostility led instead to the Misuse of Drugs Act 1971, whose schedule allotted cannabis to 'class B' status, with lower penalties for possession than those for opiates or LSD. This late-60s official 'counter-counter-culture', by denying the legalisation of drugs, helped to re-embed the notion of rebelliousness through drug use – and perhaps helped to prevent their mass use, while confirming their use by the wealthy musical elite and their attractiveness as part of an 'alternative' lifestyle.

Second chorus: rock, drugs and the commodification of cool

However, for most of popular music's listening public, there was no alternative: boy-girl pop was aimed at a mass public, but so was rock, and by the late 1960s albums were more profitable than singles, and had their own chart. It looked in retrospect, in fact, as if this commodification of 'rock rebellion' had been the inevitable outcome of the creation of the teenage consumer – after all, James Dean may have been a 'hipster hero' in the eyes of Caroline Bird, but as she says he was also rich; at the time of his death he was driving a *new Porsche*, for goodness sake. By the end of the 1960s Anglo-American rock had become part of the establishment. Broadsheet newspapers were reporting rock in the same respectful way that they covered classical music and jazz. Following the example of the Beatles, who as well as chalking up massive album sales earned vast sums in royalties as songwriters, bands like Pink Floyd – for all their gloomily anti-establishment lyrics – became multi-millionaires. It must be pointed out, though, that the establishment of the *genre* did not mean a sharing of power and wealth among all artists: while Pink Floyd and ELP went on global stadium tours and raked in the money, Soft Machine, Hatfield and the North and the other Canterbury Rock bands remained financially marginal – like almost everyone involved in popular music.

Did the commodification of the rock attitude and the increasing cultural respectability of the music mean that drug use also became 'established'? Not really. Partly thanks to the legal victories of the 1960s counter-counter-culture, despite the coded messages of dub or acid rock there was still no mass popular usage even of cannabis. In the 1970s, therefore, drugs of choice also included industrial and domestic chemicals such as solvents, which could be bought legally, and which remain associated with the moment of punk rock. However, punk had a number of parallels. 'Northern Soul' all-night dance events and 'soul weekenders' (48-hour parties held at holiday camps), where people danced to imported American soul, disco and other dance musics, raised the demands for stamina-inducing materials such as speed; and increasingly, just as in the 1920s world portrayed by Aleister Crowley, dancers also wanted cocaine, and were prepared to pay for it.

Third verse: dance and electronica

Cocaine appeared to be the drug of choice for a wide swathe of middle class people in the early 1980s. Employees working at banks in the City of London and in Manhattan often referred to the toilet facilities as 'powder-rooms' – more sales, more powder, and more Porsches seemed to be the order of the day. Meanwhile there was a dance 'revolution'.

Electronic dance music mutated throughout the 1980s. As disco's death left a vacant space for more experimental work with drum machines and samplers, a new, streamlined soundworld emerged firstly from Chicago and Detroit, later from Ibiza and the other Balearic holiday islands, then from the illegal, semi-legal and legal party worlds of the major European cities. By the end of the 1980s the new phenomenon had been christened 'rave', or 'Acid House', in a deliberate reference to the acid rock of the late 1960s. The new music was not pop, rock, soul or jazz as we knew it: like early acid rock, this music was conceived as part of a synaesthetic experience, not as something to listen to in its own right, and the experience as a whole seemed to involve the implied use of drugs, and in particular the newly-popular synthetic drug ecstasy. As with acid rock, then, the music and drugs were deliberately mutually reflexive; in Simon Reynolds' words, dance music quickly became 'a self-conscious science of intensifying MDMA's sensations' (Reynolds 1998: xxvi). The music was made from fragments, without the usual narratives of pop lyrics or jazz chord changes, and it was built above all on pulse. While in the mid-1980s most popular music shared a basic pulse of four-beat patterns at around 60 beats per minute (bpm) – the normal levels of heart beat – by the end of the decade most dance music would pulse at 120 bpm or more, sometimes far more – thus synchronising with the heartbeat rate associated with the use of speed or ecstasy. Furthermore, producers and DJs evolved a range of musical techniques, such as the panning, filtering and sweeping of drum patterns or bass lines, which are expressly designed to stimulate the bodies of the ecstasy user.

The consequences of this new formation are worth itemising. On what could be called the positive side of the phenomenon, adherents of the new music-and-drugs experience went beyond the hedonism of the moment and entered an interesting and relatively well-informed debate on ecstasy and its uses which matches the 1960s debates on cannabis, though this time without governmental input (Saunders *et al.* 1995 and 1997; Redhead 1993). The new culture made its mark partly in a revival of 1960s-style 'counter-cultural' thinking which stressed the importance of 'shamanic' drug use. In spaces such as the club Megatripolis (held weekly at Heaven in Charing Cross, central London), and the Spiral Tribe touring sound system collective, a new politics of ecoprotest was related to an imagined new collective consciousness through the new synaesthesia of drugs and dance music (McKay 1996).

The strength of this experience within UK popular culture can be gauged through its presence in films: among these are *Trainspotting* (directed by Danny Boyle 1996), *Twin Town* (directed by Kevin Allen 1997), *Human Traffic* (directed by Justin Kerrigan 1999), *Sorted* (directed by Alexander Jovy 2000), *South West 9* (directed by Richard Perry 2001), *24-hour Party People* (directed by Michael Winterbottom 2004), and *It's All Gone Pete Tong* (directed by Michael Dowse 2004). While these are all ambivalent texts – each can be read as a morality tale about the dangers of excessive drug use, though each has also been accused of glorifying the experience – they are an important register of the quotidian normality of drug use among the young, and of the continuing association between drug use and popular music: each has an associated soundtrack album.

On what could be called the negative side of Acid House, from the start the informal parties of the UK's rave scene were organised and co-ordinated by the traditional suppliers of illegal mood-altering chemicals: organised criminals. Criminals were among the organisers throughout the illegal party movement in late-1980s Lancashire towns such as Blackburn, and at the celebratory moment of 'Madchester' the early 1990s Manchester scene associated with bands such as the Stone Roses and the Happy Mondays, and which focused on events held at the Hacienda club, which was closed in 1994 on police orders thanks to the pervasive presence not just of drug dealers but of violent, armed, organised criminals (Champion 1990; Luck 2002).

Unsurprisingly, official responses to the new party scene were often hostile. After a number of pieces of early-1990s legislation the Criminal Justice Act 1994 empowered the police to arrest even small groups of people on suspicion that they might be gathering in order to hold an illegal party (though it's worth noting that the 1994 Act has led to remarkably few prosecutions). By this time, however, more ambivalent official responses included the attempted commodification of club culture through a system of licensing and control. The Henley Centre claimed in 1993 that the dance scene in Britain was worth £1.8 billion annually, about the same as book publishing; in 1996 the British Tourist Board's attempts to recruit younger visitors to Britain focused on the provision of dance clubs and rock festivals (Collin and Godfrey 1997: 267– 271). The official licensing of 'superclubs' such as Cream and the Ministry of Sound in the early 1990s have led to the formation of global brands involved in the provision of a range of leisure services and retail products such as the clubs themselves; open-air parties such as Creamfields; branded clothing; compilation CD and DVD albums; and 3G audio and video streams for mobile phones.

Perhaps the most important official response to the Acid House phenomenon, however, occurred in relation to the use of alcohol. In the three years following the large-scale arrival in the UK of ecstasy, alcohol sales in public houses fell by some 20 per cent: young people using ecstasy apparently preferred to drink water. In a repeat of the 1960s counter-counter-cultural moment, ecstasy was classified as a Class A drug, and thanks to the fierce lobbying of the drinks industry alcohol was reinvented to make it more appealing to the young. During the key year 1995 an ecstasy-related death was used to drive the mass-media campaign against the use of the drug, while the government sanctioned the televised advertising of spirits for the first time, and a number of ads representing gin, vodka and rum as young peoples' tipple followed. More subversively, 1995 also saw the introduction of 'alcopops', drinks mixing spirits with sweet flavours such as lemonade or blackcurrant. These products appeared to have been engineered to entice underage drinkers to become regular users of alcohol.

Which, in a way, takes us back to the beginning of this chapter. 1995 was also the key year of Britpop. While Blur and Oasis stormed the charts in a flurry of nostalgia and whimsy, taking the UK public back to the 1960s –

including many too young to have been there the first time – the British public also began to revert to an old drinking habit: using alcohol as a narcotic. The alcoholic strength of alcopops was relatively high by UK standards at 5–6 per cent, and the strength of beer rose to meet it. Faced with difficulties of supply and often the relative impurity of illegal drugs, some began to use the legal drug as they had used illegal drugs: to become 'out of it'. The result was not cannabis-induced relaxation, or ecstasy-inspired feelings of collective emotion, but what alcohol does best: aggression and anaesthesia. The result of the refusal to decriminalise or legalise, coupled with the reinvention of alcohol as a narcotic, gave the average UK town centre a strange new look on a weekend evening: young people went 'binge drinking' – consuming very large quantities of alcohol. The results included massive increases in male-on-male and female-on-female violence, and in allegations of 'date rape' in which the victim was either drugged surreptitiously by an assailant or so drunk after drinking all evening as to be virtually senseless at the time of the assault. While the Ministry of Sound website links to a great deal of non-judgmental information about illegal drugs, in November 2005 the original Ministry of Sound club in South London, which had been refurbished complete with cocktail bars, was awarded a 24-hour drinks licence, so its customers can now binge to the beat without thought of tomorrow.

Repeat chorus: music, drugs – and social change

'Forever seeking new stimuli, they experimented with everything from tape-loops to drugs and chance procedures borrowed from the intellectual avant-garde'(MacDonald 1995: 111). Where better to end this survey than with the Beatles, who like so many British musicians started their careers by trying to copy black American music, but who ended in a very different place. In his influential book *Revolution in the Head* Ian Macdonald argues that the band's music is influenced by whatever chemicals they were taking – there is a veritable pharmacopia of creativity here:

> With *Rubber Soul*, the Beatles recovered the sense of direction that had begun to elude them during the later stages of work for *Beatles for Sale* and which, due to their indulgence in cannabis, almost completely evaporated during *Help!* Gradually realising, from Dylan's example, that they didn't have to separate their professional work from their inner lives, they consciously experimented in much of the *Rubber Soul* material, feeling their way towards a new style – one which, defining the second half of their career together, would be inspired by their encounter with one of the biggest influences on life and culture in the late sixties: LSD.
> (Macdonald 1975: 145)

All this was also, argues Macdonald, both a part of, and in a very important way a register of, a fundamental change which occurred during the sixties. Taking a further step on from the white-as-black alienation of the Beat generation, what happened was a 'revolution in the head' in which not just a few alienated individuals moved outside the routines of the social, but a whole society held together by the decaying vestiges of religious faith and social class was replaced by an atomised and desocialised world without shared values or consensus, an era of 'personal appetite and private insecurity' (MacDonald 1975: 13). LSD itself, and LSD-inspired music, are among the watersheds of this change towards a postmodern consciousness which has replaced the politics of narrative with those of the sound-bite. New ideologies of left and right stirred from the quasi-meritocracy of the 'swinging London' of the 1960s, while popular music, created by minds under the liberating influence of a range of illegal intoxicants, assaulted head-on all and any notions about its place in the world, and the place of those who performed it. Like jazz beforehand, reggae, punk, northern soul, grunge, dance, Britpop, hip-hop, UK garage, grime, and whatever else have been among the variations on this theme: for good or ill, the consumption of drugs and the making of popular music are inseparably intertwined like the twin strands of DNA.

And it matters. During the twentieth century, and so far in this, popular music has been key to the production and circulation of the symbolic frameworks which describe and 'explain' drugs and their use. As well as the quotidian opposition between hedonists and puritans, these include narratives of the romantic artist, and his/her creativity and/or decline; of the association between pleasure and rebellion; and of the continuing symbolic importance of choice and alterity within a society which continues to grapple with the problems of recognising and valuing social and cultural difference.

References and suggested reading

Bird (1988) film directed by Eastwood, C. New York: Warner.

Cavanagh, D. (2001) *My Magpie Eyes are Hungry for the Prize: The Story of Creation Records*. London: Virgin.

Champion, S. (1990) *And God Created Manchester*. Manchester: Wordsmith.

Collin, M. and Godfrey, J. (1997) *Altered State: The Story of Ecstasy Culture and Acid House*. London: Serpent's Tail.

Crowley, A. (2000) *The Diary of a Drug Fiend* (first published 1922*).* North Beach, Maine: Samuel Weiser Inc.

Fleming, I. (1955) *Moonraker*. London: Pan.

Garratt, S (1998) *Adventures in Wonderland: A Decade of Club Culture*. London: Headline.

Harris, J. (2003) *The Last Party: Britpop, Blair and the Demise of English Rock*. London: Perennial.

Heckstall-Smith, D. (1988) *The Safest Place in the World: A Personal History of British Rhythm and Blues*. London: Quartet.

Jazz Britannia (2006) television documentary directed by Connolly, M. London: BBC, broadcast BBC4, 1 January 2006.

Kerouac, J. (1998) *On the Road* (first published 1957). Harmondsworth: Penguin.

Lambert, C. (1934) *Music Ho!: A Study of Music in Decline*. London: Faber.

Live Forever (2003) film directed by Dower, J. London: BBC/British Film Council.

Luck, R. (2002) *The Madchester Scene*. London: Pocket Essentials.

MacDonald, I. (1995) *Revolution in the Head: The Beatles' Records and the Sixties*. London: Pimlico.

McKay, G. (1996) *Senseless Acts of Beauty: Cultures of Resistance Since the 1960s*. London: Verso.

Mailer, N. (1967) *The White Negro: Superficial Reflections on the Hipster* (first published 1957). New York: City Lights Books.

Pountain, D. and Robins, D. (2000) *Cool Rules: Anatomy of an Attitude*. London: Reaktion.

Redhead, S. (ed.) (1993) *Rave Off: Politics and Deviance in Contemporary Youth Culture*. Aldershot: Avebury Press.

Reynolds, S. (1998) *Energy Flash*. London: Picador.

Rietveld, H. (1998) *This is Our House*. Aldershot: Ashgate Press.

Russell, R. (1972) *Bird Lives! The High Life and Hard Times of Charlie 'Yardbird' Parker*. London: Quartet.

Saunders, N. *et al.* (1995) *Ecstasy and the Dance Culture*. London: Saunders.

Saunders, N. *et al.* (1997) *Ecstasy Reconsidered*. London: Saunders.

Shapiro, H. (2003) *Waiting for the Man: The Story of Drugs and Popular Music* (2nd edn). London: Helter Skelter Publishing.

Shipton, A. (1999) *Groovin' High: The Life of Dizzy Gillespie*. Oxford: Oxford University Press.

Szwed, J. (2002) *So What: The Life of Miles Davis*. London: Heinemann.

Thomas J.C. (1975) *Chasin' the Trane: The Music and Mystique of John Coltrane*. New York, Elm Tree Books.

Websites:
www.cream.co.uk
www.ecstacy.org
www.ministryofsound.co.uk

6. Drugs, the family and recent American cinema

Leighton Grist

Introduction

At the beginning of *Narc* (Joe Carnahan 2002), undercover narcotics officer Nick Tellis (Jason Patric) chases suspect Elvin Dowd (Don Leis) on foot through a Detroit housing project. Tellis pursues his prey over fences, across yards, through a house, down an alley, around a corner and over a wall. Dowd grabs an innocent bystander (Lloyd Adams) and stabs him in the neck with a syringe containing a combination of heroin and other substances. Tellis fires some rounds from his pistol, Dowd again flees, the bystander goes into seizure and Tellis pursues Dowd to a playground where Dowd grabs and threatens to stab with a syringe a little girl (Meagan Issa). Tellis fires four more rounds, killing Dowd and saving the girl. However, one of Tellis's bullets also hits the girl's pregnant mother (Lina Felice), precipitating the death of her unborn child.

The scene brings us immediately to this chapter's concerns. As the chase traverses and invades domestic space, and sees a man, a woman and a living and an unborn child suffer threat and harm, it places drugs implicitly in opposition to, and endangering of, the family. *Narc*, moreover, is one of a group of American films released in the early 2000s that revolves significantly around the relation of drugs and the family. The others are *Requiem for a Dream* (Darren Aronofsky 2000), *Traffic* (Steven Soderbergh 2000) and *Blow* (Ted Demme 2001). The last released of the films, *Narc* acknowledges its group affiliation stylistically: its blue-toned shots recall the similarly toned shots that occur mainly during the Ohio- and Washington DC-set scenes in *Traffic*, a film with which *Narc* also shares an electronic Cliff Martinez score, while its pair of rapidly-edited montages of drug taking flag the numerous rapidly-edited montages of drug taking in *Requiem for a Dream*. That *Narc* has in addition been compared (Mottram 2003: 55; Richards 2003: 56) with 1970s precursors such as *The French Connection* (William Friedkin 1971) and *Serpico* (Sidney Lumet 1973) reflects the way in which the films draw from past tendencies and earlier specific examples of drug representation within American cinema. The films' grouping is further confirmed by their commonality of representational inflection and emphasis. For although the films position drugs and the family in a relation of opposition, they also suggest that of complicity, and even mutual culpability. To account for such, the films need to be referred not only to their cinematic but to their larger historical context, to be considered in terms of the socio-political conjuncture to which they give displaced articulation. This chapter, while centring upon the close analysis of the cited films, will seek to situate them both cinematically and historically, and to unpack the connotations thereof.

Drugs and American cinema

Richard Porton writes: 'Popular culture has always treated the drug culture as a threat to the solidarity of the nuclear family' (2001: 42). As much is implicit to American cinema, which from its earliest years has found in drugs and the family resonant metonyms for – reciprocally – criminality, illegality and otherness and legal and social order. Thus within silent cinema the common, and racist, association of drugs with white slavery, miscegenation and the Oriental (Stevenson 2000: 12–23). Such association can be seen no less to inform the proscription of the representation of the illegal drug trade within the 1930 Production Code that, was enforced rigorously from June 1934, worked ideologically to lend Hollywood cinema 'an affirmative cultural function' (Maltby 2003: 61). Yet what was repressed returned, whether within the exploitation sector – as in, most notoriously, *Reefer Madness* (Louis Gasnier 1936) – or within Hollywood cinema itself. Note, say, in *The Hound of the Baskervilles* (Sidney Lanfield 1939) Sherlock Holmes (Basil Rathbone)'s closing request of Dr Watson (Nigel Bruce) for 'the needle', or in *The Philadelphia Story* (George Cukor 1940) Tracy Lord (Katharine Hepburn) enquiring of C.K. Dexter Haven (Cary Grant) whether he had 'switched from liquor to dope'. Underpinning these instances is the imprimatur of, variously, the literary, the comic and the 'sophisticated'. More usually within the time's Hollywood filmmaking, drugs, like other proscribed elements, obtain coded, displaced or tacit intimation; as Michael Walker observes of *The Big Sleep* (Howard Hawks 1946), while the 'evidence' of 'censorable items', including drugs, is 'left in', the film simply declines 'to explain them' (1992: 195).

In December 1956, with Hollywood facing a declining audience and the availability of the unconstrained representations of European art cinema, the Production Code was revised to allow the treatment of previously prohibited material, including drug addiction. Before this, United Artists had released *The Man With the Golden Arm* (Otto Preminger 1955), a film that offers a for-the-time explicit representation of drug dealing, the mechanics of heroin injection and cold turkey, without the formal mark of Code adherence, the Seal of Approval. Even so, since Frankie (Frank Sinatra)'s addiction is shown to mitigate against his relationship with potential domestic partner Molly (Kim Novak), drugs and the family remain in conflict. A like correlation of increased explicitness and thematic consistency shapes the representation of drugs upon the demise of the Production Code, which in 1968 was replaced by the rating system that has fundamentally sustained to this day. Indivisible from this regulatory shift were the period's social changes, not least, in terms of the representation of drugs, the rise of the counter-culture. However, although drugs and the family are still positioned filmically as antitheses, the ideological weighting of their representation varies. Compare, for example, the representation of drugs, drug taking and their personal and social consequences in, on one hand, the likes of *Easy Rider* (Dennis Hopper 1969) or *The Strawberry Statement* (Stuart Hagmann 1970) and, on the other, that of *Klute* (Alan J. Pakula 1971), *The French Connection* or *Death Wish* (Michael Winner 1974). Across this divide, as counter-cultural lifestyles are opposed to familial mores, outlawry becomes criminality, easy sexuality becomes licentiousness and prostitution and drug-related release becomes anti-social, life-threatening addiction. Nevertheless, outside comedy, films that offer utterly non-judgemental representations of drugs and of drug use – such as that of cocaine in *Blue Collar* (Paul Schrader 1978) – remain rare. The even-handed representation of LSD use in *The Trip* (Roger Corman 1967) finds itself bracketed by a warning introductory title and voice-over and a commentatorial 'shattered' final shot of its protagonist that were imposed by the film's producing studio, American International Pictures, while in *Easy Rider* the 'untroubled' representations of cocaine and marijuana use are contrasted by the elliptical, jump-cut, visually distorted representation of its protagonists' graveyard-set acid trip.

That comedy has endured as a space permitting of the uncontentious representation of drugs is apparent whether one considers individual incidents – such as Alvy Singer (Woody Allen) sneezing and scattering a boxful of $2,000-an-ounce cocaine in *Annie Hall* (Allen 1977) – or the 'stoner' comedies that, finding a prime exemplum in *Up in Smoke* (Lou Adler 1978), have been produced up to and beyond *The Big Lebowski* (Joel Coen 1998). This correspondingly evokes Sigmund Freud's contention (1905) that jokes, like dreams, enable the expression of the inadmissible, of that which is repressed. In turn, the 1980s saw both the sustained filmic representation of drugs and their comparative thematic circumscription: a situation that, as it intersects with the decade's reactionary backlash, and continues through the 1990s, suggests drugs' certain social normalisation and a disavowal of their broader social connotations and ramifications. For example, in *Boogie Nights* (Paul Thomas Anderson 1997) and *Jesus' Son* (Alison Maclean 1999) drugs are represented copiously, but consideration of their effects is restricted to their disruption of actual, surrogate and potential family units. Not that such social disavowal is monolithic, as much of the work of Oliver Stone as a writer and writer-director demonstrates. Individual films, and their relation, present more specific connotations and tensions. Thus while in *River's Edge* (Tim Hunter 1986) and *Clean and Sober* (Glenn Gordon Carol 1988) drug taking is referred implicitly to the films' contrastingly accentuated critiques of 1980s social and economic behaviour, it is also related somewhat unreflectively to familial dysfunction, this in films whose storylines begin similarly, and uncannily, with the drug-related death of a naked young woman. In like vein, although *Drugstore Cowboy* (Gus Van Sant 1989) and *Bad Lieutenant* (Abel Ferrara 1992) offer relatively explicit and non-judgemental representations of drug use, they still uphold the drugs-family partition and its normative ideological weighting, albeit rather contradictorily: witness in *Drugstore Cowboy* the pro-drugs proselytising of author William S. Burroughs as Tom the Priest, or in *Bad Lieutenant* the film's very accumulation of represented transgression.

Nevertheless, the explicitness of its representation of drug taking – that, as in *Drugstore Cowboy*, includes the sight of skin being pierced during heroin injection – can be regarded itself to function critically, as has been the case historically, whether one considers, again, *The Man With the Golden Arm*, or the analogous, skin-piercing naturalism of *The Panic in Needle Park* (Jerry Schatzberg 1971).

Significant drug representation besides occurs in the black filmmaking that obtained increased prominence in the late 1980s and 1990s. If in part a reflection of the 'ghettocentric' actuality that the films predominantly represent, such in its representation nevertheless maintains the opposition of drugs and the family. Consider, for instance, *Jungle Fever* (Spike Lee 1991), which sees a religious father, The Good Reverend Doctor Purify (Ossie Davis), shoot and kill his crack-addicted son, Gator (Samuel L. Jackson), or *New Jack City* (Mario Van Peebles 1991), a film that, informed narratively and stylistically by the drug-related blaxsploitation cinema of the 1970s, and having as a concern drugs' perversion of childhood, foreshadows *Narc* in representing a chase that ends with a fleeing suspect being shot in a playground. *New Jack City* in addition foregrounds a correlation of drugs, drug dealing and capitalist exploitation. This can once more be traced to *The Man With the Golden Arm*, and the character and actions of the pusher Louie (Darren McGavin). Noteworthy likewise is *Easy Rider*, within which Wyatt (Peter Fonda)'s enigmatic 'We blew it' can be referred implicitly to his and Billy (Hopper)'s status effectively as drug dealers, as compromised hippie entrepreneurs. That *New Jack City* should foreground the depredations of capitalism is in turn unsurprising given it is a gangster film, part of a genre that has historically concerned itself with the same. Further, not only does the film show its gangster protagonist, Nino Brown (Wesley Snipes), watching the Stone-scripted gangster film *Scarface* (Brian De Palma 1983), in which Tony Montana (Al Pacino) attains money and power through dealing cocaine, but that *King of New York* (Ferrara 1989) similarly links drugs, gangsterism and economic dominion would appear to bear out filmically the assertion made in *The Godfather* (Francis Ford Coppola 1972) that 'narcotics is the thing of the future'. *Scarface*, *King of New York* and *New Jack City* in addition associate drugs, drug dealing and capitalist exploitation with conspicuous consumption, as does another late gangster, *GoodFellas* (Martin Scorsese 1990). Stylistically, moreover, *Good Fellas* – as it presents a chronicle of recent American history attuned to the sartorial, copious employment of voice-over and popular music and a post-*nouvelle vague* use of freeze frames at key narrative moments – provides a template that is replicated by *Blow*.

Two models

Before proceeding further, two interpretative models need to be outlined.

First, there is the 'basic formula for the horror film' propounded by Robin Wood: 'normality is threatened by the Monster' (1979: 203). 'Although so simple', the formula presents 'three variables' – 'normality', 'the Monster' and 'the relationship between the two' (1979: 204). With respect to normality, this in horror films 'is in general boringly constant: the heterosexual monogamous couple, the family, and the social institutions ... that support and defend them' (1979: 204). By contrast, the Monster is 'much more protean, changing from period to period as society's basic fears clothe themselves in fashionable or immediately accessible garments' (1979: 204). If this lends the representation of the Monster an historical dimension, Wood besides suggests that his formula can be applied to 'other genres' (1979: 204). Films that represent drugs within American cinema span numerous discrete genres, but their transgeneric commonality nevertheless invites extension of the model – with drugs as the monster – to them. It is, in turn, 'the third variable' – 'the relationship between normality and the Monster' – that Wood declares 'the essential subject of the horror film' (1979: 204); correspondingly, it is in the weighting of this relationship's representation that the genre's ideological valence can be seen to inhere. While this further reflects upon the historically shifting connotations of the representation of the relationship of drugs and the family, the representation of both also, within and across films, partakes – in its repressions and implied returns, tensions and contradictions – of the 'ambivalence' that Wood in addition proclaims concerning that of the Monster and normality in the horror film (1979: 204–205).

Second, there is the reciprocal social and discursive separation of public and private realms. Historically a division that has been referred to nineteenth-century industrialisation, this situates the private, and synonymously the family, as a refuge from, and palliation of, the ravages of the public, of the exploitative, capitalist sphere of production. Culturally, it is a split that has found paradigmatic mediation through melodrama (Kleinhans 1978; Gledhill 1987: 20 21), an aesthetic mode that has shaped the vast majority of American narrative cinema, and which remains implicit to the films to be discussed, irrespective of their formal and stylistic specificities.

Traffic/Blow/Narc

Early in *Traffic*, newly-appointed government drug czar, Judge Robert Wakefield (Michael Douglas), tells journalists that the drug problem is 'an issue that affects all families'. It is a proposition that is seemingly shared by the films under consideration. In *Traffic*, Wakefield discovers that his own teenage daughter, Caroline (Erika Christensen), is herself a drug addict, resulting in a situation that shakes his family's unity, and Helena Ayala (Catherine Zeta-Jones) finds her familial security threatened when her husband Carlos (Steven Bauer) is arrested on drug-trafficking charges. In *Blow*, a film based on the biography of real-life drug dealer George Jung (Porter 1993), not only is George (Johnny Depp), having been arrested and skipped bail, shopped to the police by his mother, Ermine (Rachel Griffiths), but a later arrest and his again skipping bail sees her disown him and an increase in tensions in his own marriage that culminate, on his imprisonment, in his wife, Mirtha (Penelope Cruz), divorcing him. Released, George's involvement in yet another drug deal sees him lose his re-established relationship with his daughter, Kristina (Emma Roberts), and, when re-imprisoned, his mother veto his request for a furlough to visit his dying father, Fred (Ray Liotta). Even the death earlier of George's fiancée Barbara (Franka Potente) is tacitly referred to drugs. Her nosebleed indexes her cancer, but can besides be read as a displaced figure for cocaine abuse, this despite George at this juncture of the narrative having as yet only dealt in marijuana. In *Narc*, Tellis's wife, Audrey (Krista Bridges), leaves him over his return to narcotics work, it having in addition been established that their relationship had earlier come under strain because of his previous, undercover work-related drug addiction. It is, moreover, a domestic situation implicitly paralleled by that of fellow narcotics officer Michael Calvess (Alan Van Sprang), around the investigation of whose death the film's narrative revolves, who is gradually discovered to have himself suffered undercover work-related addiction, which is suggested to have had a similarly negative effect upon his family's life.

In *Narc*, the manifest incommensurability of drugs and the family, and their implicit evaluation, is further underscored stylistically as the film's bleak, impersonal, workaday, dilapidated, 'cold' and blue-tinged public spaces are initially contrasted by the closely-shot, 'warm', golden-lit private space of the family, within which Tellis is, at one point, shot, in a figure of cleansing purity, holding his baby son in the shower. Like complementary connotation is supplied narratively in *Traffic* by the betrayal of corrupt Mexican anti-drug official General Salazar (Tomas Milian) to the US Drug Enforcement Agency by Tijuana policeman Javier Rodriguez (Benicio Del Toro) in return for baseball floodlighting for a park so that 'kids can play at night', safely. By contrast, Helena seeks to restore her family's security – financial and otherwise – by demonstrating to her husband's drug supplier, Juan Obregon (Benjamin Bratt), a doll made out of 'pressure-moulded cocaine' that can elude detection by the authorities, what her husband Carlos had termed 'the project for the children'.

However, this last incident is also indicative of the contradictions and ambiguities – of, to evoke Wood, the ambivalences – that no less attend the films' representation of drugs, the family and their relationship. As the heavily-pregnant Helena meets with Obregon to restore the safety and prosperity that had been, unbeknownst to her, founded upon the dealing of drugs, so Carlos's designation of 'the project for the children' obtains a familial self-reference beyond that of its cynical connotation. Not dissimilarly, in *Blow* George becomes a drug dealer as a means of avoiding the economic insecurity that bedevilled his parents' marriage. Drugs, and George's success as a drug dealer, are in turn responsible, subsequent eventualities notwithstanding, for the surrogate extended 'family' that George and his associates enjoy in the early 1970s and for his marriage to the Colombian Mirtha, this despite George being a gringo and Mirtha at first being engaged to Colombian drug dealer Cesar (Dan Ferro). As George's voice-over states: 'I was untouchable'. Maintained correspondingly is the correlation of drugs, money and, concomitantly, capitalist exploitation. As much is rendered literal in the sequence in which George and his Colombian 'business' partner Diego (Jordi Molla) are shown, on breaking cocaine into the USA, in an apartment first awash with and then filled with boxes of money. It is more widely connoted, in an extension of the film's stylistic indebtedness to *GoodFellas*, through an emphasis on conspicuous consumption, on expensive houses, furnishings, clothes, cars and so forth. Like connotations are occasioned in *Traffic* by the luxuriousness of the lifestyle that Helena seeks to preserve, or the sizeable villa that drug lord Porfirio Madrigal (Joel Torres) gifts his mistress (Salma Hayek). Even so, in *Blow* contradiction is also turned back upon itself by drugs and money being yet further linked through the representation of Ermine and Mirtha's reflective materialism as mutually disregarding of marriage and family. Ermine is represented as having repeatedly walked out on Fred and the young George (Jesse James) over her disappointed financial expectations, while on meeting Barbara and Mirtha she is interested only in Barbara's expensive engagement ring and George and Mirtha's house and furniture. She in addition admits receipt of the 'drug money' that George has sent her in the same sequence in which she shops him. Mirtha may well get her fugitive husband imprisoned when her confrontational cocaine-fuelled antics in their car lead to them attracting the attention of following police, but their point of reference is the couple's straightened financial circumstances; when George asks 'What is your fucking problem?', she responds: 'We are broke'.

In *Narc*, as Tellis becomes more involved in the Calvess investigation, and his relations with his wife become fraught, the public increasingly invades their private space stylistically, with shots tending to become wider, shadows more ominous and the lighting tinged with blue. However, although it is implied that the case presents for Tellis a means of personal and professional redemption, his economic rationale for returning to his old job, that 'This welfare, pension bullshit is not gonna cut it', also again connects drugs, money and familial security. Conversely, it is discovered that it was Calvess's lack of money that impelled him to obtain drugs by trading police badges, IDs and guns and through blowing his, and Tellis's, cover: a betrayal that precipitated the film's early, family-endangering chase. In *Traffic* the correlation of drugs and money is further lent a classed and racial aspect. When staking out the Ayala house, Hispanic DEA officer Ray (Luis Guzman) tells his black partner Montel (Don Cheadle) that he dreams about busting 'the top people, the rich people, white people'. Such finds contrasting refraction when Caroline's boyfriend Seth (Topher Grace), upon Caroline fleeing from the drug rehabilitation camp to which she had been sent by her parents, and on his being taken by Wakefield to the black neighbourhood where Seth buys his drugs, explains to Wakefield the economic and social realities of white people 'from the suburbs' entering downtown black areas looking for drugs, that narcotics embody 'an unbeatable market force': 'It's a 300 per cent mark-up … You can go out on the street and make $500 in two hours and come back and do whatever you want to do with the rest of your day'. Yet while Seth appears superciliously unaware of his own moneyed implication in the cycle of black exploitation, dependence and quietism that, despite his economics, he outlines, the film offers a classed irony in the fact that Caroline, on fleeing the camp, and through this her parents, is forced into 'lower order' crime – prostitution and stealing objects to pawn – to fund her habit.

The earlier drug taking of Caroline and her upper middle-class friends affords the association of drugs and money a further classed inflection. The suggestion is of, reciprocally, material over-indulgence and parental neglect. The parents are all prosperous professionals, but the children's actions appear to be utterly unsupervised and unaccountable: the parents of the friend, Bowman (Corey Spears), who overdoses are noted as being 'in Barbados'. Wakefield and his wife Barbara (Amy Irving) are represented as, respectively, career-orientated and ambitious, as witness his pride at being pencilled in for 'face time' with the President, and lax and over-indulgent; whereas Wakefield is initially ignorant of his daughter's drug problem, Barbara admits, to Wakefield's annoyance, that she had known for 'six months'. Exacerbating matters, Wakefield is implied to have a drink problem, and Barbara speaks of having 'tried every drug there was' in her youth. However, if we would thus appear to be returned unequivocally to the opposition of drugs and the family, Caroline and her friends' drug taking can likewise be read as a reflection of and means of compensating for familial lack, or even, in Caroline's case, a call for attention. At the drug rehabilitation camp she admits to an inchoate anger, while when Wakefield finds her and awakens her from a drug-induced sleep, she smiles beatifically and murmurs: 'Hi Daddy'. Paradoxically, drugs can be regarded as finally represented as being as much restorative as destructive of the family. As Wakefield and his wife and daughter are last represented, together, at a drug rehabilitation meeting, they are so implicitly in terms of a shared and acknowledged narcotic complicity.

Requiem for a Dream

Similar representations, correlations and connotations find more explicitly critical articulation in *Requiem for a Dream*. Described pointedly by its director Aronofsky as 'a horror film', in which 'addiction' is the Monster (Gingold 2000: 57), the film, an adaptation of Hubert Selby Jr's novel (1978), presents a foregrounded stylisation that, while working expressionistically, besides demands the film's formal negotiation. Among other devices, the film employs split screens, fades to white, cinematography that is body-mounted, noticeably wide-angled and fisheyed, superimposition, variations of both shot speed and the speed of actions within the same shot and distorted and anatomised sound. Most insistent, however, in a film containing about 2,000 rather than the usual 600–700 cuts (Brooks 2001: 49), are its multiple, rapidly-edited montage sequences. The taking of drugs is represented through variations of combinations of brief close-ups of packages being opened, substances being prepared, a syringe, a pill, a rolled-up bank-note, a spliff, drugs being ingested, blood cells and/or pupils dilating. Yet as the montages evoke the ritualised compulsion, frantic need and exhilarated release tacit to drug use, so they also relate formally not only the different illegal drugs – heroin, amphetamines, cocaine and marijuana – that Harry (Jared Leto), his friend Tyrone (Marlon Wayans) and his girlfriend Marion (Jennifer Connelly) partake of, but the legal addictions of Harry's mother Sara (Ellen Burstyn), which are represented via similarly shot and edited montages of her, *inter alia*, switching on her television, taking slimming pills, drinking coffee, being weighed and trying on the red dress that her dead husband Seymour 'liked so much'. The film, moreover, situates both illegal and legal addictions as being compensatory of familial lack. An associative linkage is offered between Sara's being chosen as a television game show contestant, her need to slim, her red dress and her unified family, with the dress, which she wore to Harry's high-school graduation, being shown as thus worn in a photograph of herself and her husband and son at the same event. She also explicitly tells Harry, whom she only wishes would 'meet a nice girl and have a baby', that with Seymour and Harry 'gone' her addictive situation gives her 'a reason to get up in the morning'. Beforehand, when Harry waits at his apartment for Tyrone to return with the 'piece' of heroin that they plan to cut and sell themselves, he looks toward the bedroom window and sees with, again, associative implication a vision of Marion standing, face to sea, on a pier, wearing – with clear Oedipal implication – a red dress resembling that of his mother. Similarly, when Tyrone, to his girlfriend Alice (Aliya Campbell)'s irritation, plays with the 'new mirrors' that his and Harry's subsequently successful drug dealing has enabled him to buy, the scene cuts to a flashback of the young Tyrone (Te'ron A. O'Neal) running to and being held by his mother (Denise Dowse), from which the sequence cuts back to Tyrone, who tells Alice that he has been 'thinking about' her.

Compounding these sequences' Oedipal connotations, Sara and Marion are also connected formally; both are shot, at different times, in low-angle, circular tracks as they walk distractedly around their apartments and, in close-up, as they apply mascara and lipstick. Such, moreover, makes comparatively explicit like connotations that are, unsurprisingly, given their concern with family, and American cinema's historical informing by Freudian psychoanalysis, barely concealed in other films discussed. Consider, again, in *Traffic* Wakefield's bedside reconciliation with his daughter that, apart from Caroline's voluptuous satisfaction, represents him implicitly – and somewhat perversely – as besting his sexual rivals, as pushing past Seth outside and ejecting a john from the hotel room in which he finds her, or in *Blow* the comparable, family-disruptive materialism of Ermine and Mirtha, which fixes George reciprocally as having 'become' his father.

Marion herself, moreover, sets her drug-founded relationship with Harry in opposition to, and as compensatory of, her own parents' materialism, complaining that money was not what she 'wanted from them', but that it was all that they had 'to give'. However, within *Requiem for a Dream* drugs are also once more related inescapably with money. For Harry and Tyrone dealing drugs is a means of eventually obtaining a 'pound of pure' heroin, the selling of which would enable them to 'get off hard knocks and be on easy street'. Besides, if more close-up, rapidly-edited montages of Harry and Tyrone dealing drugs underscore the linkage of drugs, money and, yet further, capitalist exploitation formally, and their boxfuls of money foreshadow, in lower case, those of George and Diego in *Blow*, then, as the film's montages connect illegal and legal drugs, and as Harry proposes to fund Marion's designer clothes business from his drug profits – with the montages of Harry and Tyrone dealing drugs being intercut with shots of Marion working on designs, a sewing-machine and photographs of a possible shop space – so there is an analogous, and innately critical, linkage of illegal and legal exchange. Again, this makes relatively plain that which in other films is barely dissimulated. The same is, for example, in *Traffic* implicit to Ray's verbal association of top, rich and white people, or to Carlos having passed successfully as an honest businessman and 'pillar of his community'.

As *Requiem for a Dream* proceeds, drugs also become, typically, destructive of family, whether actual or potential. With Tyrone being arrested, his and Harry's money being largely cleaned out for his bail and a gang war creating a shortage of drugs on the street, narcotic and monetary need sees Harry and Marion's relationship become strained. Sara, disappointed in her hoped-for television appearance, and taking increasing quantities of slimming pills, begins hallucinating psychotically. Tyrone, in turn, is filmed sitting on his bed looking longingly at a photograph of his mother, with Alice nowhere to be seen: with respect to which, Harry's earlier vision of Marion is interrupted, dispelled, on her turning around, precisely by Tyrone arriving back with his and Harry's 'piece'. Moreover, within *Requiem for a Dream* explicitness as implicit critique obtains a disturbing extremity. While the wasted, clammy-skinned appearance of Harry, Marion and Tyrone mirrors similar representations of addicts in the rest of the films at hand, the slimmed-down Sara becomes increasingly dishevelled and haggard. More unsettling still are the scenes, following Sara's institutionalisation, of her being force-fed or, especially, the close-up of Harry pushing a needle into the septic wound on his arm that, exacerbating the effect of previous, similar shots, Edward Lawrenson describes as 'almost unwatchable' (2000: 27). The film in addition climaxes with a relentlessly accelerating montage that cross-cuts between the four main characters, now each separated within their own infelicitous situation: Sara undergoing ECT; Tyrone, after being arrested in the South, to where he and Harry had travelled in pursuit of drugs, working on a prison gang; Harry being wheeled on a hospital trolley, then having his arm amputated; and Marion performing lesbian sex for a baying crowd – this in return for drugs. However, if drugs are represented as being but contingent in their consolation, and as ultimately ruinous, family remains unobtainable: upon the climactic montage sequence a reprise of Harry's vision of Marion sees her suddenly disappear and Harry step backwards into a dark space. Lack abides, being seemingly unassuageable.

Subsequent to Harry's reprised vision, Harry, Marion, Tyrone and Sara are shot similarly, from a high angle, as they lie on their beds, or, in Marion's case, her settee, turning on their sides and curling into a foetal position. As they imply a yearning to return to the womb, the shots invite consideration in terms of Freud's conception of the death instinct, of the striving of all organic life to return to 'an initial state from which the living entity has at one time or other departed' (1920: 310). Moreover, if that as Marion curls up she delightedly hugs the heroin received for her sexual performance reflects further upon the consolation that drugs afford, then that the shot of Tyrone is briefly superimposed over a reprise of that of his young self being held by his mother relates the characters' lack tacitly to that which Jacques Lacan posits as constitutive of desire, which Lacan describes as originating upon the loss of the maternal breast (Stam, Burgoyne and Flitterman-Lewis 1992: 127–128). Beyond such, as the association of drugs, the family and legal and illegal addiction within *Requiem for a Dream* affords a further inflection to the relation of drugs and the family across the films discussed, so this relation – as it shifts between and suggests opposition, sustenance, complicity, consolation and destructiveness – situates the familial socially and discursively as a compromised space. Add drugs synonymity with capital, and the films can be read as bespeaking an increasing erosion of the differentiation of private and public realms. True, the contamination of the private by the public could be argued to be an historical constant, and even latent to their very separation. However, its particular articulation within the films at hand suggestively implicates their particular historical and economic context; namely, that of late capitalism, which Fredric Jameson has described as being characterised by 'a prodigious expansion of capital into hitherto uncommodified areas' (1984: 78). It is correspondingly indicative, with respect to a phase of capitalism associated likewise with 'the rise of the media and the advertising industry' (1984: 78), that not only does Sara seek to restore her lost private, familial plenitude through appearing publicly, on television, before 'millions', but her preferred televisual fix is an infomercial.

Prostitution and blackness, the foreign and the domestic

Marion's sexual performance in *Requiem for a Dream* follows her being prostituted first by Harry, who impels her to get money through sleeping with her former psychiatrist, Arnold (Sean Gullette), and then by herself, when she 'sells' herself for drugs to Big Tim (Keith David), who besides hosts the 'little gathering' at which she performs. Apart from the intimations of prostitution that attend the scene of her rescue, Caroline in *Traffic* is similarly shown prostituting herself for drugs first to the dealer (Vonte Sweet) whom she had previously visited with Seth. In *Narc* addicted snitch Octavio Ruiz (John Ortiz) has been given a sexually transmitted disease by his prostitute female companion (Marilo Nunez), while Lieutenant Henry Oak (Ray Liotta), the officer with whom Tellis is partnered, tells of a drug raid during which he found a cowering little girl (Stacey Farber) whose stepfather had pimped her out 'for rent' and Tellis wonders rhetorically how long it would have been, had Calvess lived, 'before he started pimping' out his wife, Kathryn (Anne Openshaw). Yet if such relation of drugs and prostitution potentially complements the latently critical association of drugs and capitalist exploitation, it no less, in its near clichéd familiarity, and whatever the historical actuality, can be seen, following Roland Barthes (1957), to naturalise the historical, to function as a means of ideological disavowal. An analogous ideological disavowal is – again, historical actuality regardless – implicit to the extensive association of drugs and blackness. Not only are most of the characters involved illegally with drugs in *Narc* black, but Oak's overt racism invites consideration as a disavowal of that of the film itself. In *Requiem for a Dream* Big Tim is black, as is Tyrone and, in *Traffic*, the dealer to whom Caroline gives herself. Indeed, despite its convolutions regarding race and class, *Traffic* can be argued as much to uphold certain well-worn racial and cultural fears: Porton describes Caroline's 'fall' as being 'reminiscent of silent-era movies that depicted damsels sold into the white slave trade' (2001: 42). The implication of a residual demonising of otherness is, moreover, underscored by an emphasis across the films on the sources of narcotics being foreign, and more explicitly Latin American. In *Blow* the source of drugs is represented as Mexico, with respect to marijuana, and Colombia, with respect to cocaine, which a montage shows being produced, within Colombia, under the film's front credits. In *Traffic*, the source of drugs is Mexico, and the film is much exercised by the 'problem' of the USA-Mexico border: we are given shots of multiple lanes crowded with vehicles entering the USA, and verbally informed about an average of '45,000 vehicles' and '25,000 pedestrians' crossing per day into California and of there having been a 'three-fold' increase in drug trafficking. Even in the purely USA-set *Requiem for a Dream* Harry tells Sara that he is working as a 'distributor' for 'a big importer'. Admittedly, this emphasis has a basis in fact. However, although the representation of and/or a concern with the foreign provenance of drugs is apparent in earlier drug-related American films – as note, say, *Easy Rider*, *The French Connection* or *Scarface* – it is an element that occurs but intermittently.

In the films under discussion the foreign is, in addition, the source of direct threats to the family. In *Traffic* Helena has her son (Alec Roberts)'s life threatened by one of Obregon's men (Yul Vazquez), while in *Blow* Cesar tells charter pilot Jack Stevens (Charles Noland) that he has to put up his children's lives as security for his trustworthiness. Further, and further racist, mystification is, moreover, in *Traffic* apparent in the representation of Salazar. Described by Andrew O'Hehir as 'a comically nefarious Third World caricature' (2001: 54), the character is scheming, duplicitous, vicious, manipulative and callous. On meeting with Wakefield, and being asked about his 'policies towards treatment of addiction', he responds that addicts 'treat themselves': 'They overdose … and there's one less to worry about'. Nevertheless, there is also no 'treatment' representative on board Wakefield's 'plane during his fact-finding investigation of the drug 'front lines'. In turn, where Salazar is revealed to be implicated in the drug dealing that he is nominally fighting, to be wiping out the Tijuana Obregon Cartel to the benefit of the rival Juarez Madrigal Cartel, Wakefield is as drug czar likewise compromised by his daughter's addiction and his own incipient alcoholism. But if Salazar and Wakefield are thus paralleled, this serves less to implicate Wakefield and, by extension, the USA than to lessen his/its failings through comparison to a greater evil.

The films' emphasis on the foreign provenance of drugs carries similar implications. In *Traffic* Wakefield is told that the financial resources of the drug traffickers are 'way beyond' those affordable even for a country the 'size' of the USA. This implicitly returns us to the alignment of the films discussed, drugs and late capitalism: the situation outlined figures suggestively the globalisation that is concomitant with the last, before which the nation state has been claimed to have become increasingly impotent. The complicity of the USA with globalisation is, however, occluded: be this in terms of the global expansion of this or that American corporation, the deregulatory, neo-liberal economic policies fostered and imposed by the Washington-based World Bank and International Monetary Fund or, with particular pertinence to *Traffic*, the North American Free Trade Agreement that, brokered largely by, and to the profit of, the USA, eliminated trade controls between the USA and Mexico. It is further notable that Wood observes that the Monster in the American horror film has, historically, been designated 'foreign' (1979: 209). Moreover, in *Traffic* not only is American culpability displaced onto foreign destabilisation, but American involvement abroad – whether Wakefield's meeting with Salazar, the late, DEA-assisted drug seizure or Javier's promised baseball lights – is represented as socially beneficent. Even so, upon giving the evidence that indicts Salazar to the DEA, and being told that he should 'feel good', Javier says: 'I feel like a traitor'. Unanswered, the comment stands out awkwardly, but neither is it explored. Neither is *Traffic* nor any of the other films especially interested in the social and economic realities that might fuel the drug trade in Latin America. In *Blow*, head of the Medellin Cartel, Pablo Escobar (Cliff Curtis), speaks to George of Colombia being 'Beautiful ... but poor'. Yet they are words spoken both by a figure historically damned as a villain and after he has just had an informer summarily executed, while that he besides speaks of the informer's death as preventing those of 'his wife, his children, his parents, his friends' once more intimates the inimicality of the foreign and the family.

Apart from its 'foreign' problems, moreover, the USA is represented as powerless to combat drugs domestically. On Wakefield arriving in Washington in *Traffic*, his predecessor, General Ralph Landry (James Brolin), responds to Wakefield's platitudinous praise for his 'fine job' by wondering whether he 'made the slightest difference', while at a subsequent Georgetown party – cast, in part, with some real-life politicians – Wakefield is confronted with multiple opinions, but cumulatively to the effect that the 'war on drugs' cannot be won, only managed. Senator Don Nickles notes both that cutting the number of 'high-school seniors' taking drugs from 25 to ten per cent would be 'a phenomenal achievement', but that it would still leave 'ten per cent habitually using drugs'. Wakefield's literal walking out on his post during his inaugural speech correspondingly enacts his recognition of its seeming futility. That in the process he also moves from declaring, during his speech, that the war on drugs has to be won for the sake of 'our country's most precious resource, our children' to observing, extemporarily, that if there is such a war, 'then many of our family members are the enemy' and that he does not know 'how you wage war on your own family' summarises the movement in terms of drugs and the family from opposition to acknowledged complicity that is implicit mutually to character and film. However, Wakefield's apparent retreat from the political to the familial can – in another modulation of the interrelation of the public and the private – be seen to be as political as the accommodative realpolitik effectively expressed at the party, during which, as conversation covers matters of cost, profit and 'economic truth', and the represented guests include a lobbyist for 'the legal drug business' (Stephen Dunham), drugs and their dealing and capital and capitalism are yet again situated as synonymous.

Such, seemingly inescapable accommodation with drugs, with all of their accompanying connotations, raises another issue that, while worsened by the incursions of late capitalism, has a longer-standing origin: that of the absence of any substantive ideological position contesting or even significantly mitigating of capitalism available within the USA. In *Blow*, Escobar can complain about 'fucking Communists', but in the USA-set scenes the nearest to a manifest oppositional position is Fred's contention that: 'Money isn't real ... It doesn't matter, it only seems like it does'. Fred is besides represented, in contrast to Ermine, as being largely unmaterialistic, as being mainly concerned that his wife and son are happy. Fred's contention can nevertheless be seen to suggest less a programmatic statement of oppositional belief than a means of dealing with – of, exactly, accommodating oneself to – the instabilities and dissimulative plenitude of capitalism. Hence his associated philosophy that 'Sometimes you're flush, and sometimes you're bust' and that 'when you're up it's never as good as it seems, and when you're down you never think you're gonna be up again' – or his ready pocketing of the wad of $100 bills that George hands him when visiting with Barbara. Accordingly, George's admission, when 42 years old, imprisoned and having amassed and lost two fortunes, that he 'finally' understands his father's contention regarding money's irreality suggests less defiance of than a belated resignation to the way things are. This way, moreover, would appear to be that of the one-dimensional society part-described, part-predicted by Herbert Marcuse in the 1960s: a social and economic context in which 'ideas, aspirations, and objectives that, by their content, transcend the established universe of discourse and action are either repelled or reduced to terms of this universe' (1964: 27).

The family, right or wrong

For Selby, the 'dream' that his novel mourns is 'the great American dream which kills Americans dead' (Macdonald and Macdonald 2000: 32). The filmic adaptation of *Requiem for a Dream* concordantly lends the absence of an ideological alternative, of a space outside of capitalism, as its characters become engulfed within a closed, downward spiral, wherein an embrace of capitalism results in addiction, desperation, degradation and despair, a pathological edge. In turn, that the one available other space, the family, is represented, in its insufficiency, as impelling narcotically the consolation that nominally it should provide is of a piece with its fissured representation within each of the films, which, once more to adduce Wood, reciprocates that of drugs in its ambivalence. Thus while in *Traffic* Wakefield is represented as an inattentive father, he turns this around upon the family itself. Confronted by Barbara over his having to 'have three scotches just to walk in the house', he retorts: 'Otherwise I would be dying of boredom'. In *Narc* Audrey's anger when Tellis gets home late and finds her bathing their son, whom she also, on drying him, hands promptly to Tellis, implies that her displeasure at his re-entering narcotics work is in part related to her having to take a domestic role previously assumed by her husband. Tellis's irritated response that he has given their son a bath 'every day for seven months' similarly suggests a reason beyond either the redemptive or the economic for his return to his old job. Such suggests a specific historical reference: that of the changes wrought by second-wave feminism, which have seen – simplifying – both more women enter the traditional male realm of the public and a revised, more active conception of the position of men within the traditional female realm of the private. A misogynistic mediation of the changes is in turn implied in *Blow*, in which the negative representation of Ermine and Mirtha's self-centred materialism suggests retribution for their refusal to take the conventionally supportive, self-abnegating role of wife and mother. Further, if in *Blow* drugs are represented as being destructive of the family, then the family is implied to be destructive of drug-related happiness. George's voice-over summary of his surrogate family's carefree delight concludes upon him saying 'It was perfect' and a dissolve to the scene of his introducing Barbara to his parents; later, a similar voice-over summary of his initially rapturous relationship with Mirtha concludes with the same words heard over a shot of his parents arriving at his and Mirtha's house. Complementing the film's Oedipal connotations, in both instances the familial formalising of George's relationships tacitly presages the end of their joyousness; it is, moreover, during the scene with George's parents that Barbara's nose bleeds.

Moreover, in *Blow* and *Requiem for a Dream* the family is ultimately rendered a fantasy. The last scene in *Blow* represents the still-imprisoned George being visited by his now grown-up daughter (James King). The characters embrace, George professes his love, but then, as they walk hand-in-hand, his daughter is faded out of shot. A subsequent title reads 'Kristina Sunshine Jung has not yet visited her father'. *Requiem for a Dream* closes with Sara's visualised imagining of herself and Harry appearing and embracing on her preferred infomercial. A scene that caps the film's other represented visions, which include further Sara's earlier 'seeing' of her glamorised self on television, its irreality is underscored both by Sara and Harry appearing more or less as they do in Harry's graduation photograph and by Harry being introduced as having achieved a balance of the public and the private, as having his 'own private business' and being 'engaged' and 'about to get married'. The endings literalise the impossibility of an ideal of family that the films discussed represent in its actuality as being variously contingent, embattled and unfulfilling. They correspondingly suggest a division between the family as ideological construct and as existent entity. They thus have a distinct resonance within an historical context in which the family has suffered material erosion yet enjoyed continued ideological emphasis.

The connotations of this are mordantly reflected upon in *Narc*, within which Oak's violent and criminal actions are tacitly referred to as an ideological over-investment in the family. A character who is first shown attacking a suspect (Garry Robbins) in the name of the suspect's 'wife and kids', and who later vindictively berates Tellis for denying the woman whom he inadvertently shot a 'bouncing baby', he also admits to – and we see a flashback of him – beating the stepfather (Kevin Rushton) of the girl whom he discovers during the raid 'half to death'. It is further revealed that Oak, whose wife had died, childless, of cancer, both took an active interest in the girl upon her becoming a ward of state – quashing a number of, markedly, 'mostly drug related' arrests and bailing her 'out of rehab' – and that her grown-up self is Kathryn, Calvess's wife. Oak's attempt to cover up Calvess's addiction, criminality and suicide – his getting Calvess's autopsy doctored, and his willingness to frame and beat a false confession of Calvess's murder from a pair of drug dealers – is accordingly undertaken for a 'child' and family who, were it found that Calvess committed suicide, would receive 'nothing', but with whom he has but a fantastical familial relationship. Underscoring matters, that Oak attributes his beating of the girl's stepfather to his thinking of his wife and 'the baby we never had', and, especially, observes that a 'little girl being brutalised' has 'got nothing to do with rules and regulations, and everything to do with right and wrong' grants his actions an expressly ideological reference. In turn, if the intensity of Oak's familial investment once more reflects upon there being no other space, ideologically, to inhabit, then it coextensively suggests a means of personal disavowal, and arguably embodies revealing over-compensation. We are left to ponder why Oak's wanting to adopt Kathryn was refused, or why her older self did not confide in Oak regarding Calvess's problems. Given the film's emphasis on the insidious effect of police work on its actants, that Oak worked in vice, and that he discovered Kathryn naked and abused in a closet, intimates other, possibly perverse intimations. Moreover, in a film in which all flashbacks are represented as subjective, those presented as Oak speaks wistfully of his relationship with his wife (Donna Croce), which show him lying with his head in her lap, feature overripe, over-saturated colour. Yet while this returns us to the representation of the family as fantasy in *Requiem for a Dream* and *Blow*, *Narc* represents Oak's ideological embrace of the family not only as destructive and – in that it costs Oak his life – self-destructive as the drugs and the consequences of drugs that he strives to protect the family from, but as, for himself, seemingly vindicating of any number of ills. In this Oak besides presents a mirror to Helena in *Traffic*, who, apart from pursuing sustained criminality, in the name of the family demands, and obtains, the assassination of Carlos's friend-turned-prosecution witness Eduardo Ruiz (Miguel Ferrer), being a course of action that in addition sees the death of DEA agent Ray. As such compounds the negative inflection that attends the representation of family across the discussed films, so it evokes broader historical implications that are, plainly, acute.

References and suggested reading

Barthes, R. (1957/1973) *Mythologies*, trans. A. Lavers. London: Palladin.

Brooks, X. (2001) 'Requiem for a Dream', *Sight and Sound*, 11: 2 NS: 48–49.

Freud, S. (1905/1991) *Jokes and their Relation to the Unconscious*, ed. A. Richards, trans. J. Strachey. Harmondsworth: Penguin.

Freud, S. (1920/1991) 'Beyond the Pleasure Principle', trans. J. Strachey in *On Metapsychology: The Theory of Psychoanalysis*, ed. A. Richards, pp. 269–338. Harmondsworth: Penguin.

Gingold, M. (2000) 'Hooked on "Requiem for a Dream"', *Fangoria*, 197: 56–60, 95.

Gledhill, C. (1987) 'The Melodramatic Field: An Investigation', in C. Gledhill (ed.) *Home is Where the Heart is: Studies in Melodrama and the Woman's Film*, pp. 5–39. London: BFI.

Jameson, F. (1984) 'Postmodernism, or The Cultural Logic of Late Capitalism', *New Left Review*, 146: 53–92.

Kleinhans, C. (1978/1991) 'Notes on Melodrama and the Family under Capitalism', in M. Landy (ed.) *Imitations of Life: A Reader on Film and Television Melodrama*, pp. 197–204. Detroit: Wayne State University Press.

Lawrenson, E. (2000) 'Feeling Needled', *Sight and Sound*, 10: 12 NS: 26–27.

Macdonald, A. and Macdonald, G. (2000) 'Hugh Selby's Requiem for a Dream: Deconstructing American Fantasies', *Creative Screenwriting*, 7: 5: 31–34.

Maltby, R. (2003) *Hollywood Cinema* (2nd edn). Malden: Blackwell.

Marcuse, H. (1964/1968) *One Dimensional Man*. London: Sphere.

Mottram, J. (2003) 'Out of the Wilderness', *Film Review*, 627: 54–55.

O'Hehir, A. (2001) '*Traffic*', *Sight and Sound*, 11: 2 NS: 53–54.

Porter, B. (1993/2001) *Blow: How a Small-Town Boy Made $100 Million with the Medillin Cocaine Cartel and Lost it All*. New York: St Martin's Press.

Porton, R. (2001) '*Traffic*', *Cineaste*, 26: 3: 41–43.

Richards, A. (2003) '*Narc*', *Sight and Sound*, 13: 2 NS: 55–56.

Selby, H. Jr (1978/1996) *Requiem for a Dream*. London: Marion Boyars.

Stam, R., Burgoyne, R. and Flitterman-Lewis, S. (1992) *New Vocabularies in Film Semiotics: Structuralism, Post-structuralism and Beyond*. London: Routledge.

Stevenson, J. (2000) 'Highway to Hell: The Myth and Menace of Drugs in American Cinema', in J. Stevenson (ed.) *Addicted*, pp. 11–62. London: Creation.

Walker, M. (1992) 'The Big Sleep: Howard Hawks and Film Noir', in I. Cameron (ed.) *The Movie Book of Film Noir*, pp. 191–202. London: Studio Vista.

Wood, R. (1979/1985) 'An Introduction to the American Horror Film', in B. Nichols (ed.) *Movies and Methods, Volume II*, pp. 195–220. Berkeley: University of California Press.

7. Under a cloud: morality, ambivalence and uncertainty in news discourse of cannabis law reform in Great Britain[1]

Simon Cross

Introduction: high society

In January 2002, a 17-year-old British adolescent found himself the centre of international media attention. It followed revelations in the mass-market Sunday tabloid *News of the World* that he had smoked cannabis. The story became headline news across the world and included scandalous accounts of late night parties where he and other teenagers consumed cannabis and reckless amounts of alcohol. However, some reports also expressed sympathy noting that the young man had recently got in with a bad crowd. Much was made of personal difficulties he had faced coping with the death of his mother some years earlier. Of course, the nocturnal activities of teenagers do not usually fall within the sphere of newsworthiness. Unfortunately for the adolescent in question, media interest was motivated by the fact that he was third in line heir to the British throne.

The apparently boorish behaviour of Prince Harry kept the press corps preoccupied for months. In its own extensive dissection of the story, the *News of the World* referred to Harry's 'drug addiction'. It stated that 'Medical staff recognise five basic stages of addiction: contemplation, determination, action, maintenance and relapse. It is a path known well by addicts who have progressed from cannabis to heroin and cocaine' (13 January 2002, p. 4).

The theme that cannabis is a 'gateway' drug leading towards harder drug use was embedded in the *News of the World's* other Harry-related stories. Here, for example, is Amanda Evans' feature unambiguously titled 'The Route From Dope to Heroin':

> Mercifully, now Harry is clean. He has promised that his days of heavy drink and drugs are over. Drugs are the plague of the 21st century. Desperate addicts – many who just started out with a joint or two – are now responsible for unprecedented levels of vicious crime, mugging and killing for cash to feed their habits. This is a grave, everyday crisis that costs us billions, leads to incalculable pain and heartbreak – and like a relentless cancer gnaws away at the very fabric of our society.
>
> (*News of the World* 13 January 2002, p. 2)

The image of a 'clean' Prince Harry, with 'his days of heavy drink and drugs' behind him, has the appearance of a silly royal story. For example, one recalls another short-lived royal news story from the 1960s, when the British press castigated Harry's father, Prince Charles, then a 14-year-old schoolboy, for leading a group of fellow under-age school friends into a hotel bar and ordering cherry brandy!

While consumer tastes and personal vices change, moral lessons emanating from the tabloid press rarely do. The story of Prince Harry apparently in thrall to 'heavy drink and drugs' offers a titillating narrative of royal vice designed to puncture the mystique of monarchy. It also combines adulation with denigration, always the two sides of the tabloid coin when it comes to reporting the House of Windsor.

Nevertheless, the *News of the World's* coverage of Prince Harry also conveys a serious *moral* message: that cannabis is the first step on a slippery slope of drug dependency and life of crime. And while it may be hard to imagine Harry as a desperate addict 'killing for cash' (notwithstanding the fact that he is now a paid professional soldier), what matters are that Harry is publicly chastised and moral order/certainty restored: cannabis remains a gateway drug for *whoever* uses it.

The moral consensus on cannabis formally ended in 2001[2] when the then Home Secretary, David Blunkett, announced that he was considering reclassifying cannabis from a Class B to a Class C drug. However, Blunkett's eventual reclassification of cannabis in January 2004 was not monolithically articulated in terms of crime and moral deviancy. The British press, for example, were caught in a quandary about how to represent the politics and policy of cannabis reclassification.

This chapter explores the tensions, moral certainties and ambivalence that enveloped news media discourse, especially in relation to legal and mental health issues of cannabis use. As Prince Harry can testify, cannabis use is bound up with moral outrage about *where it might lead*. We begin by asking how cannabis became inscribed with moral opprobrium and note how this has helped frame the public image of the cannabis user as a moral degenerate likely to move on to harder drugs.

Seeds of moral opprobrium: a brief sketch of cannabis history and policy

According to Warburton *et al.* (2005: 113) 'cannabis laws have been a contentious issue in Britain for at least 40 years'. They are undoubtedly referring to the legalisation of cannabis debate that emerged over this period (for a summary of the contemporary parameters of this debate, see MacCoun and Reuter 2001). However, the reasons why cannabis is 'contentious' are embedded in a much longer historical drug narrative in which attitudes toward contemporary systems of drug control was forged (see also Berridge 1988). I want to briefly acknowledge this history in so far as it offers insight into contemporary vexed attitudes toward cannabis.

The connection between cannabis history and current cannabis policy and laws underpins James Mills's fascinating account of cannabis trade and prohibition during the high tide of British colonial rule in India. His book, *Cannabis Britannica* (2003), documents how colonial administration of India in the nineteenth century led to eventual prohibition of cannabis in Britain. As Mills explains, it is far from a 'whimsical tale from faraway places and long ago times [but is] directly relevant to contemporary debates about laws and policies relating to cannabis in Britain today'.

Indeed, as Andrew Blake discusses more fully elsewhere in this volume in Chapter 2 (see also Blake 1996), the seeds of British cannabis regulation involve far from successful attempts by colonial administrators in India to realise profit from imperial possession of cannabis (Britain was already skilled in generating vast revenue from its illegal opium trade with China). In India, for example, considerable political as well as commercial effort was made to tax local cannabis producers leading to widespread smuggling across the sub-continent. Both Indian and, later, British newspaper reports of this trade, and the considerable administrative efforts to control it, embedded a link between cannabis, criminality and immorality in the public imagination.

Around the mid-nineteenth century, some physicians proselytised cannabis as a treatment for pain relief. However, others were reluctant to prescribe hemp-derived medicines citing British government reports that Indian mental asylums were filled with hemp-induced lunatics (this was closely allied with the notion that insanity was intrinsically immoral). But as Mills points out, British doctors neither understood the cultural context in which Indians presented for asylum admission, nor questioned asylum admission forms that required them to assign Indian lunatics a diagnostic category in which hemp-induced madness was convenient. In short, the notion that cannabis and madness were linked has embedded itself in the medical imagination.

It was not until 1928 that proscription on cannabis supply and use was introduced in Britain. Despite cannabis being virtually unknown, the country's cannabis laws began life when Egyptian officials attending League of Nations opium conferences (1924–25) pressed for international cannabis regulation.[3] Not knowing (or indeed caring) much about cannabis, delegates supported Egyptian demands (despite British efforts to oppose them) in order to move discussion on to the international opium trade. As a result of its obligations as a League of Nations member, Britain duly introduced cannabis legislation in 1928. This set in train a framework of British drug regulation as a response to international control treaties, not domestic problems (Barton 2003).

From this moment onwards, a regulatory regime emerged in which cannabis was associated with criminality and hard drugs (Blackman 2004). Mills makes the point that when cannabis became subject to strict laws under the Misuse of Drugs Act 1971 (where it received its classification as a Class B narcotic substance) it was based on unsound historical – essentially ideological – foundations in which political, cultural and moral imperatives masqueraded as 'informed' policy making. These imperatives have each contributed to a 'war on drugs' policy discourse 'with its indifference to accuracy and inherent fear of complexity and contradiction' (Parker *et al.* 1998: 1).

Parker *et al.*'s observation that drugs policy discourse conveys 'fear of complexity' is intended as a scathing indictment of government policy on drugs in the UK. They sum up their frustration with where this leaves drug prohibition discourse: 'Cannabis may as well be heroin, a weekend amphetamine user a crazed addict, a young woman who gives a friend an ecstasy tablet a drugs baron' (Parker *et al.* 1998: 10). Like Mills, they also note that moralising about illicit drug use has led to inappropriate public policy responses to the social complexities of illicit drug use (cf. McGregor 1999).

Tearing the moral fabric: cannabis users and (im)morality in the news media

The assumption that 'soft' drugs like cannabis lead inexorably to 'hard' drugs use is more than just media hysteria. It has helped shore up political orthodoxy on the moral virtue of cannabis prohibition from the 1920s through to the current decade. Since the 1960s, this orthodoxy has been at the centre of media discourse on the dangers of illicit drug use per se. It has posed a considerable ideological challenge to those who argue for legalisation of cannabis on the grounds that recreational use 'does no harm'.

Alongside prohibition has been a media discourse about drug takers. Critical commentaries on this discourse that emerged in the early 1970s, but which retain a contemporary resonance (e.g. Young 1971; Cohen 1973), identified a 'consensual paradigm' that sees the media portray drug takers as contrasting the normal 'us' with a deviant 'them', so constructing an ideological consensus. Thus, when moral panics periodically erupt, they shroud media representations of drug takers in a spiralling escalation of a perceived threat, a manning of the moral barricades by 'right-thinking people' and the pronouncement of diagnoses and solutions by 'socially accredited experts' (Cohen 1973: 9; cf. the discussion of the 'folk devil' in Pickering 2001: chapter 7). These pronouncements invariably contain demands for a strengthening of policy responses to the problem in order to reinforce the moral barricades.

Commenting on the complex notion of 'moral' in the concept of 'moral panics', Chas Critcher (2003: 147) posits that media constructions of morality are closely aligned with social anxiety located 'less in the general public than among strategically placed elites. The media ... and politicians are permanently oriented to moral issues'. Thus, in relation to cannabis, the media – including those 'socially accredited experts' who comment about drugs issues in the media – have historically enveloped its meaning as a 'dangerous' substance such that in countries like Britain, public discourse about cannabis use is deeply bound up with social anxiety about risks of drugs use per se.

Thus, in the years following the First World War, press coverage of cannabis became enmeshed in moral concern about the cunning and cruelty of foreigners (especially Chinamen) who imported drugs like opium and cocaine into Britain and then used them to corrupt young girls into sexual decadence (Kohn 2001). Despite being virtually unknown, papers reported that hashish trafficking in London was rife. In 1923, the *News Chronicle*, for example, announced that the country faced a 'Hashish Peril' and amplified social anxiety by stating that that there was 'a very serious growth in the traffic of hashish, a deadly Eastern drug which induces madness in this country' (quoted in Mills 2003: 198). The worrying news came with a warning that while police had broken a hashish trafficking ring, a 'dope peril' remained.

The 'peril' in question was opium but the link between hashish trafficking and opium trafficking had been made explicit. Kohn (2001: 180) has argued that in the inter-war era hashish was considered a morally worse substance than opium and cocaine 'because of its perception as an agent that facilitated contact between coloured men and young white women'.[4] Thus, soon after the hashish traffic story, the *Daily Mail* informed its readers: 'Hashish: Drug Forgotten By Law' and advised that 'urgent amendments are now needed to incorporate hashish within the Dangerous Drugs Act'.

The press's agitation on this issue was short-lived, but over subsequent decades illicit drug use was periodically framed within a discourse of moral anxiety. This is exemplified in a classic construction of cannabis users as 'folk devils'. In the summer of 1960, after a decade or so in which cannabis had become increasingly fashionable as a recreational drug (see Davenport-Hines 2002), a series of press exposes introduced British newspaper readers to the unearned leisure activities of Beatniks (here, the notion of 'unearned leisure' undermines the social balance between work and play, production and consumption). According to *The People*, the devil was making work for the Beats idle hands, which included rolling 'reefers':

> When 'Beatniks' get together there is often drug-taking to be found among them. That is perhaps the most alarming feature of the new cult. The principal drugs in beatnik use are benzedrine, dexedrine and marijuana. Marijuana is a weed grown principally in Mexico and sold for rolling into cigarettes called 'reefers'.
>
> (*The People* 31 July 1960 quoted in Murdock 1980: 61–62)

While the Beats have faded from popular memory, the image of delinquent youth 'cults' claiming particular drugs as their own has continued (Kohn 1999). Cannabis, though, is no longer associated with any particular sub-culture (see Becker 1963).

Acknowledging the pattern of its slippage from its bohemian and hippy base into working class leisure styles, it is important to note that Britain is now home to the largest number of cannabis users in the European Union (Barton 2003). One recent estimate posits that as many as 2 in 5 15-year-olds in Britain have tried cannabis, while 1 in 10 of those that have tried it have used it more than 40 times in one year (European Monitoring Centre for Drugs and Drug Addiction 2004). Consequently, while cannabis use undoubtedly remains a minority activity amongst young people, the notion that the 'moral fabric of society' is being torn is difficult to sustain.

Indeed, there exists a diverse youth-oriented media in which cannabis and other drugs are celebrated and valorised (Blackman 2004). This supports McRobbie and Thornton's (1995) reappraisal of the moral panic concept, in which they question whether in today's multi-media world, a 'univocal' media voice is possible. This implies that in a world of niche and micro-media (think pro-cannabis press and websites such as *High Times* – see: www.hightimes. com) the idea that there is a univocal moral consensus against drug users is a dated concept. Their observation is all the more pertinent when one considers that cannabis users have also attracted high profile media champions.

Friends in high places: increasing social acceptance of cannabis

It is a truism of the newspaper industry that editors do not pursue campaigns they cannot win. It was a surprise then, that shortly after her 1997 appointment as editor of the *Independent on Sunday* (IOS), Rosie Boycott announced she would use the paper to campaign for the legalisation of cannabis. As she explained in an open letter to the newly installed Labour Government 'drug tsar':

> We do not advocate the legalisation of all drugs, we do not say that heroin, cocaine and Ecstasy should be freely available. What we do say is that by decriminalising cannabis the 'gateway' phenomenon, where people are led to hard drugs because the dealer who sells them cannabis also offers heroin, would end.
>
> (*Independent on Sunday* 17 October 1997, p. 23)

Boycott's use of the IOS to campaign for cannabis legalisation was widely reported by fellow members of the press corps. Some praised her journalistic acumen for self-publicity while others poured scorn on her editorial judgement. Residing in the latter camp, *The Sun* newspaper, for example, fulminated that:

> The *Independent on Sunday* has gone to pot. Its editor has launched a campaign, backed by misguided celebrities, to legalise cannabis. Home Secretary Jack Straw took about 10 seconds to knock this nonsense on the head. Straw knows that soft drugs can be the first step on the road to heroin and cocaine.
>
> (*The Sun* 20 October 1997, p. 8)

Boycott was undeterred and her cannabis legalisation campaign continued until her departure from the paper two years later.

The IOS campaign coincided with the 1997 electoral success of New Labour, though the new government ruled out changes to drug laws (Parker 2001). Nevertheless, the campaign signalled a shift in elite attitudes toward the 'otherness' of cannabis use. As an IOS editorial put it: 'The [cannabis] campaign reveals attitudes are changing amongst Britain's power elite. The *Independent on Sunday* has received a significant boost with Lord Chief Justice Bingham calling for an inquiry into the drug laws' (*Independent on Sunday* 19 October 1997, p. 22). The notion that elite attitudes were changing can also be seen in the case of another high profile figure that attempted to make punishment for cannabis possession a defining issue for the political right.

At the 2000 Conservative Party annual conference, Anne Widdecombe, in her self-styled persona as redoubtable shadow Home Secretary, proposed 'zero tolerance' policing of cannabis users (including on-the-spot £100 fines) on the grounds that it would stop users moving on to hard drugs. However, her views on cannabis as a gateway drug were spectacularly undermined when seven front bench colleagues publicly declared that they had used cannabis in their youth and had not suffered long-term effects (on this point jokes in the press were rife!). During her remaining time in the shadow cabinet, Widdecombe made no further pronouncements on drug laws.

One might view the shadow cabinet's Brutus-like response to Widdecombe as evidence that drugs are on their way to normalisation, perhaps even a form of socio-legal 'distancing' from harder drugs like heroin. But as Kohn (2001: 184) points out, if cannabis 'were to be distanced, in law and by popular consent, from other presently illegal drugs, the illicit remainder might thereby be marginalised'. In other words, making cannabis a special case for normalisation means that consumers of other drugs are likely to suffer reinforced social exclusion arising from tabloid-inspired drug scares such as that surrounding opium in the 1920s and ecstasy in the 1980s.

Kohn, unlike Widdecombe, is attuned to broader changes taking place in Britain's cultural landscape such that cannabis and other drugs are now an integral part of the lifestyle of a significant minority in the mainstream population (Shapiro 1999). In this sense, Widdecombe's political miscalculation inadvertently gave notice that the cannabis user is less 'morally isolated' – a point underlined if we consider that her zero-tolerance initiative was announced only a few months after that traditional bastion of political conservatism, the *Daily Telegraph*, published an editorial arguing that 'the Government should draw up plans to legalise cannabis both for its consumption and for its supply' (*Daily Telegraph* 30 March 2000, p. 8).

Rethinking cannabis classification

In retrospect, then, it is Boycott's and not Widdecombe's views, which appear more in tune with changing public tolerance toward cannabis use. Indeed, across the 1990s public opinion surveys of perceived harms relating to illicit drug use show that cannabis is considered the least harmful of illicit drugs (Pearson and Shiner 2002).

A survey commissioned by the Independent Inquiry into the Misuse of Drugs Act (published in 2000 and cited in Pearson and Shiner 2002) notes that teenagers tend to distinguish cannabis from dangerous drugs, regard it more or less on a par with tobacco and alcohol, and many support some form of 'decriminalisation' policy.

However, while public opinion surveys in the 1990s show increasing public tolerance toward cannabis consumption, a record number were criminalised for cannabis possession in that decade. 'By 1999, 1 in 7 of known indictable offenders were cautioned or convicted for possession of cannabis. Pressure for reform of some sort was mounting' (Warburton *et al.* 2005: 114). It came in 2001 when the Parliamentary Home Affairs Select Committee announced that it would conduct its own inquiry into drugs laws and would support reclassification of cannabis if it believed that it would break the supposed link between cannabis use and hard drug use.

Shortly after the Select Committee gave notice of its enquiry, Home Secretary, David Blunkett, made his intentions clear by announcing he was minded to reclassify cannabis from Class B to Class C. Blunkett eventually reclassified cannabis based on three proven 'tests'. Firstly, in 2002 the Police Foundation's Advisory Council on the Misuse of Drugs announced its support for reclassification (as did the politically influential Police Superintendents Association). Second, the success of the 'softly softly' pilot scheme in Brixton to seize cannabis but not arrest users was deemed successful.[5] Thirdly, the Home Affairs Select Committee report on drugs advocated downgrading cannabis to Class C status (Summerskill and Ahmed 2002).

Changes in classification of cannabis also relate to government relaxation of rules (in 1997) allowing commercial trials for cannabis-based medicine. This is in keeping with rule changes in other European countries that allow for pharmaceutical involvement in growing cannabis for medical research. Blackman (2004: 183) points to the huge profits to be made: 'It is recognized that the illegal cannabis industry of recreational and therapeutic use is worth approximately £4 billion. Both multinationals and small-time capitalist entrepreneurs see the opportunity of profits to be gained now that the British law has taken a more relaxed approach to the drug'.

Together, these elements opened a window of opportunity for cannabis law reform – a policy opportunity that occurs infrequently (Lenton 2004) because it must navigate the political realm where politicians are mindful of not being seen as 'soft on drugs'. Thus, it is not the case that cannabis reform was the outcome of contest either in public arenas or as a response to the intractability of the recreational drugs problem. As Mugford (1993) argues, changes in drugs policies relate to the State's pragmatic attempts to regulate bodily behaviour. It is noteworthy, then, that despite reclassifying cannabis to Class C, Blunkett simultaneously increased the maximum penalty for supplying all Class C drugs to 14 years' imprisonment – the same as for Class B.

Disturbed states: cannabis reclassification and themes in press discourse

The social history of illicit drug use in Britain, according to Davenport-Hines (2001: xi), is 'the history of one bad idea, prohibition'. While this a moot point, what is certain is that prohibition policies have engendered ambivalence in successive government thinking about drugs issues, which in turn reveals an uneasy alternation between criminal justice/enforcement strategies and public health/'harm reduction' approaches (see Barton 2003). Both these strategies/approaches have formed a dual track on which the motor of British policy on illicit drugs arguably chugs along.

The political significance of Blunkett's decision to reclassify the legal status of cannabis is that it challenges a hard prohibitionist line. However, we have noted that some sections of the right-wing press (e.g. *The Mail* and *Telegraph* groups) had already given support in the late 1990s for reform of cannabis laws and welcomed a 2002 report from the Advisory Council on the Misuse of Drugs (part of the Police Foundation) that showed police support for downgrading cannabis to Class C (Warburton *et al.* 2004). However, the same media groups quickly developed a hostile line once it became evident that Blunkett was *actually* heading for reform.

In the remainder of this chapter, I want to draw on this general atmosphere of press equivocation on cannabis reform to illustrate how aspects of the 'enforcement' and 'public health' approaches were framed in news discourse. In particular, two themes have been selected from an abundance of news coverage and commentary that enable us to glimpse tensions in public discourse about cannabis reform. They are, firstly, that the politics of cannabis reform has resulted in public confusion about the legality of cannabis use and, secondly, that cannabis reclassification flies in the face of medical safety warnings that cannabis use causes serious mental illness.

Hazy state: cannabis reclassification and the confused smoker

When cannabis reclassification took place in January 2004 the issue for many newspaper commentators was one of concern that cannabis users were being given confusing or mixed messages about whether it was illegal/legal to consume cannabis. Thus, for example, the *Daily Telegraph* took aim at the Government's decision to retain mandatory powers of arrest for cannabis users under the age of 18:

> It will be possible that an adult smoking cannabis in one county will get off with a warning while someone elsewhere will be arrested and gain a criminal record … Penalising users was proving a huge drain on police resources at a time when most people wanted more officers on the beat. A typical case of minor possession can take officers off the streets for five hours, cost £10,000 to bring to court and lead to an average fine of £45 … Yet under the change that comes into force next Thursday the police will still be required to arrest young cannabis users – thus defeating the original object of the change and causing total confusion among users of the drug.
>
> (*Daily Telegraph* 23 January 2004, p. 4)

As we noted above, the *Daily Telegraph*'s position on reform of cannabis laws has wavered. But this is no obstacle to its willingness to point out that cannabis policies are in 'total confusion' and that the original object of policy change (enabling police officers to avoid costly and time consuming administration) is undermined. Similarly, Simon Jenkins's polemical feature article in *The Times*, 'Drugs turn the brains of politicians into marzipan' (23 January 2004), highlights the alternation in government policy between enforcement and harm reduction as a result of political appeasement:

> Mr Blunkett has finally decided to reclassify cannabis, yet has achieved almost nothing. Before doing so – presumably to head off the right wing

[critics] – he quietly altered the penalties attaching to Class C, making them similar to Class B. Possession of cannabis thus remains subject to arrest and imprisonment. So Mr Blunkett has now the very worst of political worlds. People think that he has gone soft on cannabis when he has not. Cannabis remains illegal. The only difference is in public confusion.

(*The Times* 23 January 2004, p. 28)

Cannabis reclassification has resulted in 'public confusion' but it is only later in the article that Jenkins makes clear what he thinks could remedy this: 'Drugs must some day be legalised and controlled. In the meantime, [drugs] policy must at least make sense' (p. 28). Jenkins's view is that legalising all drugs will help reduce their consumption and criminal profits. And as he goes on to point out, this has resulted in taxpayers having to pay a £1million bill for a government advertising campaign now required to 'remind people about the continued illegal status of cannabis' (p. 28).

For the *Daily Mail* (24 January 2004), the launch of the aforementioned government advertising campaign has been forced on ministers because of unnecessary confusion that their policy change has caused. But contained in its assessment of why such an advertising campaign is deemed necessary can also be found an appeal to the ultimate *raison d'etre* for retaining cannabis as a Class B drug – its impact on children:

> Government ministers are being forced to launch a £1 million campaign to remind people that cannabis is still illegal … Many within the Government are now concerned the decision to reclassify cannabis as no more dangerous than painkillers is sending the wrong message. The United Nations drugs watchdog has already criticised the move to downgrade cannabis from a Class B to a Class C drug. It points out that Home Secretary David Blunkett's decision has caused total confusion and misunderstanding across the world. Research suggests that nine out of ten children believe that the drug is now legal in Britain, while the public is largely ignorant about the health risks.
>
> (*Daily Mail* 24 January 2004, p. 8)

The *Daily Mail* is the one national daily paper 'whose tone and agenda is closest to the 1960/1970s-style moral panic' (McRobbie and Thornton 1995: 568). Certainly, in this extract what is evident is not just the folly of reclassifying cannabis from a Class B to a Class C drug (at this stage in national press coverage, the *Mail* is the only daily tabloid newspaper *overtly* opposing cannabis reclassification per se) but that 'the wrong message' has been sent (internationally). To ground this point, and also pack it with as much moral import that the newspaper can muster, the most confused are children with the clear implication being that they will now inevitably grow up in a climate of misunderstanding about cannabis that puts their future health at risk.

Mental state: cannabis reclassification and the psychotic smoker

Of course, only the most heinous of adults (or political opponents) would put the 'future health' of children at risk, and the paper's readers are left to ponder on this despicable scenario. But what the future health risk(s) might be exactly are not discussed. A possible clue was helpfully provided by the *Daily Mail's* sister paper, the *Mail on Sunday*, a few days earlier. Revelling in its starkness, the paper's editorial asked: 'What will Britain be like when there's a whole generation hearing voices in their heads?' (18 January 2004, p. 27). Turning to newly published research on 'cannabis psychosis', it offered this sombre assessment:

> There's one clear conclusion: the younger you are when you first try cannabis and the stronger it is, the more likely it is that you will develop psychosis, delusions or manic depression. There are numerous documented instances of cannabis users claiming to have heard voices in their heads. And only last week there was a tragic example of the damage long-term cannabis use can do. Robert Dickenson, an [sic] habitual user of cannabis since he starting smoking to cope with arthritis, shot his neighbour dead in a feud over a garden hedge.
>
> *(Mail on Sunday* 18 January 2004, p. 27)

Therein lies the answer to the *Mail on Sunday's* rhetorical question: Britain will be a topsy-turvy world where the normality of neighbourliness will be replaced by the insanity of drug-induced murder. Robert Dickenson, a man whose cannabis-habit began in an effort to self-medicate, was (presumably) unaware that his cannabis use would lead to dangerous 'voices' in his head. Two days on from this article, the *Daily Mail* was less reticent about naming the mental health risks, and under the headline 'Cannabis Catastrophe', told the story of Dominique Landsdowne's cannabis-induced paranoia:

> Eleven years ago, when she was 18, the former care assistant from Swansea started smoking cannabis once a week. It very nearly destroyed her ... 'I'm positive cannabis was the cause; I became paranoid as soon as I started smoking it. I've known hundreds of people who smoke it and all of them have some kind of paranoia or a problem, whether they recognise it or not.' All of which makes it truly extraordinary that this Thursday, cannabis will be downgraded from a Class B to a Class C drug. The Home Secretary's move has delighted the drug legalisers – but astonished and horrified those, like Dominique, who know the truth about its effects.
>
> *(Daily Mail* 26 January 2004, p. 10)

Here, Dominique's testimony adds the weight of personal experience to medical criticism (outlined later in the story) that the government are to blame for encouraging people to take cannabis ('thinking it's not going to do them any harm'). Her story of cannabis-induced paranoia becomes a stick to beat the Home Secretary. Perhaps less obviously, the extract also shows how easily clinical paranoia and political paranoia can be fused! What is especially interesting about this feature on cannabis psychosis is that the writer, Melanie Phillips, uses Dominique's story to collapse a number of overlapping themes as contributory elements to the unfolding 'cannabis catastrophe':

Before she used cannabis she had not even smoked tobacco; afterwards, she also tried speed, LSD and ecstasy. 'I would never have touched hard drugs if I hadn't taken cannabis,' she says. 'Reclassification is really dreadful and sad because the Government is saying cannabis isn't that bad, so people are going to take it thinking it's not going to do them any harm.' Dominique is not alone in her concerns. Metropolitan Police Commissioner Sir John Stevens says there is a 'massive amount of muddle' surrounding the reclassification. The British Medical Association has expressed alarm that the move is sending out the wrong message. Panicked by the backlash, the Home Office has rushed out leaflets to tell the public that cannabis is still illegal and still dangerous. But it has been badly wrongfooted [sic] by recent scientific evidence suggesting that Dominique Lansdowne's experience is now horrifyingly commonplace.

(*Daily Mail* 26 January 2004, p. 11)

Herein lies a familiar moral reaction: 'I would never have touched hard drugs if I hadn't taken cannabis'. Dominique's 'horrifyingly commonplace' experience is thus rooted not in her own personal choice to consume cannabis but in a wider abrogation of political responsibility to reinforce the moral message that cannabis is 'still illegal and (consequently) still dangerous'. Conveniently, for the paper, the abstract notion of 'still dangerous' assumes human form in 'the hundreds of people who smoke it' and in whom Dominique detects paranoia, 'whether they recognise it or not'.

Similarly, in a *Times* feature article entitled 'If Cannabis is Safe, Why am I Psychotic?', Steve Boggan uses testimony from psychotic cannabis users to highlight how scientific evidence that cannabis is dangerous to mental health jars with the logic of downgrading cannabis from Class B to Class C. After outlining details of Steve Hammond's psychosis, and its impact on his family, the story makes clear that reclassification is a precursor for greater incidence of psychosis in urban centres:

Steve is one of 210,000 people in the UK who suffer from schizophrenia, and one of a growing number who believe that cannabis caused their condition. Ten years ago psychiatrists would have disagreed with him. But three weeks before the Government is due to reclassify cannabis from a Class B to a Class C drug, that view has changed dramatically. Some of Britain's most senior psychiatrists say the drug is now the 'Number 1 problem' facing mental health services. Psychiatrists in inner city areas speak of cannabis being a factor in up to 80 per cent of schizophrenia cases, and mental health specialists are bracing themselves for an increase in the problem as reclassification is misinterpreted as an assurance that the drug is safe.

(*The Times* 7 January 2004, p. 4)

Boggan's article duly summarises recent scientific evidence that links cannabis to serious mental illness. It concludes by asking whether cannabis reclassification sends out a particular message to young people about its supposed safety. Steve's father is given the final word: 'Of course it sends a message,' he says. 'After Steve became psychotic I spoke to a lot of his friends about cannabis and they all thought it was perfectly safe – and they felt that the reclassification confirmed that. Since then I have been contacted by lots and lots of parents who believe cannabis was a major factor in their sons and daughters slipping into psychosis. I have no doubt it caused Steve's'.

Conclusion

As I write these final remarks, the politics and policy of cannabis reclassification in Britain is again experiencing winds of change. The current Home Secretary, Charles Clarke, mindful of scientific evidence that strains of cannabis like skunk can cause psychosis, asked the Advisory Council on the Misuse of Drugs (ACMD) to revisit the classification of cannabis (January 2006). At the same time, the press once more defined its position on the issue in relation to the lobbying agendas of a variety of pro- or anti-cannabis groups and organisations, each of which sought to promote their own political or policy stake in the reclassification issue.

The writer Blake Morrison debated the issues at stake in typically measured fashion. Writing in *The Guardian* newspaper (16 December 2005, p. 23), Morrison noted how new scientific studies on 'cannabis psychosis' had resulted in a surprisingly quick embrace of the research amongst pro-medical mental health charities. He proceeded to identify high profile liberals whose pro-legalisation of cannabis position had recently become realigned with the drug prohibitionists:

> A ... spectacular volte-face has been that of Rosie Boycott, who as editor of the *Independent on Sunday* in 1997 led an influential campaign to legalise cannabis: 'if alcohol is a tiger', the paper declared, 'then cannabis is a mouse. Everyone has probably known someone whose life – or family – has been blighted by alcohol, heroin or cocaine ... Certainly no one has ever been disfigured by a joint.' By the summer of 2005, though, Boycott did know people whose lives and families had been blighted by cannabis; she made a television programme and wrote a long and detailed piece in the *Daily Mail* entitled 'The Cannabis Catastrophe' that explained why 'cannabis users today are playing Russian roulette with their mental health'.
>
> (*The Guardian* 16 December 2005, p. 23)

In her original *Daily Mail* article (18 May 2005, pp. 11–12) Boycott outlined her past political opposition on cannabis prohibition and noted that her *Independent on Sunday* campaign had led to the reclassification of cannabis. She then asked: 'So what is it that had changed the relatively mild drug which so charmed my generation into today's monster'? Her answer is that skunk was responsible for turning some young people into 'crazed killers'. She then called 'for a new cannabis campaign – one that makes it clear that smoking skunk can destroy some young lives for ever'.

Boycott's concern that new strains of cannabis might be a trigger for mental health problems is justified, though it remains an open scientific question as to whether skunk causes psychosis (see the discussion of recent scientific reports on cannabis psychosis in Henderson 2005). But as this chapter has shown, attitudes toward cannabis and its users have historically been informed not by scientific judgment but moral concern about where it might lead. In this context, Boycott's claim that smoking skunk leads some young people to become 'crazed killers' revitalises debunked notions of 'reefer madness' (see Davenport-Hines 2002) whereby cannabis consumption inevitably leads the user to a life of criminality and moral degeneracy.

It also remains uncertain as to what Boycott's 'new cannabis campaign' might aim to achieve and where and how it might be promoted. The most obvious promotional vehicle is the press but as this chapter illustrates, cannabis is a weed that can and does grows to monstrous proportions when cultivated in print. Indeed, those who use cannabis in print form, whether enthusiasts or opponents, often report effects that go well beyond the natural impact of its psychoactive properties.

For example, tension, contradiction, as well as some political paranoia, appeared evident in the few days between the ACMD handing over its report to the Home Secretary and the public announcement of Clarke's decision on cannabis classification. Thus, some members of the ACMD publicly threatened resignation if Clarke reclassified cannabis back to Class B status. They need not have worried.

In the end, Clarke's decision was to retain cannabis's Class C status and announce a £1 million information campaign to remind the public that cannabis remains illegal and also a risk to mental health. In the context of mounting political concern about the future social (including health) costs of cannabis psychosis, one can view this either as a judicious use of public money or a case of preaching to the converted. Whilst this is a moot point, then, what *is* certain is that it will not remove the cloud of morality, ambivalence and uncertainty that hangs over the cannabis user.

Notes

1 Thanks to Dr Michael Pickering for comments on an earlier draft of this chapter.
2 This is not to say that there has been inter-agency consensus between the Home Office (historically responsible for the criminal law and punishment of drug users) and various incarnations of the Department of Health (responsible for providing the medical treatment of illicit drug users). Indeed, there has been an evident 'power struggle' over the implementation of British drug policy between criminal punishment and medical treatment (see the discussion in Barton 2003: 131–132).
3 They appear to have done so primarily for domestic political purposes, i.e. as a reaction against continuing British involvement in opium trafficking in Egypt following the country's political liberation from British rule.
4 A similar moral anxiety about miscegenation can be found in US news media in the same era. In the 1920s, prohibitionists in the Federal Bureau of Narcotics identified marijuana use by Mexican migrant workers and blacks as a major new criminal menace (drugs and sexual relations between white women and non-white men were

a heady combination for journalists). By the mid-1930s, anti-marijuana propaganda in US newspapers cited public demand for tough news laws to control cannabis use.

5 A key figure in the Brixton cannabis pilot scheme was Metropolitan Police Commander, Brian Paddick. Paddick's management of the Brixton scheme coupled with his open acknowledgement that he is gay rendered him a high-profile target for the tabloid press. This intensified when his employers, following allegations by his former partner that Paddick had allowed cannabis use in his home, suspended him. He was eventually exonerated and resumed his post.

References and suggested reading

Barton, A. (2003) *Illicit Drugs: Use and Control*. London: Routledge.

Becker, H. (1963) *Outsiders: Studies in the Sociology of Deviance*. New York: Free Press.

Berridge, V. (1988) 'The Origins of the English Drug "Scene", 1890–1930', *Medical History*, 32: 51–64.

Blackman, S. (2004) *Chilling Out: The Cultural Politics of Substance Consumption, Youth and Drug Politics*. Maidenhead: Open University Press.

Blake, A. (1996) 'Foreign Devils and Moral Panics: The Anglo-Indian Opium Trade with China', in B. Schwarz (ed.) *The Expansion of England: Essays in Postcolonial Cultural History*, pp 232–259. London: Routledge.

Cohen, S. (1973) *Folk Devils and Moral Panics*. St Albans: Paladin.

Critcher, C. (2003) *Moral Panics and the Media*. Buckingham: Open University Press.

Davenport-Hines, R. (2002) *The Pursuit of Oblivion: A Social History of Drugs*. London: Phoenix Press.

Henderson, M. (2005) 'One in Four at Risk of Cannabis Psychosis', *The Times*, 12 April, p. 7.

Kohn, M. (2001) *Dope Girls: The Birth of the British Drug Underground*. London: Granta.

Lenton, S. (2004) 'Pot, Politics and the Press-reflections on Cannabis Law Reform in Western Australia', *Harm Reduction Digest*, 23: 223–233.

McRobbie, A. and Thornton, S. (1995) 'Rethinking "Moral Panic" for Multi-mediated Social Worlds', *British Journal of Sociology*, 46 (4): 559–574.

MacCoun, R.J. and Reuter, P. (2001) *Drug War Heresies: Learning from Other Vices, Times, and Places*. Cambridge: Cambridge University Press.

MacGregor, S. (1999) 'Medicine, Custom or Moral Fibre: Policy Responses to Drug Misuse', in N. South (ed.) *Drugs: Cultures, Controls and Everyday Life*, pp 67–85. London: Sage.

Mills, J. (2003) *Cannabis Britannica: Empire, Trade, and Prohibition 1800–1928*. Oxford: Oxford University Press.

Mugford, S. (1993) 'Social Change and the Control of Psychotropic Drugs – Risk Management, Harm Reduction and "Postmodernity"', *Drug and Alcohol Review*, 12: 369–375.

Murdock, G. (1980) *Adolescent Culture and the Mass Media*, Final Report to the Social Science Research Council. Leicester: Centre for Mass Communication Research.

Parker, H., Aldridge, J. and Measham, F. (1998) *Illegal Leisure: The Normalization of Adolescent Recreational Drug Use*. London: Routledge.

Pearson, G. and Shiner, M. (2002) 'Rethinking the Generation Gap: Attitudes to Illicit Drugs among Young People and Adults', *Criminal Justice*, 2 (1): 71–86.

Pickering, M. (2001) *Stereotyping: The Politics of Representation*. London: Palgrave.

Shapiro, H. (1999) 'Dances with Drugs: Pop Music, Drugs and Youth Culture', in N. South (ed.) *Drugs: Cultures, Controls and Everyday Life*, pp 17–35. London: Sage.

Summerskill, B. and Ahmed, K. (2002) 'Blunkett will Legislate to Downgrade Cannabis'. *The Observer*, 21 April 2002, p. 1.

Warburton, H., May, T. and Hough, M. (2005) 'Looking the Other Way: The Impact of Reclassifying Cannabis on Police Warnings, Arrests and Informal Action in England and Wales', *British Journal of Criminology*, 45 (2): 113–128.

Young, J. (1971) *The Drugtakers*. London: Paladin.

8. The symbolic framing of drug use in the news: ecstasy and volatile substance abuse in newspapers

Paul Manning

Introduction

Declining circulations and the proliferation of alternative 'new media' sources of news might lead one to question whether newspapers should continue to be regarded as significant examples of popular culture. But the role of the newspapers in popular culture cannot be assessed simply in terms of circulation figures; newspapers remain important because of the way in which they contribute themes, phrases, imagery, inferential frameworks, to the circulation and reproduction of popular ideas. Journalism is still part of, not separate from popular culture (Dahlgren 1992: 18). This chapter is concerned with the symbolic frameworks that organise the representation of substance misuse, or illicit drug consumption, in national newspapers. Surprisingly, there are relatively few recent textual studies of the ways in which the consumption of different substances is represented in news discourse, one exception being Giulianotti (1997).

In this analysis, symbolic frameworks found in contemporary news discourse are understood to consist of four elements that organise the symbolic representation of drugs as substances and the cultural practices associated with their consumption. These symbolic frameworks will usually contain symbols of *location*, or, in other words, they will signify particular places or spaces where different kinds of substance misuse will occur. These frameworks will also symbolically represent, or signify, particular *behaviours and identities* that are associated with particular kinds of substance misuse. In other words, these symbolic frameworks highlight the cultural practices associated with drug consumption or substance misuse, and associate particular social groups or identities with the consumption of different kinds of substances. Thirdly, these symbolic frameworks contain *substance images*; they signify the actual substances consumed in particular ways, together with the drug paraphernalia, equipment, or technologies of consumption. Finally, these symbolic frameworks are likely to include symbols that suggest particular *causes* and particular *consequences* for readers in 'making sense' of different patterns of drug consumption or substance misuse.

The symbolic association of particular patterns of drug use with certain kinds of people, particular social groups and identities, certainly *has* been

150

frequently explored before (for example, Reeves and Campbell 1994; Kohn 1992; Musto 1973). Some attention has been given to the symbolisation of drug paraphernalia or equipment (Manderson 1995). These studies all illustrate the way in which understandings of drug consumption have been frequently racialised and gendered; in seeking to understand substance misuse as a cultural practice, both political and news discourses in the US and Britain have frequently associated drug use with particular *kinds* of people, consuming drugs in particular locations and in particular ways. And the perceived risks, both to the individual and society, are often estimated through the prism of these symbolic frameworks. Perception of risk seems to depend partly upon what kind of people are involved in illicit or licit drug consumption, and upon the ways in which they are doing it. Thus, to take one example discussed in earlier chapters, opium swallowed by bourgeois women as a medicinal compound within the home in the late-nineteenth century was accepted with some reservations by polite society; opium smoked by Chinese migrants in opium dens, a few decades later was most certainly not (Musto 1973). Risk here was contingent upon ethnicity, gender, and location.

This chapter will explore the differing symbolic frameworks involved in newspaper reporting of volatile substance abuse (VSA) and ecstasy. VSA can involve a bewildering range of substances widely available in shops or in the home. Glue sniffing was strongly associated with the youth subcultures of the 1970s but many of the solvents have been removed from the manufacturing process and the use of glue in VSA has declined. On the other hand, use of gas fuels (mainly lighter fuel) has increased significantly, while aerosols (hair spray, air freshener, etc.), paint, petrol, domestic cleaning agents, etc., are also frequently used. St. Georges Hospital, South London, lists 1,959 separate substances in its analysis of data between 1971 and 1999 (Field-Smith, Taylor, Norman *et al.* 2001). Unlike the consumption of officially classified, illicit drugs, VSA does not involve the use of illegal substances but only their consumption in unsanctioned ways. VSA is, thus, an illustration of the blurring of the boundaries between licit and illicit substance use identified by Measham, Aldridge, and Parker, as a feature of contemporary Britain (2001: 16).

The chapter begins by noting the disproportionate attention devoted to the risks associated with ecstasy and the relative lack of national newspaper interest in VSA despite a significantly greater 'risk', if measured by annual mortality rates. The intention is to show that the symbolic frameworks used to represent ecstasy and VSA in newspaper coverage point to widely shared cultural assumptions that partly explain the lack of attention given to VSA. However, the reproduction of these symbolic frameworks, and the associated cultural assumptions, depends in part upon processes that are political and material, as well as cultural. Indeed, the forces at play along each of these three dimensions interplay to produce the reproduction of symbolic frameworks. These ideas will be developed further in the second half of this chapter.

The invisibility of VSA and the over-representation of ecstasy

The news media preoccupation with the dangers of ecstasy and the inclination of certain sections of the media to represent ecstasy in terms of a moral panic framework have been well documented (Wykes 2001; Palmer 2000; Jenkins 1999). The intensity of news media coverage often has an important influence upon government thinking and resource allocation. Critics suggest that the intermittent periods of intense news media coverage of ecstasy, often structured around the 'Leah Betts template', have disrupted the development of coherent harm-reduction strategies and prompted the government to revert to enforcement approaches to appease sections of the press (Measham, Aldridge and Parker 2001; Shapiro 1993). But the intensity of media interest in the risks or threats posed by some drugs can mean that other substance related risks are neglected. The history of VSA policy is a case in point, not only in the UK but in other countries, too (D'Abbs and Brady 2004). The year 1990 represented the peak of VSA-related deaths in the UK when 152 deaths were recorded (Field-Smith et al. 2001: 19) and yet significant policy measures to address the problem only emerged in the late 1990s when regulations concerning the sale of solvent-based products and lighter refills began to be tightened and the Home Office added VSA to the 'templates' or targets specified for regional Drugs Action Teams.

In earlier research (Manning 2006), a simple quantitative content analysis was used to demonstrate the over-representation of ecstasy in national newspaper coverage and the significant under-representation of VSA. The study included the years 1993, 1996, 1999 and 2003 and searched 18 national daily and Sunday English and Scottish papers for news reports including 'significant mentions' of either ecstasy or VSA. Further details of the research are to be found in Manning (2006). In 1999, for example, 212 reports appeared concerning ecstasy but only 46 concerning VSA, while in 2002, 663 items concerned ecstasy and only 50 dealt with VSA. In 1993, 145 ecstasy stories appeared and only 32 VSA stories and in 1996 the respective figures were 464 and 12.

In what sense do these figures indicate an over-representation of ecstasy and an under-representation of VSA? An expectation that news coverage 'represented reality' in a perfect correspondence is, of course, highly problematic. And to treat drug-related mortality data as perfect measures of the 'the extent of the problem' would be equally problematic, though there are good reasons to suppose that the official mortality data underestimates, rather than overestimates actual deaths (Bland and Taylor 1998). Nevertheless, the extent to which there is a lack of correspondence between the distribution of news items and the relative risks of ecstasy and VSA is important. If we compare drug related mortality results we find that despite the relative lack of newspaper interest, VSA represented a significantly greater risk of death. In recent years, the numbers dying through VSA have dropped considerably from the 1990 peak to just 47 in 2004 (Field-Smith et al. 2006: 6). And yet even now, VSA produces a higher mortality rate with a total of 148 deaths in England and Wales between 2001 and 2003 (Field-Smith et al. 2006), compared to 143 for ecstasy (European Monitoring Centre for Drugs and Drug Addiction 2005).

During the period in which the newspaper content analysis took place, the disparity was even more striking. According to the Office of National

Statistics (ONS), 78 people died in England and Wales, as a consequence of taking ecstasy between 1995 and 1999 (ONS 2001). In Scotland, between 1996 and 1999, there were 22 ecstasy-related deaths recorded in the official figures (Drugscope 2002, drawing upon Jackson and Cole 2000). In the same period, there were at least 388 VSA-related deaths (Field-Smith, Bland, Taylor *et al.* 2002). In other words, VSA deaths were usually four or five times greater than ecstasy-related deaths during the 1990s. Based upon an estimate of the population regularly using ecstasy, again drawn from the British Crime Survey, Drugscope calculated that the risk of death from taking ecstasy was approximately 0.00005 per cent – roughly the same as riding a horse or driving a car. According to the European Monitoring Centre for Drugs and Drug Addiction (ECMDDA) ecstasy contributes approximately 0.8 per cent of drug related deaths in England and Wales each year (ECMDDA 2005).

VSA is a particular problem for younger teenagers and, at least, 20 per cent of VSA related deaths are first time users (Johns 1991). VSA is a serious problem, both for substance abusers and their families. VSA is associated with poly-drug use, crime and other behavioural problems experienced by young people (Goulden and Sondhi 2001). Neither VSA, nor ecstasy use, produce the death toll associated with opiates (more than 700 per year in the UK). Nevertheless, one might anticipate that this issue would be of interest to the national news media, given the ratio of four or five VSA deaths to every ecstasy-related death through the 1990s to 2002. To reinforce the point, the majority of VSA-related deaths occur within the home (59 per cent according to Field-Smith *et al.* 2006: 17). There is plenty of material here for stories with a human interest angle but few opportunities were taken to frame VSA news stories in terms of the 'the threat to our young', or the 'menace within the home'. VSA involves the illicit consumption of everyday household commodities, frequently stored within easy reach of young children, and yet, the content analysis demonstrated how infrequently these kinds of news narratives were developed.

Marginalisation, power and cultural reproduction: explaining the invisibility of VSA

An explanation for the relative invisibility of VSA in national news coverage has to explore the ways in which structures of power and disadvantage intersect with the processes of cultural reproduction through which cultures, including popular cultures, are made and re-made. The symbolic frameworks that represent drug consumption and substance misuse are part of this and, as we shall see below, they also contribute to the processes that render VSA invisible in national news coverage.

Power and systematic disadvantage work in three ways relevant to this analysis. We need to examine the politics of news sources and the strategies employed by organisations seeking to promote their own agendas in mainstream news agendas. Secondly, we have to think about the position of those most likely to be involved in either VSA or ecstasy use. Thirdly, we have to consider the ways in which structures of power intersect with the cultural assumptions made by journalists in their work and as they select and construct drug news

(a) News sources and official definitions

One of the reasons that the death of Leah Betts as a consequence of taking ecstasy in 1995 become so well-known was that her parents were determined to publicise the risks, as they understood them. They encouraged the circulation of the 'death bed' photograph of their daughter that offered news organisations a powerful set of symbols with which to construct the framework of ecstasy as a deadly threat, and they established the Leah Betts Trust, which developed an active, sophisticated news media strategy (Palmer 2000: 20–22). However, this, in itself, cannot explain the over-representation of ecstasy in news and the under-representation of VSA. There are at least three comparable organisations, established by parents who have lost their children through VSA. All three – Solv It, the Chantelle Bleau Memorial Fund, and Lee O'Brien Solvent Trust – have grown to the point where they are in dialogue with government ministers and journalists. A fourth organisation, Re-Solv, was established with funding from the solvents industry but now receives income from a variety of sources, including the EU. Its political influence has been strengthened through the appointment of a former Conservative MP as director.

So the policy field is populated with news media-active organisations seeking to move both ecstasy and VSA further up the news agenda. There is a large literature that explores the politics of news sources and concludes that while more politically marginal groups can secure access to news media agendas in particular instances, through the skilful use of material and symbolic resources, over the longer term the powerful are able to exploit the routines of news production to privilege their definitions of events and their agenda priorities (Schlesinger and Tumber 1994; Manning 2001). According to Critcher (2003: 59), ecstasy continues to be regarded as problematic by the powerful because the symbolic meanings associated with it transgress norms of risk avoidance and bodily discipline. Now these 'pleasures' may also be available to those involved in VSA (MacClean 2005) but this may be one illustration of the way in which symbolic frameworks can intersect with structures and processes of power. The symbolic framework in which VSA is commonly 'understood' by the powerful may not encourage VSA to be associated with the same bodily excess.

Governments can, of course, shape news agendas through the way in which departments define priorities and allocate resources. For journalists, the exercise of power is by definition newsworthy. Specialist correspondents in the relevant fields of health, home affairs and criminal justice will take, at least in part, their information through the flows generated by initiatives and debates associated with particular state departments. The tightening of regulations concerning the sale of lighter refills (1999) was not likely to capture correspondents' imagination unless the government accompanied this with a louder policy fanfare. VSA, as we have seen, has only recently been added to the Drugs Action Team (DAT) template, which drives strategy and objectives for regional DATs. Even the Advisory Council on the Misuse of Drugs annual report has given VSA relatively little attention. In short, then, part of the explanation for the virtual absence of VSA stories in the national newspapers is to do with the configuration of power relations in the substance misuse policy arena.

(b) VSA and the marginalised

There is a process of double marginalisation at work in the case of VSA. Young people from a variety of backgrounds may become involved with VSA but those most marginalised are most likely to resort to it (MacClean 2005; D'Abbs and Brady 2004; Collinson 1996; Ashton 1990). But secondly, experiencing frustration in trying to get agencies to help seems to be a common experience for parents in lower socio-economic groups (Jagger 1996). Estimates of the extent of VSA vary. The European School Survey project which gathers data on those aged 16 in the year of the survey concludes that 12 per cent of their UK respondents had 'lifetime experiences' of using inhalants (ESPAD 2006). An earlier self-report study suggested that up to 22 per cent of those aged between 14 and 15, living in the north-west of England had been offered solvents but that those from lower socio-economic groups were more likely to be in 'offer situations' (Measham, Newcombe and Parker 1993).

The desire to use illicit or licit drugs to alter states of consciousness may be common amongst young people from all social backgrounds, but access to supplies of illicit drugs is not evenly distributed but dependent upon economic resources, age, and to an extent, gender. VSA is a 'blocked drug opportunity' strategy for those who lack either the economic resources, or social networks, necessary to obtain sufficient supplies of alternative, recreational drugs. This is why VSA normally declines with age (Ramsey et al. 2001), though there has been a recent increase in deaths amongst older teenagers (Field-Smith et al. 2006). As young people grow older they normally acquire more money and more access to the local supply networks for a wider range of recreational drugs. It is the most marginalised of the young, those with least access to economic and cultural resources, who are most likely to resort to VSA. Those excluded from school, school refusers and particularly female truants, persistent and minor offenders, runaways, and the young homeless are all more likely to turn to VSA (Goulden and Sondhi 2001). Standardised mortality ratios rise the further one travels from the south-east towards the north of the UK (Field-Smith et al. 2006). Boys may contribute almost four times as many deaths as girls but it is the least visible, most marginalised and most distant from the metropolitan political and media elites who are most likely to be involved in VSA. We know that ecstasy use is not associated only with the economically marginalised (Riley and Hayward 2004: 244). In the minds of journalists might it be that ecstasy is regarded as more newsworthy because it is understood as a threat even to 'respectable', middle-class families, in contrast to VSA? This question brings us back to the symbolic frameworks within which different substances are constructed, understood, and, of course, represented in news media.

(c) Journalists, power and the symbolic frameworks of substance misuse

National news journalists are recruited from an increasingly narrow social background according to recent research undertaken for the Sutton Trust. Over half (54 per cent) of the leading 100 print and broadcast editors, columnists, and news presenters within UK news organisations were educated privately and almost half (45 per cent) went to either Oxford or Cambridge Universities (Major 2006: 4). While the staff within the metropolitan media elites are drawn from increasingly narrow and privileged backgrounds, they can have little first-hand knowledge of the experiences of the least visible, most marginal young people at risk from VSA. Michael Schudson once argued that we should pay more attention to the 'cultural givens', or underlying assumptions that shape the way journalists understand the world because they were the source of the 'generalised images and stereotypes' that organised news copy (1991: 151).

These 'generalised images and stereotypes' are likely to contribute to the construction of the symbolic frameworks in which particular kinds of drug consumption or substance misuse are 'understood' and represented in the news media. Schudson suggested that we returned to Mary Douglas's work on taboo and pollution in order to explore the 'cultural givens' underpinning journalists' practice and we have already noted the value of this approach in relation to exploring drugs as popular culture in Chapter 1 (Manning in this volume). The news media will play an important role in classifying drug consumption as trangressive pollution (Giulianotti 1997; Manderson 1995) which, of course is indicated in the phrase 'substance *mis*use' – the inappropriate use of substances, or 'matter out of place' as Mary Douglas defined pollution (1966). Substance misuse and the drug paraphernalia, or equipment, associated with it, can generate powerful cultural images precisely because of the transgression of taboos about pollution and this has obvious relevance for VSA. As Manderson argues:

> Why does there seem to be something particularly unpleasant about solvent sniffing, which is a problem in some Australian aboriginal communities, or in the sniffing of gas from pipelines running across Inuit territory, or in the drinking of Lysol or methylated spirits … Partly, perhaps, because of the desperation it suggests amongst those who would do such a thing. But, then again, why do we think this behaviour desperate? Because such a drug utilizes, for a very different purpose, something whose function we had thought to be clear. Glue and disinfectant have their place in all our houses, but their use as intoxicants threatens, as cocaine use or pill popping do not, the boundary between the normal and the deviant.
>
> (Manderson 1995: 802)

As argued throughout this volume, the symbolic construction of drug consumption and substance misuse is always inextricably bound up with discourses of power, identity and inequality (Boyd 2002; Humphries 1999; Reeves and Campbell 1994). The cultural reaction generated by the transgressive nature of glue sniffing and VSA is likely to be intensified by the marginalised status of the social groups involved. These groups are 'pathologised', together with the substances they consume, and this is shown clearly in the examples of news reporting discussed below. One journalist explained that VSA-related deaths lacked news value because, 'It's such a grubby, horrible kind of death ... not the kind of thing to appeal to the "thrivers and strivers" this paper is pitching for' (Manning 2006: 56). In contrast, while the dangers of ecstasy are fully acknowledged in press reports, those taking ecstasy are not 'pathologised'. Quite the reverse, ecstasy is represented as the threat to the normal.

The marginality of those involved in VSA, their powerlessness, and distance from media elites, provides the context for the construction of the symbolic frameworks discussed in the second half of this chapter.

Four symbolic frameworks: the construction of VSA and ecstasy news

The content analysis described in Manning (2006) also provided a source of examples for a further qualitative analysis of the underlying symbolic frameworks organising news coverage of VSA and ecstasy. Four frameworks were identified and the analysis approached their construction by examining four dimensions:

- *Location* – where substance misuse was represented as taking place.
- *Behaviours and identities* – the kinds of people involved, their friends or relatives, and the way in which they were represented as behaving.
- *Substance images* – how particular substances were described in terms of their qualities and appearance, potency, dangers, or benefits.
- *Causes and consequences* – the reasons suggested as to why substances were 'abused' or 'consumed' and the consequences of doing so – in other words, a narrative structure for each news story.

VSA stories were almost exclusively organised around the first framework but examples of ecstasy stories were found constructed around all four.

(1) Social pathology

This framework was used to organise a large proportion of VSA stories, particularly VSA-related deaths. It was found in local and regional papers and in a great deal of the national coverage. Stories constructed around a social pathology framework typically described a *location* for VSA stories which involved images of alleys, sheds, rubbish strewn public spaces, or even sewers. VSA stories rarely featured in the national press but, interestingly, when they did it was sometimes in an international location. For example, *The Times* included a story about the murder of street children in Rio which reported that the latest killings had followed police interventions to remove pots of glue from the sewers where the children lived (*The Times* 1993). Similarly, the *Daily Mirror* described the Duchess of York's visit to an area of Moscow where homeless children lived in 'a stinking, disease-infested cellar', 'where the stench of glue and excrement was near-overpowering' (*Daily Mirror* 2002). With domestic stories, there was a similar stress upon the squalid nature of both the environment and the substances involved. One story, for example, under the headline, 'Why I Shopped My Son' featured a prominent picture of a mother standing in a rubbish strewn alley, the implication being that *this* was where solvent abuse took place. Smaller photographs below featured a derelict set of garages and a small public park (*Stroud Citizen* 1999). What is important here, of course, is that over half the VSA-related deaths each year occur, not in squalid alleys or sheds, but within the home.

The *behaviours and identities* were congruent with the location. According to Jagger (1996) there is an ambivalence in agency responses to VSA behaviour, with an inclination to see first time or light use as 'normal experimentation', but more sustained use as problematic. However, in most of the news discourse, VSA was represented as simply a sign of pathology and associated with crime, drug use, and violence. Those involved were frequently represented as coming from low-income households, disorganised estates, or backgrounds where truancy was the norm. The case of 'Rat Boy', for example, attracted the attention of national papers in 1993. Under the headline, 'Hell of Mother at Her Wits' End', the *Mail on Sunday* ran a full feature:

> They caught him, caged him, then caught him again. The 13 year old burglar they call the Rat Boy is once more in custody after being captured roaming the lift shafts and stair wells on the Newcastle estate he has terrorised for years. Glue sniffing, smoking drugs, truancy, stealing from everyone including his own family, are all among the achievements of this boy who still cannot read or write.
>
> (*Mail on Sunday* 1993)

The animal-like image of young solvent abusers continued in more recent coverage. The *Daily Mirror* described the young homeless in Moscow as 'feral youngsters', commenting that 'the only way they can escape from where they are living is glue' (*Daily Mirror* 2002). The case of the Bulger killing occurred in 1993 and journalists were keen to offer 'glue sniffing' as a possible explanation for the behaviour of those responsible, even though the parents of the two killers rejected the suggestion and little evidence supported it (*The Independent* 1993; *Daily Mail* 1993; *The Times* 1993b). Other examples, included 'The Teenage Thief who Stabbed a Teacher – Solvent Sniffer Grins as a Judge Jails him for Life' (*Daily Mail* 1993b). Government initiatives were sometimes interpreted as reinforcing this picture of what those involved in VSA were like. For example, national papers reported a central government plan to assess the risk of vandalism and burglary at schools in terms of a series of indicators, including levels of solvent abuse (*The Independent* 1996).

The *substance images* in the reporting of VSA were predictable. The *Daily Mirror* report of the Duchess of York's visit to the Moscow cellars featured a colour shot of a young boy in a football shirt smeared in filth and glue, with grime all over his face, holding a plastic bag, presumably containing glue. But along with the unpleasant, grubby and toxic nature of the substances themselves, some stories also highlighted the danger, or 'menace lurking on our shop shelves' (*Stroud Citizen* 1999). The *causes and consequences* were congruent with both the images of solvents and the description of the behaviours and identities. While some more reflective pieces made connections between the poverty and marginalised nature of the locations and the reasons why young people might turn to VSA – for example, *The Independent*'s account of 'Rat Boy' (*The Independent* 1993b) – the dominant 'explanation' focused upon individual pathology. And the consequences of VSA were linked to the image of the substances as possessing a powerful toxicity. One of the St. George's Hospital research team was quoted in the *Daily Mirror*: 'There are no other drugs that cause such a sudden death. It can happen the first time you abuse or it may never happen. It is like a game of Russian roulette'. To reinforce the point, the story focused upon the example of 'Darren' who died within ten minutes after sniffing aerosol deodorant (Palmer 1996). Another powerful example was the story of a boy who was burnt to death when the petrol he was sniffing caught fire (*The Independent* 1993c). However, there were few reports of specific cases of VSA-related deaths in the national newspaper coverage and in terms of *consequences*, the more common theme related to problems of social disorder, as in 'Glue Sniff Wreckers Stormed by Riot Police', a *Daily Mail* report about disturbances at a children's home (*Daily Mail* 1993c).

Another consequence of this symbolic framework was to suppress and deny the possibility that either VSA or ecstasy use could be a source of pleasure or that the experience of that pleasure could be, in some ways, empowering for those who were routinely marginalised (MacClean 2005). Perhaps, the denial of pleasure was easier to secure in the case of VSA because it 'more obviously' transgressed rules or taboos around the appropriate use of substances. There were some ecstasy stories that approximated to the social pathology framework but comparatively few. A feature by Melanie Phillips in *The Guardian*, for example, focused upon the St. Anne's district of Nottingham, examining links between decline in the local economy and the growing drugs and sex industries. Ecstasy featured here (Philips 1993). Similarly, *The Times* reported on ecstasy dealing in the 'run-down' Hulme district of Manchester (*The Times* 1993c). However, the social pathology framework organised only a very small minority of ecstasy reports.

(2) The threat to the innocent

Reporting of the death of Leah Betts in 1995 provides the template here (Palmer 2000; Wykes 2001). As Palmer argues, the circumstances of this story had a strong appeal in terms of mainstream news values – an 'innocent girl' with bright prospects and a happy, prosperous family background, took an ecstasy tablet at her own eighteenth birthday party, and died subsequently after some days in a coma. The power of this story lies in its suggestion of a threat to the family and the domestic sphere. Ecstasy is represented, here, as a drug that can penetrate the 'safety' of the home with terrible and disruptive consequences for even the most harmonious and respectable families. The *location* for this symbolic framework, then, is the home, though sometimes 'innocent' young people, from 'good homes' are represented as entering 'clubland' where they are no longer protected by the family and are vulnerable as a result. Significantly, in terms of *behaviours and identities*, many of the stories following this kind of framework stressed either the academic promise of those whose lives had been ended, or ruined by ecstasy, or their young age. For example:

A-LEVEL GIRL, 19 KILLED FOUR IN ECSTASY SMASH
Families' fury over 2-year jail sentence
A girl student who killed four people when she fell asleep at the wheel after an all-night rave was jailed for two and a half years yesterday.

(*The Sun* 2001)

Similarly, in *The Sun*, once again, there was a full page report of 'pretty Anita' under the headline, 'Dead After taking Just One Tablet of Ecstasy', alongside a picture of the girl and the grieving parents. The article reported, 'A prison officer's 17-year-old daughter collapsed and died after her first taste of ecstasy yesterday. Pretty blonde Anita passed out after taking the drug at a night club' (*The Sun* 1999). The fact that it was the girl's first time underlined her 'innocence'.

Even children could be victims of ecstasy because it had the power to threaten or penetrate the home. Thus, several papers reported 'Jade – the Youngest Victim of Ecstasy' (*Daily Mirror* 2002b; *The Guardian* 2002) who died last year after swallowing ecstasy tablets found at a friends house. For *The Sun*, this was a front page, national tragedy, which it communicated with a picture of a smiling Jade and the headline, 'Weep for Her, Weep for Her Country' (*The Sun* 2002). While the Leah Betts case generated large amounts of coverage organised around this symbolic framework, it was by no means the first. Dance clubs and, of course raves, had been identified as zones of danger since the late 1980s. Hence, in 1993, *The Sunday Times* highlighted the case of a young teenager who died after attending a 'rave' in Glasgow and the call made by doctors to ban 'rave events' (*Sunday Times* 1993). Cohen and Young (1980) pointed out a long time ago that in news narratives, where innocents are portrayed as being at risk, there usually is a role for the 'evil' individual seeking to lead 'innocents' astray. In the case of Leah Betts, there were loud calls to find the 'pusher' who had sold the deadly tablet. In the more recent case of 'Jade', Jane Moore in *The Sun*, demanded that action be taken against those 'drug takers today who feel no shame' and allow children to be exposed to the risks of drugs at home (Moore 2002).

As we shall see below, ecstasy as a substance can be represented in other ways but within this symbolic framework, the stress is upon the strength and potency of the drug. In the case of Jade, there were references to a 'super strong "Ferrari"' form of the drug – a form that systematically attacked her vital organs' (*The Sun* 2002). In the same case, the *Daily Mail* described it as 'a drug that sent the senses haywire' (2002). The *Sunday Times* report referred to 'the deadly cocktail' swallowed by Laura Hay – a term used in a number of ecstasy reports (*Sunday Times* 1993). Of course, as suggested by the examples above, with this framework, while the *causes* were related to 'evil pushers', or careless 'drug takers' who left tablets around the home, the *consequences* for the innocent were represented as terrible in terms of death or the ruining of educational promise. Victims died and others went to prison instead of university.

A number of cases of VSA-related death *could* have be represented in terms of this framework, and occasionally they were but not very often. One example was provided by the *Daily Mirror* in a 1996 health feature article. Under the headline, 'Solvents are Secret Killer', the story reported the death of a young man found by his mother on the bathroom floor at home (Palmer 1996). The emphasis, here, as with ecstasy stories was upon the threat to the home from without, and the disruptive consequences for family. However, very few VSA stories were constructed through this symbolic framework.

(3) Recreational drugs and the 'chemical generation'

Popular red tops found it difficult to understand ecstasy as anything but a dangerous threat but in some broadsheet papers there was evidence of an attempt to come to terms with the normalisation of recreational drug use. This makes it much more problematic to represent ecstasy use as something deviant, dangerous, or beyond the parameters of 'normal, everyday life'. In terms of *location*, the arenas of dance culture and the venues for 'rave' events were no longer understood as menacing, but rather as normalised leisure venues for young people. The term, 'chemical generation' appears to have first been used in an *Observer* supplement report on the arrival of a new and powerful 'dance drug' which claimed the lives of three young people (*The Observer* 1999). However, the piece used this as a peg around which to hang a discussion of the normalisation of soft drug use, and the point that every weekend, 'thousands' of 'reasonable and respectable young adults' used dance drugs as a matter of routine for 'the weekend that *we* design with drugs'. In terms of both *location* and *behaviours and identities* this symbolic framework was very different to those constructed around the 'threat to the innocent'. Here, ordinary and normal, rather than innocent or vulnerable, young people *chose* drugs, such as ecstasy, as a way of planning their recreation. A *Sunday Times* article, 'Rave New World' introduced a former commodity broker who had given up the City to run his own rave events promotion company. The article acknowledged that ecstasy was part of the routine experience for those attending (*Sunday Times* 1993b); another *Sunday Times* report summarised the findings of the Henley Centre report which indicated that young people now spent more money on drugs than going to the pub (*Sunday Times* 1993c) and this story, in turn, was given a gendered angle by *The Independent* which suggested that women were choosing dance culture and 'Es', over smoky pubs (*The Independent* 1993d). As if normalisation implied bourgeoisification, *The Sunday Times* lifestyle feature section, 'Morgan Weekend Trippers', announced that 'ecstasy dinner parties are all the rage now', adding that 'unlike the 1960s drug abuse is recreational rather than revolutionary and increasing among young people' (*Sunday Times* 1993d).

In this symbolic framework, the *substance images* are rather different to those found in other frameworks. While ecstasy can be represented as highly dangerous and potent, there are some alternative images. After all, ecstasy tablets are frequently produced with faces, smiles or other designs intended to amuse the consumer. In news discourse organised around the 'recreational drug' framework, ecstasy was sometimes constructed as 'the technological tool' (*The Observer* 1999) that 'the chemical generation' employed to facilitate their modern leisure experiences, together with the music, bottles of water, and so on. In contrast to the previous symbolic frameworks, the *causes and consequences* are understood as rather more benign. There were some darker thoughts about the implications of recreational drug use expressed in some articles organised around this framework. In one reflective piece, *The Guardian* quoted one woman as saying, 'I just looked at us all dancing away and suddenly thought, it's like *Brave New World*, because really there was nothing radical about it. It was like we were just enslaved to this pleasure machine and that made me rather sad.' (*The Guardian* 1993). However, in the main this framework constructed stories in a way that attempted to reach out to a younger readership by offering to complicity share the knowledge that using E's was both pleasurable and widespread. A lifestyle feature in *The Sunday Times* described, 'Londoner's insatiable desire to see in Sunday mornings' fuelled by ecstasy and amphetamines (*Sunday Times* 1993e), while *The Independent's* Weekend Style Page discussed outdoor rave events and asked, 'people bang on about the dangers of drug taking but when did any of these kids get so much fresh air?' (*The Independent* 1993e).

(4) Drug smugglers and criminals

A large proportion of ecstasy stories involved reports of ecstasy smuggling, dealing and the associated crime, including violent crime and murder. A number of stories suggested a globalised *location* for drug trafficking, with reports of police or customs seizures of ecstasy originating from China, India, Russia, Amsterdam, Rotterdam and Ibiza. Others located ecstasy dealing in the London's East End or gangland Essex. However, reports usually constructed the *identity and behaviour* of ecstasy influenced criminals in conventional crime reporting terms, based upon arrests or trials. There were plenty of 'gangland criminals' and one 'Ecstasy Gang Supergrass' (*The Independent* 1993f). There were some interesting examples of the ways in which the frameworks constructed in cinema, television, and other agencies of popular cultural reproduction can be appropriated by news media. Thus, the *substance image* in some of these stories was akin to the imagery in films like *Traffic* (Boyd 2002) and *Layer Cake*. Ecstasy, like cocaine, was a valuable commodity, presented in some smuggling stories as almost exotic, but in all cases something that was associated with crime and danger. In other stories, the image of the drug was determined by the way in which dealers or smugglers were portrayed. In the *Daily Mirror*, for example, if the global smugglers operated an 'evil trade', then the drug itself had to be a dangerous, 'killer drug' (*Daily Mirror* 2002c). Given that so many stories constructed around this symbolic framework originated from court cases, customs or police action, it is hardly surprising that the *causes and consequences* were usually discussed in terms of crime and punishment.

Conclusion

We have looked at the examples of the representation in news discourse of VSA and ecstasy for two reasons. Firstly, because this provides a striking contrast in terms of the symbolic frameworks within which two patterns of substance misuse are placed. The distinction between the fate of the 'promising' young people whose lives and families have been damaged by ecstasy and the 'feral', 'pathologised' youngsters associated with VSA provides a powerful further illustration of the familiar point that the symbolic construction of drug consumption is inextricably bound up with discourses of marginalisation, class, 'race' and gender. The chapter has also provided an illustration of the way in which the cultural and symbolic intersect with the material and political: the reproduction of these symbolic frameworks is shaped by the politics of news sources and architecture of government departments, the social composition of media and political elites, and crucially, the material and symbolic exclusion of particular social groups. But, in turn, these patterns of media representation impact upon and can distort government policy and the allocation of resources for harm reduction strategies.

The second reason concerns the broader theme of this volume. The construction of the symbolic frameworks of drug consumption and substance misuse discussed here, within newspapers, is itself, part of the broader reproduction of popular cultures. An important question to ask is, 'what kind of bearing do these symbolic frameworks have upon the understandings and frameworks embraced or constructed by particular social groups?' Is there any congruence, for example, between the symbolic frameworks constructed in news discourse here and the 'picturing' of substances, or the meanings attached to drug consumption by particular groups of young people? Studies exploring these kinds of themes frequently focus specifically upon particular groups of drug users rather than considering a wider focus upon how drug images or drug meanings are shared by those on the fringes of drug using social networks, or within wider social networks (Leeming, Hanley and Lyttle 2002: 170). If the normalisation of recreational drug use is occurring, it is important to explore how the symbolic frameworks of drug consumption are circulated through 'normal' communities and social networks. We need to explore how popular drug cultures are constructed and reproduced.

We have seen that the symbolic frameworks reproduced in news discourse are constructed in ways that reinforce moral evaluations not only of kinds of substances, but also of the ways in which substances are consumed and the people consuming them. In other words, hierarchies are constructed involving both moral and aesthetic elements. VSA, for example, is understood as repulsive because of the nature of the substances used, the way in which they are used, and the kind of people associated with it. Although ecstasy was constructed as highly risky or dangerous, it was not represented as 'dirty' or 'grubby' in the same way as solvent abuse. There is plenty of evidence to suggest that amongst groups of drug consumers, 'taste hierarchies' exist regarding drugs and methods of consumption and these may be associated with class and identity. Groups rationalise or normalise their own drug practices and condemn those of others; there are 'good drugs used in the right way' and drug practices labelled 'bad' (Sterk-Erifson 1996: 64). The language and imagery used by drug consumers is important, both reflecting and shaping their cultural practices, and their own ambivalence. Thus, marginalised groups of young people in Australia may see inhaling paint aerosols as a 'scummy-arsed drug' but they also call this 'chroming' which has a superior ring to 'paint sniffing' (MacClean 2005).

To develop this argument a little further by drawing upon contemporary social theory (see Chapter 1), we know that individuals develop drug styles as part of the process through which they construct their self-narratives (Collinson 1996). These narratives are constructed as individuals negotiate the tensions, constraints, and opportunities, afforded by late modernity. In this era, as McRobbie and Thornton (1995) argue, the fragmentation of mainstream media and the growing importance of new and alternative media, mean that it is unlikely that news discourse alone will fix particular images or symbolic frameworks in the minds of young people. Nevertheless, there is some evidence that despite a healthy scepticism with regard to the news media, young drug consumers do still draw upon them in a rather confused way for drug information (Hammersley, Khan and Ditton 2002: 145) and that fashions in drug consumption can be affected by mainstream media coverage (Parker, Aldridge and Eggington 2001: 13). A useful next step could be to explore in more depth the interplay between drug consumption, media consumption and wider cultural practices; to consider whether elements of the symbolic frameworks discussed above do provide some of the resources that individuals draw upon in constructing their drug styles or wider self-narratives, and to explore these processes in the context of the reproduction of popular cultures.

References and suggested reading

Ashton, C.H. (1990) 'Solvent Abuse; Little Progress After 20 Years', *British Medical Journal*, 300, 20 January.

Bland, J.M. and Taylor, J. (1998) 'Deaths Due to Volatile Substance Misuse are Greatly Underestimated', *British Medical Journal*, 316: 146.

Chritcher, C. (2003) *Moral Panics and the Media*. Buckingham: Open University.

Cohen, S. and Young, J. (eds) (1980) *The Manufacture of News*. London: Constable.

Collinson, M. (1996) 'In Search of the High Life: Drugs, Crime, Masculinities and Consumption', *British Journal of Criminology*, 36 (3): 428–444.

D'Abbs, P.H. and Brady, M. (2004) 'Other People, Other Drugs: The Policy Response to Petrol Sniffing Among Indigenous Australians', *Drug and Alcohol Review*, 23: 253–260.

Dahlgren, P. (1992) 'Introduction', in P. Dahlgren, and C. Sparks (eds) *Journalism and Popular Culture*. London: Sage.

Daily Mail (1993) 'The Evil and the Innocent', 25 November, p. 36.

Daily Mail (1993b) 'Teenage Thief Stabbed Teacher for Trying to be a Hero', 29 October, p. 7.

Daily Mail (1993c) 'Glue Sniff Wreckers Stormed by Riot Squad', 11 May, p. 5.

Daily Mail (2002) 'The Girl who was Killed by Ecstasy', 16 July, p. 7.

Daily Mirror (2002) 'Fergie and the Gluesniffers – Duchess Meets Russia's Sad Street Kids', July 12, p. 25.

Daily Mirror (2002b) 'Jade, 10, Youngest Victim of Ecstasy', 16 July, p. 5.

Daily Mirror (2002c) 'On the E Trail – How the Killer Drug Gets to the UK', 30 July, p. 17

Douglas, M. (1966) *Purity and Danger*. London: Routledge and Kegan Paul.

Drugscope (2002) 'Drugscope UK Drug Report 2001', at website: www.drugscope.org.uk/druginfor/drugsearch/ds_report_results/ (accessed 30.3.2003).

EMCDDA (European Monitoring Centre for Drugs and Drug Addiction) (2005) *United Kingdom Focal Point Report 2005 National Report to the European Monitoring Centre for Drugs and Drug Addiction*, at website: www.nwph.net/nwpho/Publications/emcdda.2005.focalpoint.pdf (accessed 16.8.06). London: Department of Health and the EMCDDA.

ESPAD (2006) *European School Survey Project on Alcohol and Other Drugs*, at website: www.espad.org/summary.asp (accessed 16.8.06).

Giulianotti, R. (1997) 'Drugs and the Media in the Era of Postmodernity: An Archaeological Analysis', *Media Crime Society*, 19 (3): 413–439.

Field-Smith, M.E., Butland, B.K., Ramsey, J.D. and Anderson, H.R. (2006) *Trends in Death Associated with Abuse of Volatile Substances 1971–2004 Report 19*. London: St. Georges Hospital Medical School, University of London.

Field-Smith, M.E., Bland, J.M., Taylor, J.C., Ramsey, J.D. and Anderson, H.R. (2002) *Trends in Death Associated with Abuse of Volatile Substances 1971–2000 Report 15*. London: St. Georges Hospital Medical School.

Field-Smith, M.E., Taylor, J.C., Norman, C.L., Bland, J.M., Ramsey, J.D. and Anderson, H.R. (2001) *Trends in Death Associated with Abuse of Volatile Substances 1971–1999 Report 14*. London: Department of Public Health Sciences and Department of Cardiological Sciences Toxicology Unit, St George's Hospital Medical School.

Guardian, The (1993) 'Agony', Features, 7 September, p. 3.

Guardian, The (2002) 'Girl, 10, Believed to be the Youngest Victim of Ecstasy', 6 July, p. 2.

Goulden, C. and Sondhi, A. (2001) 'At the Margins: Drug Use by Vulnerable Young People in the 1998/99 Youth Lifestyles Survey', *Home Office Research Study 228*. London: Home Office Research Development and Statistics Directorate.

Hammersley, R., Khan, F. and Ditton, J. (2002) *Ecstasy and the Rise of the Chemical Generation*. London: Routledge.

Independent, The (1993) 'Mother Can't Believe that 'Devious' Child Killed', 25 November, p. 3.

Independent, The (1993b) 'How Rat Boy Made His Name', 9 October, p. 14.

Independent, The (1993c) 'Boy Died in Petrol Sniffing Prank', 3 March, p. 7.

Independent, The (1993d) 'Living Page Feature', 28 October, p. 26.

Independent, The (1993e) 'Saturday Night: Last of the Summer Raves', Weekend Style Page, 28 August.

Independent, The (1993f) 'Ecstasy Gang Supergrass Escapes 20-Year Sentence', 21 December, p. 5.

Independent, The (1996) 'Hi-Tech Security Coming to Schools', 9 September, p. 5.

Jackson, G.W.L. and Cole, S.K. (2000) *Drug-related Deaths in Scotland*. Edinburgh: General Register Office Scotland.

Jagger, E.A. (1996) 'The Policing of Glue-Sniffing', *British Journal of Criminology*, 36 (2): 237–254.

Jenkins, P. (1999) *Synthetic Panics: The Symbolic Politics of Designer Drugs*. New York: New York University Press.

Johns, A. (1991) 'Volatile Substance Abuse and 963 Deaths', *British Journal of Addiction*, 86: 1053–1056.

Leeming, D., Hanley, M. and Lyttle, S. (2002) 'Young People's Images of Cigarettes, Alcohol, and Drugs', *Drugs: Education, Prevention and Policy*, 9 (2): 169–185.

MacClean, S. (2005) 'It Might be a Scummy-arsed Drug but it's a Sick Buzz: Chroming and Pleasure', *Contemporary Drug Problems*, 32, Summer: 296–318.

McRobbie, A. and Thornton, S. (1995) 'Rethinking "Moral Panics" for Multi-mediated Social Worlds', *British Journal of Sociology*, 46 (4): 559–574.

Mail on Sunday (1993) 'Hell of Mother at Her Wits' End', 2 May, p. 28.

Major, L.E. (2006) *The Educational Background of Leading Journalists*. London: The Sutton Trust.

Manning, P. (1999) 'Categories of Knowledge and Information Flows: Reasons for the Decline of the British Labour and Industrial Correspondents' Group', *Media Culture Society*, 21 (3): 313–336.

Manning, P. (2001) *News and News Sources: A Critical Introduction*. London: Sage.

Manning, P. (2006) 'There's no Glamour in Glue: News and the Symbolic Framing of Substance Misuse', *Crime Media Culture*, 2 (1): 49–66.

Measham, F., Aldridge, J. and Parker, H. (2001) *Dancing on Drugs: Risk, Health and Hedonism in the British Club Scene*. London: Free Association Books.

Measham, F., Newcombe, R. and Parker, H. (1993) 'The Post-Heroin Generation: Youth Culture May Be Outpacing Today's Drug Service Establishment', *Druglink*, 8 (3): 16–17.

Moore, J. (2002) 'Drug Takers Today Feel No Shame and No Fear. That's Why Jade Died', 17 July, p. 11.

Observer, The (1999) 'Real Life: The Chemical Generation', 24 January, p. 26.

Office of National Statistics (2001) 'Deaths Related to Drugs Poisoning: England and Wales, 1995–1999', *Health Statistics Quarterly*, Spring.

Palmer, J. (1996): 'Solvents are Secret Killer – Mirror Health: Dangers of Solvent Abuse', *Daily Mirror*, Mirror Health Section, 14 October.

Palmer, J. (2000) *Spinning into Control*. Leicester: Leicester University Press.

Parker, H., Aldridge, J. and Egginton, R. (2001): *UK Drugs Unlimited: New Research and Policy Lessons on Illicit Drug Use*. Basingstoke: Palgrave.

Philips, M. (1993) 'This is Radford Road in Nottingham', *The Guardian*, Features, 27 February, p. 21.

Ramsey, M. Barker, P. Goulden, C., Sharp, C. and Sondhi, A. (2001) 'Drug Misuse in 2000: Results from the British Crime Survey', *Home Office Research Study 224*, Home Office Research Development and Statistics Directorate.

Riley, S. and Hayward, E. (2004) 'Patterns, Trends and Meanings of Drug use by Dance-drug Users in Edinburgh, Scotland', *Drugs: Education, Prevention and Policy* 11 (3): 243–262.

Schudson, M. (1991) 'The Sociology of News Production', in J. Curran and M. Gurevitch (eds) *Mass Media and Society*. London: Arnold.

Schlesinger, P. and Tumber, H. (1994) *Reporting Crime: The Media Politics of Criminal Justice*. Oxford: Clarendon Press.

Sterf-Elifson, C. (1996) 'Just for Fun? Cocaine Use Among Middle Class Women', *Journal of Drug Issues*, 26 (1): 63–76.

Stroud Citizen (1999) 'Why I Shopped My Own Son', 12 January, frontpage.

Sun, The (2001) 'A-Level Girl, 19 Killed Four in Ecstasy Smash', 16 June, p. 7.

Sun, The (1999) 'Dead after Taking Just One Tablet of Ecstasy', 19 May 19, p. 15.

Sunday Times (1993) 'Doctors Call for a Ban on Raves', 5 December, Home News.

Sunday Times (1993b) 'Rave New World', 21 November.

Sunday Times (1993c) 'Where is Elicit Ness When We Need Him?', Feature, 31 October.

Sunday Times (1993d) 'Morgan Weekend Trippers', Features, 17 October.

Sunday Times (1993e) 'The Wide Awake Club', Features, 11 July.

Times, The (1993) 'Policeman Arrested Over Murders of Rio Street Children are Freed', Overseas News, 26 July.

Times, The (1993b) 'My Son is Devious But He is Not a Killer', Home News, 25 November.

Times, The (1993c) 'Armed Gangs Recruit Boys on Mountain Bikes for Deliveries', Home News, 15 November.

Wykes, M. (2001) *News Crime and Culture*. London: Pluto Press.

9. Drug dealers as folk heroes? Drugs and television situation comedy

Paul Carter

Normalisation of drugs in sit-coms

Ideal (Baby Cow Manchester for BBC 3 2005) was one of the first productions from BBC Comedy North, a unit set up in 2003 to 'develop and nurture the next generation of comedy talent in the North of England' (BBC Press Office 2005). It was commissioned for BBC 3. This digital station had originally been delayed in its approval by the Department of Culture, Media and Sport because it had failed to demonstrate that it would be suitably distinctive. BBC 3 finally launched in February 2003, promising to be 'a mixed genre channel primarily aimed at serving the needs of 25–34 year-old viewers with a high level of original production. It had the explicit aim of trying to reconnect this group with the BBC's output in particular and public service broadcasting in general' (Hewlett 2004: 4). The programme hit a zeitgeist of normalisation of cannabis use following the Labour government's downgrading of cannabis from a Class B drug to a Class C in January 2004 which, despite claims that it did not equate to a decriminalisation, may well have changed the image of the drug in popular culture and public understanding. Programmes such as *The Mighty Boosh* (Baby Cow for BBC 3 2004) and *Shameless* (Company Pictures for Channel 4 2004) had already begun to show on television the use of cannabis as a normal part of many people's lives.

However, before this time, it is difficult to imagine a sit-com being produced and shown by the BBC about a central character whose sole occupation carries a maximum prison sentence of 14 years. *Porridge* (BBC 1973–77) does not count because all its characters were being punished – and to confirm the effectiveness of the system there was a short-lived, follow-up series entitled *Going Straight* (BBC 1978). There are few areas of illegality which produce as many diverse opinions as drugs and *Ideal* is an important development in British television because it is the first sit-com to feature a drug dealer as its main protagonist. The BBC often finds itself in the difficult position of being required to act as the custodian of Reithian principles of broadcasting and simultaneously at the cutting edge of entertainment and culture. The 'minority' digital channels give the BBC the opportunity to take risks and it has resisted attempts to widen the target audience for BBC 3 (BBC 2004).

However, despite having risk taking as part of its remit, it is interesting to consider how the channel handles a subject such as drug dealing to make it appear acceptable.

Through a close textual analysis of the first episode of series one of *Ideal* this short chapter will consider how narrative and *mise-en-scène* work to attempt to demonstrate the normalisation of the use of cannabis and maintain an empathy with the target audience while acknowledging the illegality of its subject material and making 'small-time' drug dealing appear as unglamorous as possible.

Ideal

Moz

There is a great deal of emphasis of the small-time nature of the dealing within *Ideal*. As late as the second running of the second series in July 2006, the BBC website is still describing the protagonist, Moz (Johnny Vegas) as a 'hapless, small-time dope dealer' (BBC 2006). Graham Duff, who writes *Ideal* and also plays the character of Brian, has stated that the use of drugs within the programme is purely a dramatic device, '*Ideal* isn't about drugs, it's about the people who have this one thing in common and how their lives interact due to their shared need. Moz is a typical dealer in that he seems to have lots of friends but in reality they're just work acquaintances who are obliged to spend time with him'. This is, of course, in total accordance with the normal structure of situation comedy – what makes it unusual is its use of an illegal situation as its premise. Duff is rather disingenuous both in his writing and in his publicity surrounding the series. It is quite obvious that cannabis is central to the plot and drives the humour of the series, just as its 'knowing' nature is directly aimed at its target audience of 25–34 year olds.

'The Rats' – the first episode of series one is an obvious attempt to deglamourise the life of a drug dealer and to position Moz at the very lowest level of dealers. The episode begins with a shot panning over dirty plates, a half glass of lager and an ashtray. As Moz reaches down to answer a mobile phone he knocks over the lager and a puddle forms on the bare floorboards. Everything about this shot suggests squalor and it is interesting, therefore, that the required BBC logo appears associated with it. The first long-shot reinforces the idea of squalor as Moz sits on the side of the bed to take the call. It is from a potential customer, Craig, but Moz does not demonstrate the greed we would normally associate with drug dealing, and asks Craig to phone him back. It quickly becomes clear that is more about laziness rather than scruples and he climbs back into bed and asks his girlfriend Nicki (Nicola Reynolds) for sex. On being turned down Moz demonstrates a clear division of labour – 'you make a brew, I'll make a bong'. The clearly domestic nature of this situation – and the equation of tea and cannabis – is the first indication of how strong the normalisation of the drug is going to be in this programme. The drug is no threat to the domesticity of Moz's home – it is an integral part and, soon, will be shown to even enhance it.

The next shot shows Moz smoking a bong as the cheerful, simple theme music (Song of the Oss by Candidate) begins and a knock at the door brings the response from Moz 'oh well, time to clock on'. Upon being asked to ignore the caller, Moz replies, 'can't can I? Trying to run a business here'. This would appear in direct contradiction to his earlier refusal to deal with the phone caller, but would suggest that he has a genuine feeling of a 'working day' and that his dealing is his job – a day-to-day routine. The title sequence then begins with the word 'Ideal' appearing and disappearing as smoke – smoke is important to this programme. It had originally been planned to title the programme *I Deal* but this was dropped – possibly for being too obvious an allusion to drugs. The single word title can be taken not only to suggest Moz's occupation but also as an ironic reference to his anything but utopian lifestyle – and takes on a possibly literal meaning when formed from the cannabis smoke.

As the title fades there is a sequence which is vital to the positioning of Moz. Jenny (Sinead Matthews), frighteningly working as a child-minder but unsure of the name or gender of the baby on her lap, is in negotiation with Moz and it is at this point, just over two minutes into the episode, that he sets out his stall – and his morals.

Jenny: *Can I get a sixteenth for Gary an' all? He says if you lay it on him he'll drop the money round Friday.*

Moz: *Lay it on 'im? I'll lay 'im out. Rulo uno – no cash no 'ash.*

Jenny: *That's what I thought.*

Moz: *Rulo duo. I don't do 'teenths do I?*

Jenny: *Of course... that's what I said to 'im.*

Moz: *I don't do euros neither – if it ain't got a picture of big Liz on it I don't wanna know.*

Jenny: *Can you get any e's?*

Moz: *Nah. It's just hash and weed innit.*

Jenny: *LSD?*

Moz: *Nah.*

Jenny: *MDNA?*

Moz: *Stop chucking letters at me. I'm not Carole Vordemann am I?*

Jenny: *Ketamine? I love ketamine.*

Moz: *No.*

Jenny: *Whizz?*

Moz: *Jenny, all I can do you is blow.*

Jenny: *What you mean coke? Oh, do us a gram then.*

Moz: *No, blow – hash and weed. That's it. That's all I sell. That's all I do. But you know this. We've talked about this before haven't we?*

This humorous, but matter of fact dialogue cleverly combines the business side of Moz's life with his principles. He does not give credit, he does not deal in very small amounts and Jenny supplies a long list of drugs in which he does not deal. His reasoning for this is left up to the viewer, but we are given a strong indication that these decisions are choices and not imposed on Moz through monetary or legal restraints. He does not deal in small amounts because he cannot be bothered; he does not deal in 'harder' drugs because he has some morals. There are some other significant aspects in this exchange which help to position the programme with its target audience. There is no need to elaborate on what the slang terms for drugs mean – the writer assumes an understanding by the viewer.

Legal or not legal?

The first suggestion of the illegality of his trade comes with the arrival of his second customer of the day, Colin (Ben Crompton), a petty crook who is, as he keeps reminding everybody, 'on probation'. Moz is obviously unimpressed by Colin's tales but shows worry when told that he obtained probation by turning in his acquaintances. Colin is very open about his illegal lifestyle, offering a stolen mobile phone in exchange for drugs. Moz refuses despite the phone being worth more than the price of the deal, 'D'ya think this is Multi-coloured Swap Shop? No cash – no 'ash.'

Although money is discussed, it is never seen being exchanged in the first episode and very rarely throughout the series. Again this emphasises the 'amateur' status of Moz – particularly when his supplier is revealed. The squalid nature of Moz's life and, by association, that of drug dealers in general, is emphasised over and over again in this first episode and is epitomised by the discovery of rats in his flat. This leads to an argument between the couple which results in Nicki hitting Moz and giving him a bloody nose. Although there has been violence near the surface already in this episode as Colin described his tactic of 'glassing' himself to impress people, this outbreak of domestic violence comes as something of a shock. The combination of being of the receiving end of a left hook, having a bloodied nose and not being able to find a clean t-shirt almost completes Moz's degradation. As he bleeds over dirty crockery in the sink and Nicki plugs his nose with toilet paper there can be no doubt in the viewer's mind that the world of the small-time drug dealer is not glamorous.

However, Moz does attempt to bounce back. Answering the door to his next customers – Brian (played by the writer Graham Duff) and his latest partner Matt (Kris Mochrie) – Moz is happy to accept Brian's suggestion that his bloody nose is due to '… too much coke?' and even goes on to claim that he has none left to sell because he has snorted it all. Whether this is aimed at the young Matt or at both of them is unclear – as is why Moz should suggest that he deals in Class A drugs after earlier making his position so clear. He goes on to say that he is '… having a bit of trouble … with me bitch'. This is the first time that Moz slips in to anything which could be considered to be 'street talk' or the slang which may be expected of a stereotypical drug dealer and it sounds ridiculous in his Mancunian accent. Duff is clearly setting Moz up as a character of fun and working towards creating a distance between the character and the public's perception of a drug dealer. This distance is increased by the revelation of the source from where Moz gets his drugs.

Only ever known as P.C., Moz's apparently sole supplier is a police constable who is having an affair with Nicki and obtains drugs by confiscating them. An earlier sit-com – *Early Doors* (Ovation Entertainments and Phil McIntyre

Productions for BBC 2) also used the idea of police misappropriating confiscated material by having the two policemen Nige (Peter Wright) and Phil (James Quin) either dealing in stolen goods or smoking confiscated dope in the back room of The Grapes – the pub which is the location for the series. It is possible that these examples of low level police corruption mirror street concern that police officers keep the materials they confiscate – a concern which increased with the downgrading of cannabis, since the drug could be confiscated without an offence being reported.

P.C. is another character young enough to be considered part of the grouping around Moz and to be identified within the target audience. P.C. is first seen as a silhouette through the frosted front door – to the audience this is a bust not a delivery. The joke is continued as P.C. produces a 'weight' of home grown skunk from his cap. There is no discussion of payment for the consignment, despite the fact that it would appear that Moz has placed an order for part of it. The audience is not aware of P.C.'s relationship with Nicki at this stage and so may find it difficult to comprehend his apparent altruism. This tactic within the writing could be seen as an attempt to dilute some of the criminal aspects of the situation. The stereotypical nature of P.C. makes him representative not only of a police force but, within this situation comedy, of all authority – and, with the exception of a brief appearance of an equally incompetent WPC, is the only authority figure to feature in this series. His access to the flat and his relationship with Nicki makes his authoritarian threat extremely ambiguous and neatly mirrors the continuing ambiguity concerning cannabis as an illegal or 'semi-legal' substance after its reclassification. The revelation of Moz's supply line reinforces the moral confusion of the situation, as though what is happening here is some sort of victimless or white-collar crime – no more than a redistribution of assets.

P.C. is shown as being not only corrupt but also incompetent as he fails to spot that Cartoon Head (James Foster), the local serial killer is washing blood from his knife in the kitchen. The fact that this is a point of tension for the audience demonstrates that there is a clear distinction between normalised crime – the supply and use of 'soft drugs' and unacceptable crime – murder. The police are shown to be complicit in one and incompetent in the other.

After P.C. delivers the new supplies, they decide to sample them and this is where the programme could be accused of condoning or glamorising. As they begin to smoke music starts and there is a watery wipe which indicates both the passing of time and the effect of the drugs. The montage sequences are a motif of the series which are normally associated with the taking of drugs. There is no doubt about the pleasure which is being derived from the smoking of cannabis.

Cartoon Head's appearance adds to the surreal – or possibly stoned – feel of the episode. Permanently hiding behind a mask of a cartoon mouse in a bizarre attempt to conceal his identity, he never speaks although he must be capable of speech since he is the unseen half of a telephone conversation in a later episode. He is seen letting himself into the flat with a key and the first view of him is his bloodied hand opening the door. The sinister underscore is obviously meant to add tension but, surprisingly, Moz is not perturbed by either his arrival or his appearance. Indeed, Moz demonstrates a previously unseen strength of character as he admonishes Cartoon Head by telling him, 'I don't want you practising round here'. It is unclear to what he is referring – it could be housebreaking or something to do with his mask. Moz's relaxed style, even when Cartoon Head shows him his blood-stained hands, could be a symptom of the drug taking, but the combination of the childish mask and the attitude of the scene, suggests to the audience that this is not as sinister as it may appear. Moz casually tells Cartoon Head that he knows where the sink is so that he can wash his hands. It would appear that this is a common event, as Moz looks in a box in the kitchen while Cartoon Heads rinses his hands and surreptitiously removes a large bloodied knife from inside his jacket.

All this time P.C. is stoned in the living room. His cheerful greeting of Cartoon Head – who speedily hides the knife behind his back, demonstrates the policeman's incompetence or, possibly, the way in which the skunk he has just smoked makes him incapable of doing his job properly.

Despite all the, now obvious, illegal activity surrounding him, Moz manages to remain a strangely sympathetic figure. This is due partly to the farcical nature of the script – emphasised at this point of the episode by a scene where Moz searches through Nicki's drawers for a clean shirt and discovers, and utilises in several humorous ways, an assortment of sex toys. Vegas's performance is also important. Never playing far from his well-known stand up comedy persona, he appears in many respects victim rather than perpetrator – a position demonstrated by his next clients, two attractive young women who persuade him to drop his rules and provide drugs on credit. The illegality of Moz's occupation is emphasised by the arrival in his flat of Psycho Paul (Ryan Pope), the rival dealer from whom P.C. has confiscated the drugs and who arrives to take them back by brandishing a large screwdriver. 'It's a Philips screwdriver – they're the worst', he tells an obviously frightened Moz.

There is genuine menace in this scene and despite an attempt by Moz to defuse the situation by following Colin's earlier advice and glassing himself – with a plastic glass – it results in Moz being left with no stock at the end of the episode. It does not entirely work as a 'crime doesn't pay' message but it does work towards the demonstration of the unglamorous nature of the role of a drug dealer. It is quite obvious, from the way he lives and dresses, that Moz does not make any more than a humble living from his dealing. The first indication of Moz exhibiting stereotypical dealer traits and behaviour comes in episode six of the first series, 'The Party', which is, in many respects a turning point. Moz is shown wearing a silver cannabis leaf on a heavy silver chain – the first indication of any sort of 'bling' in the series. It is also the first time that drugs harder than cannabis feature and it is P.C. who introduces cocaine into the flat by sharing a line with Nicky in the bathroom before they have sex. There would appear an attempt at creating a connection between the two events – hard drugs and illicit sex. Meanwhile, in the kitchen there is an explicit, detailed showing of 'hot-knives' a rapid and particularly potent method of smoking cannabis resin. The scene is such a clear 'how-to' demonstration that it would appear to be in opposition to the general normalising of drugs within the series. It is almost as if, after five episodes of normalising cannabis and integrating it into a domestic situation the producers feel that there is a need to move out of the cosy atmosphere they have created and to take more risks.

Regulatory bodies have worried in the past about the demonstration of drug-taking methods rather than the normalising of drugs and the old Independent Television programme code included the sentence 'The same caution should be applied to solvent abuse and detailed demonstration of methods of illegal drug-taking that could be easily imitated should be avoided' (OFCOM 2006). This is not included if Ofcom's Broadcast Code of 2005 which instead states that the use of illegal drugs 'must not be condoned, encouraged or glamorised in other programmes likely to be widely seen or heard by under-eighteens unless there is editorial justification' (OFCOM 2005). The BBC is required to comply with this code and it might find it difficult to demonstrate that a sitcom on BBC 3 is not aimed at young people including under-18s and so the attempt to deglamorise cannabis is obviously important.

Conclusion

There is no doubt that its subject material puts *Ideal* at the cutting edge of television production, helping BBC 3 to fulfil its remit of risk-taking for its target audience of 25–34 year olds, but the risks appear severely mediated by the attempts – mainly successful – to show the life of someone who lives by selling illegal drugs as squalid and unattractive. It seems unlikely that this was anything other than a deliberate policy to allow the sympathetic portrayal of the dealing and use of a widely accepted but undeniably illicit substance. The inclusion of other crimes within the series – particularly serial killing – acts as a juxtaposition to further reduce the impact of the centrality of drugs to this programme. *Ideal* is not the only programme to have as its main subject small-time dealing in cannabis. 2005 also saw the production of a US series for the Showtime cable network called *Weeds*. Protagonist Nancy Botwin (Mary-Louise Parker), is left widowed in an upper-class Californian suburb and decides to maintain herself and her two young sons by dealing in cannabis. The programme was quickly also shown on Sky in the UK, and was very different to *Ideal*, critics comparing it more with *Sex and the City* (HBO 1998–2004) and *Desperate Housewives* (Touchstone Television 2004). Writing in *The New Yorker*, Nancy Franklin states it 'can't be called courageous, since the premium-cable networks have little to lose when they venture into controversial territory, but it is nonetheless daring' (Franklin 2005).

Ideal would appear at first glance to be both courageous and daring, and the BBC would seem bold to have commissioned a Christmas special and to repeat the first series on the more mainstream BBC2, but a deeper investigation uncovers a timidity in its treatment and acceptance of the normalisation of recreational drugs.

References and suggested reading

BBC (2004) *Independent Reviews of the BBC's New Digital Television and Radio Services – An Initial Response from the Board of Governors of the BBC*, November 2004, website at: www.bbc.co.uk/info/policies/pdf/digital_bbcresponse.htm (accessed 11.8.06).

BBC (2006) website at: www.bbc.co.uk/bbcthree/tv/ideal/index.shtml (accessed 11.8.06).

BBC Press Office (2005) website at: www.bbc.co.uk/pressoffice/pressreleases/stories/2005/05_may/31/funland.shtml

Franklin, N. (2005) 'Dealing Housewives', *The New Yorker*, 5 September.

Hewlett, S. (2004) *DCMS Review of BBC Digital Services*, Department of Culture, Media and Sport. London: DCMS.

OFCOM (2005) website at: www.ofcom.org.uk/tv/ifi/codes/bcode/ (accessed 11.8.06).

OFCOM (2006) website at: www.ofcom.org.uk/static/archive/itc/itc_publications/codes_guidance/programme_code/index.asp.html (accessed 11.8.06).

10. Junk, Skunk and Northern Lights – representing drugs in children's literature

Andrew Melrose and Vanessa Harbour

Introduction

The coupling of children's literature with controversial subjects such as sex and drugs should perhaps be considered as a cultural oxymoron, a combination that immediately signals an end of innocence and thereby an end to childhood itself. However, there is another side to the argument which suggests that when addressing such topics, children's literature is exactly where it should be located. What must be considered here is the place of the book in cultural context. Narrative, story, is not without controversy in any culture but it also has a function in culture; story is one of the truly multicultural issues in the world. '*Homo historia*, the history of our existence as a species is translated through stories, *homo fabula*, by our very nature we are a storytelling species who live, breath, sleep and eat stories as part of the narrative of our very being' (Melrose 2002), we exist through story which lies at the very heart of experience and this has to be considered in context. What we are discussing here is popular culture as old as the human race itself and in particular one still widely *read* and admired by children, who internalise the experience of the story as they look for positive outcomes. A story is a place where children can learn without risks or peer pressure, where they can trace the lived out experience of others which they may make their own, and having read the books, may then make informed decisions about the rights and wrongs of drug taking (say). Thus, children's books can be intellectually and emotionally challenging, encouraging the readers to develop understanding, judgement and maturity. Children's literature can often now be seen to be the instigator in debates on controversial aspects of modern life for the maturing reader: which quite possibly explains why often children's literature elides seamlessly into the adult market.

Of course, this idea is still fraught with difficulties. Jacqueline Rose (1994) talks about the impossibility of children's literature and Jack Zipes (2002) says it doesn't exist, and what they actually are referring to is *writing for children* from *adult writers* who do the job. Children's literature, stories written for children are inevitably created and owned by adults on the child's behalf: thus the responsibility for those stories is one which needs to be handled with care and that is the real issue. It's not whether issues such as sex and drugs should be represented but how. Italo Calvino once wrote that:

> Literature is not school. Literature must presuppose a public that is more cultured, and *more cultured than the writer himself*. Whether or not such a public exists is unimportant.
>
> (Calvino 1986: 85)

The public, being in this case children, are almost guaranteed to be more cultured with regard to their knowledge of drugs than the authors writing for them. It is an acknowledged given that despite the perceived loss of innocence, children of the twenty-first century are already surrounded by images of drugs, either through a media context, in the school playground, or in particular the internet. In fact it might reasonably be conjectured that these newest forms of communication make this 'the age of the adolescent' and taking this into a cultural context, the songs of innocence and of experience have moved on since William Blake tried to define childhood early on in the nineteenth century. Therefore, it is not useful to be thinking that somehow teenagers are some inexperienced, second-rate repositories for second-rate stories. They *need* the best and it behoves writers to give it to them. They are also very astute judges, just as critical of books as their adult counterparts and (in our experience) they can spot a fraud a mile away. But ask yourself this: why would any writer want to give them less than the best and perhaps just as crucially, do writers know what that is? In representing realism, what is real for the twenty-first century teenager – who is legally speaking still a child.

Writing fiction for children is never easy (Melrose 2001) but out of all the age groups the teenager is the most difficult to pin down. What is a teenager, after all? A young adult: a new adult: an old child: what is it? Teen fiction is one of the most fraught and, at the same time, exciting ends of the writing for children scale particularly because of the range of issues that can be dealt with. It is exciting mainly because these are children on the cusp of adult sensibility with the experiences of adulthood coming at them as fresh and exciting possibilities. In terms of their reading, you are just as likely to get a 13-year-old girl reading Hilary Mantel and a 14-year-old boy reading Irvine Welsh and *vice versa*. While a great many of potential readers will be studying texts by Shakespeare, Austen and Melville through school-based lessons, rather than reading the latest *Point Horror* from Scholastic, although that too has its attractions. And therefore, before any writer even gets into the fraught area of 'representation' they would need to address those confusing paradoxes that call themselves teenagers – and if this also appears rather paradoxical then that is because teenagers are oxymoronic, confused and curious and extremely interesting and depressing and fascinating and sad and happy and every other invective, subjective and objective term that can be introduced to try and describe them. So how do you write for them? How do we represent them and then how do we deal with their issues, the unsayables such as sex and drugs, in a way they will come to appreciate without an understanding of them and their issues in cultural context?

The role of fiction

What any writer has to acknowledge from the beginning is that the life of an adolescent is a period of intense growth and exploration as they seek to acquire an identity. As part of this phase, some adolescents experiment with drugs and sex, partly because they are readily available but also because they are subject to peer pressure and feel the need to conform; in any representation there is a need to get this into perspective.

Teenagers also tend to have a solipsistic attitude to life and indeed to the exclusion of all others, particularly during times of trouble. It can be a period when they seek solace and answers to questions they are hesitant about asking out loud. This is where fiction can come into play. Having already established that narrative is culturally implicit, issues can be addressed and reached through fiction, rather than (say) risking a lecture from adults, who, they perceive, do not take the time to listen or the effort to answer them, as is suggested by Charles Sarland in his essay 'Ideology, Politics and Children's Literature'.

> ... research evidence uncovers a complex picture of the young seeking ways to take control over their own lives, and using the fiction that they enjoy as one element in the negotiation of cultural meaning and value.
>
> (Hunt (ed.) 1999: 50)

Fiction is an opportunity to escape whilst examining issues of real concern to them like drugs; though they are not always looking for a perfect solution they are looking to read texts that challenge 'dominant social values', (Cogan Thacker and Webb 2002: 113) giving them opportunities to form their own decisions about life through realism.

Teenagers, as previously mentioned, are surrounded by drugs and sex, not just in the guise of abstract debates (in the liberal press) or polemical diatribes (in the illiberal) but as schoolyard norms. Any parent who believes that their child is unlikely to be exposed to such things, and therefore should not see them represented in the fiction they read, are sadly deluded. Both are available readily across the social spectrum. Neither of them are exclusive activities for either the very poor or the very rich. Nor are they confined to the city streets, rural villages have as great a problem with drugs and sex as any city housing estate. Books, therefore, need to reflect this. Parents hope they can trust their child but they are reliant on them being well enough informed to be able to make a reasoned and sensible decision about what is best for them. This judgement is not going to be based on some government sponsored literature nor any lecture that a parent/teacher has given. It is going to be based on information that they have ascertained through various mediums. Reading realistic books must form part of that culture of information.

But realism has to be realistic without being didactic. Any adolescents worthy of retaining any sense of credibility among their peers (a crucial factor in being an adolescent) would eschew the didactic among those peers (even if they do claim to embrace it to please willing parents). Therefore, if books are to deal effectively with drugs and sex issues they must do so without being edifying. They should provide an opportunity for teenagers to explore different sides of society (their society, one that represents them) without actually having to become involved in the grittier aspects of it (and isn't this what we all do to some extent). As such books can be used to help adolescents understand or empathise with their situation or environment. J. Appleyard (1994: 95) suggests that 'A story that doesn't give you the answers is better than a story that gives you a solution but doesn't leave you with anything to think about.' Such books should challenge teenagers and leave them asking questions. Parents and teachers should also be well informed enough to be able to answer their subsequent questions without turning it into a lecture. Even if the teenager is not likely to follow the advice at least they are thinking about it. By deciding that books should not touch 'delicate' subjects just drives these issues underground, where nobody can make an informed judgement and mistakes are made.

Representation of drugs in literature

The first book to really break the mould of apathy and deal with drugs in depth, causing substantial controversy, was *Junk* by Melvin Burgess which won the prestigious CILIP Carnegie Medal. In a harrowing tale, set in a squat in Bristol, where the voices of Tar and Gemma are mixed into a multi-voiced, cross section of inner-city drug taking, you are given a dual message. One is that Gemma looks likely to survive and the other is that despite some effort by the end of the book, Tar looks fit to be a casualty. Julia Eccleshare (Hunt (ed.) 2003: 548) said Burgess's handling of the subject was 'an open-minded and non-judgemental stance on the way of life of the young addicts and their various, largely unsuccessful, attempts to break out of the cycle of drug use'. It is hard not to agree with this but the problem with the novel is the overbearing, reified idea that drug taking is something that happens elsewhere. A squat in Bristol is not a leafy Winchester suburban garden, it is not next door, it is not the school your child goes to, *it's a squat in Bristol*, which allows the parents in us to breathe a collective sigh of relief. Burgess's drug culture, for all its representational bravery, becomes 'other', something that happens over there and elsewhere, on the margins of an otherwise civilised and moral society, in other words and in that sense we are not escaping much further than 'where the wild things are' and Maurice Sendak's famous picture book of the same title (written for pre-school children). So the problematic issue of representation still exists in this form of representation and the need to get beyond the childish.

Kerosene, by Chris Wooding and perhaps less so, *Trainspotting* by Irvine Welch, take the culture of drugs into the arena of the disaffected youth. In *Kerosene* (a book essentially about pyromania) dope-smoking isn't some kind of cathartic escape but more of an incidental idea in the story, relating to disaffection and an exercise in adolescent mood changes and time wasting. The drug issue just exists as part of the culture which Cal, the book's central protagonist, inhabits. And yet for the reader it has a resonating authenticity on teenage culture, where time appears to be endless and the youthful ever young, which might even be explained by the author, himself, writing on the novel:

> This book was just pure catharsis. I was having a bad few months of it one winter at University, and some days I was just walking around like Cal does in the book, unable to meet anyone's eye. A lot of people found these passages particularly well-observed, which is kind of them; but I think I had an advantage, as I was in the unpleasant position of feeling that way at the time I wrote them. Cal was just an extrapolation: what would it be like to feel like that all of the time?
>
> (Wooding undated)

Wooding was a 21-year old undergraduate when he wrote *Kerosene*. It is unlikely he would have had the same time to have 'a bad few months' were he older and taking a route through society as a graduate. But is this the only way the space between the writer and the reader can be filled. By writing so age-wisely close to the experience in the first place? Or is there another path which can be fashioned from this, nurturing the idea that to be an adolescent is not about being young but being understood?

A growing genre

Following on from *Junk, Trainspotting* and *Kerosene* over the past few years there has been an increase in the number of books that include drugs. These are often written by authors who base them in the area where they live thus identifying problems and providing empathy with teenagers of the area. It needs to be noted that their portrayal of hard drugs tends to fit into the symbolic frameworks which are often reproduced by the media (Manning 2003) – conforming to the stereotypical 'location, behaviour and identities, substance images, causes and consequences' (Manning 2003).

One recent book is *Candy* by Kevin Brooks, published in 2005. It appears to take its lead from *Junk* where it deals with heroin addiction, a runaway and a dysfunctional family. The novel looks at a classic boy meets girl story of Joe who meets Candy at King's Cross in London (and the location should be noted here for its cultural inference). Candy is a runaway who has fallen into prostitution and heroin addiction and is controlled by a thuggish pimp called Iggy. The book follows Joe's obsession with Candy and his attempts to help her. There is a graphic and harrowing description of the withdrawal symptoms that Candy suffers whilst trying to come off heroin:

> She couldn't keep still for a second. She was either too hot or too cold. She was sweating … then shivering. Sweating … shivering. Hugging herself. Bashing the pillow. Swearing … cursing … shouting … screaming … spitting … coughing … sniffing … sobbing ….
> Suffering.
> It wasn't pretty.
>
> (Brooks 2005: 279)

Nothing in this text glamorises drugs, it highlights the criminal aspects and the desperation of a drug addict to good effect. However, once again the drug addict is portrayed as 'other' and apparently removed from 'normal' everyday life consequently not a perceived threat. Thus conforming to the idea that the media's concept of the 'them' (drug users) and 'us' (non-users). This, as previously discussed with regard to *Junk*, reinforces these perceived stereotypes (Cross 2006).

Bali Rai's *The Whisper* also published in 2005 takes an uncompromising approach to drug dealing in a multi-cultural society. The language used is a streetwise dialogue aimed presumably at attracting teenagers. It continues the story of a group of youngsters who are accused of being informers. One of the 'crew' has become involved in a family drug-dealing business and abandons his friends. The readers become aware of his increased need for drugs as they have less and less impact when he takes them, in particular with reference to cocaine:

> Jas watched Dee as he chopped up lines of coke, desperate for some. His head was crawling with spiders and that sweet voice, the whisper that called to him all the time, sounded like it was a siren going off in his brain. He leaned over quickly and snorted two fat lines of white powder, hoping for the rush to be instant, like the first time. It wasn't.
>
> (Rai 2005: 201)

In the main you are witness to cocaine being used whilst being aware of heroin being sold. The society this is centred within is a deprived area with an ethnic majority which once again conforms to the symbolic frameworks of drug use as suggested by Manning (2003). It is worth noting that where cannabis is used it tends to be by the adults and almost implied as incidental and acceptable similar in attitude to *Kerosene*. Once again there is no glamorisation of the drug world; it is seen to be violent and destructive. Whilst undertaking this literature review this is the only book that actually mentions VSA (Volatile Substance Abuse):

> ... walking past a gang of youths who, if they had been rich, would have been at home in bed by midnight. Thirteen-year-olds on the prowl, looking for people to mash up just for the hell of it. Bored and high on home-grown or glue.
>
> (Rai 2005: 169)

This portrayal conforms exactly to the symbolic frameworks discussed in this volume. They are young and underprivileged hanging around a grimy deprived area (Manning 2003). Writers seem to be automatically picking up on a moralising message without appearing to be dictatorial. Both these books connect drugs with violence and crime thus reinforcing government messages relating to drugs issues. But the reified issue of drug culture as 'other' still persists.

Kidulthood

This theme is continued to the extreme in *Kidulthood* (2006) written by Noel Clarke and based on his screenplay. It has to be asked whether it has been written for shock value rather than realism. The ease with which two of the female characters offer sexual favours in exchange for drugs which can then be sold in order to fund a shopping expedition certainly wakes the reader up. The story is based around a group of 15-year-olds who are having a day off school after one of their classmates commits suicide following severe bullying. It is contained within the 24 hours and examines decisions taken by this group of teenage students when they arrive at the same party. Once again the story complies with stereotypes with the majority of characters being black and from a deprived area. The story is driven by sex, violence and peer pressure all of which teenagers can relate to. The blurb on the back maintains it is a tale of 'powerful modern-day morality' though this could be arguable as it seems to be couched in violence, portraying possibly an acceptable view of violence and drugs. Needless to say, the book and the film courted controversy which of course is an added incentive for any teenage to seek it out. The fact that the novel has an incredibly large font size, making it easy to read, also seems to target the story away from adulthood and straight to *kidulthood* and there is a sense of cynical marketing manipulation on view. But what also has to be considered here is this: is the product being manipulated to suck in the teenage audience or do the audience desire the product being offered?

Kidulthood is not the only book to have warnings of explicit content on the front or to have courted such intense controversy. Julie Burchill with *Sugar Rush* was slated for a liberal attitude to drugs and alcohol, though it is nowhere near as explicit as any of the other books mentioned previously. *Sugar Rush* follows Kim whose mother has run off with a toy-boy and she is forced to change from her posh private school to a local comprehensive where she develops a crush on Sugar. The reader experiences through Kim's point of view the conflict of having feelings for another girl. Alcohol and cannabis are used in abundance in order to ease Kim's problems which is a likely if somewhat disturbingly realistic approach (for these adults). Kim does take an ecstasy tablet whilst at a disco against drugs, thus complying with the symbolic framework of ecstasy being 'represented as the threat, which can destroy the innocent and fragment families' (Manning 2003). The fact that Burchill handles this threat by ensuring that ecstasy is not glamorised, as Kim collapses in the middle of the dance floor therefore highlighting the dangers, still allows the representation of hard drugs within children's literature to appear as showing no signs of normalisation or acceptance. Once again (and oddly from Burchill – who was/is a well-known biographical, chronicler of her own and her associates' normalised drug use in her newspaper columns), they are represented as a forum for teenagers to explore the dangers without participating (which as a representation it defies the realism of the statistical analysis of those who experiment with drugs during their teenage years – rendering it rather abnormally unrealistic).

Normalisation

In a recent report it has been suggested that there has been a process of normalisation where 'the use of illicit drugs is now simply perceived to be part of growing up for many young people' (Smith and Fitchett 2002). But, it appears to have become almost invisible within literature, contradicting Cross's opinion that 'cannabis can and does [always] grow to monstrous proportions when cultivated in print' (Cross 2006). Teenagers see cannabis as different from the literary portrayal of drugs, almost innocent and on a par with tobacco and alcohol. There is rarely violence or even drug dealers involved in the chain that links them to drugs because often a teenager's first experience of cannabis is with friends or family. Cannabis is used in a predictable way in Alan Gibbons's *The Lost Boys' Appreciation Society* to highlight Gary's torment when his mother dies unexpectedly and he goes 'off the rails', bunking off school and hanging around with other dope users as a means of rebellion. This was published in 2004 but two other books have been published recently which imply the normalisation referred to, where cannabis is mentioned but plays no real part in the story, it is irrelevant and invisible. Anne Cassidy's *Looking for JJ* (2004) is about a child murderer who is trying to re-establish a new life as a teenager. There is no mention of drugs except in one incident in order to provide a stereotypical portrayal of students:

> The argument at the table had finished when she got back and the lads were sitting quietly, their beers in front of them. One of them was passing a joint around, each person inhaling and passing it on.
>
> (Cassidy 2004: 61)

The story could quite easily proceed without this incident. The mention of cannabis is used to imply a normality. Rachel Anderson in *This Strange New Life* also uses cannabis to stereotype students in her story of a family whose two sons develop ME which is once again incidental to the story. Andy's father implies that it is because of cannabis that he has become ill but can no longer justify this when his other son who has never used drugs or alcohol experiences the same symptoms. In both these books cannabis is neither portrayed in a negative or positive light. It is just there, part of everyday living. Part of the culture.

Age of readership and censorship

It is interesting that all these books are aimed at the 12+ age group (children's literature is invariably linked to age – this is crucial in writing for children because the ten-year readership of children, 4 to 14, suggests that the child reader is a variable one, governed by experience and cognitive ability) and that the only censorship applied is either done voluntarily by the author or the publisher. Hence children's literature has a chance to push at the boundaries of contentious issues like drugs, sex and violence openly, unlike other media where tight censorship is applied. For example the novel *Kidulthood* is aimed at 12+ plus yet the film of the same story has a certification of 15, as do other drugs-based films such as *Layer Cake* and *How High*. The argument for this is interesting but is questionable; it actually has much more to do with the perception of culture. Books are still seen as belonging to a higher cultural idiom than film (in an old fashioned high culture/low culture debate). Whilst undertaking this research we found that computer games that involve drugs, for example *Grand Theft Auto Sans Andreas,* receive a certification of 18 and is not (supposedly) available to all but the late teenagers – and the even lower culture of the game in relation to cinema issue is still in obvious view (though of course, as this collection of essays does reveal, drugs are the lowest cultural denominator in certain arguments).

Melvin Burgess has suggested that fiction for people in their teens

> should be dangerous, thrilling, intoxicating, experimental, daring – but above all intensely personal.
>
> (Burgess undated)

This is a useful idea. Reading is an intensely personal experience from which the reader takes as much or as little as they need. Further, reading as a cultural experience tends not to have the same implied shared experience (and thereby peer pressure) of film going. The reader is then able to interpret information based on their current knowledge and judgement as a private issue and one of personal choice.

The adult child/child adult is growing in maturity and experience and if teenagers weren't so judgemental then censorship would have to be applied to so much more. If, a totalitarian censorial view was applied to literature many of the most successful books would need to be changed. For example, Philip Pullman's *Northern Lights* would need to be renamed as it is known that Northern Lights are also a cannabis seed that produces a very potent plant. J.K. Rowling would be taken to task over several of Harry Potter's escapades where he and his friends frequently produce and take mind altering potions. The important thing is that authors provide children with authentic stories even if they are based on fantasy as children have 'a forward-looking curiosity about people, events and consequences' (Meek 2005).

It is a good thing children are such discerning readers and the fact that the censor acknowledges this affirms that a growing sense of responsibility and maturity is acknowledged in them. Official censorship is almost a voice of reason among the self-appointed, censorial authorities that have become the national press (it is not censorship that is worrying but the censors – and the self-appointed do much to disgrace their own self-appointment). That teenagers are capable of making their own decisions about drugs means that the ongoing debate about representation has be put into context. Storytelling and thereby literature is part of the very fabric of civilised culture going back centuries. Drugs in children's literature is one of the great taboo subjects and all too often the debate that surrounds it is more about the sound of raised voiced opinions than reasoned debate (as Simon Cross in Chapter 7 in this volume explains in more depth). Like sex, drugs in children's literature usually has people split into two camps; the 'don't mention it in front of the children brigade' and 'we have to get it out in the open crew'. Hence novels like *Junk* by Melvin Burgess are panned and praised in equal measure. Taking a look in critical and cultural context, this chapter has tried to address the whole nature of representation as it exists and where it needs to go with a view to summarising the debate and the success (or not) of the representation. On one hand there is FRANK, a government-sponsored service that provides free and confidential advice about drugs and alcohol. Its information is informative but fact laden and precisely the sort of information which teenagers, who believe they know better, switch off from. On the other there are the texts we have looked at which tend to highlight the violence and criminality rather than touching on the normalisation and getting on to dealing with the side issues that linger therein, like health issues for example. There is a crying need for balance and a position between the two.

Parent v teenager

The parental versus teenage experience is a matter of dealing with facts and specifics in the face of opinions. Drugs, such as cannabis, and under-age sex are issues about which many people have very definite views; therefore inevitably, if you choose to write about the issue within a fictional piece you are going to upset some and appease others because your approach is or is not in accordance with their opinion. Therefore, it is vital to offer a balanced and accurate view within any narrative, teenagers are going to want to know why people do drugs but also need to know what the likely results could be.

Any adult that argues against drugs and tells of the dangers is likely to have the argument that alcohol is equally as dangerous used against them. It is difficult to stop people drinking on health grounds as they find it pleasurable. Most teenagers who are seeking to rebel are going to be able to argue their point, that drug taking is also pleasurable. They will not want to admit to the dangers. The same as adults do not like to admit the dangers of drinking to excess. These issues have to be written about seamlessly so that they are not even aware that this is what they are reading about.

The assumption is that if teenagers read about sex and drugs they are going to go and try them. As such this 'moralising discourse that assumes a direct relationship between the reading of fiction and aberrant behaviour rejects the attempt, on the part of the authors, to invite (and expect) children to think for themselves' (Cogan Thacker and Webb 2002: 141). Are we guilty therefore of assuming that teenagers are stupid? Does an adult go out and commit murder just because they enjoy detective stories? Teenagers are just as capable of deciding what is right and wrong, possibly more so than any adult. They have a fine tuned sense of justice at this age which is yet to be tarnished by society's influence, and indeed have had less opportunity to escape punishment for misdemeanour. When's the last time you drove faster than the permitted speed limit – to the imminent danger of us all?

Writing for teenagers

Writing teenage fiction has a wide brief and while graphic does not have to be explicit, the stories have to be real, even if fantasy. They have to be able to deal with everything life throws at them with a sense of purpose. Futile nihilism may sit well with gothic rock or Kurt Cobain acolytes, but to what extent it should figure in teen fiction is a question of responsibility. And yet, inside such a story there can exist a sense of worth and meaning which helps to keep even the most militant from committing themselves to a life of complete loss.

Thinking about the early teens, by now the young adults, for that is what they most certainly are, especially when we realise that childhood, as a legally defined term is not much older than the last century, are now conscious of, and trying to make greater sense of their own and other people's personalities. As Nicholas Tucker writes:

> At whatever level of complexity, however, stories for the eleven to fourteen age-group usually reflect their audience's increasing pre-occupation with the need to acquire a consistent sense of identity ... readers are now chiefly interested in more adult-seeming behaviour.
>
> (Tucker 1981: 145–146)

And to this end, they are beginning to understand the world in more abstract terms, where metaphor and metonym, relationship and simile take on a new resonance, along with adult realities. But worryingly, what happens when the experience of the adolescent growing out of this is greater than the writer/ parent? Having followed the decriminalisation of cannabis debate with interest, the issue of 'skunk' is already moving out of our cultural sphere, other than as an abstract and academic thesis. How do we make the connection without being involved? We are not the only ones who find it problematic. Nick Hornby once asked, 'How cool was Will Freeman?':

> This cool: he had slept with a woman he didn't know very well in the last three months (five points). He had spent more than three hundred pounds on a jacket (five points). He had spent more than twenty pounds on a haircut (five points) ... *He had taken Ecstasy (five points), but in a club and not merely at home as a sociological exercise (five bonus points)* ... (emphasis added).
>
> (Nick Hornby 1983: 13)

Ecstasy in a club, how cool is that? Is Hornby's middle-aged Will Freeman, a man resolutely hooked into repressed youth, even a close commentator of youth itself? What chance, then, the dry as dust academic writer (or indeed the tabloid hack) who is trying to represent this alien's dilemma?

Adele Geras in an essay on fiction for teenagers (Powling (ed.) 1994: 193–194) once advised:

> I have one word of warning for writers of stories for teenagers: *beware of being too trendy and up-to-date.* Nothing has less street-cred than yesterday's

slang, and you may find yourself hoist with your own petard if you try to be up-to-the-minute in the matter of pop-groups and so on ... do your own thing. It's better than putting on a fancy dress of grooviness which any teenager will see through instantly.

(Adele Geras 1994)

This seems rather obvious but it still begs the question, how up-to-date is up-to-date? Do adults know, indeed can we know who the reader is? It is easier to remember that teenage readers are mature readers who know what and who they like. For all their sex, drugs and rock and roll reputation, they are erudite, currently one of the best read, computer and internet literate generations ever, and well tuned in to world events, major issues and opinions. Their access to information is already happening quicker than the average writer can keep up with. Thus the writer/adult/parent is already having to address a highly sophisticated being.

Research

Consequently a vital aspect of writing for teenagers is research. As has been previously stated teenagers are very astute at picking up errors or weaknesses in a narrative. They will readily pass judgement on the verisimilitude of a text from which they are seeking a reflection of their culture. In that 't[T]he difference seems to be that for adolescents realism is now an issue; they have discovered that a story's truthfulness to life is not something a reader can take for granted but must make a judgement about' (Appleyard 1994: 108). Therefore any detail embedded in a narrative has to be accurate as a teenager could be using this information to assist them to make life influencing decisions.

Here lies a problem. The information on drugs varies enormously and changes frequently and particularly with reference to cannabis. For example, when the authors googled the word 'cannabis' it showed 7,510,000 sites relating to the drug which also changes daily. However, as the internet is not regulated as such these sites cover every argument for and against the drug imaginable. Thus it is possible to use the internet to say whatever you want, as you will find a site that agrees with your opinion somewhere however far fetched your argument may be. Though it should be highlighted that over the past few years the government and media stance on drugs has altered as has the medical viewpoint on the consequences of taking cannabis and the only and best way to keep abreast of these changes is via the internet, you must be aware of which sites you are going to. As an author it is important to be mindful whose site you are using for research as whichever organisation/ company/support group has produced the website is likely to influence the content.

The result of all these changes is that there is a great deal of confusion created by the media and the government, consequently many teenagers, parents and teachers are likely to have no idea what the legal position is or what the consequences of taking a drug like cannabis are. Therefore an author has an obligation to write narratives that use information that is as precise as possible rather than exacerbating the confusion.

Another important aspect of research when writing for teenagers is getting to know them by talking to them. Knowing your audience is crucial to any writing, of course, but you cannot assume to know the teenager just because you have been one once. Yes, you probably can remember what it was like but you will have no concept of contemporary pressures and issues that they have to face. Do not insult them by assuming you do. Listen to what they have to say and also what is not being said – read between the lines. Teenagers come in all shapes and sizes with as many different interests and viewpoints. Just because they wear what appears to be a uniform, depending which group they belong to, does not mean that their opinions are identical. Any author needs to understand that it is a teenager's prerogative to make errors, even if they are the repetition of a previous generation's failings. The teenager will see them as different so once again it is an author's responsibility to provide accurate information that can act as damage limitation for those mistakes.

Italo Calvino (1996: 112) also suggested that writers need to 'set themselves tasks that no one else dares imagine'. Therefore authors should take the opportunity when writing for teenagers to push the boundaries allowing them to explore possibilities at a safe distance where the only limitation is their imagination. Obviously then an effectively researched text can be used to dissolve prejudices and allows the reader to empathise with situations, as is suggested in the essay 'Images of Childhood' (Wyse, Hawtin (ed.) 2000: 11): '… what a reader experiences in real life might be seen as similar to the happenings in a book and this might create comfort or even inspiration'. As such, teenagers can take from a book what they need at any particular moment in their lives. If the author is trying to convey a researched-based educational message it should be hidden so that it is not obvious that any narrative is didactic or the reader as previously mentioned will 'switch off'.

And this appeal to the imagination is an important one. Adolescence, it has been suggested, is just a state of mind and as such the imagination has to be appealed to. As Erik Erickson (Macdonald (ed.) 2004: 34) stated in *Childhood Society*:

> The adolescent mind is essentially a mind of the moratorium, a psychosocial stage between childhood and adulthood, and between the morality learned by the child and the ethics developed by the adult.
>
> (Erik Erickson 2004)

Teenagers are searching for who they are, knowing they are not children but also not feeling capable of being a fully fledged adult.

Conclusion

Should it not be the mode of representation that is addressed here? If the idea that a 'story' is to share wisdom the issue of representation is surely the most serious consideration. This brings us back to fiction and the idea that it can begin to represent a teenager's world while offering solutions to problems as part of the story being told – not as a didactic message but as a by-product implicit in the narrative. In other words it runs counter to the Baudrillard (1985) idea that '... the commodity form is the first great medium of the modern world' and is a counter-commodity idea which entertains the teenagers own sense of identity as outsiders (and a skilled writer may be able to persuade them that only they can see the connection). It may, indeed, become commodified in time, *Trainspotting* became a huge commercial hit, and it did so on the back of its representation of a counter-culture (without reclaiming the characters – what chance has Rent Boy staying off drugs in Amsterdam?). Representing drugs as part of a culture need not be as intrusive as it is in *Trainspotting* but as included and as implicit as the current reputed, middle class, cocaine trade in the City of London (giving a new slant on the gag: 'something for the weekend, sir'). Also, drawing incidental awareness and attention to drugs by including them in a story allows the issues surrounding it to be addressed as part of the cause and effect of its inclusion.

Ultimately the responsibility of the author lies in the safety of the child/ adolescent/teenage reader. But how much a novel can influence such readers is not the question, the simple fact is that fiction's responsibility to its reader lies in the simple notion that a writer must write *for* children, not *at* them or *to* them. Peter Hunt (1992: 1) almost casually remarked that, 'Children's literature is an amorphous, ambiguous creature; its relationship to its audience is difficult', but the clear message here is know your audience. Robert Lesson (1985: 161) in an analogy between the writer and the storyteller tells us that in the actual experience of storytelling, 'you match story to audience, as far as you can'. The caveat, 'As far as you can', reveals the indeterminate parameters it addresses and the problems faced. 'Junk, skunk and northern lights' is a title used to hook the reader in, a story for the teenage audience has to have a similar hook if the story is to have any audience at all and indeed such a title might appeal to such an audience – were we trying to attract them to this chapter. Nevertheless, it has to be able to connect in cultural context and the issue of drugs in isolation will not suffice. They have to be weaved into the fabric of the story if they are to present a realistic view of the story. In the meantime, northern lights has been described as 'the strongest weed in the world', available to any teenager as easily as clicking here, it might be a good place to begin research: www.maryjanesgarden.com/northern_lights.php

References and suggested reading

Anderson, R. (2006) *This Strange New Life*. Oxford: Oxford University Press.
Appleyard, J.A. (1991) *Becoming a Reader: The Experience of Fiction from Childhood to Adulthood*. Cambridge: Cambridge University Press.
Baudrillard, Jean (1985) 'The Ecstasy of Communication', *Postmodern Culture*, H. Foster (ed.), pp 126–134. London: Pluto Press.
Brooks, K. (2005) *Candy*. Frome: Chicken House.
Burchill, J. (2004) *Sugar Rush*. London: Young Picador.
Burgess, M. (2003) *Junk*. London, New York: Puffin Modern Classics.
Calvino, I. (1986) *The Uses of Literature* trans., P. Creagh, New York: Harvest/Harcourt Brace & Company.

Calvino, I. (1996) *Six Memos For the Next Millennium* trans., P. Creagh, New York: Harvest/Harcourt Brace & Company.

Cassidy, A. (2005) *Looking for JJ*. London: Scholastic.

Clarke, N. (2006) *Kidulthood*. London: Bloomsbury.

Cogan Thacker, D. and Webb, J. (2002) *Introducing Children's Literature*. London, New York: Routledge.

Cross, S. (2006) 'Under a Cloud: Morality, Ambivalence and Uncertainty in News Discourse of Cannabis Law Reform in Great Britain', in P. Manning (ed.) *Drugs and Popular Culture: Drugs, Media and Identity in Contemporary Society*, chapter 7. Cullompton, Devon: Willan Publishing.

Eccleshare, J. (2003), in P. Hunt (ed.) *International Companion Encyclopedia of Children's Literature*, p. 548. London, Routledge Falmer.

Gibbons, A. (2004) *The Lost Boys' Appreciation Society*. London: Dolphin Paperback.

Hornby, N. (1998) *About a Boy*. London: Indigo.

Hunt, P. (ed.) (1999) *Understanding Children's Literature*. Abingdon, New York: Routledge.

Leeson, R. (1985) *Reading and Writing*. London: Collins.

Macdonald, P. (2004) *The Oxford Dictionary of Medical Quotes*. Oxford: Oxford University Press.

Manning, P. (2003) 'News and the Denial of Volatile Substance Abuse: How News Coverage Reflects and Reproduces the Meanings Attached to Drug and Substance Misuse', *British Sociological Association Annual Conference*, 12 April 2003, University of York.

Meek Spencer, M. (2005) 'Growing up in Reading. The Balance of Fictive Reality and the Real World: The Reader's Lessons', *New Review of Children's Literature and Librarianship*, 11 (2): 130–145.

Melrose, A. (2001) *Storykeeping: The Story, the Child and the Word in Cultural Crisis*. Carlisle: Paternoster.

Melrose, A. (2002) *Write for Children*. London, New York: Routledge Falmer.

Powling, C. (ed.) (1994) *The Best of Books for Keeps*. London: Bodley Head.

Rai, B. (2005) *The Whisper*. London: Corgi Books.

Rose, J. (1994) *The Case of Peter Pan or The Impossibility of Children's Fiction* (revised edn). London: Macmillan.

Sarland, C. (1999) 'Ideology, Politics and Children's Literature', in P. Hunt (ed.) *Understanding Children's Literature*. New York: Abingdon.

Smith, A. and Fitchett, J.A. (2002) '"The First Time I Took Acid I was in Heaven": A Consumer Research Inquiry into Youth Illicit Drug Consumption', *Management Decision*, 40 (4): 372–382, at website: www.nottingham.ac.uk/mumba/p372.pdf (accessed 10.5.06).

Tucker, N. (1981) *The Child and the Book*. Cambridge: Cambridge University Press.

Welsh, I. (2004) *Trainspotting*. London, Vintage.

Wooding, C. (2003) *Kerosene*. London: Scholastic Point.

Zipes, J. (2002) *Sticks and Stones*. London: Routledge.

Websites:

Burgess, M. 'What is Teenage Fiction: Novels are All about Relating and Understanding', at website: www.web.onetel.net.uk/~melvinburgess (undated).

www.maryjanesgarden.com/northern_lights.php (accessed 28.1.06).

Wooding C., at website: www.chriswooding.com/kerosene_book.html (undated).

Part 4

Identities, Cultural Practices and Drugs

Introduction

Paul Manning

The chapters in this fourth part of the volume focus upon aspects of the cultural practices associated with illicit and licit drug consumption. Each explores examples of the ways in which drug consumption can be understood as a popular cultural practice, embedded with other practices, as part of everyday life (South 1999). In each chapter, we find that concepts of identity have an important bearing upon how drug use is understood and related to other elements of popular culture. Each chapter provides important clues as to the processes at play when individuals integrate their 'drug styles' within the self-narratives that, according to the contemporary social theories discussed in Chapter 1, they continually construct and re-construct. While Chapter 11 considers the relationship between ethnicity, urban music and drug use, Chapters 12 and 13 place gender in the foreground. Chapter 14 retains a focus upon gender, but returns to the question of how distinctions between the licit and the illicit in drug use are policed but also subverted.

In Chapter 11, Oluyinka Esan explores the representation of drug use in urban music but she emphasises that this has to be done by placing both urban music and the cultural practices associated with illicit drug consumption in a wider political-economic and social context. In talking about drug use, urban music draws upon symbolic frameworks that are produced and reproduced through everyday popular cultural practices at the micro-level. These practices are, in part, a response to the experience of social exclusion and marginalisation that provide important themes in urban music. Drug experiences are, in one sense, part of the broader experiences of urban life which are overlaid by the interplay of gender, ethnicity, class and age. In reflecting upon their lives and in constructing their self-narratives, the urban young may draw upon both urban music and their own drug styles for symbolic resources with which to make sense of things. But as Oluyinka Esan suggests, the influence of urban music has extended far beyond the marginalised housing estates of the metropolis. The global commodification of urban music, thanks to the transnational music industries and MTV, has ensured that urban music and its symbolisation of drug use resonate and register with young people located in a diverse range of contexts and locations, including affluent small towns in middle England, as well as the decaying suburbs of Los Angeles. As Oluyinka Esan notes, these cultural processes are supported by the infrastructure of the night time leisure economy, the clubs and pubs, that are important venues for the consumption of urban music. If recreational drug use has been normalised this is, in part, through the interplay of music and cultural practices within these settings.

Chapter 12 serves as an important reminder and corrective. In their development of the 'normalisation thesis' Parker, Aldridge and Measham make it clear that this concept refers to 'soft', 'recreational' drugs, consumed in 'sensible' quantities. It is easy, however, to allow a conceptual slippage that erodes the distinction between this pattern of drug consumption, and drug styles that are actually much more disruptive. Self-report surveys usually suggest that regular opiate use is concentrated amongst a very small proportion of the population (1–2 per cent) and that even amongst communities of regular drug users, opiate users represent no more than 5 per cent at most. Nevertheless, they contribute by far the highest number to the annual totals of drug-related deaths (around 600 annually or approximately 55 per cent of drug related deaths in England and Wales, according to the European Monitoring Centre for Drugs and Drug Addiction (EMCDDA) 2005). Heroin users are often heavy poly-drug users and the imperatives associated with their drug styles often produce chaotic effects disrupting the other dimensions of their lives. In this light, Hollywood's preoccupation with the danger and threat posed to the family, as discussed in Grist's contribution (Chapter 6), is all the more powerful because it refers, albeit in a highly ideological way, to a 'reality' found in the lives of 'hard' drug using families. However, Sarah Goode, in Chapter 12, is able to show that women who use heroin, frequently engage in daily struggles to 'normalise' their drug styles. They apply desperate strategies to contain the chaotic consequences of opiate-dependency and to minimise the disruptive consequences of 'being a junkie' for themselves, and their families. As Sarah Goode notes in reviewing her interviews, these women are continually attempting to repair the damage done to their identities by their drug habits. This provides a rather different perspective upon the concept of the relationship between drug style and self-narrative. It is tempting to focus upon the ways in which drug styles, through the symbolic frameworks within which substances are embedded, provide symbolic resources for the construction of self. However, Sarah Goode's chapter provides a sharp reminder that in constructing biographical accounts, regular 'hard' drug users may have to manage hugely magnified tensions and contradictions; tensions that may threaten to tear open their family lives, as well as profoundly disrupting the process of constructing self-narrative. Their concern to maintain a symbolic barrier between their drug styles and the lives of their children and families contrasts sharply with some studies of male poly drug users (Collinson 1996).

Chapter 13 retains a focus upon gender but in the context of drug use and the body. As recent social and cultural theory has noted, the conceptualisation of 'risk' is a feature of contemporary cultural practices (see Chapter 1), and the relationship between 'risk', health and the body is now a familiar topic (Lupton and Tulloch 1993), as is its application to drug cultures (Measham, Aldridge and Parker 2001). Just as social forces exist to control, regulate and discipline other patterns of risk taking, Elizabeth Ettore in Chapter 13, suggests that women who use drugs are subjected to specific disciplinary discourses because they are women. Women are expected to maintain control of their bodies in order to meet expectations to do with femininity and mothering; drug use subverts this control and presents the transgressive prospect of 'embodied deviance'. We can interpret the women in Sarah Goode's previous chapter as examples. Elizabeth Ettore offers a theoretical framework for exploring the processes through which 'embodied deviance' related to drug use unfold. In doing so, she returns to the idea of pollution discussed in Chapter 1 and the value of postmodern theory as a tool for making sense of these disciplinary processes. We can see here, then, further examples of the symbolic frameworks within which drug substances and drug users are encoded and 'understood', and in particular, the importance of the 'the body' as a signifier within these frameworks.

If Chapter 13 returns us to the variety of disciplinary processes at work in the disciplining or regulation of drug use, and in the policing of the identities of those involved, Chapter 14 offers a rather hopeful account of the negotiation and subversion of these disciplinary forces. Here, Laura Hübner, also shows that one of the consequences of these instances of resistance is a further blurring of the distinction between illicit and licit drug consumption across the zone of pain relief in labour. At what point does the use of drugs for pain relief become 'excessive', and what if male partners, as well as women in labour, avail themselves of the narcotic potential of 'gas and air'. This is a wonderful reminder that in everyday cultural practices, definitions of 'legitimate' and 'illegitimate' drug consumption can be resisted, challenged and re-invented.

References and suggested reading

Collinson, M. (1996) 'In Search of the High Life: Drugs, Crime, Masculinities and Consumption', *British Journal of Criminology*, 36 (3): 428–444.
EMCDDA (European Monitoring Centre for Drugs and Drug Addiction) (2005) *United Kingdom Focal Point Report 2005 National Report to the European Monitoring Centre for Drugs and Drug Addiction*, at website: www.nwph.net/nwpho/Publications/emcdda.2005.focalpoint.pdf (accessed 16.8.06). London: Department of Health and the EMCDDA.
Lupton, D. and Tulloch, J. (1993) '"Life Would be Pretty Dull Without Risk": Voluntary Risk Taking and its Pleasures', *Health, Risk and Society*, 4 (2): 113–124.
Measham, F., Aldridge, J. and Parker, H. (2001) *Dancing on Drugs: Risk, Health, and Hedonism in the British Club Scene*. London: Free Association Books.
South, N. (ed.) (1999) *Drugs: Cultures, Controls and Everyday Life*. London: Sage.

11. Echoes of drug culture in urban music

Oluyinka Esan

Introduction: old tunes, new beats

We may not give much thought to it, but the connection between music and drugs is one that has been around for longer than we care to admit. They are both features of a vibrant youthful scene. In this chapter we shall examine the way in which drug consumption is represented in urban music, a genre selected due to its popularity amongst youth, a high-risk group in the consumption of drugs. In this context, drugs refer primarily to illicit substances such as cannabis, cocaine, and amphetamines.

Urban music has also been selected as the focus for this discussion because of its notoriety. We shall argue that this music genre contributes to the demonisation of urban youth, particularly (but not exclusively) black males. The chapter thus facilitates an understanding of the construction of ethnicity in an aspect of popular culture; the use of stereotypes and how this informs the politics of identity.

In some traditional societies, music and drugs were evident in certain religious festivals which can be regarded as being equivalent to the (modern) social scene. The use of drugs may be evident in many ways, possibly in the dexterity of the performers; such as the nature of the dance or the delivery of the music. The Rastafarian movement is one which is well known to endorse the use of certain substances, perhaps due to the popularity of Reggae musicians such as Peter Tosh, and Bob Marley who sang about the merits of marijuana in particular. These performances were subversive acts; political statements against colonial authorities and also for spiritual enhancement. In such work, music was made to resonate with adopted attitudes to drugs. The repetitive throbbing beat per minute that characterises dance club music (associated with raves and the use of ecstasy) is another example, though that particular subculture is beyond our focus here.

Studying the representation of drugs within music gives an indication of practices and attitudes within and around the cultures of drug consumption, thus giving an insight into such cultures. Other signifiers which indicate the preferred substances and attest to the different historical and cultural specificities will be explored further in this chapter. As this is the 'MTV generation' it is important that where possible, the visual and aural signifiers of music are taken into consideration; an acknowledgment of the different ways in which music is consumed.

Defining urban music

Urbanity as a concept speaks of a physical location and a way of life. Though the music industry has its own operational definition for urban music, which shall be discussed shortly, it is worth examining the peculiar elements of that spatial dimension known as the urban landscape. This is crucial since spatial structures and other economic and political processes inform relationships, quality of life and the experiences that inspire creativity. Urbanisation is a feature of modern social arrangements with the division of labour, industrialisation and high levels of social alienation compared to the more cohesive communal life known in rural areas. Urban areas are massive, densely populated and, therefore, places of diversity. 'Heterogeneity or diversity are inscribed on the landscape in the appearance of location, of housing [commerce], signage, parks and other facilities and other forms of infrastructure' (Stevenson 2003: 32). As life experiences are structured by factors like race, ethnicity, age and lifestyle, the inequalities amongst urban populations is made manifest in access to wealth and other social infrastructure. Physical structures thus give an indication as to the stratification of the occupants.

The equivocal nature of social development in post-industrial society is exhibited in social inequality. Whilst neo-liberal economic reforms may have shored up the economy in the UK and the US, the accompanying expansion of the differences in society, as seen in the squeeze on the working and middle classes particularly in the 80s was remarkable. It is still debatable whether the reversal in the relative decline in the economy witnessed in recent years has brought about improvement in the living standards of all citizens (Middleton 2004) so social inequalities persist. Such inequalities were global; they translated into poverty and dysfunctional traits that characterise the urban poor for whom the glamour of urban life remains a mirage.

Contradictions in post-industrial societies, where many live on the fringes of opulence yet experience hardship, breed a range of creative activities including music. These are also sites of political and cultural struggle.

> ... subcultures arise as attempts to resolve collectively experienced problems resulting from contradictions in the social structure, and they generate a form of collective identity from which an individual identity can be achieved outside that ascribed by class education and occupation. This is nearly always a temporary solution and in no sense a real material solution, but one which is solved at the cultural level.
>
> (Brake 1985: ix)

The global distribution of music provides a forum for a wider range of audiences to share their experiences. Cultural theorists have, in recent times, 'sought to understand urban cultures as it is lived and experienced and cities as sites of difference and resistance rather than as repertoires of negative effects of social political and economic structures and processes' (Stevenson 2003: 135). Urban music is another front on which to engage with the renewed interest in urbanism, and urban life.

Both in terms of the performers and the consumers, urban music scene is youthful. In the UK these are consumers of MTV Base and BBC Radio 1 Extra, also to be found on varied internet music sites. There are strong ethnic connotations on the label though urban music fans cut across racial lines. It is generally agreed that urban music consists of hip hop, rhythm and blues (R & B) and garage. It refers to inner city (street) music, much of which is of American origin. By inference or convention it has become a dominant signifier for music of black origin; which avoids negative racial connotations. The genre thus encompasses 'gangsta' rap, dance hall (reggae, raga) soul music, and other genres which are more specific to black artists. The contentions around this construct must be acknowledged, in that it does not include rock/heavy metal which may present a different (race tainted) experience of urban life. Yet this limitation on the categorisation need not be a problem in this context; as it only helps to maintain focus.

Youth culture as frame – the musical score

To suggest that the urban music scene targets an audience of young people; the same high-risk group for drug use (and abuse) is more than a presumption. It has been acknowledged by the United Nations Office on Drugs and Crime.[1] In the first of its annual reviews of the global situation of drug abuse amongst youths, a UN Commission document (1999) identifies this stage of growth as being very crucial.

> The transition from adolescence to young adulthood is a crucial period in which experimentation with illicit drugs in many cases begins. Drugs may have strong appeal to young people who are beginning to struggle for independence as they search for their identity. Because of innate curiosity; thirst for new experiences, peer pressures and resistance to authority, sometimes low self esteem problems in establishing interpersonal relationships, young people are susceptible to the culture of drugs.
>
> (UN Commission document 1999, para 14: 4)

If as argued young people are attracted to both, in the consideration of music and drug culture, it is only fitting that due attention be given to the peculiarities of youth culture. The youth and adolescence stage is known to be the period for exploration and experimentation. 'Adolescence and early childhood is a period for reshaping values and ideas, and exploring one's relationship to the world, and is therefore an important source of secondary socialisation' (Brake 1980: 25).

Whilst acknowledging the variation in the patterns of drug use presented in different parts of the world, the UN report (1999) suggests that drug use amongst young people cuts across nationalities and social positions, albeit with slight variations. Such evidence confirms the case of the normalisation of drugs. Yet though the practice may be universal, drug use and abuse has different meanings. There are incidents of drug use amongst young people on the fringes of society, and the evidence also indicates the high prevalence rates of the use of drugs amongst the socially adjusted populations particularly in the industrialised societies. Drugs are also consumed to escape the harsh realities of life, such as unemployment, neglect, violence and sexual abuse, as found amongst marginalised urban youths in developing societies. In the event that drugs are used to ease the pain of an arduous existence in spite of the threat of legal sanctions, the practice acquires meanings unique to the users. It may be evidence of wretchedness to non-users, but a means of liberation to users. Likewise, certain classes of narcotics are packaged as part of particular social lifestyles, causing drugs to adopt a meaning other than the official. In spite of the regulatory policies in force, some drugs are recreational and exclusive due to the high costs; others seem benign. With seeming justification for drug use from both ends of the social spectrum, it is no wonder that drug use has either stabilised at a high prevalent rate, or is on the increase amongst young people around the world.

The media have also helped to confer status on certain drugs over the years. Ecstasy is a controlled substance which acquired a particularly notorious reputation in the media (Manning 2006; Redhead 1997). The negative publicity of the raves and acid house cultures in the news media particularly in the 90s – the decade of dance, has been well documented (Measham and Brain 2005). These authors identify alcohol as the latest substance in the wave of media coverage about drugs around which the latest moral panic may be created.

Although they show the youth subculture was responsible in part for the new *culture of intoxication*, they showed that the issue was more complex than the media representation revealed. Thus we see that there is a liberal policy in Britain that seeks to exploit the potential in the night time economy (revenue from longer pub opening hours, for instance). It is feared that whilst this promotes the *culture of intoxication* it may not always be reflected in reports about the increasing censoring of individual liberties, and infringements on the public peace. Such factual reports offer particular constructions of young people. This pattern shows alcohol as a substance which should raise concern, yet the fact that it does not always feature as a drug demonstrates the constructedness of norms, and underscores the significance of the context in which drugs are situated. Clearly the drug culture is complex and it includes a range of substances, illicit and legal; with varying patterns of consumption and effects. From the mild sedation to euphoria, from hallucinations to wild bursts of energy, the pleasures of drugs are discernible. (Drugscope 2004; ISDD 1997) Drugs also vary in the degree to which they are tolerated by the cultural/moral guardians.

As evident in regulatory practices implicit in the classification of mass media content, there are concerns about the consumption and behaviour of young people. This is ostensibly to preserve young individuals, keep them from self harm, and to uphold agreed standards in society; thus maintaining the status quo. A similar assumption is to be found in the debates over media influence. Even with more liberal positions that acknowledge the sophistication of young people in their exposure and response to media messages, there are still reservations about what media savvy young people do with the media. In the final analysis, such reservations are an expression of hegemonic struggle; which group will control popular opinion. According to Brake subcultures challenge dominant cultural ideology. 'Youth subcultures attempt to solve problems which they are only able to do in an imaginary way, because they are never able, given the peripheral class position of youth, to tackle the fundamental problems of class access to education and occupation' (1985: 6). Youths, therefore, use subcultures to express pride in their identity and aspirations with such style that the dominant groups are forced to engage with them. Youth subcultures are thus to be viewed as maps of meanings, to interpret how youths relate with the authorities that subordinate them. Urban music thus offers an insight into attitudes and response to drugs.

Youths have always used music in defining themselves. The tendency for people at this stage to test the boundaries through their music is not strange. Bennett (2000) in a review of literature on the culture of resistance amongst the youth shows the long association with crime and deviance. The inadvertent connotation of criminality (folk devils) in media constructions of youth as a distinct category from adult life (othering) has been documented (Cohen 2002; Campbell 2004; Young 2005). The suggestion that criminality is a pathological condition of adolescence and youth thus occurs irrespective of the orientation brought to the study of youth. Whether we focus on the influence of the local context on the youth, or we regard subcultures are sites of struggles, youth cultures are awash with meaning. Meaning is not always readily apparent; it has to be teased out (Hebdige 1979). Consequently in studying youth culture, there is the need to appreciate the antecedents to the symbolic expressions of the youth. We should seek to understand the stylistic innovations and the subversive potentials expressed in the voice (sounds) and appearance of the youth as evident in their music.

Music in youth culture is thus more than mere entertainment; it is a haven for free expression, subject to artistic license which defines itself, as it redefines prevalent values. According to Blake (2003), hip hop is a global phenomenon that appeals to almost all ethnicities and is synthesising a new culture that goes beyond race, education, and income. To buttress this argument one needs only to consider the extent of the cultural industries which devote themselves to the service of this population segment; fashion trends, automotive designs, movies, television programming, magazines, video games and music. The overlaps within the management and organisation of these businesses show how these multi-billion industries work in tandem to fuel particular lifestyles.

Urban music and drug culture: the harmony

In the earlier definition of urban music, the central position of hip hop culture had been identified. This culture is rooted in the traditions from the Bronx in New York. It includes particular musical techniques, the dexterity in the use of language over samples of music, street poetry or artful (candid) expressions.

200

Though it has acquired the reputation of being a black genre, in its origins on the streets, it was a forum for black and Hispanic youth to express their respective cultures and issues of concern. The genre is known for its boastful lyrics that betray the fantasy of the community of artistes. It is notorious for its explicit language, expressions of anti-white sentiments, and reflections of everyday including the use of the violence (verbal and physical), 'dope' and the inevitability of incarceration or untimely death. The music video is an influential medium for transmitting the hip hop culture and this includes the visual side of the performances; the dressing, the (break) dancing, look, and walk that complement the talk and the musical groove. The genre is associated with excessive materialism, jewellery ('bling') flashy cars, opulence and parties which contradict the visual and lyrical references to the poverty experienced in the neighbourhood. In this way it calls attention to the incongruence in lifestyles that are built around the drug business.

To appreciate the signifiers that evoke images of the drug culture, it is useful to understand the practices in the drug arena. South (1999) shows how important it is to attend to the evidence in the banal aspects of living as these have often been appropriated in the drug arena. This argument is justified in George's (2005) account of hip hop, which offers detailed insight into the drug culture. His account corroborates the ethnographic study of a teenage-cocaine gang in New York (Williams 1990). An inventory of descriptors can be drawn from these. This includes iconic references, a range of indicators and symbolic codes.

It is possible to find iconic references to actual drugs, and referents of the various forms of drug use in film. In music the explicit verbal references to the use of drugs is one to be considered, rather than actual images of the joint of marijuana; the cocaine powder, crack in vials, and heroin being based or injected. *Cocaine* by Dillinger is an example of a musical text in which there were such unabashed references to an illegal substance. In the 70s hit he declared 'I've got cocaine, running around my brain'. As a refrain to a song which re-defined New York as a place of fun and by cunning use of puns, a place of danger and life on the edge, the style of the music encouraged the listener to chant the declaration along with Dillinger. One can argue then that this is an example of how music helped in the valorisation of drugs.

The use of the rhyme helps to make the statement more memorable creating a catchphrase amongst the fans. The phrase has no apparent link with the dialogue about New York in the music, yet it manages to offer a 'feel good report' of the substance.

> *whatever the time I walk in the rain,*
> *Man oh man I feel a pain*
> *I feel a burning pain keep on burning in my bloody brain*
> *I've got cocaine*
> *Running around my brain*
> *I wanna meet my soul brotha and my soulsister*
> *I want you to hold me tight because I'm dynomite*
> *I've got cocaine running around my brain …*
> (*Cocaine*, Dillinger)

Marley's *Kaya* was similar in his expression of the desire for a joint of marijuana, referred to in this context as *Kaya*, 'Got to have kaya now' is the phrase which kept recurring in the call response style of singing. Marley also describes how good he feels, in his altered state:

> *I feel so high, I even touch the sky*
> *Above the fallin' rain!*
> *We-e-ell, I feel so good in my neighbourhood*
> *So, here I come again*
> *I've got to have Kaya now!*
> *I've got to have Kaya now!*
> *I've got to have Kaya now, for the rain is fallin'*
> (*Kaya*, Bob Marley)

Kaya is one of the other names for marijuana. Peter Tosh (1976) had made popular some other aliases for this substance in another reggae track *Legalize It*. Using such vernacular terms makes these no less direct references in the community of users though the information may be obscure to 'outsiders'. This illustrates how exclusive space is carved out for subcultures as a means of rivalling the more dominant cultures.

The illegal substances were on a high pedestal, especially with the endorsement from men of such stature. Unlike the playful context set for Dillinger's *Cocaine*, the skanking rhythm and tempo (in *Kaya* and *Legalize it*) convey a sense of a carefully considered position rather than a flippant outburst; a reflection of marijuana's place in Rastafarianism.

By the 1980s a shift in attitude to hard drugs was evident in music. *The Message* by Grandmaster Flash, one of the pioneers of hip hop presented a sober appraisal of life in deprived neighbourhoods; a cautionary tale. It details the dreary lifestyle in the ghetto – the physical squalor, the indignity of individuals, the insecurity in the home, betrayal by family members, and the supremacy of money which is in short supply for some. This is a sharp contrast from the myth of America as the land of opportunity. The values exhibited by the characters presented cannot be reconciled with the puritan ethics. The value of education is in question; the sense of morality is the same, and in all the chaos the drug culture is evident though not eminent as the Grandmaster clearly condemns these – 'junkies in the alleyway', 'school children smoking reefer', 'thugs, pimps, pushers and big money makers', 'smugglers, scrambles, burglars, gamblers, pickpockets, peddlers and even pan handlers' who delude the children into a life of self destruct. The wry laughter that comes up at the end of the stanzas in this rhyme, further underscores the seriousness of his contemplation and the warning it carries. His indignation is unmistakeable in the chorus as well.

> *... sometimes I think I'm going insane, I swear I might*
> *Hijack a plane!*
> *Chorus*
> *Don't push me cause I'm close to the edge,*
> *I'm trying not to lose my head*

It's like a jungle sometimes, it makes me wonder
How I keep from going under.
(*The Message*, Grandmaster Flash)

Such lyrics and the pattern of the beat created no false illusions about the menace of drugs. This was no ordinary party song; there was more to it than just fun. Devoid of the glossy style that has become a standard in music video industry, the glamorisation of drugs is not as readily apparent. The use of realism in the video (dilapidated buildings, dirty streets, overgrown grass, apparently aimless people, and police harassment) aids the social commentary on the state of America. The shadow cast on the images by the tall buildings around adds to the dreariness of their life. This is poles apart from the visions of suburbia, America the land of the free. However, the tough stance taken by Flash is still consistent with the myth of America as the home of the brave.

Without accompanying videos, earlier music texts relied on the images on the album covers or the direct experiences of reception for the visual cues that they associated with the songs. These have been known to contain images of drugs. An example is Peter Tosh on a marijuana farm with his smoking pipe. A clear blue sky was the backdrop; thus placing this within a discourse that positions marijuana as a product of nature. The casual pose makes this look usual. The dreadlocks of the artist further helps to anchor this meaning within the context of Rastafarianism. Marley's *Catch a Fire* reissue sleeve (2001; original 1973) shows the musical legend with his *spliff* in his mouth. The simple layout, shows a close up of Marley's face. This is a mug shot in black and white, like an official passport photo, though one side of his face is more prominent due to the lighting. That Marley seems so relaxed in smoking the joint makes it seem like a normal act. The sleeve for Dillinger's *Cocaine* is likewise full of candour. Though there is no drug apparent, this a hazy shot of the man who can hardly open his eyes, and is fairly obscured by a puff of smoke. With the lighting in the background and the canted angle shot, he could well be in the clouds, indicative of his being high.

References to drug culture may be subtle or oblique due to the regulation of media content, stylistic preferences or use of restricted codes. With negative official attitudes towards drugs, open display or endorsement of drugs has to be curtailed though substances like alcohol and cigarettes are still on open display. As argued earlier, use of restricted codes makes it more difficult for one outside the community to recognise the signs but with help from other sources of information, the cryptic codes can be accessed. Signs associated with drug culture are now shared more widely, due to democratised new media but the consumption patterns of these sources may still maintain the hegemonic tensions.

Indicators such as the puff of smoke, physiological evidence of altered states evident in their facial features or reconstructed through the performance of the camera work, the tone and tempo of the music, the energy in the dance are useful signifiers. Some codes are re-appropriated signifiers, like the use of beepers that had hitherto been associated with doctors. 'In the monarch bar you can tell the dealers by the beepers clipped to their belts and by the way they handle money; they don't simply take out one bill to pay, but display the entire wad, counting off the bills in rapid strokes' (George 2005: 23).

The above quote also calls attention to the ostentatious use of money, indicating other signifiers that occur in the musical videos. Big cars, plush furniture, jewellery, designer wears, hooded sweatshirts (hoodies) and baseball caps, and scantily clad women are other acknowledged markers of a drug culture that feature as part of the visual narratives in much of urban music. The twinning of drugs and crime means that the evidence of violence (guns, baseball bats) is also a hint of drug culture. This pattern is illustrated in the work of 50 Cent.

> ... I'm not the type to get knocked for d.w.i.
> I'm the type that'll kill your connect when the coke price rise
> Gangstas, they bump my shit then they know me
> I grew up around some niggas that's not my homies
> Hundred gs I stash it (what) the mack I blast it (yeah)
> Ds come we dump the diesel and battery acid
> This flows been mastered, the ice I flash it
> Chokes me, I'll have your mamma picking out your casket, bastard
> I'm on the next level, right lane forget bezzle
> Benz pedal to the metal, hotter than a tea kettle.
> (What Up Gangsta, 50 Cent)

Evident in that verse is the use of slang[2] which demonstrates the ruthlessness in the drug business. This character is a hard man. He is prepared to do anything to evade authorities; he would cheat, even kill for profit. Human life has very little value in this arena. He is also boastful and ostentatious as attested to by the references to his Benz and diamonds (ice). This is a tactic for maintaining respect. Loyalty within the crew (friends/gang members) is expected as is fitting amongst 'outlaws'.

Other more tangible signifiers are to be found in the *mise-en-scene*. The use of steel doors for instance may be indicative of efforts to evade authorities; likewise the use of alley ways, stair wells, basements and other secluded locations especially when accompanying shady movements or specific paraphernalia for processing or consuming drugs (like aluminium foil, vials) is implicating. These are useful markers of the drug culture to look out for (Williams 1990; Shapiro 1997; George 2005). Whilst they may be non-verbal, their 'silent' testimony in the constructed images of the drug culture must not be undermined if we are to understand the normalisation of drug culture or the stereotyping of black youth. The tendency for musical videos to rely on stereotypes and share narrative conventions with films helps to create associations with this genre. This type of intertextuality further entrenches previous patterns of representation. With such strong use of realism there is a danger of confusing the simulacra with the reality. In some cases the association is direct as with Warren G & Nate Dogg's *Regulate* (1994) which was part of a soundtrack for the film *Above the Rim* (directed by Jeff Pollack 1994). The film belongs in the crime genre; a dramatisation of the relationship between three brothers – a basketball star, a security guard and a drug dealer.

Samples from the film were used in the music video conflating the lines of demarcation. *Regulate* offers a sober reflection on the culture of vice and violence, with a definite indictment of drug use at the end.

> *It's a G – funk era*
> *funked out with a gangsta twist*
> *If you smoke like I smoke*
> *then you high like every day*
> *and if your ass is a buster*
> *213 will regulate.*
> (*Regulate*, Warren G & Nate Dogg)

The use of the partying mode in videos (McDonald 1999), along with certain looks of pleasure that can connote both drug use and sexually suggestive dance routines, make it difficult to distinguish those acts which connote the drug culture from those which do not. Nelly's *Hot in Here* has no overt references to drugs but with the intense partying – the dance, the sweat, the slow motion sequences, the use of the blue colour filters, moans of pleasure, the visual effect of flames and sparks from the loudspeaker there is a strong sexual innuendo. This is comparable with the reports of ecstasy driven raves. According to Henderson (1999: 40) young women and drugs came together as a package – '... music, drugs, dancing, social interaction, a feeling of belonging, style and fashion, auto eroticism, flirtation – but the appetite for the pleasures of this nocturnal culture was outstanding'. She argues that the young women (and men) were not just moral reprobates or passive victims, but social actors who elected to reject the norms on drugs for a bit of fun that ultimately leads to substance dependency and attendant evils.

Montell Jordan's *This Is How We Do It* is another video which emphasises eroticism in the fun. In this case the editing and the camera work suggests that these are people under the influence of drugs; juxtaposition of medium shots of young ladies in yearning mode, particularly the one grinding herself against the wall.

With its references to magic and the 60s, as evident in the dressing and the props employed in this spoof of a game show, Black Eyed Peas' *Don't Phunk With My Heart* is bound to look whacky. Yet the psychedelic style and the (aural and visual) imagery from exotic (Eastern) location implicate this video. The use of the synthesiser and out of synch mimes by the performers convey the impression of an altered state. The surrealist style of Fatman Scoop's *Be Faithful* is likewise, and this is made worse by the absence of a clear narrative in the lyrics. The track is reminiscent of early practices in MCing, where the motive is simply to excite and entice people to dance. The fact that Chris Brown's *Run It* is performed in a restricted space robs it of its innocence. This may be no more than adolescent adventure featuring dance offs amongst rival groups in the 'hood' as break dancing was an integral part of hip hop culture in its early days on the street. It is the lyrics and the cutaways from the dancing floor that confirm explicitly the (sexual) nature of the desired acts. This is no surprise as sexual adventures go with the adolescents' territory. Sex in gangsta mentality is an act of power, control, and domination (George

2005). The lust for sex and not love may thus be quite indicative of drug use and the power relations and hierarchies that emerge from this culture. The fact that such gatherings are targeted by drug dealers provides further justification for such association with the drug culture, but it does not have to be so. Implicating these tracks on the basis of circumstantial evidence illustrates the potential for mislabelling black youths.

Afroman's *Because I Got High* is a self confession; the narrative is in the first person detailing the debilitating effects of drug dependence. The fact that a person is unable to perform even the simple routines in life; cleaning his room, succeeding in school, holding down a job even having sexual pleasure, maintaining a home, wife and children, just because of his drug dependence makes this seem like a cautionary tale. The lyrics alone suggest that this is a condemnation of drug use, yet the video suggests otherwise. There is a lack of remorse; rather a playful tone is used. The visual narrative is somewhat comical, hinting of the carnivalesque and encouraging viewers to dance with this clown and others like him.

Lil Kim is a female rapper whose *Lighters Up* is a celebration of collective identity, in spite of the perceived wrong doings in the community. A variety of urban centres with large ethnic populations around the world were invited to join in the show of solidarity. The accompanying montage offers a candid view of Brooklyn; with a range of interior and exterior shots. There is a sense of pride in this community in spite of apparent impoverishment. Even when the community was clearly subordinated; there is evidence of subtle defiance of the authorities – facial gestures, inscriptions on T-shirts, including the image of Bob Marley. Reference to the drug culture was casual but due to censorship acts satellite television viewers[3] – get a tame version. This light hearted treatment of otherwise grave issues can be said to contribute to the normalisation of drug culture, but it may also be due to the need for entertainment. In any case, the political underpinnings of this pattern of representation should not be lost. This is an example of a community telling its own story; maintaining a dignity no matter how warped its reality may seem within the dominant ideology. Perhaps the in-your-face style of presentation is a stab at the conscience of the dominant elites; a deliberate challenge of normality.

Conclusion – musical beats and echoes

This chapter began with the suggestion that music resonates with drug culture. This has been established within a particular ethnic niche and is consistent with existing literature (Giroux 2004; George 2005; Lippman 2005). The existence of such links in various niches of music; in rock or punk, acid house, club or dance scenes has also been documented. The universality of the experience may be explained in part by the pursuit of fun characteristic of youth. Fun appears to be defined as social interaction and whatever else will enhance the experience. It is the risqué – drugs, sex, and inevitably crime. This pursuit of fun undermines the seriousness of drugs issues, presenting drugs as merely another aspect of a phase in life.

We have argued here that the struggle for identity that occurs for youth is partly responsible for the harmony between the drug culture and urban youth music. This may be another reason why such music transcends lines of race, nationality, class, and gender. The wide acceptance of youth, music whether due to deliberate marketing efforts or induced by shared concerns, contributes to the circulation of the redefined norms on drugs. As has been argued, music is a vehicle for conveying the resistance to dominant values; it has been a forum for contesting the official or dominant positions on drugs. The symbolism in these performances indicative of deeper hegemonic struggles should not be lost.

The struggle for identity also explains the shifts that are evident in the industry. It has been argued that each generation identifies its music and this is reflected in the drugs that are fashionable. 'If drugs of choice fluctuate in part due to changing wider fashions in music, style and leisure, in part it is because each generation wants to make its own mark on the world rather than follow in its parents' and older siblings' footsteps' (Measham and Brain 2005: 266). This suggests that identity informs the choice of substances consumed, whilst also explaining the limited range of substances referred to in the selected music texts. It sheds light on the shifts in style and discourse evident in the samples discussed.

Music is a vehicle for ideological struggle, although its entertainment value is clear. Urban music offers a social commentary whether this is politically motivated through the deliberate use of realism or betrayed in what appears to be fantasy. It is clear that the social, economic and political experiences provide much of the inspiration for the performers and their audiences who make meaning from them.[4] Two broad classification can be made of the attitudes to drugs in the sample examined; outright indignation against drug use, and casual resignation. These have transcended different generations. It can be argued that the very conduct of the debate has contributed to the normalisation of drugs. Irrespective of the stance which may have been taken, the perpetual reference to drugs within entertainment must be investigated for its role in the normalisation of drugs culture.

Though this was not explored, compromises instigated by the commercial interests should not be undermined. The construction of black masculinity as sexualised, dangerous 'other' is consistent with a tradition for marketing black culture over the years. The routine conventions of production also account for the observed representational practice. The continued use of stereotypes, along with the appropriation of artefacts from everyday life and the potential mislabelling both consumers and music of black origin was noted in the chapter. It is most disconcerting to see how normalisation of these cultures may criminalise entire communities.

The influence of the observed patterns of representation must be the subject of another exercise. This should consider how audiences interpret the texts; what is defined as the text, do audiences simply listen, view or do they read information on the cover; do they make use of web-based resources, for example, to interpret the music. Relevance of audience experience should be noted. Such knowledge enables evaluation of the censoring of music genres. With changing perceptions of illicit substances, politicisation of the drugs issue and inconsistent policy of drug control, it is no surprise that there are still alarming proportions of drug use.

The study has utilised a small purposive sample in identifying existing patterns. It is evident that there are echoes of drug culture in music. This has been so perhaps before the rumours of obscure references to marijuana in *Puff the Magic Dragon*, and the unequivocal advocacy of the Rastafarians. Contemporary urban music is only having its day.

Notes

1 See section on 'Who is Using Drugs' at website: www.unodc.org/unodc/en/drug_ demand_who.html, and for more facts on drug abuse, see website: www.unodc. org/unodc/en/drug_demand_abuse.html
2 'DWI' – driving with intoxication; 'connect' – connection or business associates; 'mack' – uzi (submachine gun) or pimp/ladies man; 'homies' – homeboys (close friends); 'ice' – diamond or cocaine; 'g' – thousand ($) (see website: www.rapdict. org).
3 In this case Kiss (Sky channel 350).
4 It is worth noting that following the renowned *Cocaine*, Dillinger went on to make a track *Say No to Drugs* (1993), having done *Marijuana in my Brain* (1979).

References and suggested reading

BBC News (2003) 'Hip Hop Radio Leads Digital Race' 23 October 2003.

BBC News (2005) 'Brits Debate Over "Urban" Music', 2 November 2005.

BBC Annual Report 2005.

Bennett, A. (1999) 'Hip Hop am Main: The Localization of Rap Music and Hip Hop Culture', *Media Culture & Society*, 21: 77–91.

Bennett, A. (2000) *Popular Music and Youth Culture: Music, Identity and Place*. Basingstoke: Macmillan.

Blake, R. (2003) 'Beyond the Bling: A Look at Hip Hop, African American Leadership and the Black Church', in C. Taylor (ed.) *Online Journal of Urban Youth Culture*, at website: www.juyc.org/current/index.html

Brake, M. (1980) *The Sociology of Youth Culture and Youth Subcultures: Sex and Drugs and Rock 'n' Roll?* London: Routledge and Kegan Paul.

Brake, M. (1985) *Comparative Youth Culture: The Sociology of Youth Culture and Subcultures in America, Britain and Canada*. London: Routledge and Kegan Paul.

Campbell, N. (2004) 'On Youth and Cultural Studies', in N. Campbell (ed.) *American Youth Cultures*, pp 1–30. Edinburgh: Edinburgh University Press.

Cohen, S. (2002) *Folks Devils and Moral Panics*. London: Sage.

Coleman, R. (2005) 'Surveillance in the City: Primary Definition and Urban Spatial Order', *Crime Media Culture*, 1 (2): 131–148.

Drugscope (2004) *The Druglink Guide to Drugs: A Guide to The Non-Medical Use of Drugs in Britain*. London: Drugscope.

George, N. (2005) *Hip Hop America*. New York: Penguin Books.

Giroux, H.A. (2004) 'Disposable Youth/Disposable Life', in N. Campbell (ed.) *American Youth Cultures*, pp 71–87. Edinburgh: Edinburgh University Press.

Hall, S. and Winlow, S. (2005) 'Night-time Leisure and Violence in the Breakdown of the Pseudo–pacification Process', *Probation Journal*, 52 (4): 376–389.

Hayward, K. and Yar, M. (2006) The 'Chav' Phenomenon: Consumption, Media and the Construction of a New Underclass', *Crime Media Culture,* 2 (1): 9–28.

Hebdige, D. (1979) *Subculture: The Meaning of Style.* London: Methuen Books.

Henderson, S. (1999) 'Drugs and Culture. The Question of Gender', in N. South (ed.) *Drugs: Cultures, Controls and Everyday Life,* pp 36–48. London: Sage.

Institute for the Study of Drug Dependence (1996) *Drug Misuse in Britain.* London: ISDD.

Jeffres, L. (2002) *Urban Communication Systems: Neighbourhoods and the Search for Community.* Cresskill, N.J: Hampton Press Inc.

Lippman, L. (2005) *The Queen of the South: How a Spanish Bestseller was Written about Mexican Narccorridos, Crime Media and Culture,* 1 (2): 209–213.

Manning, P. (2006) There's No Glamour in Glue: News and the Symbolic Framing of Substance Misuse', *Crime Media Culture,* 2 (1): 49–66.

McDonald, P. (1997) 'Feeling and Fun: Romance, Dance and the Performing Male Body in Take That Videos', in S. Whiteley (ed.) *Sexing the Groove Popular Music and Gender.* London: Routledge.

Measham, F. and Brain, K. (2005) '"Binge" Drinking, British Alcohol Policy and the New Culture of Intoxication', *Crime Media Culture,* (December 2005) 1: 262–283.

Meyer D. *et al.* (1999) *The Urban Condition: Space, Community, and Self in the Contemporary Metropolis.* Ghent Urban Studies Team.

Middleton, R. (2004) Book Review, *Economic History Review,* LVIII, 4: 790–792.

Murji, K. (1999) 'White Lines: Culture, Race and Drugs', in N. South (ed.) *Drugs: Cultures, Controls & Everyday Life,* pp 49–65. London: Sage.

Philo, S. (2004) 'Be Childish, Be Irresponsible, Be Disrespectful, Be Everything this Society Hates: Punk, Youth and Protest', in N. Campbell (ed.) *American Youth Cultures,* pp 209–236. Edinburgh: Edinburgh University Press.

Redhead, S. (1997) *Subcultures to Clubcultures.* Oxford: Blackwell.

Shapiro, H. (1999) 'Dances with Drugs: Pop Music, Drugs and Drug Culture', in N. South (ed.) *Drugs: Cultures, Controls & Everyday Life,* pp 17–35. London: Sage.

Snyder, G. (2006) 'Graffiti Media and the Perpetuation of an Illegal Subculture', *Crime Media Culture,* 2 (1): 93–101.

South, N. (1999) 'Debating Drugs and Everyday Life: Normalisation, Prohibition and 'Otherness' in N. South (ed.) *Drugs: Cultures, Controls & Everyday Life,* pp 1–16. London: Sage.

Stevenson, D. (2003) *Cities and Urban Cultures.* Maidenhead: Open University Press.

United Nations Commission on Narcotic Drugs (1999) *Reduction of Illicit Demand for Drugs: World Situation With Regard to Drug Abuse, With Particular Emphasis on Youth and Drug Abuse,* E/CN.7/1999/8.

Williams, T. (1990) *The Cocaine Kid: The Inside Story of a Teenage Drug Ring.* London: Bloomsbury.

Young, J. (2005) 'Moral Panics, Margate and Mary Poppins: Mysterious Happenings in South Coast Eastside Towns', *Crime Media Culture,* 1 (1): 100–105.

Discography

2Pac (2005) *Ghetto Gospel,* Interscope Records.

Afroman (2001) *Because I Got High,* Universal.

Beyonce (2005) *Check On It,* Sony.

Black Eyed Peas (2005) *My Humps,* Interscope Records.

Black Eyed Peas (2005) *Don't Phunk with My Heart,* Polydor.

Black Eyed Peas featuring Tipa (2004) *Hey Mama,* Interscope Records.

Bob Marley (1978) *Kaya*, Island Records.
Chris Brown featuring Juelz Sanatana (2005) *Run It*, Jive.
Destiny's Child (2005) *Bootylicious*, Sony.
Dillinger (1976) *Cocaine in my Brain*, Trojan.
Eminem (2005) *When Am Gone in Curtain Call*, Shady Records.
Fatman Scoop (2003) *Be Faithful*, Mercury UK.
Grandmaster Flash (1982) *The Message*, Castles.
Ice Cube featuring Mack Tan & Ms Toi (2004) *You Can Do it*, All Around the World.
Juelz Santana (2005) *There it Go*, Def Jam Recordings.
Kanye West (2005) *Gold Digger*, Roc-A-Fella.
Lil Kim (2005) *Lighters Up*, Atlantic.
Mariah Carey (2005) *Get Your Number*, Island Def Jam Music Group.
Montell Jordan (1995) *This is How We Do It*, Def Jam Recordings.
MVP (2005) *Roc ya Body*, Positiva.
Nelly & Justin Timberlake (2002) *Work It*, Universal Records.
Nelly (2002) *Hot in Here*, Universal Records.
Peter Tosh (1976) *Legalize It*, Virgin Records.
Rhymefest featuring Kanye West (2005) *Brand New*, J Records.
Sean Paul (2005) *Ever Blazing*, Atlantic Records.
Snoop Dogg (2004) *Who Am I*, Simply Vinyl S12.
The Game & 50 Cent (2004) *How We Do*, G-Unit/Aftermath/Interscope Records.
Warren G & Nate Dogg (1994) *Regulate*, Death Row Records.
Will Smith (2005) *Switch*, Interscope Records.

12. Drugs and identity: being a junkie mum

Sarah Dalal Goode

Introduction

This chapter will focus on the voices of women as they explore and make sense of their daily experiences as mothers who are dependent on heroin and other substances. As drug use becomes an increasingly 'normal' part of everyday life, it becomes also an increasingly important part of family life, with more and more families having one or both parents, and even grandparents as well, who are dependent on illicit drugs. In contrast to other chapters in this volume, and in distinction to the normalisation thesis proposed by Parker, Aldridge, Measham and others which suggests that recreational drug use is now a 'normal' part of everyday life which creates few problems and requires little managing, this chapter takes a somewhat different approach. It is concerned with the struggle of parents to maintain 'normal' family behaviour despite the impact of parental substance use. The chapter aims to examine the ways in which families may struggle to 'normalise' behaviour that is inherently disruptive of 'normality' and, in particular, the chapter explores the way in which parents may simultaneously (and paradoxically) try to portray their behaviour to their children as being both 'normal' and 'abnormal'.

To explore the relationship between women's identities as mothers and their identities as drug users, this chapter draws on interviews with 48 women in the West Midlands area of England (for further details, see Goode 2000). Through the interviews, themes are drawn out on the women as 'reluctant non-conformists', often working hard to maintain their family's well-being and struggling to maintain control and autonomy in the face of significant barriers.

As explored in depth elsewhere in this volume, the relationship between drug use and everyday life is profoundly complex. Back in the 1970s one commentator suggested that 'America doesn't *have* a drug-culture, America *is* a drug-culture' (Ashley 1972: x, emphases in original), and one might now suggest the same is true of Britain. While theorists may argue whether or not drug use has indeed become 'part of everyday life', it is undeniable that it is of 'enormous contemporary importance – whether as symbol, social problem, or fashion accessory' (South 1999: 6, 7). As one aspect of this phenomenon, within British families the latest figures suggest that there are now between 250,000 and 350,000 children who have parents with problem drug use (Advisory Council on the Misuse of Drugs (ACMD) 2003), with additional estimated figures ranging from 920,000 children (Callingham 2004) to 1.3 million children (Prime Minister's Strategy Unit 2004) who live in homes where one or both parents has an alcohol problem. This is therefore a situation which potentially affects in excess of 1 in 11 of all children living in the UK (Turning Point 2006), and with an additional 20,00 young people every year set to become adult problematic drug users (Home Office 2005) the situation will continue to grow. There is increasing awareness in Britain of the problems faced by these families (ACMD 2003; National Society for the Prevention of Cruelty to Children (NSPCC) 2003; Kearney *et al.* 2003), and there is growing recognition of the need to understand the experiences of these families in greater depth, in order to provide appropriate help.

Learning about the lives of drug-using women

A small number of studies have begun to tell us about the experiences of substance-dependent adult women, including those who are mothers. The first notable early study was that conducted by Marsha Rosenbaum in the US, published as *Women on Heroin* in 1981. Rosenbaum noted how women's 'careers' as drug-users, unlike that of men, tended to 'funnel' down into an increasingly narrow set of options, presenting women with ever-bleaker choices about how to earn money and how to manage their relationships and their families. While men found it relatively easy to move back from a deviant drug-using lifestyle into a more socially-valued 'normal' lifestyle, women found that their identities as 'junkies' tended to stick and, once labelled, they were unlikely to regain a more valued social identity. Another significant finding from Rosenbaum's early study was that mothers tended to hold very conventional views on the centrality and importance of mothering. They tried hard to do their best for their families and would develop strategies to protect their children from the worst consequences of their drug-using lifestyles. These early findings, on women's more problematic status as drug-users and on their efforts as mothers, have been replicated in more recent studies in North America (Colten 1982; Kearney *et al.* 1994; Murphy and Rosenbaum 1999), Canada (Boyd 1999), Sweden (Lalander 2003), Scotland (Taylor 1993; McIntosh and McKeganey 2002), and England (Goode 1993; Klee *et al.* 2001).

However, national and regional differences are significant in the experiences of drug-using women. In Britain, heroin use, which had remained dormant from the 1960s, experienced a resurgence ironically concurrent with Margaret Thatcher coming into power in 1979. The rise of Thatcherism (and the concomitant demise of heavy industry and mining) coincided with a surge in imported heroin, particularly smokable brown heroin, changing the way in which people encountered heroin and developed addiction. Tam Stewart's book, *The Heroin Users*, and Geoffrey Pearson's *The New Heroin Users*, both published in 1987, provide us with a picture of British heroin use at the moment when it was arguably becoming a culturally mainstream activity for the first time. The heroin-related death of supermodel Gia Carangi in 1986, and the publication of Irvine Welsh's novel *Trainspotting* in 1993 subsequently helped to resurrect the almost-forgotten beatnik iconography of the junkie as glamorous anti-hero – at least for those who were young, sexually attractive, or rich. Stewart and Pearson, meanwhile, had presented portraits of junkies before junkiedom was fashionable again. While Stewart focused on heroin users who had started using heroin and other drugs in the 1960s or 1970s (the remainder of the hippie generation of users), Pearson explored the lives of those young people in their early 20s for whom 'dragoning' or smoking 'brown' sat alongside drinking a bevvy of ale with their mates in their conventional working-class lifestyles. It is these conventional users – and now the children and, in some cases, the grandchildren of this generation – whose lives are examined in this chapter.

The position of women in the British heroin scene has been regarded as marginal from its inception (Perry 1979): this is despite the fact that use of those opiates preceding heroin – opium and morphine – was seen as an activity significantly if not predominantly involving women (Berridge and Edwards 1981; Kohn 1992). Dorn and South, for example, writing of the illicit drug scene in London in the early 1980s, refer to women's 'relative absence' and comment that women 'are in fact marginalised and isolated in this subculture just as in the dominant culture', going on to remark that their 'isolation and difficulties can be very seriously compounded if they also have children' (1985: 84). Pearson's (1987) study, while dwelling at length on the experiences of both women and men, touched only in passing on the children of those he interviewed and, perhaps surprisingly for a Professor of Social Work, made no reference at all to social services' intervention. In contrast, Stewart, who estimated that a third of all heroin users are women (1987: 33), showed a great awareness of heroin users' family life and paints a deft pen-portrait of the junkie mother:

> In working-class households, women traditionally see to the chores and raise the kids. Unemployment and drug addiction do not necessarily alter this. I have seen female addicts scurry about the house struggling to keep going while their men sprawled about in peaceful drugged slumber like sated lions on a hot afternoon. ... [The woman] has to balance the books, making sure that the children are fed and seeing that the supply of smack does not run out. There will usually be no money left over to pay the launderette. The kids run around in track suits that double as pyjamas, and a few urgent bits of washing hang dripping around the fire. A woman with a home to run can become very exhausted ... The man often looks five years younger than he really is and the woman looks ten years older.
>
> (Stewart 1987:106)

While Chapter 13 of this volume by Elizabeth Ettorre focuses on the issue of drug-dependent women and men in treatment, this chapter concentrates on the women's daily lives in their families, and the texture of living as a 'junkie mum'.

West Midlands women and drug use study

The material for this chapter originated in a doctoral study of drug and alcohol-dependent mothers in the West Midlands. The study focused on mothers who were self-defined as having either a current or recent severe problem with drugs, including alcohol and, in all, 54 participants were interviewed, including 48 women and 6 of their partners or family-members. The women were recruited through drug and alcohol agencies, probation services, and a GP surgery, and agreed to participate in voluntary, anonymous and confidential interviews. Contact with the participants ranged from a one-off interview of around half-an-hour, conducted in a secluded office, to repeated visits to the women's homes over a period of up to two years, in which a number of the women spent a considerable amount of their time talking with the researcher about many aspects of their lives. The women felt able to talk about their situations which were often intensely painful and which they handled with tenacity and with great courage. They were encouraged to explore a number of aspects of their everyday lives and experiences, using a combination of semi-structured interviewing, narrative accounts, and instruments such as autobiographical life-maps and questionnaires to prompt questions and consider key moments in their lives. The interviews were transcribed and the methodology of grounded theory was used to identify and pursue emerging themes within the data. All names given are pseudonyms and identifying details altered to ensure confidentiality.

Twenty-nine of the women used primarily opiates, nine used amphetamines, and one used 'pills' – a mixture of illicitly-purchased prescription drugs including tranquillisers and anti-depressants. The remaining nine women were or had been primarily dependent on alcohol.

The ages of the interviewees ranged from 20 to 59 years. There was a total of 105 offspring mothered by the women in this sample, with ages ranging from newborn to adult. Just over half the mothers (27 out of 48) had a fairly small family of either one or two children, but family sizes ranged from one up to five children. Some of the women interviewed had only adult children and, of these, seven of the women were now grandmothers.

The following case study of one research-participant, Annie, illustrates some of the issues with which these mothers struggled.

Case study: Annie

Annie: 'It's really hard to really know just how wrong it is when you're actually the person who's doing the wrong'.

At the time that the study ended, Annie was a grandmother in her mid-30s, with children aged from 6 to 15, and a grandchild a few months' old. Annie had been drug-dependent for over 10 years. She had a partner living with her, although the relationship was sometimes difficult, and she was involved in the care of her children and her grandchild. Her other activities included raising money through dealing cannabis and through sporadic shoplifting. As with many of the mothers in this study, Annie held strongly to traditional views on how a wife and mother should behave. She did not see herself as a member of any kind of deviant or alternative subculture, but rather saw herself as attempting, and failing, to live up to normative cultural expectations on being a mother – nurturing and protecting her children, keeping her house clean, and providing a role-model for her children. Annie wanted to be a good mother: she also wanted to continue taking drugs, mainly cannabis, injectable methadone and injectable amphetamine, prescribed by the drug agency and also bought illicitly from others.

The following quotations from interviews with Annie explore some of the painful tensions inherent in continuing to use drugs on a daily basis while at the same time remaining strongly committed to a traditional view of normative motherhood. These quotations illustrate themes which will form the basis for discussion for the rest of this chapter. Some expletives have been deleted from the transcript, which is otherwise verbatim. In this extract Annie is talking about her use of injecting:

> ... if anybody was to tell me what had gone on in my house – if somebody were to tell me what I *know* goes on, I think I'd be shocked by it. Like I'll sit on the pouffe and do me 'medicine', inject me 'medicine', and the kids will come in and I'll say to them, 'Just go out a bit while I'm having me medicine', and – but they'll know what I'm doing, although I sort of cover meself by saying, 'Go out', I mean they *can* still walk in and they know ... they do sometimes and say, 'I just want this'. They don't take any notice, but I mean it's terrible really – but like I say I cover meself because I – I cover me conscience cos I do say to them, 'Just go out a bit while I'm having me medicine', and it's bullocks! They shouldn't even be bloody – they shouldn't even *know* that that's how I have to do it, or they shouldn't be aware that it's okay to – you know, that it's alright to inject because people *don't* inject themselves, do they? You go to hospital to have an injection! I don't want them to think that it's alright to ... it's sort of me saying it's alright for me to do it, but *you* can't. I mean I can't teach them not to do things if I'm sat there doing it. But I really don't – I mean at the time I don't believe that I'm putting them – I don't believe that I'm encouraging them to do it, which is *crap* because I *must* be, you know, it's only obvious.

In the following extract Annie refers to the effects of her heroin and methadone use, so that she is 'gauching' (or 'on the nod'), sleepy and unresponsive to her children:

> ... if somebody ever took a video of me gauching, I think I would die ... if I could see myself, or see my kids ... if somebody put a video in my room, you know, from morning till night and around me when I was wrecked – or when I *chose* to be wrecked – and how my kids were, and how I was, I'm sure I would stop, I really am sure ...

Here Annie discusses her failure to provide an appropriate role-model for her children and her lack of protection for them from 'wrong' behaviour such as drug taking and swearing:

I was watching [a television programme] the other day ... a woman was selling draw [cannabis] – she was just stood there cutting the block [1lb weight] and the little kids was walking about, and it looked terrible! And I looked at it, and I thought, 'What an irresponsible mother! You know how *them* kids are going to end up!' And I thought, 'Well, that's exactly what I do too, in front of my kids', you know, I'd think nothing of bringing in my cutting board here and cutting up me quarter into bits for the week – although it ain't a *block* or whatever, it's nothing that I wouldn't think of doing. It's like when Jeremy shouts at the kids, I say to him 'Don't talk to them like that, it sounds horrible' and he says, 'Well, look at you, you're – you're always swearing at them'. And I say, 'But they know me, they know I don't mean it'. But I mean it's still the same, but because I do it all the time it's like, well, no, they wouldn't think like that of me because they know that I – but I mean they *don't* know, do they, they just – you know, and it's really hard to really know just how wrong it is when you're actually the person who's doing the wrong. You gotta – I've gotta see meself, because I wouldn't believe that I was ever that bad, unless I did see meself. It's only because it's obvious that I've *gotta* be that bad – if things are wrong you normally stop doing them, don't you, really?

These extracts highlight Annie's confusion over what is normal in terms of what she does every day and what is normal in terms of morality and expected standards of childrearing. Her practice of mothering is very much at odds with her own beliefs about mothering, but what is it that we do generally expect of mothers in contemporary society?

What do we expect of mothers?

Annie shares a general social understanding of what we expect from mothers, but what exactly is it that mothers are supposed to do? What are the elements that make up the role of 'mother' in contemporary Western society? From research on motherhood which has been done, it can be seen that there are at least two primary imperatives of normative motherhood in contemporary society. One is to love one's children and the other is to take responsibility for one's children. These two imperatives can be seen as the distinction between 'caring about' and 'caring for' first articulated by Carol Smart (Smart 1991; Boyd 2002).

Attempting to break down this theme of responsibility into its constituent elements suggests that one aspect of taking responsibility as a mother includes the expectation of being available for one's children (Dally 1982). Other elements include taking on the practical daily work of caring for, disciplining, and 'bringing up' the child, identified by Ruddick (1990: 61) as the three maternal practices of 'protection, nurturance, and training'. Training can be seen as including role-modelling (Kearney *et al.* 1994). We therefore can identify two main components of mothering: loving (or caring about), and taking responsibility (or caring for), and within the component of taking responsibility, four elements including availability, protection, nurturance, and training (or role modelling). There are therefore five main activities which mothers are expected to do as part of their role. (These mothering activities are not directly equivalent to fathering activities, although they may be broadly similar to gender-neutral 'parenting' expectations.) Moreover, for most mothers most of the time, this work of taking responsibility – including being available, protecting, nurturing, training and role modelling – is expected to be conducted almost invisibly, without fanfare or acknowledgement, and without lapses and failures, merely with what Graham has termed 'unobtrusive competence' (Graham 1982: 103).

In this study, issues around motherhood were most significant to those women whose children were around school-age and thus at the age where they are beginning to explore questions of responsibility and independence with their parents, but have not yet reached the stage of moving into independent living. This is the age when the nurturing aspects of motherhood may be beginning to decrease (relative to early childhood) but the role-modelling aspects are increasing in importance (Kearney *et al.* 1994).

What impact do these expectations of motherhood have on junkie mothers? How did the mothers in the study talk about loving, being available for, protecting, nurturing, training and role modelling for their children?

Drug and alcohol-using mothers and their relationships with their children

Generally, the women in this study, whether or not they currently had a partner, expressed very traditional notions of being a wife and mother. Stella, for example, commented wistfully, 'ideally I want to wake up and do housework and cook the tea ready for my man and kids and all that'. No respondent in this sample expressed any view significantly at variance with the prevailing accepted notions of being a 'good' wife and mother, with the possible exception of Carrie, who spoke about her relationship much more as a 'partnership' than did the other respondents, so that she said of her partner: 'We're as one. He changes the nappies, he baths the kids, you know, he does what *I* do. He'll cook a meal every night'. Nevertheless, Carrie still very much subscribed to traditional concepts of being a good mother and took pride in the fact that her home was not like a 'junkie's home'.

By far the most common view among the respondents was that their children generally had had a positive impact on their lives, often a calming and stabilising influence, motivating them to stay away from criminal activities and drug taking. Stella, reunited with her children after they had lived with their father, commented how, 'I just feel complete again now', and Penny candidly admitted, 'I enjoy them being at home when I don't send them to school. It's company I think as well'.

Being available for their children, and protecting them from harm, was a more problematic experience for these mothers. Protection, to be effective, is dependent on access to power. While these mothers had responsibility, they did not have power in the sense that often they could not control the impact of criminal justice and social services interventions, housing crises, money and other resources. At times they could not even control who came into their homes or even what happened to their own bodies. These women often experienced powerless responsibility, struggling to maintain authority and control within a context of poverty, homelessness, ill-health, and violence and abuse from those around them. Nevertheless, they remained committed to traditional notions of 'good mothering', that mothers should take on the traditional tasks of good housekeeping, should be available for their children, and should be able to communicate with them and be confided in. They also emphasised the importance of maturation, attempting to protect their children from inappropriate maturation (including knowledge about drug use and criminal behaviour) while at the same time encouraging them in appropriate maturational tasks and preparing them for independence and adulthood.

Protection and disclosure

While the mothers encouraged their children's maturation, they also attempted to protect their children by not disclosing their own drug use. Stella was the only mother in the sample who discussed her drug use openly with her children, perhaps partly because she was also one of the most confident mothers in her belief that she was able to make things right for her children:

> I feel that the more she knows, the more likely she is *not* to follow in my footsteps, as well. [My daughter has] come up to the bedroom and caught me, but I haven't … like, scuffled it away. I need her to – as soon as she's seen it, I've gone, 'This is heroin, and this is what it's doing to me, and I'm trying and –'. She basically knows, basically. I wouldn't sit there and smoke it in front of her, but it was because she caught me and she needed to know.

Patricia expressed the more representative view, which was that her children knew nothing about her drug use other than that she and her partner used 'medicine', even though they 'know if the kitchen door's shut they've got to knock on the door and then they'll get in trouble if they walk in there without knocking on the door, which they do', and her children had seen her and her partner injecting, and had seen methadone bottles and injectable ampoules 'all over the place! [laugh]'. She explained that, if her children asked about her and her partner's use of methadone, she would reply:

> Medicine. Simple as that. Just medicine. I think they have been told before it's just medicine, trying to make out it's not *bad* what we're doing, because … cos it *is*, you know what I mean, it's like a diabetic has to take drugs every day.

However, once the mother's substance-use was known about, the knowledge could prove damaging and hurtful for their children. For example, Marlene related a painful incident that had occurred with her neighbour, who had shouted at her in public with her children nearby, and called her 'a drugged-up drunkard'. Cathy related an incident at school: 'it ended up with some girls and they circled her and was saying that Mummy's an alcoholic and all that stuff. It made her cry and all that. That made me feel really bad … since then she's changed schools'.

It was not only outsiders who could inflict pain through such disclosure, however, and Alison told how her partner jeered at her in front of her children:

> ... when we have a row he always brings it up and throws it into me face, 'Well, are you going to go down and get some drugs, now, are you?' [jeeringly]. You know, and all this. And he says it in front of the kids, which is not very nice, you know what I mean, for a five or six-year-old sitting there listening to this – saying about his mum being on drugs.

Being a role model: the problem of what is 'normal'

Another key responsibility of motherhood is to act as a role-model for one's children, and it is here that the women found the most difficulty in teasing out what is 'normal'.

Returning to Annie as a case study, it is clear that Annie shares the social understanding that mothers should not take illegal drugs in front of their children – that this behaviour is incompatible with the accepted norms of the role of mother (Kearney *et al.* 1994) – but at the same time she finds it hard to place herself in that category of 'drug-taking mother', because her own drug-taking is such a very normal and unexceptional part of her everyday life. For Annie, within her personal and family life, her drug taking activities are no longer deviant, they are compatible with her self-identity as a good mother until some external event acts as a prompt to remind her of the external social reality that drug taking is sanctioned and stigmatised and that what she is doing is therefore quite definitely not 'normal'. Only at this point is she confronted with an alternative identity of herself as a 'drug-taking mother' and therefore as 'bad', a self-identity she has difficulty either *applying* to herself or *denying* as relevant to her actions. As she says, 'I've gotta see meself, because I wouldn't believe that I was ever that bad, unless I did see meself. It's only because it's obvious that I've *gotta* be that bad'. It is 'obvious' only when she is confronted by the external label 'drug-taking mother' and realises that it must apply to her, therefore she is forced to the conclusion that 'I've *gotta* be that bad', and even then there is tension and ambivalence: 'if things are wrong you normally stop doing them, don't you, really?' As a 'good mother' Annie would stop doing something that was 'bad' and 'wrong'. She does not stop drug-taking. Annie therefore struggles with the implicit paradox that either she is 'good' and therefore what she is doing cannot really be 'wrong', or else it is 'wrong' and she is therefore 'bad' for continuing.

Annie's struggle to negotiate and define her primary identity – either as 'good mother' or as 'irresponsible mother' – epitomises the struggle faced by many substance-using mothers. Most of the time, Annie is able successfully to split off the definition of 'dirty, desperate' drug users from her own self-definition. As Annie says, 'I always think of, like, drug users – dirty, desperate people, but then when I think of myself I don't think like that'. However, this strategy of splitting herself off from a stigmatising identity suddenly breaks down when Annie is confronted and challenged by someone else, either literally as when her partner points out that she swears at the children at least as much as he does, or in her imagination when she pictures to herself what she must look like to other people, as she sits 'gauching' in front of her children, or cutting up a block of cannabis, or sitting injecting her methadone as her children wander in and out of the living room.

It was not only her drug use which posed a challenge for her ability to model 'normal' behaviour for her children. She had also often taken her children shoplifting with her in the past, and her view regarding her own children shoplifting in the future was:

> I would rather them shoplift for money than take it off a person or go burgling or anything like that. If they're going to be desperate for money then that is the way I would rather them earn it [sic], to be honest. If you're going to be a criminal then I can't see anything wrong with – obviously it's wrong, you know, because – but, you know, it's the, uh – it's just easy money, really.

Annie's straightforward attitude did not appear to be shared by the other two respondents who discussed shoplifting and their children. They both generally expressed ambivalence about shoplifting, taking pride in their own skill but hoping their own children would not follow suit. For example, Deborah stated, 'I want to be normal really, and I don't want kids growing up knowing their mum goes out lifting. And I'd never do it so Agnes could see'. Mandy, when asked how she would feel if her son began shoplifting, replied:

> That's a hard one, innit. Cos when *you* do it … I would be angry at him doing it. I would. Because I teach him not to touch things that aren't his. I hope I'd be understanding with him as well … you don't want your kids to do wrong, do you, you want your kids to do better than what you've done. That's the whole idea of it all.

Thinking about what they wanted for their children in the future, the mothers hoped that in fact they were not role models for their children, but contra role-models. Cathy was therefore pleased that her daughter specifically wanted not to be like her:

> I did explain to her how important it was that she does not become like Mummy, you know, with the drinking and that. And I do think that now she realises and that, she knows it's not normal and that. But she often did say, 'I'm not going to drink like my mother does'.

Sandra also was explicit about not being a role model for her children, yet teaching them her moral code:

> I think because they've seen what it's done to me they are very, very careful. Very careful indeed. So I don't worry about them. We talk about it now and they – like I said to them, 'Don't follow my example, don't

do as I do. Do as I tell you'. And they accept that. They accept the fact that too much drink is not a good thing.

When it came to opiates, respondents felt strongly that they did not want their children following in their footsteps. As Heather said, when asked how she would feel if she found her son was taking heroin when he was older: 'Oh God, I'd be heartbroken. Oh God, I'd be devastated. I'd feel it was all my fault'.

Stella was far more sanguine about her children not following her example:

> I also think and I hope – this is just me – that I may have done my kids a favour by being who I am and what I've done because I know that my daughter's also said to me, 'I don't ever want to be like you, Mum'.

Several of the respondents pinned their hopes on drugs no longer being a 'novelty' to their children, but for Annie at least this had already proved a forlorn hope:

> I thought, well if they're brought up around it, it's not a novelty to them, so they won't wanna explore or – it'll be nothing to them, but I was wrong then, cos Angela stole a quarter of me draw not so long ago. I thought she would never do that. I thought, you know, that – she's seen it all. If people ever come to her who was on about draw, she'd think, 'Well I seen much more than that, that don't impress me'. That's what I thought, like, but it didn't!

Meanwhile, Beth tried to keep her lifestyle as 'normal' as possible, so that her children would not feel different from other children:

> I don't want my problems to become their problems, you know. Because that easily happens to people. They use drugs and then like it becomes the kids' problems, and if you begin to live a life so different to everybody else, which isn't fair because they're not the ones – it's not their choice, is it. I like to try and keep the kids out of all that, not let my drug using affect them. I just want them to feel like other kids do.

These two quotations epitomise two different strategies of protection for children, which left the respondents on the horns of a dilemma. If they presented their drug use as 'normal' and not a 'novelty', children might be less inclined to experiment and thereby get into difficulties themselves in future. However, the strategy of 'normalising' a drug-using lifestyle was also seen to have inherent dangers, as it led to 'a life so different to everybody else', where children could no longer distinguish between normal and deviant lifestyles. As Heather explained: 'I feel that if I don't sort of sort something out now he's going to feel like it's normal to do them sort of things, isn't he. He's just going to feel it's quite normal to take drugs'. She clearly feels that she has failed as a parent because she has been unable to provide her son with a 'normal' upbringing due to her drug use. Her drug use stops her feeling 'normal', and harms her son by distorting his understanding of what is 'normal' and not giving him a 'normal' childhood, so that he is justified, in her view, by responding with delinquency:

> There's nothing more that I'd like in this world, is just to wake up and be normal again. I stop myself from smacking him or punching him because I think, 'Heather, it's your fault why he's like that. If you hadn't had the lifestyle you've had he wouldn't be – he may be not like that. If you'd have been a normal parent he might not be like that'.

Cathy, as an alcohol user, shared these concerns, and confessed that, when her children were 'taken into care it's the first time that she [daughter] thought that things was, you know, not normal. She thought that it was normal, like'.

Beth, who is currently using the strategy of deliberately not allowing drug use to be seen as 'normal' in her home, explained what had happened to her eldest son:

> … he'd be left with my mum, and then like when I come back he'd see me, you know, all out me face type of thing. And that was how he looked at me, and that was the norm. The norm. Although he was so different from everybody else, it was normal for him to be that way.

She later spoke about her distress when she realised that, as an adult, he was addicted to opiates:

> when Alex started using drugs to that degree I knew he was because it was all there, all the signs and everything. But I didn't want to believe that he was, you know. It took a lot for me to actually accept that he was doing it. And I know I kept thinking to myself, 'Well surely to God he'd have learnt by my mistakes. He's seen what I've gone through. So how can he? He wouldn't do it, not to that degree', you know what I mean. And it wasn't until he got registered that I accepted that he actually was in a mess with the drugs.

From the above quotations, it can be seen that, in relation to their current substance-use and their fears for their children in the future, the mothers are struggling with a major dilemma about what is 'normal'. They are attempting to present themselves as 'not normal' to their children ('don't do what I do') while simultaneously attempting to retain their authority as 'normal' parents inculcating a moral code for their children to follow. Thus they try to maintain a 'normal' family lifestyle for their children – so they would not feel different from others – while at the same time, within that lifestyle, they do their best to demarcate their own substance-use as 'not normal' and thus not to be emulated (although also not defined as a potentially desirable 'novelty').

These mothers are reluctant non-conformists. They cannot offer their children the comfort of a conventional, 'normal', lifestyle. At the same time, they cannot draw on the potential resource of an alternative, self-consciously counter-cultural or radical lifestyle. They do not delight in deviance and criminality. They are not making a political statement. They are not attempting to build a brave new world. They are simply getting by. Their use of substances (particularly opiates and amphetamines) is reminiscent, not of rebellion, but of medication. It links to the nineteenth-century use of laudanum, opium and morphine (Berridge and Edwards 1981); the prescribing of barbiturates and benzodiazepines (Cooperstock and Lennard 1979; Helman 1981) or the more recent popularity of selective serotonin re-uptake inhibitors such as Prozac (Kramer 1993; Wurtzel 1995). This view is reinforced by the fact that the women sometimes forgot that what they were doing was illegal. Stella and her partner were clearly astonished when the police arrested them for possession of heroin on one occasion. While other participants perhaps did not go so far as to forget that they were committing a serious offence in their use of heroin, nevertheless they too appeared to view its illegality merely as a necessary evil, and their use of opiates and other illicit substances as a normalised and everyday part of life along with their use of cigarettes, alcohol and tranquillisers.

Conclusion

The identity issues involved in being a junkie mum, which have been discussed in this chapter, are of the greatest significance for women such as those in this study: women who are mainly still relatively young parents, aged in their late 20s to mid 30s, with school-age children living at home. The women are in many cases either the sole or *de facto* head of the family. These factors heighten the salience of the women's identity as 'mother', and exacerbate the difficulties when this self and social identity fails.

What is significant, both on a theoretical level and for those working with such mothers, is the emphasis that the women themselves place on their identity as mothers. It is not the case that, as some theorists of the underclass have argued (Murray 1990) these women are lacking in adequate socialisation and engagement with normative ideologies of being a wife and mother. On the contrary, their identification with such traditional normative roles appears strong, despite their perceived or actual inability to fulfil such roles. Their struggle to maintain their role as a mother while remaining substance-dependent is both genuine and painful. An observer may notice the self-deceptions involved in the women's narratives, but the self-deceptions themselves serve to point up the women's continuing investment in their identities as mothers – they have not given up entirely. It is their remnants of self-belief, however delusive, which offer hope that agencies working with these women can assist them in working their way out of despair and failure and back into a sense of competence and autonomy. It is the women's normative family-based aspirations which may be able to provide a powerful resource for change, if drug and alcohol agencies and other professionals are able to validate and valorise their identity as 'mothers' over their identity as 'junkies' or 'alkies'.

James McIntosh and Neil McKeganey, in a study of recovery from drug addiction (2002), emphasise the significance of a 'spoiled identity' (following on from Goffman 1968) in the addict's motivation to quit drug use. They state: 'the theme which dominates our interviewees' accounts is their concern to repair an identity severely damaged by drugs and to recapture a sense of value and self-respect; in other words, a desire to regain a positive sense of self' (2002: 44). The motivation to quit requires 'a sense of a future that is potentially different from the present' (2002: 153). For women, this identity crisis is likely to be more severe than it is for men, as research from Rosenbaum (1981) onwards has repeatedly shown how women, once their identity is 'spoiled', find it more difficult to regain a valued social status. Perhaps, rather than anything dramatic, it can be the small comforts and achievements of daily family life which can provide the resource for women to regain a valued sense of self.

Adele, who was talking with the researcher and drug worker about taking heroin to help her get the housework done, began to explain: 'I don't feel very energetic and I can't do all the things that I wanna do in the house, and when [partner's] around I don't feel right, I feel like I should be getting up and doing things, and getting the ironing done'. At this point she was interrupted by the drug worker commenting, 'What's so special about the piggin' ironing!'. For many women in contemporary British society, there is very little special about such mundane household tasks, but one may conclude that, if the 'piggin' ironing' represents one of the very few normative activities which an individual feels able to access, then there may in fact be something very special about it: feeling validated for doing the ironing well, or doing the housework well, or doing childcare well, may, for some women such as Adele and the other mothers in this study, provide the small but essential first steps back into a valorised social and self-identity, and back into 'normal' life.

References

Advisory Council on the Misuse of Drugs (ACMD) (2003) *Hidden Harm: Responding to the Needs of Children of Problem Drug Users*. London: Home Office.

Ashley, R. (1972) *Heroin: The Myths and the Facts*. London: St James Press.

Berridge, V. and Edwards, G. (1981) *Opium and the People: Opiate Use in 19th Century England*. London: Allen Lane.

Boyd, S. (1999) *Mothers and Illicit Drugs: Transcending the Myths*. Toronto: University of Toronto Press.

Boyd, S. (2002) *Child Custody: Caring and Social Policy*. Oxford: Oxford University Press.

Callingham, M. (2004) *Survey for NACOA* (National Association for Children of Alcoholics), summary available from NACOA, Bristol, website: www.nacoa.org.uk

Colten, M. (1982) 'Attitudes, Experiences and Self-perceptions of Heroin-addicted Mothers', *Journal of Social Issues*, 38 (2): 77–92.

Cooperstock, R. and Lennard, H. (1979) 'Some Social Meanings of Tranquilliser Use', *Sociology of Health and Illness*, 1: 331–347.

Dally, A. (1982) *Inventing Motherhood: The Consequences of an Ideal*. London: Burnett.

Dorn, N. and South, N. (1985) *Helping Drug Users: Social Work, Advice Giving, Referrral and Training Services of Three London 'Street Agencies'*. Aldershot: Gower.

Goffman, E. (1968) *Stigma: Notes on the Management of Spoiled Identity*. Harmondsworth: Penguin (originally published (1963) Englewood Cliffs: Prentice-Hall).

Goode, S. (1993) Heroin-using Mothers: A Sociological Perspective, a dissertation submitted for the degree of MA in Sociological Research in Health Care, Sociology Department, University of Warwick.

Goode, S. (2000) 'Researching a Hard-to-Access and Vulnerable Population: Some Considerations on Researching Drug and Alcohol-Using Mothers', *Sociological Research Online*, 5 (1): www.socresonline.org.uk/5/1/goode.html

Graham, H. (1982) 'Coping: Or How Mothers are Seen and Not Heard', in S. Friedman and E. Sarah (eds) *On the Problem of Men*. London: Women's Press.

Helman, C. (1981) '"Tonic", "Fuel" and "Food": Social and Symbolic Aspects of the Long-term Use of Psychotropic Drugs', *Sociology of Science and Medicine*, 15B: 521–533.

Home Office (2005) *Preventing Drug Misuse*, webpage published 24 August, at website: www.homeoffice.gov.uk/drugs/drugs-misuse/preventing-drug-misuse/?version=1>

Kearney, M., Murphy, S. and Rosenbaum, M. (1994) 'Mothering on Crack Cocaine: A Grounded Theory Analysis', *Sociology of Science and Medicine*, 38 (2): 351–361.

Kearney, P., Levin, E. and Rosen, G. (2003) *Alcohol, Drug and Mental Health Problems: Working with Families*. London: Social Care Institute for Excellence.

Klee, H., Jackson, M. and Lewis, S. (eds) (2001) *Drug Misuse and Motherhood*. London: Routledge.

Kohn, M. (1992) *Dope Girls: The Birth of the British Drug Underground*. London: Lawrence and Wishart.

Kramer, P. (1993) *Listening to Prozac*. London: Fourth Estate.

Lalander, P. (2003) *Hooked on Heroin: Drugs and Drifters in a Globalized World*. Oxford: Berg.

McIntosh, J. and McKeganey, N (2002) *Beating the Dragon: The Recovery from Dependent Drug Use*. Harlow: Prentice Hall.

Murphy, S. and Rosenbaum, M. (1999) *Pregnant Women on Drugs: Combating Stereotypes and Stigma*. New Brunswick: Rutgers University Press.

Murray, C. (1990) *The Emerging British Underclass*. London: IEA Health and Welfare Unit.

National Society for the Prevention of Cruelty to Children (NSPCC) (2003) *Response to National Alcohol Harm Reduction Strategy Consultation*. London: NSPCC.

Pearson, G. (1987) *The New Heroin Users*. Oxford: Basil Blackwell.

Perry, L. (1979) *Women and Drug Use: an Unfeminine Dependency*. London: Institute for the Study of Drug Dependence.

Prime Minister's Strategy Unit (2004) *Alcohol Harm Reduction Strategy for England*. London: Cabinet Office.

Rosenbaum, M. (1981) *Women on Heroin*. New Brunswick: Rutgers University Press.

Ruddick, S. (1990) *Maternal Thinking: Towards a Politics of Peace*. London: Women's Press.

Smart, C. (1991) 'The Legal and Moral Ordering of Child Custody', *Journal of Law and Society*, 18 (4): 485.

South, N. (ed.) (1999) *Drugs: Cultures, Controls & Everyday Life*. London: Sage.

Stewart, T. (1987) *The Heroin Users*. London: Pandora.

Taylor, A. (1993) *Women Drug Users: An Ethnography of a Female Injecting Community*. Oxford: Clarendon Press.

Turning Point (2006) *Bottling it Up: The Effects of Alcohol Misuse on Children, Parents and Families*. London: Turning Point.

Welsh, I. (1993) *Trainspotting*. London: Secker and Warburg.

Wurtzel, E. (1995) *Prozac Nation*. London: Quartet.

13. Women, drugs and popular culture: is there a need for a feminist embodiment perspective?

Elizabeth Ettorre

Introduction

Illegal drugs have distinct social spaces in popular culture, while public opinions and social attitudes towards drugs use may vary significantly depending upon where, when and who is using drugs as well as the type of drug used. Drugs become visible as culturally shaped substances affecting human behaviour. However, for drug users, while the experience of their drugs use has a symbolic value, they themselves become symbols of deviant, abject individuals. As a threat to white, male, middle class values, drug use is emblematic of one's failure to engage properly with conventional society. When women are included in this representation, scholars (see, for example, Ettorre 2005, 2004, 1992; Measham 2002; Evans *et al.* 2002; Raine 2002; Murphy and Rosenbaum 1999; Sterk 1999; Stevens and Wexler 1998; Henderson 1996, 1997, 1999; Hunt, Joe-Laidler and Evans 2002; Anderson 1995, forthcoming; Kandall 1996) challenge traditional assumptions which lack an awareness of gender dynamics in the drugs field. In this shifting context, women appear in the drugs world in different ways than men and connections between women's pursuits in the illegal and conventional worlds are able to be made (Anderson 1998).

Here, I want to frame the issue of women, drugs and popular culture in a new light, as I introduce the notion of female embodiment in considering the complexities of this issue. Within the social sciences, the body as a theoretical concern is a relatively recent development. In particular, 'second wave' feminist work on women's health appealed to feminist social science scholars during the 1970s and allowed for the development of the body as a vital theoretical notion. While the body has become the site for 'the life project' within late modernity, bodies are cultural and social beings – fleshy entities where we inscribe normalised as well as stigmatised identities. Bodies are the means that experience all sorts of embodiments and why we can speak of the consuming body, the labouring body, the sporting body, the drug using body, etc. The body is a central point for struggles over power: a foundation of social identities which are inscribed upon our social, cultural and corporeal lives. Social behaviour at all times manifests itself in the fleshy human form – in a variety of forms of embodiment.

In this chapter, I analyse various core gender notions related to women drug users' bodies through the lens of embodiment. These notions include: *postmodern approaches, pollution, dependence, affective dimensions of risk*, and *power*. In analysing the five above mentioned notions, I will establish theoretical links with ongoing work in the drugs field and I do this through a feminist lens. Given that I want to offer a feminist, embodiment perspective, I scrutinise the effects of these core gender notions on women's drug using bodies. The assumption running throughout this chapter is that a clear knowledge of major embodiment issues in the experiences of women drug users needs to be valued in the drugs field. Exploring the connections between the female body, the technologies of drugs use and these core gender notions should offer us a lucid understanding of the contested character of cultural representations of drug use. Additional gender notions such as *pleasure, sexuality, resourceful activities, self-governance, risk reduction, leisure* and *reproduction* could have been added to my paper's schema. However, given the focus of this chapter and my self-imposed limit on the discussions, I plan to analyse these additional notions in future discussions outside of this chapter. In keeping with other contributions in this text, I want to build upon a schema in which the production of sensitive, collective explorations of the complex ways in which drugs use and popular culture come together is possible. For myself, I acknowledge that in these explorations there are problems and nuances involved when defining women's relationship to drug use as a feminist issue. But, I understand that implicit in our explorations are attempts to offer new cultural approaches. In this way, I see my task as offering a feminist approach which includes the notion of female embodiment.

The discussions in my chapter follow from analyses of the five core gender notions (outlined earlier). I will examine and define each core gender notion in turn and as I do, I will allude to how each particular notion leads to an awareness of gendered embodiment. My aim is to outline how operationalising these respective notions enable us to shape a gender sensitive or feminist perspective on women, drugs and popular culture. In the concluding part of my chapter, I thread together the beginnings of a feminist embodiment viewpoint on women, drugs and popular culture by making links with additional feminist ideas such as involvement in: an 'ethics of understanding', core activities, cultures of emotions, and challenging the drug misuse orthodoxy.

Envisaging core gender notions

The postmodern approach: finding our bodies

In recent work (Ettorre 2004) I have argued that two approaches co-exist in the drug field today: the classical and postmodern. I contend that there are differences between these two approaches and that in the main, they represent two bodies of thought, which have emerged over time in the drugs field. The postmodern approach offers more useful ideas and concerns because this approach has dealt more effectively with persistent systems of social inequalities. For example, social inequalities based on class, gender, ethnicity, ability and age are not only recognised but also respected as theoretical categories. Thus, the postmodern approach begins to deal with ethics and the fundamental human rights and needs of users (Ettorre 1992: 57). This approach focuses on drug use as a social issue that is culturally shaped into a social problem, reflective of 'disreputable pleasures' (O'Malley and Vlaverde 2004) and demonstrates how when social policies are grounded in erroneous premises, these can have harmful social consequences (Brownstein 1995: 45).

Trained experts are needed as much as drug users themselves. The latter are lay experts with a recognisable voice who experience drug use and its problems. Users are also the consumers of drugs that become intertwined with the cultures of everyday life (Ruggiero 1999). Consumption cultures are poly-drug cultures where users may or may not consume their drugs of choice, but at least they use a substance that makes them feel high or provides wanted psychotropic effects. Parker and Measham (1994) have referred to this particular type of consumption as the 'pick 'n' mix' scene. These drug cultures have a specific impact on young persons (Ettorre and Miles 2001), given that their lives occupy distinctive social spaces in the paths of consumption, reproduction and production, located in specific gender, sex, class and race contexts (Griffin 1997). Local narratives of normalisation that focus on consumers with specific needs and demands tend to be at variance with local policies of containment and control, shaped by surveillance systems such as the criminal justice system, customs and social services. Community-based services within the context of multi-agency responses become routinised (Teeman, South and Henderson 1999).

The postmodern approach may view drug users as transgressors but only in so far as their rule breaking is indicative of their experiencing poverty, unemployment, homelessness, victimisation and/or violence. In effect, social exclusion is a key factor in shaping the transgression of drug use (Pearson 1999). In this approach, safer sex and harm minimisation strategies are catchphrases as well as practices that attentive users will exploit with their significant others, within their peer groups and/or in public, rave, dance or consumer settings. All users, whether those using soft or hard drugs, have human rights and privileges that are not dependent on whether or not they discontinue using drugs. Here, I contend that the postmodern approach appears as the more compassionate approach given that voices of users are heard rather than silenced and, furthermore, inequalities, in particular those of class, gender, race and ethnicity, are acknowledged.

Within the postmodern approach, there are many ways to view the body and its theoretical development. In this context, Shilling (2005: 2–5) argues that body has become: 'commercialised', displaying a 'hyper efficient' performing self; a means of discriminating on the basis of gender; an object of various forms of control; surrounded by uncertainty given that there is a weakening the boundaries between itself and those of machines and a conceptual resource. For our purposes, I am interested not so much in how women's drug-using bodies are discriminated against (I take that for granted), rather I am concerned how we are able to conceptualise women's drug-using bodies in a way which enables us to advance our study of drugs and more importantly allows us to contextualise the boundaries between gendered drug-using bodies and popular culture.

To do this we need a discursive outline of the theoretical linkages in our cultural understandings of pollution, dependence, affective dimensions of risk and power. This is what I attempt to do in this chapter. For me as the author, the postmodern body itself in whatever physical form it is experienced positions women as both morally faulty and existentially immobilised. The bodies of males and females are constructed not simply as different but these bodies are differentially constructed (Shildrick 1997: 14). Shildrick contends that we must not overlook the persistence of masculinist values as a social form and the privileged construction of masculinity and male bodies over femininity and female bodies. Translating this to the drugs world means that we recognise gendered female bodies with visible, if not limited access to being valued in our drug using cultures have an important part to play in transforming our social worlds.

Pollution: challenging a 'contaminated' view

In earlier work (Ettorre 1992), I spoke of a hierarchy of drugs implying strong moralising features embedded in the popular discourse on drugs. Implicit in this hierarchy is the view that some substances are better as well as more polluting both chemically and culturally than other substances. In a classic piece, Warburton (1978) defined internal pollution, the 'state when the security of the internal environment of our bodies is destroyed'. While Warburton noted that internal pollution had received scant attention in the drugs field at that time, he argued that it was easy for those with a knowledge of drugs in society to blame over-prescribing doctors; criticise the marketing strategies of the pharmaceutical or the alcohol industry and see the breakdown of governments to curb, if not control the illegal global trade in heroin. While Warburton's ideas are rather outdated, he characterised a notion which thrives in contemporary society. For him, the consumers of drugs were to be blamed for internally polluting their bodies which became the interior environments for contamination. More importantly for him, drug users conspired in this pollution process by insisting in the up taking of drugs. While this moral judgement was made and drug users were seen to pollute themselves as well as their social environments, they involved themselves in a subtle discrimination process.

Let's translate this view on internal pollution which still exists today to women drug users. Those women are seen as 'polluted women' and they become main targets in the above discrimination process. Furthermore, why is it that women more than men drug users are targets of this discrimination process? In another classic piece, Mary Douglas has defined pollution as 'a type of danger which is unlikely to occur except where the lines of structure (i.e. cultural boundaries) are clearly defined' (Douglas 1966: 113). She suggests these cultural boundaries are more clearly defined for women than for men. Given this, we could argue that the consequence of transgressing these boundaries (i.e. polluting their bodies through drugs, becoming out of control, etc.) for women drug users is social exclusion on a grand scale. In a real sense, these women have polluted or soiled identities. Furthermore, pollutants such as drugs are coded as dirt or symbolic matter out of place and as a result, drug-using women can be seen to engage in a state of ritual impurity which is dangerous to themselves or others and which inheres in certain life events and conditions (i.e. reproduction) (Jewkes and Wood 1999).

We all know or should be aware at least of the low, irreversible status of the female drug user. While women have the disagreeable social function as carriers of difficult emotions, historically they have been punished when these emotions were overstated or they appeared too troublesome (Chesler 1994). Additionally, in the private/female sphere of domestic life, women, particularly mothers are the primary emotional copers – a reality which has a long-term effect on women's psychic lives (Ernst 1997). These social functions and resultant cultural practices have particular consequences for women drug users. Regardless of when, where, how and why women take drugs, they are viewed as having polluted their identities and their bodies as women. In turn, they have contaminated the private space of family life and the public space of communal cleanliness. In a popular sense, women drug users' bodies are eminently polluted.

Additionally, if she is pregnant, as are some women drug users, she characterises a body which is 'doubly polluted'. She is doubly polluted because she consumes illegal drugs contaminating her body. In turn, these drugs are seen to have contaminated her foetus. Unlike non-drug using women's bodies, pregnant drug users' bodies are viewed as lethal foetal containers. Murphy and Rosenbaum (1999) have shown how pregnant drug users are the focus of social policy concerns and the targets of treatment regimes and the law. Whether their babies are taken from them after birth or they are told to have an abortion, be sterilised or so on, these bodies are viewed as not fit to reproduce. In this context, Carter (2002) contends that women drug users bear three 'stigmata' – 'they are immoral, sexually indiscrete and inadequate care givers'. Furthermore, these stigmata become even more punitive when they use drugs during pregnancy.

Recalling the hierarchy of drugs, we see that there is a range of drugs from 'good or more socially acceptable' such as alcohol and tranquillisers at the top of the hierarchy to 'bad or unacceptable drugs' such as cocaine, amphetamines and heroin at the bottom of the hierarchy. This hierarchy is dependent on our cultural value systems and 'primitive' notions of pollution and purity and affects notions of the body for both men and women substance users. However, I would argue that the cultural delineation of the public and private spaces of our social lives places women's bodies more than men's bodies in a socially vulnerable position if they choose to consume an illicit drug. While the female body is the epitome of women's reproductive nature, drug use is seen as an assault on women's bodies. A drug-using woman becomes the cultural representation of a contemporary woman who does not care enough about her body. (This is an understatement.) Indeed, she is a polluted body *par excellence*.

Dependence: learning to swing both ways

A very basic thread of feminist thinking is that women more than men are socialised into dependency and as Gilligan (1987) has noted a 'woman's place is in a man's life cycle'. This idea of women's dependency must be understood in cultural, economic, social and political contexts as multi-pervasive. In related contexts (Ettorre 1989a, 1989b, 1992), I have detailed the tandem definitions of 'dependency' and discussed with special reference to the drugs field, the delicate and complex implications of these dual meanings for women. To aid an understanding of these subtleties, I will explain below my original ideas presented in those previous, related contexts.

Briefly, the etymological roots of the English word, dependency comes from Latin – the words *'de'* and *'pendere'*, meaning to hang down from. However, there are two meanings for 'dependence' in the English language: dependence refers to 'habit' or 'addiction' and 'a subordinate thing'. For women, the former meaning (habit or addiction) is what I have referred to as the unacceptable face of dependency, while the latter meaning (of the 'subordinate thing' kind) is the acceptable face of dependency as well as a cultural norm for many women. For example, dependency (of the addiction kind) is socially 'unacceptable' when it gets in the way of woman's social functioning as mother, daughter or worker, etc., while dependency (of the 'subordinate thing' kind) is seen as valued or culturally good enough when it involves being dependent on a man, men, male sexuality, male protection or male superiors.

For any woman, the cultural expectation that she will conduct herself in traditional, that is, dependent ways is clear. Nevertheless, an incongruity exists between the cultural expectation for women to be dependent and the need for all women to be in charge of their lives. For example, women, by being dependent on male kinship structures, such as the family, can be viewed as being constrained if not controlled by man (whether consciously or not) (Yanagisako and Collier 2004). While being constrained structures her life, she is seen in control. In this context, a woman drug user may consciously choose to use an addictive substance in order to cope with or control an oppressive, controlling situation such as her family life, relationship, etc. or even to be better mothers (Baker and Carson 1999: 360). Regardless of how she sees herself, she is viewed as 'a woman out of control' and not a 'normal' woman. The basic cultural message for a woman is that at all times, she should be in control of herself, mindful of her partner, her children, her home responsibilities and her work. If she feels strung out, stressed or unable to cope, she should avoid addictive substances.

On a more wide-ranging level, this issue of dependency becomes more multifaceted when we consider that women's dependent status is contingent upon their being at the same time depended upon by others. For women deeply involved in the social organisation of caring, giving care and helping others is a fundamental part of being a dependant. Her caring body is viewed not only as a dependent body but also a dependable body. In some ways, this illustrates the cultural complexities of dependency for women. Perhaps, in this light, we can see that in relation to women drug users the word, dependency, has various hues of meanings and cultural representations in both public and private spaces and with regards to female embodiment.

Affective dimensions of embodied risks: finding cultures of emotions

As a form of 'embodied deviance' (Urla and Terry 1995), drug use shapes bodies of individuals and determines their low social status and presumed lack of moral agency. A drug using body becomes a means of expression for solving a variety of problems that all bodies must face. But these problems become exaggerated because of drug use. All bodies are implicated in societal tasks that can cause trouble (Turner 1996). These have been referred to as 'the 4 Rs' (Scott and Morgan 1993) – restraint, representation, regulation and reproduction. In earlier work (Ettorre 2004), I discussed in detail how these bodily tasks relate to drug users with special reference to women drug users. In these prior contexts, I contended that the drug-using body needs to be seen as the place where we organise tasks of self-control, self-image, regulation and reproduction within the context of awareness of risk. Drug-using bodies are culturally and politically shaped by practices of containment and control as well as difference and risk. I argued that in the drugs field, we need to place the body as the focal point of our analyses and that as Turner (1996: 67) notes bodies are not gender-neutral systems but they are shaped by gender. In making these claims, I highlighted the complexities of gender as a process and an institution and maintained that the bodies of women drug users appear as 'broken bodies'. I used the term, 'broken bodies' in order to bring up the idea that Western ways of thinking have been based on separating ourselves as cultural and moral actors from our bodies and how we have become disembodied in our ways of theorising. I noted further that because morality is highly mediated by gender, it is based on the exclusion of female bodies from extensive moral agency. Women experience a fragmented morality of the body – in moral terms, women's bodies are not whole; they have become 'broken'. I claimed that there is a visible need to bring whole bodies back into the drug field and that academic feminists have exposed that the traditional neglect of the body reflected a masculinist social science that naturalised bodies and sanctioned control of male over female bodies. In this way, I attempted to document the types of regulation, restraint, provocation and resistance experienced by gendered bodies confronting drugs.

While the moral outrage levelled against women drug users is one more deployment in the stigmatisation of women's drug-using bodies, this can also be an occasion for these female bodies involved to privilege their performativities of disgust (Ahmed 2004) (i.e. drug use); to access their own raw materials of emotion and awareness; to consume actively and to creative a particular lifestyle that has traditionally remained undeveloped or repressed in a drug-using environment. To consume drugs is to open oneself up to risk (Collison 1996). However, the consuming, emotional body of the female drug user creates space for an imaginative form of femininity: illegal pleasures may become escapes from powerless and domination in everyday life and a type of consumption of desire. Drug use for this woman becomes a culturally resistive and oppositional response in her experience of powerlessness.

This conception is significant if we are to comprehend drugs as popular culture.

Power: revolt of the 'bio-underclass'

Up until recently, explanations about women offered in the drugs field have been uncritical and ahistorical. A systematic enquiry into this issue must highlight key individual and social factors which offer full accounts of the day-to-day experiences of women drug users. We need to be able to explain comprehensibly the structural roots of power and for women, the issue of power whether cultural, social, political or economic is most important.

In contemporary theory, power is a contested concept. However, with regards embodiment theory, power has a specific pivotal point: the body is the product of power relationships. As Turner (1996: 63) argues, the body as an object of power is produced in order to be controlled, identified and reproduced and power over the materiality of the body can be divided into two separate but related issues – disciplines of singular bodies and regulations of populations. Thus, power manifests itself through bodily disciplines or technologies of the self and regulatory regimes targeting populations.

For example, since the Enlightenment, the embodied subject has been located at the central focus of the practices and techniques of rational domination. This body has been at the core of productive control and manipulation that marks the order of discourse in modernity and the concurrent sexualisation and medicalisation of the body in a new configuration of power, biopower (Bradotti 1994: 58). Modernity is the sacred era of biopower – the age of constant normativity. Biopower is all about the power of normativity over the living organism; the force which produces and normalises bodies to serve prevailing relations of dominance and subordination and the total control and manipulation over living matter – specifically human living matter (Braidotti 1994: 58). In this age of biopower bodies are enclosed by many disciplinary regimes and strategies of attention in a relentless, incessant effort to assemble and normalise them.

The bodies of women drug users are constantly disciplined within the moralising discourse on drugs. They are sexualised and medicalised as a 'bio-underclass' (Baker and Carson 1999: 349) and their access to cultural, social, political or economic power is mediated not only by their damaged views of themselves (Dale and Emerson 1995) and their own despair (Spittal and Schechter 2001) but also by their lack of access to an extensive range of material, cultural and social resources needed to live a satisfying life (Kandall 1996).

Women, drugs, and popular culture through the lens of feminist embodiment

In this brief concluding part of my chapter, I begin to weave together a feminist embodiment perspective on women, drugs and popular culture. I want to do this by making connections with additional ideas on gender. While the gender notions, *postmodern approach, pollution, dependence, affective dimensions of risk*, and *power* work together to construct powerful images of women drug users in popular culture, these notions do allow for a level of struggle, inconsistency and instability in finding female embodiment through other activities such as involvement in: an 'ethics of understanding', what Anderson (2005) has called 'core activities' (Ettorre, forthcoming), cultures of emotions, and challenging the drug misuse orthodoxy.

While the body in a postmodern context is viewed as a site of intersection between power, the corporeal flesh and the individual as a subject to and of truths, we must not overlook the gendering of truths in this power/knowledge nexus (Shildrick 1997). When we weave these ideas together with ideas in the drugs world, we must continue to be vigilant in noticing how drug using bodies may stand for something fundamentally male or fundamentally female and how this can be taken as a biological and moral given. It is paramount that a postmodern approach on drugs use offers a critical embodiment approach incorporating a vision of popular culture which upholds the importance of gender as a key theoretical issue as well as an embedded social practice. In our postmodern approach, we need an 'ethics of understanding' gender issues and a methodology which preserves a vision of gender as both a social process and a cultural institution. By crafting an 'ethics of understanding', we create an 'ethical moment' (Shildrick 1997: 216) in which we discard modernist notions of static bodies and a complete self-identity marked by these bodies. In this space, a feminist ethics on drugs use which encompasses embodied selves will be able to develop.

We saw how a drug using woman becomes the cultural representation of a contemporary woman who does not care enough about her body and that she appears as a polluted body particularly if she becomes pregnant. She is perceived as uncaring of herself, her body, others around her and embodies shame. She is a failure in female embodiment and not dependable. Linked with the notion of dependence, her 'polluted' caring body is viewed not only as a dependent body but also as a body which should be dependable *vis a vis* her significant others. Here, it is interesting to note with special reference to the sorts of core activities (e.g. control of the household; their purchasing 'power'; subsidising men's use and engaging in dealing) that women drug users are involved in (Anderson 2005) how these core activities can be conceptualised as resources or 'embodied' caring work (Ettorre, forthcoming). Additionally, in focusing on these core activities as embodied resources, we are able to move beyond traditional assumptions surrounding women's contribution to drugs cultures.

In looking at the affective dimensions of risk or more simply drug-using women's 'culture of emotions', we see permeable boundaries existing between precarious emotions and past, present and future risks in her drugs using world. For these women, embodied emotions can be an important resource which challenges the drug misuse orthodoxy. Indeed, embodied emotions can be a form of pleasure as evidenced in Hinchliff's (2001) research which found that when ecstasy was used as a form of independent pleasure by women, these drug-using women did not view their actions as deviant. Do we see this as scandalous or equally as an important issue that is productive of social and cultural theory?

In relationship to power, the body can be seen as the end-product of a whole system of power relations (Armstrong 1987: 66). Nevertheless, embedded within these social and cultural processes, marking the boundaries between normal and deviant bodies, we see the cultural components of the drug misuse orthodoxy which shapes abnormal drug-using bodies as distinct from normal non-drug using ones. In these processes a variety of disciplinary strategies attend to female drug-using bodies to construct and attempt to normalise them. We need to challenge this orthodoxy and expose these disciplinary strategies in an attempt to break free from outdated social theories and cultural representations. Bringing the body into our work allows us to make this challenge and expòse.

In conclusion, bodies need to be seen as sites where narratives of risk, identity, knowledge of emotions and bodily management converge and not as gender neutral, non-determinate systems. A major stumbling block is that our work needs to be done with the explicit intention of demonstrating how creating a sensitive postmodern approach, understanding pollution, upholding the complex notion, dependence, recognising the affective dimensions of risk, and being aware of the dynamics of power are culturally dependent 'embodied processes' for us as drugs use theoreticians. Thus, there is a need for a resurrection of the body in our work and the breathing of 'epistemological' life back into our neglected frames. Our work should be about the affirmation of gendered corporeality – making the distinct claim that the body and specifically embodied emotions, risk, power, knowledge shaped by gender exist very centrally in our drug risk discourses.

References and suggested reading

Ahmed, S. (2004) *The Cultural Politics of Emotion*. New York: Routledge.

Anderson, T. (1995) 'Toward a Preliminary Macro Theory of Drug Addiction', *Deviant Behavior*, 16: 353–372.

Anderson, T. (1998) 'A Cultural Identity Theory of Drug Abuse', *The Sociology of Crime, Law and Deviance*, 1: 233–262.

Anderson, T. (2005) 'Dimensions of Women's Power in the Illicit Drug Economy', *Theoretical Criminology*, 9 (4): 371–400.

Baker P.L. and Carson A. (1999) '"I Take Care of my Kids": Mothering Practices of Substance-abusing Women', *Gender and Soc*, 13 (3): 347–363.

Braidotti, R. (1994) *Nomadic Subjects: Embodiment and Sexual Difference in Contemporary Feminist Theory*. New York: Columbia University Press.

Brownstein, H. H. (1995) 'The Media and the Construction of Random Drug Violence', in J. Ferrell and C. Sanders (eds) *Cultural Criminology*, pp 45–65. Boston: Northeastern University Press.

Carter C.S. (2002) 'Prenatal Care for Women Who are Addicted: Implications for Gender-sensitive Practice', *Affilia – Journal of Women and Social Work*, 17 (3): 299–313.

Chesler, P. (1994) *Patriarchy: Notes of an Expert Witness*. Monroe, Maine: Common Courage Press.

Collison, M. (1996) 'In Search of the High life: Drugs, Crime, Masculinities and Consumption', *British Journal of Criminology*, 36 (3): 428–444.

Dale, B. and Emerson, P. (1995) 'The Importance of Being Connected: Implications for Work with Women Addicted to Drugs, in C. Burck and B. Speed (eds) *Gender, Power and Relationships*. London: Routledge.

Douglas, M. (1966) *Purity and Danger*. London: Routledge and Kegan Paul.

Ernst, S. (1997) 'The Therapy Relationship', in M. Lawrence and M. Maguire (eds) *Psychotherapy with Women: Feminist Perspectives*, pp 11–35. Basignstoke: Macmillan.

Ettorre, E. (forthcoming) *Revisioning Women and Drug Use: Gender, Power and the Body*. Houndsmill: Palgrave Macmillan.

Ettorre, E. (2004) 'Revisioning Women and Drug Use: Gender Sensitivity, Embodiment and Reducing Harm, *International Journal on Drugs Policy*, 15: 327–335.

Ettorre, E. (1992) *Women and Substance Use*. Houndsmills, Basingstoke: Macmillan.

Ettorre, B. (1989a) 'Women, Substance Abuse and Self-help', in S. MacGregor (ed.) *Drugs and British Society*. London: Routledge.

Ettorre, B. (1989b) 'Women and Substance Abuse: Towards a Feminist Perspective or How to Make Dust Fly', *Women's Studies International Forum*, 12 (6): 593–602.

Ettorre, E. and Miles, S. (2001) 'Young People, Drug Use and the Consumption of Health, in S. Henderson and A. Petersen (eds) *Consumption of Health*. London: Routledge.

Evans, R.D., Forsyth C.J. and Gauthier, D.K. (2002) 'Gendered Pathways into and Experiences Within Crack Cultures Outside of the Inner City, *Deviant Behavior: An Interdisciplinary Journal*, 23 (6): 483–510.

Gilligan, C. (1987) 'Woman's Place in Man's Life Cycle', in S. Harding (ed.) *Feminism and Methodology*, pp 57–73. Bloomington and Milton Keynes: Indiana University Press and Open University Press.

Griffin, C. (1997) 'Troubled Teens: Managing Disorders of Transition and Consumption', *Feminist Review*, 55: 4–21.

Henderson, S. (1996) 'E Types and dance divas: gender research and community prevention', in T. Rhodes and R. Hartnoll (eds), *AIDS, Drugs and Prevention: Perspectives on Individual and Community Action*. London: Routledge.

Henderson, S. (1997). *Ecstacy: Case Unsolved*. London: Pandora.

Henderson, S. (1999) 'Drugs and Culture: The Question of Gender', in N. South (ed.) *Drugs: Cultures, Controls & Everyday Life*. London: Sage Publications.

Hinchliff S. (2001) 'The Meaning of Ecstasy Use and Clubbing to Women in the Late 1990s, *International Journal of Drug Policy*, 12 (5-6): 455–468.

Hunt, G., Joe-Laidler, K. and Evans, K. (2002) 'The Meaning and Gendered Culture of Getting High: Gang Girls and Drug Use Issues', *Contemporary Drug Problems*, 29 (2): 375–411.

Jewkes, R.J. and Wood, K. (1999) 'Problematizing Pollution: Dirty Wombs, Ritual Pollution and Pathological Processes', *Medical Anthropology*, 18 (2): 163–186.

Kandall, S.R. with the assistance of Petrillo, J. (1996) *Substance and Shadow: Women and Addiction in the United States* (second edn. 1999). Cambridge Massachusetts: Harvard University Press.

Measham, F. (2002). 'Doing Gender – Doing Drugs: Conceptualizing the Gendering of Drug Cultures', *Contemporary Drug Problems*, 298 (2): 335–373.

Measham, F., Aldridge, J. and Parker, H. (2001) *Dancing on Drugs: Risk, Health and Hedonism in the British Club Scene*. London: Free Association Books.

Murphy, S. and Rosenbaum, M. (1999) *Pregnant Women on Drugs: Combating Stereotypes and Stigma*. New Brunswick, New Jersey: Rutgers University Press.

O'Malley, P. and Valverde, M. (2004) 'Pleasure, Freedom and Drugs: The Uses of "Pleasure" in Liberal Governance of Drug and Alcohol Consumption', *Sociology*, 38 (1) 25–42.

Pearson, G. (1999) 'Drug Policy Dilemmas: Partnership, Social Exclusion and Targeting Resources' in A. Marlow and G. Pearson (eds) *Young People, Drugs and Community Safety*. Lyme Regis: Russell House Publishing.

Raine, P. (2001) *Women's Perspectives on Drugs and Alcohol: The Vicious Circle*. Aldershot: Ashgate.

Ruggiero, V. (1999) 'Drugs as a Password and the Law as a Drug: Discussing the Legalisation of Illicit Substances', in N. South (ed.) *Drugs: Cultures, Controls & Everyday Life*. London: Sage Publications.

Scott, S. and Morgan, D. (1993) *Body Matters*. London: The Falmer Press.

Shildrick, M. (1997) *Leaky Bodies and Boundaries: Feminism, Postmodernism and (Bio) Ethics*. London and New York: Routledge.

Shilling, C. (2005) *The Body in Culture, Technology and Society*. London: Sage.

Spittal P.M. and Schechter, M.T. (2001) 'Injection Drug Use and Despair Through the Lens of Gender', *Canadian Medical Association Journal*, 164 (6): 802–803.

Sterk, C. (1999) *Fast Lives: Women Who Use Crack Cocaine*. Philadelphia: Temple University Press.

Stevens, S.J. and Wexler, H.K. (eds) (1998) *Women and Substance Use: Gender Transparency*. New York and London: The Haworth Press (published simultaneously as *Drugs and Society*, 13 (1-2) 1998).

Teeman, D., South, N. and Henderson, S. (1999) 'Multi-impact Drugs Prevention in the Community, in A. Marlow and G. Pearson (eds) *Young People, Drugs and Community Safety*. Lyme Regis: Russell House Publishing.

Turner, B. (1996) *The Body and Society* (2nd edn). London: Sage Publications Ltd.

Urla, J. and Terry, J. (1995) 'Introduction: Mapping Embodied Deviance', in J. Terry and J. Urla, (eds) *Deviant Bodies: Critical Perspectives on Difference in Science and Popular Cultures*, pp 1–18. Bloomington, Indiana: Indiana University Press.

Warburton, D.M. (1978) 'Internal Pollution', *Journal of Biosocial Science*, 10: 309–319.

Yanagisako, S.J. and Collier, J.F. (2004) 'Toward a Unified Analysis of Gender and Kinship', in R. Parkin and L. Stone (eds) *Kinship and Family: An Anthropological Reader*, pp 275–293. Oxford: Blackwell.

14. The drugs of labour: the contested nature of popular drug use in childbirth

Laura Hübner

Introduction

While preceding chapters debate the extent of illegal drug use amongst young people and, by implication, the centrality of illegal drugs in youthful popular culture, this chapter highlights examples of the contested nature of common and popular *legal* drug consumption. Childbirth is taken as an example of a site where the cultural and the physiological intersect and where popular cultural discourses compete with medico-technical discourses to define access to legal drugs.

People remain divided about the intrinsic worth of pain-relieving drugs during childbirth. The elaborate histories of childbirth reveal tensions and contradictions not only in the healthcare system and where it meets the wider culture, but also specifically in the boundaries of 'normal' or legal drug use, raising questions about morality and ethical practice. Many of the debates and media representations concerning pain-relieving drugs and childbirth centre on the body, its functions and limitations in relation to the mind, but more specifically the female body as it functions politically, socially and morally within shifting cultural norms and expectations. Trend and fashion, influenced by cultural, economical and religious factors, and how these impact on gender, age, class and ethnicity, often dictate the sway of these debates and representations, prescribing who has and who should have access to which drugs, when the drugs should be used or administered and – most controversially – who has control over usage, and the range of choice available. Therefore, what becomes coded as acceptable, and legal, practice in terms of access, use and administration during the three stages of labour and birth[1] is not fixed, but liable to change.

The aim here is not to present a rallying call for preferred birth-giving practices, as a number of articles have done, for example arguing from feminist and humanitarian concerns.[2] Instead, this chapter analyses a range of materials including medical and academic texts, alongside popular media texts such as books on pregnancy and birth, websites, maternity packs, magazines and newspaper articles to investigate cultural and statutory forms of control upon legal drug consumption where it concerns the specific case of childbirth.

The campaign for natural childbirth

Historical developments in the approach to childbirth are complexly linked with shifting levels of value and approval that a culture places on pain. British physician and obstetrician W. Tyler Smith's sensationalist response in *The Lancet* (1847: 321–323) to the case of a young French woman, whose inhalation of ether as pain relief during childbirth made her experience sexual fantasies and behave untowardly, sparked off a moral debate regarding femininity and national purity: 'To a woman of this country the bare possibility of having feelings of such a kind excited and manifested in outward uncontrollable actions would be more shocking even to anticipate than the endurance of the last extremity of physical pain' (Smith 1847: 322). That taboo thoughts and exhibitionist behaviour might be triggered during the sacred event of childbirth was unthinkable for many in the UK at the time.

Opponents of anaesthesia in any form of surgery, dentistry and obstetrics often drew on moral and religious doctrines to argue in favour of pain, valuing labour and childbirth pain above and beyond other forms. In a number of religions, painful suffering is associated with divine punishment and sacrifice. For example, when James Young Simpson (1811–1870) administered chloroform to labouring women, he was met with vehement disapproval, with opponents citing the Bible, stating that the pain of childbirth is women's punishment for Eve's Fall: 'In sorrow thou shalt bring forth children' (Genesis 3: 16). Criticisms were largely quenched when Dr John Snow (1815–1858) administered chloroform to Queen Victoria on 7 April 1853 at the birth of her eighth child, Prince Leopold, and again four years later at the birth of her last child, Princess Beatrice. Philip Rhodes emphasises the moral and religious significance of this event in influencing the wave of popular opinion: 'The Queen was head of the Church of England and a devout christian, carrying immense moral authority' (Rhodes 1995: 83). However, as will be discussed later in this chapter, the idea that pain in childbirth is natural and therefore somehow beneficial lingers on in many of the current debates and discourses surrounding drug use.

In sharp contrast, English obstetrician Grantly Dick-Read (1890–1959), practising in the 1920s, founded his theories upon the belief that there is, and should be, no pain during childbirth, so long as it is allowed to progress naturally, without fear. Dick-Read first published his controversial views on childbirth in 1933 in *Natural Childbirth*, expanded as *Revelations of Childbirth*, leading towards the fourth and last edition completed in 1959, *Childbirth Without Fear*,[3] reprinted in 2004. Central to Dick-Read's theory of natural childbirth is the 'Fear-Tension-Pain Syndrome'.[4] He argues that, if women are instructed in the correct manner using breathing and relaxation techniques so that pain-relieving drugs are rendered unnecessary, there would be no pain during labour, except in a minority of cases (the 5 per cent that he categorises as 'abnormal'). According to this theory, it is the *fear* of pain that causes actual pain via the 'medium of pathological tension' (Dick-Read 2004: 45).

In its promotion of women's choice, knowledge and control in childbirth (routes that would later be taken up by the feminist cause) Dick-Read's work has had a tremendous influence upon the current writings and practices of childbirth. Binary oppositions evident in his writing – such as man/woman, doctor/midwife, unnatural/natural – have remained prominent in the fight against what has been seen as the increasing intervention by men in the delivery of babies. Dick-Read campaigned for women's access to knowledge about the processes of pregnancy and childbirth, using warfare imagery to convey the sense of an emergent struggle:

> Never before in the history of man has he faced so great a power of militant women, exercised in a claim so justifiable and a demand so overwhelming. They are militant today in pursuit of their health and happiness in natural childbirth ...
>
> (Dick-Read 2004: 17)

Dick-Read (2004: 106) rightly condemns the system whereby women are forced to take drugs, such as the chloroform mask being forced onto the face, whether wanted or not. As Andrew Claye outlined in 1939:

> ... in the last few years there has been a definite move towards universal obstetric analgesia in this country, helped financially and otherwise by the National Birthday Trust and encouraged by the investigations of the British College of Obstetricians and Gynaecologists.
>
> (Claye 1939: 95)

With surgical interference and the use of drugs in labour becoming virtually compulsory, many people felt that a call for women to take control was urgently needed.

Although Dick-Read's work was timely, its negation of the agonising pains of 'normal' childbirth was rooted in an equally cast-iron perception of gender roles. His reverence for 'motherhood' and for the 'male instincts of preservation and protection when in its presence' (Dick-Read 2004: xi) hark back to a Victorian division between men and women:

> Is there any love so unselfish and so inspiring as the love of a mother for her child? To healthy minded women it is the realisation of their highest ambition, the fulfilment of their instinctive urge and the ultimate perfection of their bodily functions.
>
> (Dick-Read 2004: 20)

Dick-Read further universalises the female by tracing the life of a young woman through to becoming a mother, whereupon 'every girl' will find herself (passively) in love, marry and 'if all goes well' conceive and prepare 'to bear her child' (Dick-Read 2004: 21). Prior to this, he draws a vivid picture of his original inspiration, the 'woman in Whitechapel' who first got him thinking about the values of natural childbirth, in a 'low hovel' at 2.00 or 3.00 in the morning 'by the railway arches' with rain pouring in at the broken window. He recounts how his patient lay covered only in sacks 'refusing the mask of chloroform' and how the baby was born with 'no fuss or noise' (Dick-Read 2004: 19). He embellishes his story by narrating the woman's later explanation for this refusal; she 'did not answer at once, but looked from the old woman who had been assisting to the window through which was bursting the first light of dawn; and then shyly turned to me and said: "It didn't hurt. It wasn't meant to, was it, doctor?"' (Dick-Read 2004: 19).

This universalising of the female contradicts Dick-Read's overt insistence upon free will and the notion of treating each case as an individual. Moreover, the story of the poor woman in Whitechapel mythologises the impoverished female as a key to an untamed, primitive truth of womanhood and childbirth. There is also a religious tone that draws to a climax at the end of the book, when he claims that the highs of natural childbirth are the closest connections of the body with 'the most inexplicable manifestation of the spirit of nature' (Dick-Read 2004: 190), visualising the doctor as 'the devil standing in the guise of liberator of the oppressed' (Dick-Read 2004: 191). It will be seen later in this chapter that this spiritual elevation continues in much of the current discourses of natural childbirth.

Dick-Read is extremely forward-thinking in his insistence that there should always be an anaesthetic or analgesic apparatus to hand in all labours, and that women should where necessary be instructed in its use, implying some degree of female control during childbirth. However, his work is as reductive as it is liberating, and his categorisations of: (1) normal or natural childbirth, (2) average or cultural labour, and (3) abnormal or surgical delivery are too rigid, suggesting an element of blame upon the woman who fails to be instructed in the right (natural) way. In the final parts of the book, troublesome, sleepless and 'green nappy babies' are attributed to 'negative', or unnatural, women (Dick-Read 2004: 277) thus constructing unnatural women as, essentially, the cause of future ills that will be associated with their offspring.

Popular culture and the natural/unnatural divide

At the end of the nineteenth century suffragettes campaigned for all women who wanted it to be given anaesthesia during childbirth. In turn, the twentieth century saw feminists fighting for 'natural childbirth' following the course of figures like Dick-Read. Many supporters of 'natural childbirth' associate the use of drugs in childbirth with the disenfranchisement of women under the power of (male) obstetricians. Jan Williams discusses the transition of childbirth from the female to the male domain: 'The transformation of midwifery from the control of women themselves with a midwife, meaning 'with-woman', to domination by obstetricians, from the Latin *obstare* meaning 'to stand before', is both rich and fascinating ...' (Williams 1997: 234). Any institutional administration of drugs might be seen to conflict with the philosophy that, since birth is a natural process, labour should proceed at its own pace with as little medical intervention as possible.

There is no official consensus for what constitutes 'natural childbirth'; the term is as confused and contentious as 'natural' and 'nature', and politically as dangerous. On a general level, the term 'natural childbirth' can be used to signal that the baby was born via the 'normal' (vaginal) route, as opposed to via abdominal surgery (Caesarean section), with implicit emphasis on differentiation (*not* a Caesarean) and the 'moment' of birth itself – disregarding, for example, how long first and second stages of labour might have been endured 'naturally' prior to this.

However, there are a range of more purist interpretations of 'natural childbirth' in popular cultural discourses. At its most extreme it implies complete abstinence, a birth without any forms of medical intervention or drugs. Controlled breathing, yoga (or active standing, squatting or kneeling positions), being at home and birthing pools are amongst methods of pain relief most associated with a purist interpretation of natural birth. Notably, 'alternative' or 'complementary' methods, such as those incorporating hypnosis, acupuncture, reflexology and homeopathy, are also often located within the 'natural' category.

A completely purist approach to 'natural childbirth' is taken by French obstetrician and researcher Michel Odent who introduced the idea of birthing pools and home-from-home birthing rooms. He developed the maternity unit at Pithiviers Hospital in France in the 1960s and '70s, and founded the Primal Health Research Centre in London, which looks at the long-term effects of the earliest experiences of newborn life, from labour and birth through to the first hours post-partum. His work has featured in medical journals such as *The Lancet*, and in television programmes including the BBC documentary *Forty Minutes: Birth Reborn*, broadcast in March 1982. He has published a wide range of scientific papers, and books (in 21 languages), including *The Scientification of Love* (1999), *The Farmer and the Obstetrician* (2002) and *Birth and Breastfeeding: Rediscovering the Needs of Women during Pregnancy and Childbirth* (2004). His 'Foreword' to the 2004 edition of Grantly Dick Read's *Childbirth Without Fear* universalises birthing experiences, in search of the 'authentic midwife' making comparisons between women across the world and between women and other mammals. His thesis here, as throughout his work, emphasises the importance of 'the cocktail of "love hormones" a woman releases when giving birth' (Odent in Dick Read 2004: viii) over the 'strict standard protocols' of the medical world (Odent in Dick-Read 2004: vii), arguing that natural love hormones, such as oxytocin, produced during the three stages of labour and birth to strengthen contractions, are essential ingredients for the future of a healthy civilisation.

Odent's theories filter into the popular sphere directly and indirectly. For instance, he has a column in *Mothering* the 'Natural Family Living' magazine in the 'Ask the Experts' section, answering questions about labour and water birth (featured on the website: www.mothering.com). Throughout his work, he advocates using birthing pools to facilitate the release of oxytocin and thus reduce the need for pain killers, suggesting that long labours are caused by the wrong hormonal balance. As an 'Expert' for *Mothering*, Odent directs readers to the Birth Works website (which has links with the Primal Health Research Centre at: www.birthworks.org/primalhealth) where studies are underway on the possible correlations between the mother's use of analgesics during childbirth and the statistical likelihood of the child becoming addicted to amphetamines (in the case of entonox) or opiates (in the case of pethidine) in later life. The worth of these statistical findings is still being debated at midwife and obstetric conferences across Europe and the US.

Odent consistently promotes the values of a natural over an unnatural high during childbirth. In his article 'The First Hour Following Birth: Don't Wake the Mother!' in *Midwifery Today*, Odent focuses on the importance of the natural release of oxytocin to maintain uterine contractions and bring about the delivery of the placenta, against the common practice now of a medical injection of synthesised oxytocin (or syntometrine or syntocinon) used to speed up this process, in the hope of avoiding complications such as haemorrhaging. Odent argues that medical injections of oxytocin and other administrations of drugs during childbirth block the 'love hormones' that are naturally released, in effect inhibiting – if not destroying – the bonding process between mother and baby. Odent argues that oxytocin is an essential, altruistic natural hormone, released also during sexual intercourse and lactation. His mode of language is striking, as he adopts terms commonly associated with the recreational practice of illegal drug-taking, thus emphasising the natural and unnatural divide. For example, he values the biological process whereby mother and baby 'are impregnated with opiates', where the baby is 'naturally programmed to find the breast and the mother is 'still "on another planet"', instinctively knowing how to hold the baby.[5]

Childbirth, particularly as experienced by 'first-time mothers', is often presented as a rite of passage, a spiritual ritual leading towards the altered state of 'mother'. The ways in which cultures define this ritual ensure that boundaries between acceptable and unacceptable, or legal and illegal, drug use during birth remain fluid, negotiated as they are around political, religious and social factors as well as medical and physiological considerations. Odent argues throughout his work that, although his research is politically incorrect, it has important implications for the future well-being of society (see for example his book *Birth Reborn: What Childbirth Should Be* (1994)). Thus, according to Odent, culture is determined by the body. Biological determinism, as defined by Lynda Birke, is the view that 'something about a person's *behaviour* or *capabilities* is caused by some aspect of their biology' and that 'If biology is the basis ... then it will tend to show through however much we try to change things through learning' (Birke 1992: 68). But the political implications of Odent's work go beyond this, insinuating that the body is easily changed and therefore – for moral reasons – should not be tampered with, that childbirth 'should be' (should remain) a certain way. The call for an unveiling of a 'true' childbirth is rife in popular culture, but as Paula A. Treichler argues, there is no 'true nature' or 'real meaning' of childbirth:

> The word *childbirth* is not merely a label, provided us by language, for a clear-cut event that already exists in the world; rather than describe, it *inscribes*, and makes the event intelligible to us. We cannot look *through* discourse to determine what childbirth 'really' is, for discourse itself is the site where such determination is inscribed.
>
> (Treichler 1990: 132)

The question of whether to use drugs during childbirth becomes tied to questions about the essential nature of womanhood and motherhood, and the extent to which there should be a moral duty to experience, or relieve, pains naturally. Much of the debate therefore hinges on what is encoded and packaged as natural or unnatural. But it also hinges on our understanding of pain, which in its rawest sense must surely feature as another powerful block to any natural love hormones, especially considering the short and long-term traumas that can be brought on by extreme pain, and further physiological complications that can emerge during a painful birth that will not progress. Even an uncomplicated vaginal birth necessarily involves, at the very least: strong labour contractions, pushing the baby out, post-partum contractions leading to the delivery of the placenta, postnatal contractions to reduce the size of the uterus and postnatal pains in the perineum area. As Christina Mazzoni points out, 'Although it is constructed as liberating, the rhetoric of the natural can subtly and not so subtly constrain, shape, and even reduce the experience of maternity' (Mazzoni 2002: 157).

The 'rhetoric of the natural' implicitly relies upon a series of symbolic frameworks that employ medical or biological determinist discourses and that surface in the symbolic frameworks of popular culture and media. The elevated status of the natural birth, for instance, seeps into the mainstream, often aligned with an Odentian understanding of the 'authentic' or natural midwife. The *Daily Mail* leads the debate at the time of writing this chapter with the headline on 8 May 2006 'Mothers "Should Know the Pain of Childbirth"'. Health Reporter, Emily Cook writes:

> WOMEN should experience the pain of childbirth and not rely on painkillers to get them through, midwives will claim this week.
> Taking drugs during labour can leave new mothers feeling they have 'missed out' in some way on a satisfying experience.
> As a result, they can find it harder to bond with their babies straight after the birth.
>
> (Cook 2006: 28)

The report refers to The Royal College of Midwives (RCM) 2006 Annual Conference and Exhibition, which took place at the Riviera International Conference Centre, Torquay, in May 2006.[6] The RCM runs a campaign to lower intervention and Caesarean ('Campaign for Normal Birth' or 'The Big Push for Normal Birth') maintaining that these should be the last, rather than the first, choice. The College website under the section 'Coping with Pain' prioritises 'Natural Pain Relief' and does not discuss the use of pain-relieving drugs (www.rcmnormalbirth.net/). Instead, the focus is on ways of taking the woman's mind off the pain, for example by massage, conversation, and making jokes, at least in the earlier, less painful stages. Later on, according to this campaign, it is crucial that stress hormones created by fear or intervention do not block the release of the woman's 'pain relieving endorphins', which 'have a similar effect to opiate drugs (drugs like heroin and morphine work by engaging the endorphin receptors in the brain)'. This kind of advice can be extremely empowering. In addition, an active upright position, with the mind looking inwards in a focused manner can often help the gravitational mechanisms of labour and birth to progress. However, a hint of failure is directed at women who use analgesic pain relief:

All births can be rewarding. Even the woman who has a caesarean section under general anaesthetic still has the miracle of a newborn baby. But certain kinds of birth may be more rewarding than others. A woman who goes through labour without analgesia or intervention will experience a birth with the full potential of which she is capable, enjoying one of nature's great 'highs' thanks to her increased levels of endorphins.

(www.rcmnormalbirth.net/, accessed 8.5.06)

The *Daily Mail* report on the RCM conference ends with an advert for their special guide to alternative pain relief at www.dailymail.co.uk. The site features Naomi Coleman's article 'How to Face the Fear of Labour' (2 October 2002) in response to the new mother and baby survey[7] out that week. Using terms reminiscent of Grantly Dick-Read, Coleman draws on the advice of experts from two of the largest childbirth organisations in the UK, where natural products are big business: Janet Balaskas, founder of the Active Birth Centre, featuring details of how to order a birth ball, or hire a birth pool from the Active Birth website; and Belinda Phipps from the National Childbirth Trust (NCT).

The NCT, a registered charity, is in contact with around 300,000 parents and parents-to-be,[8] through over 380 branches and groups across the UK. The word is also spread via a range of antenatal classes, helplines and social and educational events, as well as books and leaflets produced by the NCT. There are also links to products and services, and people do not have to be a member to go along to NCT events.

Daniel Miller (1997: 69) asserts that while the letters NCT stand for National Childbirth Trust, it might more appropriately be called the Natural Childbirth Trust, because of the compulsive concern with nature evident in most active members and literature. In actual fact, the 'N' stood for 'Natural' when the trust was initially formed in 1956, founded upon ideas associated with Grantly Dick-Read. It became 'National' in 1961. The concern with nature is perhaps not quite so prominent now as Miller suggests, since much of the literature on pain relief includes a range of methods including: breathing and visualisation, position, massage, water, complementary therapies, TENS,[9] gas and air, pethidine and epidurals, though admittedly the order of this sequence privileges the drug-free. However, writing openly as someone who attended NCT-like classes, living in north-west London as a middle-class academic, Miller captures a 'truth' in the sense of a popular conception of the NCT and the experiences and feelings of members who have attended NCT preparation and postnatal classes.

The structure of NCT classes clearly depends on the local branch, and the content is often determined by the specific interests of group members, but Miller speaks for those who have been encouraged to avoid 'interventions' such as painkillers (Miller 1997: 69) and for those who ironically had 'hitherto devoted themselves in large measure to escaping from the constraints of biology and family' (Miller 1997: 69). The NCT is a social organisation and can become a lifestyle choice. Women who attend antenatal classes often go on to meet as a postnatal support group for years, organising childminding and babysitting circles, where many of the discourses on the natural filter through into postnatal concerns for the purity of the infant's consumption practices, supporting breastfeeding and ways of avoiding sugary drinks.

The cultural and economical capital of the body, and of the natural as it collides with science, is realised in much of the current media, from leaflets about yoga and birthing balls available in hospital waiting rooms through to television programmes and advertisements. For example, the documentary *Life Before Birth* (Channel 4, 22 April 2006), celebrating the innovative techniques developed by Professor Stuart Campbell to produce footage of foetal development within the womb, is set to a voice over and poetry by Roger McGough which marvel at the body's natural endorphins, and the importance of the baby's experiences of birth.

Nature has long been a commodity. The latest advertisement features in pregnancy and parenting magazines continue to capitalise on its sales appeal. For example, the whole page spread on the TENS machine (transcutaneous electrical nerve stimulation), in 'Anne's *Guide to...* Pain Relief: Are you feeling TENS' in *Practical Parenting* magazine, plays off the natural faculties of this battery-operated machine, which is wired to electrodes and taped onto the back, against the artificiality of drugs:

> These gentle impulses stimulate your body to release its own natural painkiller, endorphins, and by stimulating the nerves, pain signals are blocked before they reach the brain (often referred to as the 'gate theory') ... A TENS machine offers the chance of a drug-free pain relief, allowing you to stay alert and keep mobile. It's completely natural, doesn't affect your body in any way and is easy to self-administer.
>
> (Anne Richley *Practical Parenting*, March 2006: 42)

Thus, sticking electrodes onto the body is coded as more natural than medicine. A technical scientisation of nature is used to display drugs as unnatural, corrupting substances, inhibiting the body's alertness and mobility, thus perpetuating the myth of failure and passivity related to drug use in childbirth. Advertisements for birthing balls, birthing pools and yoga mats play on ideologies of drug-free birth as more active, working through the identity of the woman to that of the emerging mother. Mothers are encouraged in advertisements and DVDs to use their birthing balls and yoga mats after the birth, in healthy play with their babies.

The contemporary ritual of childbirth: is there any choice?

Ninety-six per cent of women in the UK today give birth in hospital.[10] While some of the defining features of 'natural childbirth' are currently embedded into the system, home births are still an extreme minority, and it is illegal for a woman to give birth without the presence of a midwife. It is exceptionally rare to (choose to) give birth outside of one of these two pre-arranged locations – the home or hospital.

From the moment that pregnancy is declared to the doctor, the woman becomes part of the pregnancy and birth system, and will usually comply with a succession of appointments with the midwife, doctor or consultant depending on the individual case and regional preference. *The Pregnancy Book* provided by the NHS is given free to all first-time mothers in England, and all women are asked to complete the personal section of a pregnancy and birth booklet which is then filled in by the doctor or midwife at each visit, monitoring physiological developments such as blood pressure and blood iron levels. The woman is encouraged a few weeks prior to the expected due date to write a birth plan (a form on the booklet usually provides space for this) outlining preferences for, among other things, a birthing partner, birthing positions and pain-relieving drugs. Jan Williams sees the issuing of birth plans as perpetuating the illusion of choice:

> ... in reality, free choice does not exist. Birth plans may be seen as a public relations exercise in medical hegemony.
>
> (Williams 1997: 241)

However, choice inevitably involves some degree of limitation, a selection of one thing over another, from a limited range. It is also difficult to judge the extent to which a woman's wishes are met, since wants and needs can change significantly through the event of childbirth.

The format and wording used in the NHS *Pregnancy Book* in many respects typifies the majority of contemporary popular literature aimed at pregnant women and their partners, published in the UK,[11] and can therefore be seen as forming part of a prevailing discourse in birth giving practices. The section 'Pain Relief in Labour' (2001: 91–94) opens with the statement 'Labour is painful', in contrast to Dick-Read and some of the later proponents of natural childbirth that suggest that pain is fear-induced. However, the continuing statement, that women should therefore learn about what is available, implies that the call for women to take control, sparked off by Dick-Read and later feminists, has had a profound influence upon current practices. The hierarchy of pain relief as set out here also implies that this level of control is positioned within a limited choice, that the woman's experience is framed within precise boundaries.

The sections 'Types of Pain Relief' and 'Alternative Methods of Pain Relief' connote a sense of normal and 'other' (alternative). Top in the hierarchy of normal is 'self-help', which involves methods such as relaxation, breathing and keeping mobile, significantly all elements of 'natural' childbirth. This is followed by 'gas and air' (entonox), the TENS machine,[12] the 'intramuscular injection of a pain-relieving drug, usually pethidine' (a morphine-like narcotic that alters the perception of pain), and finally, the epidural anaesthesia, which numbs the feelings of pain from the birth canal to the brain, 'So, for most women, an epidural gives complete pain relief' (2001: 92).[13] Alternative methods, including acupuncture, aromatherapy, homeopathy, hypnosis, massage and reflexology, are marginalised and are only appropriate within a secure medical framework; women are advised to: let the hospital know beforehand, discuss ideas with the doctor or midwife, use a trained practitioner and contact the Institute for Complementary Medicine (2001: 93).

Pain-relieving drugs made available by the NHS are thus allotted an implicit hierarchy. The structure of this hierarchy is governed to some extent by what is deemed medically 'safe'. For example, pethidine can make some women feel sick and if it is given too close to the time of delivery, it may affect the baby's breathing making an antidote necessary. However, in the case of childbirth, as with other instances that implicate the legal drug debate, medical preferences are not fixed.

Popular childbirth books commonly foreground the 'fulfilling' nature of childbirth.[14] Michelle Stanworth argues that the pressures on women to 'regard motherhood as the fulfilment of their lives ... have different impacts on women in different circumstances and women respond to them in varying ways, depending upon their social circumstances, their health and their fertility, and according to opportunities and meanings derived from ethnic and social class cultures' (Stanworth 1987: 3). Stanworth goes on to highlight that 'it is difficult to find a position on motherhood from which we can say clearly and unambiguously what women want or need' (Stanworth 1987: 4). The same is true with childbirth. Indeed, women are often self-reflexively split between competing discourses, seeing childbirth as something just to get through safely, but also experiencing some level of jubilation or failure/loss/ lack/blame depending upon the level of exhilaration felt through the final stages of birth. In terms of pain relief, much of this is dependent on what certain 'drugs' come to *mean*, where even the meanings of 'safe' and 'healthy' are culturally determined. The symbolic power of a drug's image and the construction of symbolic frameworks of drug use help to inform consumer choice.

Attendance at classes can be empowering, but women also choose not to subscribe to NCT codes, or to attend NCT groups, or to participate in NHS ante-natal weekends and breastfeeding evenings. Women may choose to consume illegal substances, such as cannabis, to help endure painful contractions, sometimes even in the presence of the midwife if they are sympathetic to this form of pain relief. Women who have hitherto taken illegal drugs at festivals and clubs might choose to push for a natural home birth and a birthing pool. Part of the reasoning behind these diverse 'choices' seems to be the need to forge a sense of control, to some extent informed by the popular images of particular drugs and the implicit hierarchies they represent.

Articles, such as Cook's report in the *Daily Mail* (mentioned previously) – 'Mothers "Should know the Pain of Childbirth"' – are written to provoke debate and stimulate controversy, and immediate responses to anti-drug articles are likely to include retorts that it is the woman's right to decide which forms of pain relief are required, and at what stages of labour.[15] The debate continues through to the weekend newspapers. The article 'Mummy State: Childbirth Revolution' fills the front-page of the *Independent on Sunday*, leading with a quote from Patricia Hewitt, Secretary of State for Health, 'I want all women to be offered the choice of a home birth and a choice of pain relief'. Here, the 'revolution in childbirth policy that will reverse decades of medical convention' advocates a system whereby home birth and pain relief 'choices' are not seen as mutually exclusive (Marie Woolf and Sophie Goodchild, *Independent on Sunday*, 14 May 2006, p. 1). The cover story of

Observer WOMAN magazine (Mimi Spencer's 'How Pregnancy Went Public', 14 May 2006, pp 20–27) calls in Caroline Flint, director of the Natural Birthing Centre in Tooting, in an anti-intervention attempt to endorse 'intuition' over 'information': 'We've lost the idea that women are mammals – and mammals are exceedingly good at having babies' (2006: 24).

Conversely, the *Mail on Sunday*'s magazine *You* features an article, 'When Birth Trauma Goes beyond the Baby Blues' (Jane Phillimore, *Mail on Sunday*, 14 May 2006, p. 42), arguing that use of pain-relieving drugs can prevent post-traumatic stress disorder (which is all the more significant considering the newspaper's usual promotion of, and investment in, drug-free childbirth). Phillimore reports:

> Rosie felt that her antenatal care was ineffective: 'I came away from classes thinking that I'd be able just to pop this baby out. But all the talk that natural is best, of "positive pain" – it just wasn't true in my case'. … 'In Britain there is a culture that all a woman has to do is relax during labour and everything will be all right,' says Felicity Reynolds, emeritus professor of obstetric anaesthesia at St Thomas's Hospital in London. 'As a result women overestimate their ability to cope with the pain. They need to be told that birth will be painful, but that there is a system of pain relief that can help them.'
>
> (Phillimore 2006: 42).

The Birth and Motherhood Survey 2005 commissioned by the *Mother and Baby* magazine (www.motherandbabymagazine.com)[16] reports that: 75 per cent of women say their labour was 'more painful than they ever imagined', 53 per cent finding it 'far more shocking than they thought'. A third of the women answered that 'antenatal classes hadn't properly prepared them for the childbirth experience in Britain today', 43 per cent saying that they 'had been encouraged by the classes to "avoid pain relief"'. 'Only 5 per cent' ended up having a 'completely natural birth'. It is clear then that a complex network exists, where diverse popular cultural discourses compete with medical and statutory discourses to define what choice – and the wanting of choice – actually *means*.

Thus, the intersection of medical, ideological and commercial discourses do not always provide entirely compatible definitions or understandings of the world and this can, in turn, generate important tensions within the symbolic frameworks that represent 'legitimate' drug consumption. Significantly, these tensions are similar to those inherent in the popular symbolic frameworks of 'illegitimate' drug use, as discussed in previous chapters.

Celebrating the unnatural: the case of 'gas and air'

'Entonox' is a mixture of oxygen and nitrous oxide, which is commonly (erroneously) known as 'gas and air'. In the UK today, the context of childbirth provides a forum for acceptability where 'gas and air' is seen as safe and harmless, and thus tends to be associated with completely 'natural childbirth'. It appears in the range of popular books published on childbirth in the UK as the least harmful form of analgesic, determined largely by its medical sanction: it is mild and does not seem to cross the placenta; there is no official evidence of long-term damage to mother or baby; plus it contains oxygen that is sometimes seen as good for the baby. However, other elements about the drug that signal its safety and naturalness sit within social, rather than medical or physiological, parameters. For example, it is self-administered and therefore under the woman's control, it is easy to use, it dulls rather than deadens the pain, the 'highs' are short-lived (breathed out within seconds), its portability means that it can be used in any position, standing and walking, it can be used during a home birth and while sitting in a birthing pool.

Experimentation with the short-lived unnatural highs associated with entonox are much celebrated in popular cultural discourses, via anecdotes between friends. Shared experiences, enabling individuals to take on a mildly subversive role by relating how good the drug is and how 'out of it' they managed to get, resemble stories of recreational illegal drug use.[17] Both 'legitimate' and 'illegitimate' forms of drug use, then, are partly about the popular images we have of the substances we consume. Being able to self-administer 'gas and air' can make the experience mischievous, facilitating a light 'them and us' approach to authority. While these informal anecdotes are scarcely documented, comments by participants on the Baby Centre website (www.babycentre.co.uk/tips/542569.html, accessed 6.4.06) serve as a fairly representative example of the way that informal discussions progress:

> I had gas and air during labour. It made me feel extremely 'out of it' for about a minute. The midwives were trying to ask me questions and I found I had to get my brain and mouth to coordinate in order to answer them!!!!
>
> (6 January 2001)

Conscious allusions are made to recreational drug use and illegal substance abuse, in terms of words used and reported behaviour, as Aileen's comments indicate:

> I think the point about timing the entonox is critical i had a normal delivery with my daughter using 'gas and air' and found that i was high between but not during contractions, mind you it would be great stuff to have at a party.
>
> (aileen, 14 February 2001)

Further connotations of illegal drug use are evident in the debates about the best methods for consuming the substance, whether by the mouthpiece or mask: 'i had entonox with my first, i thought it was excellent, being on another planet. i think its far better through a mask' (jane, 1 March 2002) and 'i agree with jane the gas is great the mask allows you to breathe properly, although i had to much and kept droping it' (lizzi, 5 March 2002).

The participation of the partner is another predominant factor in informal anecdotes about gas and air, similar to the comments made here: 'I had entonox when my wife was having a baby the stuff is great i used it out of a mask' (andy, 20 April 2001) and:

> I don't like feeling sick or dizzy so leave the gas'n'air to my husband, who is hysterical to watch. Especially when the midwife comes in and he tries to act straight!
>
> (Julie, 31 May 2001)

What is striking is the sense of mild rebellion, problematising some of the standard distinctions between legitimate and illegitimate drug use:

> I used it with both my births and found it great. You can't overdose with it and the high only lasts about a minute. I sucked it almost continually through my contractions. My husband thought it was great as well! I would thoroughly recommend it.
>
> (Vicky, 28 October 2001)

Vicky consciously subverts the recommended practice of breathing in only as a contraction is coming on, by taking the drug 'continually' thus heightening its intoxicating effects.

Conspiracy theories abound on this chat room as the dialogue moves onto possible reasons why entonox is not so widely used in the US, whether the NHS have fallen for a cheap alternative or whether there are more dangerous aspects to 'gas and air' than previously thought. A link directs readers to the Birth Works website, and thus to the opposite camp that celebrates a drug-free childbirth. While similar informal anecdotes about use of other legal drugs, such as pethidine, exist, they are less widely celebrated, possibly due to the less sociable attributes of opiates, and to the formalised method of usage; pethidine has to be injected by the midwife or obstetrician, usually at a specific stage of the labour, and the experience is not shared with a partner. These celebratory anecdotes about 'gas and air' illustrate the creative ways in which individuals negotiate childbirth.

Conclusion

To conclude, the female body at the final stages of parturition symbolises a boundless site of contestation, when ideologies of womanhood meet those of motherhood, fuelled by moral and religious discourses. Debates on the use of legal drugs as pain relief during childbirth are encoded with judgements on self and a sense of identity. Pain-free childbirth remains controversial, entrenched with dilemmas connected to drug use and body ownership. Common quandaries about drug taking – over boundaries between legal and illegal, acceptable and unacceptable, self and unself, natural and unnatural – are all the more intense during transitional, liminal phases such as birth and death. Should playing host to another body mean that a woman possesses a moral duty to be 'present' (to be mentally or spiritually there) at the birth of her child? How much will it damage the bond between the mother and child if she is drugged up and 'out of it', rather than breathing through her contractions and following the natural flow of her body, and that of the unborn – and born – child?

Childbirth is a social rite. Certain forms of medical intervention can increase the likelihood of further intervention; even walking into a hospital can bring on adrenaline and stress hormones that slow down labour. This chapter provides an illustration of the point that drug consumption is regulated by cultural as well as statutory mechanisms and that both impact upon self and identity. It illustrates the dualistic relationship of body and mind, the interconnectedness of cultural and emotional experiences and the fluidity between legitimate and illegitimate forms of drug consumption. Popular conceptions and representations of drug use in labour, and the images of labour-related drugs, are encoded within symbolic frameworks produced and reproduced as part of popular cultures. These symbolic frameworks are characterised by tensions and contradictions in much the same way as the symbolic frameworks evident in popular media representations of illegal drugs and drug use that have been explored in preceding chapters. The way in which a drug becomes labelled, packaged, promoted, taken or administered is determined by cultural perspectives on what the body is and what it should be. Competing tensions, between what might be seen as puritanical and libertarian approaches to drug use, often manifest themselves within individuals as conflicting desires for choice. Because it is impossible to detach medico-technical discourses from cultural popular discourses, battles between puritanical and libertarian stances on drug use remain unresolved.

Notes

1 The first stage is usually defined as starting with the softening of the cervix and the onset of labour contractions right through to the full dilation (to about 10 cm) of the cervix. The second stage is the pushing stage, beginning when the cervix is fully dilated, and lasting until the birth of the baby. The third stage consists of the delivery of the placenta, after the baby is born.

2 See, for example, Oakley, A. (1980) *Women Confined: Towards a Sociology of Childbirth*. Oxford: Martin Robertson & Company Ltd. For instance, in the final chapter 'Proposing the Future', Oakley draws a list of 'Proposals' under 'Birth':
(1) an end to unnecessary medical intervention in childbirth;
(2) the re-domestication of birth;
(3) a return to female-controlled childbirth;
(4) the provision of therapeutic support for women after childbirth.
(Oakley 1980: 295–296)

3 In 1954 Dick-Read conducted an extensive tour investigating childbirth practices of African tribes, resulting in the book *No Time for Fear*.

4 'The Fear-Tension-Pain Syndrome' is the subheading to the fourth chapter 'Anatomy and Physiology' in *Childbirth Without Fear* (Dick-Read 2004: 45).

5 The article was first published in *Midwifery Today*, Issue 61, Spring 2002, and posted onto the website (www.midwiferytoday.com/articles/firsthour.asp, accessed 7.5.06).

6 The website for this conference (www.rcmconference.co.uk, accessed 1.5.06) states that this is the 124th conference run by midwives for midwives, attended by 800

delegates from around the UK. It also claims to activate considerable practical changes: 'The Royal College of Midwives seeks to inform and influence the development of policy that affects both midwives and the women and children for whom they care.'

7   The survey reported that 96 per cent of women give birth in hospital, and that a large proportion use pain relief (38 per cent – epidural, 41 per cent – pethidine). Genevive Fox's 'So What did You Expect? A New Survey has Found that Most Women Find Childbirth Painful and Shocking. Is this News?' in *The Guardian*, 2 October 2002, argues that pain-relieving drugs should be encouraged rather than seen as the last resort.

8   Membership of the NCT costs £36 a year per couple.

9   TENS is a 'transcutaneous electrical nerve stimulation' machine, as explained later in this chapter.

10 This is usually seen as part of a rising proportion of British babies being born in hospital, since the rise in 1927 to 15 per cent. However, according to Michelle Stanworth's research, it rose to a staggering 99 per cent in 1985 (Stanworth 1987: 10) suggesting that there has been a small but significant increase in home birth more recently.

11 For example: Murkoff, H., Eisenberg, A. and Hathaway, S. E. (2002); Stoppard, M. (1999) and Hunter, A. (1998), and magazines such as *Mother and Baby* and *Prima Baby & Pregnancy*.

12 In some books this will be found in the 'other section' the alternative methods section, since its lessening of pain is debatable, and it is only offered in some hospitals. Again, the woman has most of the control here, holding and activating the small battery powered obstetric pulsar connected by wires to electrodes that are taped on to the back giving small, safe amounts of current.

13 There is no mention in this section of general anaesthesia, which now tends to be used only in Caesarean cases (although even in this instance an epidural or similar spinal anaesthetic tend to be used). The Caesarean-section is only mentioned (2001: 101) at the end of the labour and birth section, under 'Special Cases' (and is therefore doubly 'othered'): it will 'only be performed where there is a real clinical need for this type of delivery' usually in the case of an emergency. In this context, the 'elective Caesarean' (planned in advance) is only recommended if labour is judged to be dangerous (2001: 102), in contrast to the *Too Posh to Push* debate over whether it is too easy to opt for a Caesarean, especially for the rich and famous. (See, for example, 'Stop the Too Posh to Push Births', *Daily Mail*, 26 April 2004.)

14 It is hard to find a pregnancy and birth book that does not foreground 'fulfilment' and 'satisfaction', but see, for example, the NHS *Pregnancy Book* (2001: 93) and Miriam Stoppard (1999: 6–8).

15 For example, Emily Cook's report in the *Daily Mail*, 'Mothers "Should Know the Pain of Childbirth"', was rebuked live on *The Wright Stuff* (Channel 5), 8 May 2006. The retort being that a painful birth is not likely to be conducive to a 'satisfying experience'.

16 The website claims that '3,000 mothers and pregnant women were questioned over 11 TV regions … making it the biggest National Survey ever of feelings about pregnancy, birth, maternity care and motherhood.'

17 Incidentally, the recent trend of inhaling nitrous oxide-filled balloons sold in clubs, festivals and dance venues has been reported in the British press, for example: Terry Kirby 'Laughing Gas, the Legal Drug Sweeping Clubland', *The Independent*, 14 January 2006.

References and suggested reading

Baby Centre website: www.babycentre.co.uk/tips/542569.html (accessed 6.5.06).

Birke, L. (1992) 'Transforming Biology', in H. Crowley and S. Himmelweit (eds) *Knowing Women: Feminism and Knowledge*, pp 66–77. Milton Keynes: Polity Press.

Birth (2006) Channel 4, 22 April.

Claye, A. (1939) *Evolution of Obstetric Analgesia*. Oxford: Oxford University Press.

Cook, E. (2006) 'Mothers "Should Know the Pain of Childbirth"', *Daily Mail*, 8 May 2006, p. 28.

Dick-Read, G. (2004) *Childbirth Without Fear*. London: Printer and Martin Ltd.

Hunter, A. (1998) *The Queen Charlotte's Hospital Guide to Pregnancy and Birth*. London, Sydney, Auckland 10, Parktown 2193: Random House.

Lesnik-Oberstein, K. (2003) 'On "Wanting" a "Child" or: An Idea of Desire', in N. Segal, L. Taylor and R. Cook (eds) *Indeterminate Bodies*, pp 22–35. Basingstoke and New York: Palgrave Macmillan Ltd.

Mazzoni, C. (2002) 'Maternal Impressions: Pregnancy and Childbirth', *Literature and Theory*. Ithaca, New York and London: Cornell University Press.

Miller, D. (1997) 'How Infants Grow Mothers in North London', *Theory, Culture and Society*, 14 (4): 67–88. London, Thousand Oaks and New Delhi: Sage.

Mother and Baby Magazine at website: www.motherandbabymagazine.com (accessed 4.5.06).

Murkoff, H.E., Eisenberg, A. and Hathaway, S.E. (2002) *What to Expect When You're Expecting*. London, New York, Sydney, Tokyo, Singapore, Toronto, Dublin: Pocket Books.

Oakley, A. (1980) *Women Confined: Towards a Sociology of Childbirth*. Oxford. Martin Robertson & Company Ltd.

Odent, M. (2002) 'The First Hour Following Birth: Don't Wake the Mother!', at website: www.midwiferytoday.com/articles/firsthour.asp (accessed 7.5.06, first published in *Midwifery Today*, Issue 61, Spring 2002).

Phillimore, J. (2006) 'When Birth Trauma Goes Beyond the Baby Blues', *You* Magazine, *Mail on Sunday*, 14 May, p. 42.

The Pregnancy Book (2001) London: NHS, Health Promotion England.

Rhodes, P. (1995) *A Short History of Clinical Midwifery*. Cheshire: Books for Midwives Press.

Richley, A. (2006) 'Anne's *Guide to…* Pain relief: Are you feeling TENS', *Practical Parenting*, March 2006: 42.

The Royal College of Midwives, website at: www.rcmnormalbirth.net/ (accessed 8.5.06).

Smith, T. (1847) 'A Lecture on the Utility and Safety of the Inhalation of Ether in Obstetric Practice', *Lancet*, 1: 321–323.

Spencer, M. (2006) 'How Pregnancy went Public', *Observer WOMAN* Magazine, 14 May, pp 20–27.

Stanworth, M. (1987) 'Reproductive Technologies and the Deconstruction of Motherhood', in M. Stanworth (ed.) *Reproductive Technologies: Gender, Motherhood and Medicine*, pp 10–35. Cambridge: Polity Press.

Stoppard, M. (1999) *The New Pregnancy and Birth Book*. London, New York, Sidney: Dorling Kindersley.

Treichler, P.A. (1990) 'Feminism, Medicine, and the Meaning of Childbirth', in M. Jacobus, E. Fox Keller and S. Shuttleworth (eds) *Body/Politics: Women and the Discourses of Science*, pp 113–138. London and New York: Routledge.

Williams, J. (1997) 'The Controlling Power of Childbirth in Britain', in H. Marland and A.M. Rafferty (eds) *Midwives, Society and Childbirth: Debates and Controversies in the Modern Period*, pp 232–247. London: Routledge.

Woolf, M. and Goodchild, S. (2006) 'Mummy State: Childbirth Revolution', *The Independent on Sunday*, 14 May, p. 1.

Part 5

Drugs, Normalisation and Popular Culture: Implications and Policy

Introduction

Paul Manning

Chapter 15, the final contribution to this collection, shifts the focus from the cultural practices associated with drug consumption at the micro-level, back to the relationship between political practices and illicit drug use. In this, it returns to and develops themes explored in the Chapters 2 and 7 of the volume, namely the response of the government to evidence of widespread recreational drug use, but in doing so it extends the discussion to consider whether or not we can detect evidence of normalisation in the very development of government policy. In other words, is it the case that government policy, despite the alternations and tensions between harm reduction and enforcement strategies, has in effect moved to a position of accommodation? This is the point at which the dimensions of popular cultural practices and symbolic representation touch policy development within the state. As Richard Huggins suggests, if it is possible to detect a move towards a position of accommodation to recreational drug use in the policy development process, this is likely to be prompted by much more than a simple reading of the quantitative evidence provided by surveys of use and exposure to 'offer situations'. It is likely to reflect a recognition of the process of cultural accommodation discussed first by Parker, Aldridge and Measham (1998) in their original formulation of the 'normalisation thesis'. In other words, governments and civil servants, as much as journalists and cultural commentators, must acknowledge the extent to which 'sensible' drug use is culturally embedded within popular cultures.

15. Systemic 'normalisation'? – mapping and interpreting policy responses to illicit drug use

Richard Huggins

Introduction

> We have no intention of legalising any illicit drug. All controlled drugs
> are dangerous and nobody should take them.
>
> (UK Government Updated Drug Strategy 2002: 6)

This chapter explores recent developments in policy initiatives, especially
criminal justice responses, to illicit drug use in the UK. The chapter surveys
general and specific policy and legislative developments and the recent creation
of what Parker has called the 'new drugs interventions industry' (Parker 2004:
379). It does so whilst exploring the context of the 'normalisation' of drug use
debate (Davis and Ditton 1990; Measham *et al*. 1994; Parker *et al*. 1998, 2002;
South 1999) to ask if the current policy framework provides evidence of a
(particular) response to the 'normalisation' of drug use or, if not normalisation
of use, a particular form of 'normalisation of the drug user'? (Berridge 1993).
As such the chapter does not necessarily seek to establish that drug use
– particularly Class A drug use – has been normalised in and of itself, but
rather to suggest that policy responses, in terms of systemic criminal justice
responses and the extent to which responding to drug use has become a
central priority for many areas of public policy and statutory agencies, may
represent evidence of a shift to an acceptance of normalisation. This may be
especially the case when located within the wider context of the cultural fabric
of what are sometimes called 'high crime)' societies and the degree to which
drug use, criminal justice responses and crime discourses have contributed to
such developments (Garland 2000; Estrada 2004).

Clearly, the UK government has increasingly seen drug use as a major
concern and area for policy action (Bennett 1998, 2000; MacDonald 1999;
Audit Commission 2002). The 2002 Updated Strategy suggests that the current
position is that at least four million people use at least one illicit drug each
year and 'around one million use at least one of the most dangerous drugs
(such as ecstasy, heroin and cocaine)' (Home Office 2002: 6). Furthermore,
estimates of the number of 'problematic drug users' in England and Wales
appear to range from around 250,000 to 360,000 individuals depending on the
source (Home Office Drugs Strategy Directorate 2002; Bernhaut and Peters

2006). It is estimated that drug misuse costs society between £10 billion and £18 billion a year in social and economic costs and that there are strong links between problematic drug use and crime (Godfrey *et al.* 2002). Consequently, the government is convinced that tackling drugs will reduce crime, improve the life of all communities and save considerable resources. In order to achieve this the government has, since the mid-1990s, pursued a more strategic, integrated and joined-up approach to tackling drugs which will be examined in this chapter.

This chapter starts from a number of conceptual standpoints that draw on a broad and developed literature. The first is that the significance of and responses to illicit drug use (as a social, criminal or health 'problem') has a long and contested history and many scholars have focused on the politics, significance and effects of drug control and drug policies (for example, see Berridge and Edwards 1981; Berridge 1984, 1993, 1996, 1999; Courtwight 1982; Courtwright 2001; Gossop 2000; Carnwarth and Smith 2002). Second, for a number of commentators the significance of and responses to illicit drug use can be seen as socially constructed rather than one that has specific and actual characteristics and, if nothing else, we are well advised to acknowledge the long-term historical and social contexts of drug use and misuse (Terry 1931; Sonnedeciler 1962; Levinthal 1985; Berridge 1984, 1989, 1996, 1999). Furthermore, social and cultural contexts and expectations have a strong influence on how drug use and experience is shaped (Zinberg 1984) as well as how such use is interpreted, defined and then regulated.

Finally analysing, discussing or simply trying to make sense of contemporary drug use, its links to and with crime and responses to such use is complex and is made so by the highly contested nature of the key terms involved and the culturally situated natures of both 'crime' and 'drug use' (Christie 2004; Ferrell and Sanders 1995; Ferrell and Hamm 1998; Ferrell 1999; Ferrell and Websdale 1999; Presdee 2000; Lalander 2003; Measham 2004). It is, therefore, important to consider the social, historical, political and cultural contexts of use and responses to such use to develop our overall understanding of the social meaning of drug use and related behaviours. Indeed, the symbolic meaning of drug use and the reflection of such symbolic meaning in popular media products adds further complexity to the whole discussion (Giulianotti 1997; Huggins 2006; Manning 2006). This chapter works from the premise that policy and policy responses should also be understood from cultural perspectives (as well as political and legislative) and that such an approach can help us understand the cultural meaning and significance of crime and drug use and that have particular value to the analysis and understanding of current responses to drug use in contemporary society.

In particular the chapter will consider the development of strategic responses to drug use in the UK in the form of policy documents and prescriptions including *Tackling Drug Misuse* (1985), the emergence of national and sub-national strategies in the mid-1990s, such as *Tackling Drugs Together: A Strategy for England 1995–1998* (Department of Health 1995) in England, and the development of New Labour's 1998 *Tackling Drugs to Build a Better Britain* (President of the Council 1998) and the updated version of this strategy in 2002. The chapter will also focus on the development of the Criminal Justice

Interventions Programme, the Drug Interventions Programme and the impact of the Drugs Act 2005.

In doing so the chapter will discuss what the effect, nature and intent of policy developments and regulation have been and the degree to which they can be said to represent evidence for the existence of a level of 'normalisation' of drug use in the UK, the degree to which such developments represent evidence of a shift in the regulatory and policy culture regarding drug use in the UK and the ways in which such developments might be seen to relate to other aspects of structural shifts in social and political control in contemporary UK and the emergence of what can be seen as a more systematic approach to the monitoring and maintenance of social control (Christie 2004; Garland 1997, 2001; Rose 2000).

'Normalisation' of drug use: some key issues

> Foremost among the reasons why Prestbury's adult citizens worry about congregations of local youths is drugs.
>
> (Girling *et al.* 2000: 111)

The 'normalisation' thesis developed as a way of explaining the apparent increase in drug use and prevalence which characterised the findings of a number of studies (see for example, Measham *et al.* 1994; Parker *et al.* 1998, 2002; Aldridge *et al.* 1999). The thesis represents a relatively clear argument put forward by a number of commentators in the early 90s, that drug use, and in particular, recreational drug use had become a 'normalised' element of, in particular, youth culture and everyday life as drugs and their use had themselves become so commonplace and a key element of youth, consumer and leisure cultures (Measham *et al.* 1994; Shiner and Newburn 1997, 1999; Parker *et al.* 1998, 2002; Hammersley *et al.* 2002; Webster *et al.* 2002; Chatterton and Hollonds 2003; Rumgay 2003; Gourley 2004; Jackson 2004; Measham 2004; Sanders 2005). In addition such 'normalisation' was accompanied by other changes such as increased availability, experimentation by young people from across all social groups suggesting some changes in central structural determinants (Measham 2004). As noted elsewhere in this chapter, in addition to the quantitative increase in drug use a number of commentators (Inciardi and Harrison 1998; South 1999) have suggested that the cultural visibility and significance of drug use has also changed with 'drugs' occupying a more central reference point within popular cultural texts and products.

The thesis – as discussed by Parker *et al.* 1998 – adopted six key indicators of change. These included, drug availability, drug trying or lifetime prevalence of use, current or regular drug use, future intentions to use, being 'drugwise' and the cultural accommodation of illicit drugs and associated behaviour. In this way the thesis offers a useful attempt to 'initiate a conceptual reconsideration of motivations and meanings of drug use in recent years' (Measham 2004: 209). As Measham notes, some discussions of the normalisation thesis have tended to overlook the scope of the thesis, in terms of indicators beyond the quantitative elements of 'actual' use and have, perhaps, sought too hard for evidence of actual use rather than a broader recognition of the significance of the cultural accommodation of use. I would add one further indicator; the systemic response to drug use as a reflection of official, policy and cultural accommodations to drug use.

Measham's (2004) recent contribution provides a useful summary of the discussion and tries to extend the debate by exploring the value that cultural criminology can or could play in explaining the significance of contemporary drug use in ways that quantitative survey data does not. Thus, cultural criminological approaches can enhance drug research by encouraging a wider consideration of historical and cultural context of illicit consumption and also the broader cultural contexts of consumption, control and leisure use time. Thus for South (1999), drug use is increasingly located within the highly consumerist cultures of contemporary society and consequently the whole issue of drug use has become a more complex one to analyse and understand due to changes both in the organisation of everyday life and drug use itself. Consequently, drug use has ceased to be located at the margins of social experience and has become part of the 'paramount reality' of everyday life (1999: 3).

Clearly, South's argument, at least in part, draws on the emergence of the notion that drug use has become widespread, everyday and to some extent 'normalised', although the actuality of the extent of normalised drug use is disputed (see for example, Shiner and Newburn 1997, 1999). South, amongst others, argues that use and visibility has become more pronounced than in earlier periods. In this sort of analysis it is not so much the levels of drug use that have significantly increased but the symbolic and representational prevalence of 'drugs' that has also increased. Thus, he argues:

> Whether or not as individuals we actually use drugs, we now live in a cultural, media and consumption environment saturated with references to and images of drugs, as well as explicit and implicit connections between drugs and various other consumption items. What is more significant about late modernity and the quest to control and reduce use and misuse of drugs is not simply the question of 'how many people actually use them?' Rather, it is the sheer volume of social activity concerned with, or referring to, drugs. Daily examples include, expressions of cultural, media, political, medical and enforcement engagement, attention and reaction.
>
> (South 1999: 7)

I think the interventions by authors such as South (1999) and Measham (2004) are particularly important for they usefully develop the arguments and analysis of the idea of normalisation. Furthermore, in emphasising the cultural dimension and importance of drug use, in terms of how it impacts on users and non-users, how it impacts on the 'everyday', suggests that what can be said to constitute normalisation and what would constitute evidence of normalisation may take various forms. While it is important not to overplay all this, one can note the potential impact of normalisation, especially in relation to the implications such a development would have for drug policy, service and treatment provision and criminal justice responses. Of course, it can also be argued that it is precisely the far-reaching implications of the 'normalisation' thesis that make it so potentially controversial and significant as the remainder of this chapter will explore.

Tackling drugs – drug legislation and policy responses in the 1920s–1970s: the rise and fall of the 'British System'

Clearly there is not space here to engage in a detailed mapping of regulatory and policy responses to drug use and misuse in Britain and there are a number of useful and informative studies that cover this area in detail (for example, Berridge and Edwards 1981; Berridge 1984, 1996, 1999). However, it is valuable to give brief consideration to general trends in policy and regulatory development in the period 1900–80 to provide a background for later, more strategic responses in recent years.

Following a period in which drug use was generally unregulated the late nineteenth and early twentieth century witnessed a slow growth of policy development and regulatory practice including developments such as the Pharmacy Act 1868, the Inebriates Act and the Lunacy Act 1888, as the medical professions and public health discourses gained ground although dealing with levels of domestic use was not a key government concern (Berridge 1979, 1999). In fact the early to mid-twentieth century was a period in which supply and use was relatively limited and small-scale and, consequently, official responses were also limited (Berridge 1999). This period of regulation can be characterised as one in which the British government sought to respond to international expectations – especially those of the USA – in terms of developing international treaties and regulatory regimes rather than as a response to actual or perceived domestic use (Ruggiero and South 1995) a trend that still to some extent characterises responses to illicit drug use in many European states (European Monitoring Centre for Drugs and Drug Addiction (ECMDDA) 2005).

Although full regulation of domestic use was established in the passing of the Dangerous Drugs Act 1920, the 1920s have also been characterised as the period in which the 'British system' of drug control emerged under the influence of the Rolleston Committee. This advocated the prescription of heroin and morphine to provide a medically regulated supply to manage and then reduce addiction. This response is often contrasted with that common to other countries, such as the US which tended towards more penal and criminal justice responses to drug use leading some to posit that Britain has tended to take a more health and harm reduction based approach to illicit drug use (Parssinen 1983). However, the scale of response in Britain can also be more readily seen as a response to the actual and perceived level and threat of drug use which resulted in the acceptance of 'narcotic drug maintenance in the 1920s because the addict population was small, elderly and dying off' (Parssinen 1983: 220).

The 1960s witnessed an acceleration of government responses to drug use and misuse which included the creation of the Inter-departmental Committee on Drug Addiction (the Brain Committee) charged with reporting on aspects of drug supply and use in Britain. Although the first Brain report suggested that little was changing in terms of the extent of drug use in Britain, the number of addicts notified to the Home Office was rising and the Brain Committee was reconvened in 1964. This resulted in the publication of a second report in 1965 which made a series of important recommendations which would influence the development and passing of the Dangerous Drugs Act of 1967 and the subsequent Misuse of Drugs Act 1971.

In general terms there is clear evidence of significant growth in substance use in the UK throughout the 1970s and into the 1980s. Numerous studies demonstrate increased distribution, use and shifts in demographic profile of users throughout this period (see, for example, Lewis *et al.* 1985; Pearson *et al.* 1986; Dorn and South 1987; Robertson 1987; Parker and Newcombe 1987; Parker *et al.* 1988; Measham *et al.* 1994) which can be seen to evidence a significant and rapid growth of substance misuse across the UK. Linked with concerns around the spread of HIV in the mid-1980s (see for example, Advisory Council on the Misuse of Drugs (ACMD) 1988), changes in the political and socio-economic climate of the UK in the 1980s and shifts in the global production and distribution of illicit drugs, the issue of substance misuse took a much more serious guise in this period and, consequently, an increased amount of attention from legislators and statutory agencies.

By the 1990s, as South (1999) notes, Britain had developed a 'poly-drug' culture of readily available drugs reflected in the development of a more hedonistic youth culture. In this sense drug use became, symbolically if nothing else, commonplace and 'everyday'. Once again a sweep of research and surveys suggested that drug use was a much more common feature of contemporary living resulting in the presentation of the notion of 'normalisation' (Measham *et al.* 1994; Parker *et al.* 1998; South 1999; Hammersley, Khan and Ditton 2002; Parker *et al.* 2002). Importantly, South (1999) notes that this 'emerging debate about 'normalisation' or otherwise is one of tremendous significance, not least in its implications for drug laws and the planning and provision of services'. As observed earlier, this is particularly relevant when we consider that social policy responses, in part at least, reflect the way in which a social problem is defined and thus, examination of such policy can tell us a great deal about the perceived nature of a social problem at any given time.

In recent years the heightened concern about substance misuse in general and the relationship between such use and, in particular, certain forms of acquisitive crime has led to an increased emphasis on the value of targeting problem drug users who are in direct contact with the criminal justice system either at arrest, sentencing, custody or post-custody (Hough 1996; Kothari, Marsden and Strang 2002; Bean 2004a, b, c). Despite the undoubtedly problematic and complex relationship between drug use and criminal offending (Bean 1994; Hough 1996; Seddon 2000; Simpson 2003) the attraction of targeting substance misusers through the criminal justice system has become a key element of current government policy and strategy in the UK as well as a number of other countries around the world. The logic is simple, the criminal justice system offers an ideal opportunity to target drug interventions due to the high number of problem drug users who find themselves within it

(Bennett 1998, 2000). Such official response to the issue of drug use and crime is further backed by popular assumptions that there is a direct and causal link between drug use and crime (for examples see the British Crime Survey or local studies, such as Girling *et al.* 2000).

For example, since the emergence of arrest referral schemes in the 1980s such approaches have become highly popular with government and law enforcement agencies in recent years and appear to offer a highly effective way of exploiting the opportunities provided by entry into the criminal justice system by those offenders who are using illegal substances and whose offending and drug use may be linked (Hough 1996; Edmunds *et al.* 1998, 1999; Sondhi *et al.* 2002; O'Shea and Powis 2003; Sondhi and Huggins 2005). Indeed, current government drugs strategy places significant emphasis on the role of arrest referral in tackling Class A drug users 'who account for 99% the costs of drug misuse in England and Wales and do most harm to themselves, their families and communities' (Home Office Drugs Strategy Directorate 2002: 4) and currently all police forces in England and Wales now offer arrest referral schemes of varying characteristics and models.

For McSweeney, Turnball and Hough (2002), the opportunities provided by the criminal justice system for intervention are clear and they highlight the value of proactive schemes and the voluntary nature of such interventions. For these authors, the increasing success of referral and diversion schemes is reliant upon 'proactively identifying, assisting and supporting drug users at the point of arrest, and referring them to appropriate and adequately resources treatment services' (2002: 3). Thus the criminal justice system provides a valuable opportunity to contact problematic drug users who have little previous exposure to treatment but they also acknowledge potential limitations if continuity of care and support is not maintained at each stage. In terms of the effectiveness of particular schemes one key variable has been the availability of appropriate treatment services for arrest referral schemes to refer back to (Kothari, Marsden and Strang 2002). Capacity and availabilty of treatment services and the micro-management of treatment and service budgets and provision at a local (Drug Action Team) level are critical and suggests that significant variables will exist when arrest referral schemes are mapped against available services and treatment options within any given locality (Parker 2004; Sondhi and Huggins 2005).

In many respects the significance for our discussion rests not so much on what may or may not be effective as an intervention, but more importantly how policy and systemic responses to drug use and misuse can been seen to reflect the way in which social problems (in this case drug use and misuse) are conceptualised and defined (MacGregor 1999). Not unlike many policy areas in the UK drug policy can be characterised as possessing significant levels of continuity and consistency in the approaches and prescriptions of different UK governments and administrations, especially since the mid-1980s. Although it might be argued that drug issues have became much more politicised in the 1980s and 1990s, it is also clear that there exists a significant political consensus around illicit drug use, misuse and indeed, crime and to a great extent what to do about it all which has tended to place great emphasis on criminal justice responses.

Development of strategic responses to illicit drug use in the UK 1990–2002

The launch of *Tackling Drug Misuse* (1985) represents an important development in drug policy in the UK as it can be seen as the first publication by national government of an overarching strategic response to substance misuse and a significant move beyond legislative responses alone. This paper identified five main areas of activity and action, including education, prevention and treatment, but was mainly focused on enforcement actions. Subsequently the Conservative government introduced a series of drug strategies for the constituent elements of the UK in the mid-1990s. The strategy for England and Wales placed a focus on community-based crime prevention approaches and established multi-agency, partnership working, through the creation of Drug Action teams.

Evidence of policy continuity can be found in the Labour government's 1998 strategy document *Tackling Drugs to Build a Better Britain* (Office of the President 1998) which built directly on previous policy initiatives but also represented the development of the first cross-cutting strategy (Home Office Drugs Strategy Directorate 2002). The 1998 strategy identified four key themes which have become central to the development, implementation and monitoring of drug use and misuse. These four themes are: to help young people resist drug misuse in order to achieve their full potential, to protect communities from drug-related anti-social and criminal behaviour, to enable individuals with drug problems to overcome them and lead healthy drug and crime free lives and to stifle the availability of illegal drugs. Although it is possible to detect a broad and encompassing approach to tackling illegal drug use in this strategy that includes community development, social inclusion and exclusion, drugs prevention and treatment, the 1998 strategy clearly placed detection, enforcement and crime-reduction at the centre of drug policy.

The government makes significant claims for the success of the 1998 strategy which includes increases in the number of schools with drug policies, substance misuse as part of the National Curriculum, the development of Positive Futures, Connexions, local Young People's Substance Misuse Plans, Progress2Work launched in 2001, Communities Against Drugs initiatives and the spread of arrest referral scheme to all police forces.

This trend continued in 2002 with the publication of the government's Updated Drug Strategy (Home Office 2002) which, once again, sought to build directly on earlier strategic approaches. In doing so the government signalled its ongoing commitment to joined-up and integrated approaches to tackling drugs and to significant increases in planned direct annual expenditure to support responses to drug use and committing the government to increasing annual spending to nearly £1.5 billion by April 2005, an uplift of 44 per cent (though the actuality of such increases has been challenged and the uplift for 2006 was considerably less than many had expected or predicted). The increase in funds would be directly linked with a tougher focus on Class A drug use, a stronger focus on education prevention, enforcement and treatment to 'prevent and tackle problematic drug use' (Home Office Drugs Strategy Directorate 2002: 4) and a renewed commitment to reducing availability, an expansion of services within the criminal justice system (for example, testing, arrest referral and expanded community sentences), more focused targeting and a whole set of revised delivery targets.

The Updated Drug Strategy demonstrates a considerable attempt to develop an overarching response to drug use which ranges from highly localised responses through national and regional level responses to major transnational initiatives. At local level this includes the targeting of middle markets, the disruption of local supply markets, high profile specialist action against suppliers in particular communities with specific or pronounced drug use problems and increases in the penalties for dealing and trafficking. At the national level action includes the strengthened provision to seize assets and proceeds from drug-related crime through the Proceeds of Crime Act 2002, the launch of a new and high profile communications campaign FRANK in 2003[1] and a new and intensified focus on crack with the introduction of a National Crack Plan in December 2002 which was followed by a series of crack audits and plans which detailed local, statutory and agency responses to crack use. Major transnational initiatives have included the enhancement of joint EU co-operation, the development of more effective drug liaison with producing and transit countries and the development of specific country based strategies and initiatives including a strategy to tackle drug-related crime in the Caribbean and closer working with the Afghan government to reduce opium production with the aim of eliminating production completely by 2013 (Home Office 2002). In addition, for the government at least, progress since 1998 can also be traced through increased organisational developments including the creation of the National Crime Squad, the National Criminal Intelligence Service, the Drug's Strategy Unit and the Concerted Inter-Agency Drugs Action Group (Home Office 2002).

As stated these developments are significant because they represent a shift to a systemic and strategic response for the first time and one that goes far beyond legislative responses charactersied by, for example, the Misuse of Drugs Act 1971. Furthermore, the totalising nature of the strategic response – ranging from local to transational levels – is further evidenced through the objectives, indicators and focus given within the strategy and supporting documents which establish the role of an ever-increasing number of services and agencies, such as Connexions, in identifying young people with drug problems, the creation of named drug workers within all Youth Offending Teams (YOTs) and the expansion of treatment services within the Youth Justice System. Through the development of such responses 'tackling drugs' has become central to or at least a significant element of public policy and for many agencies increasing the scope, range and extent of their activities and targets either directly or indirectly related to substance misuse.

The development of the Criminal Justice Intervention Programme (CJIP) and the Drug Intervention Programme (DIP): 2005 and beyond

The strategic responses highlighted above have been further developed through the launch of the Criminal Justice Intervention Programme (CJIP) and subsequently the Drug Intervention Programme (DIP) (Home Office Drugs Strategy Directorate 2004; Home Office 2006). DIP is a 'critical part of the Government's strategy for tackling drugs'[2] and builds directly on the CJIP which was launched in 2003. CJIP aimed to integrate a broad set of interventions (including arrest, assessment, treatment and aftercare) in a stated attempt to break the drugs-crime cycle. This scheme is now funded at around £165 million pounds per year and the intention is that such an approach will develop into the 'normal way' of working with drug-misusing offenders across England and Wales. The programme, seen as a world-first by the Home Office, is a multi-agency response involving criminal justice agencies, health and treatment agencies, including the National Treatment Agency (NTA)[3] and the Department of Health, the Department for Education and Skills (DfES) (DfES 2004) and a range of voluntary agencies which seeks to provide an integrated, 'joined-up' and effective system of interventions for substance misuse. The pursuit of 'joined-up' approaches has been a key characteristic of New Labour's approach to social policy (Clark 2002) and as such CJIP and DIP represent examples of broader trends in the New Labour approach to modernising and reforming public and statutory agencies and policy. But more than this they also represent clear examples of the extension of criminal justice and social order issues and regulation into wider areas of public policy.

Not surprisingly the Home Office has high hopes for such an approach and stresses the fact that 'everyone can win' in that drug-using offenders can access treatment and support, communities will suffer less crime and the taxpayer saves money as criminal justice costs are reduced. Despite the complexity and disputed nature of the relationship between crime and drug use explored earlier in this chapter the government is convinced that the DIP programme offers the best chance to break the 'destructive cycle of drugs, offending and prison' and asserts that areas piloting the intensive programme have experienced faster falling crime rates than elsewhere (Home Office 2006). DIP works on the basis that early capture and treatment of drug using offenders, with rapid access to the right sort of treatment, backed by actual and potential sanctions available through the criminal justice system will provide an effective and joined-up response to drug use. In this sense the development of DIP can be seen as a significant extension of criminal justice based responses to and a reflection of both official and popular notions of the current size and nature of the UK 'drug problem' and very much as a problem associated with crime rather than other broader interpretations.

DIP is a highly systemised and systemic response to drug misuse and criminal offending aiming to provide a complete and proactive set of intervention, from arrest to release and aftercare. At arrest an individual is offered the opportunity to see a non-police drugs worker who can provide information, referral to treatment or other support. In some areas 'enhanced' arrest referral schemes operate which offer a more developed, structured and extensive range of support and interventions and also some arrest referral schemes have become central to the delivery of intensive DIP interventions.[4] What can be readily seen as a voluntary or elective process has been increasingly backed by the development of drug testing on arrest, firstly in 97 police Basic Command Units throughout England and Wales, and then more widely through the Drugs Act 2005. In this approach individuals detained for 'trigger offences'[5] can be given a drug test looking for evidence of the Class A drugs most readily associated with criminal activity namely, heroin, cocaine and crack cocaine.

The use of drug tests and arrest referral as ways of detecting and initially identifying drug using offenders and their treatment needs is followed by a series of what might be seen as both carrot and stick processes designed to strongly encourage offenders to engage in treatment. This includes conditional cautioning which attaches specific conditions related to rehabilitation, treatment or restoration to the granting of a police caution. In addition, DIP works closely with the Prolific and Priority Offender Programme (PPO) (launched in 2004) which now covers all Crime and Disorder Reduction Partnerships and seeks to identify, target, monitor and 'rehabilitate' those offenders who are considered to cause most harm to themselves and their communities. The close working of DIP and PPO schemes is supposed to be facilitated through the sharing of information, joint case management and shared treatment referral and provision.

The opportunities for intervention continue in the courts with the use of test results to feed into sentencing decisions including restrictions on bail, drug treatment and testing orders and community orders. Restrictions may be placed on access to court bail if a offender refuses a drug assessment or follow-up treatment. Drug Treatment and Testing Orders (DTTO) were introduced in the late 1990s and despite disputes over the consistency of their implementation and management and over their effectiveness they have often been highlighted as a significant element of the government's response to repeat offending and drug use. DIP aims for greater use of such sentencing and DTTOs have been replaced – for new offenders – by the community order which was introduced by the Criminal Justice Act 2003 and came into force in April 2005. This sentence offers a broader range of options for both courts and individuals which are designed to provide a more flexible response to the seriousness of the offences committed and for the treatment requirements of the individual offender, including a drug rehabilitation requirement. Those who receive a prison sentence present can engage in treatment and support processes and central to prison-based interventions has been the development of CARAT (Counselling, Assessment, Referral, Advice and Throughcare) services and the development of Intensive Treatment Programmes aimed at moderate to severe drug misuse problems and related offending behaviour.

The various developments at each stage of the criminal justice system have been accompanied by the development of a national framework aimed at providing consistency and continuity of care of drug-misusing offenders aimed at joining-up DIP, the NTA, prisons and the National Offender Management Service (NOMS) in an attempt to develop a more effective cross-service case management approach.

Official documents place considerable emphasis on the extent and effectiveness of throughcare and aftercare aspects of DIP and the systematic support of offenders and drug misusers in terms of supporting rehabilitation and reintegration. CJIT (Criminal Justice Integrated Teams) are charged with delivering or brokering the provision of appropriate services in relation to aftercare including housing, support with benefits, managing finances, employment, education and training, access to mental health services and so on.

The developments of CJIP and DIP outlined here have been backed by the passing of the Drugs Act 2005 which seeks to increase the effectiveness of DIP by introducing a new range of enhanced police and court powers to deal with drug misuse. This 2005 Act has witnessed the further extension of criminal justice based responses as seen with the creation of a new civil order to run alongside anti-social behaviour orders (ASBOs) aimed at tackling drug-related anti-social behaviour, introduction of testing on arrest (rather than on charge), the requirement of individuals with a positive test to undergo assessment by a drugs worker, one introduction of an intervention order, which is attached to ASBOs issued to adults whose anti-social behaviour is drug related which requires individuals to attend drug counselling. The 2005 Act has also allowed for extensions of police custody for those who swallow drugs in secure packages to increase evidence recovery, allows a court or jury to draw adverse inference where an individual refuses to consent to an intimate body search, x-ray or ultrasound, requires courts to take account of aggravating factors, for example dealing near schools, when sentencing, and has amended the Anti-Social Behaviour Act 2003 to give police the power to enter premises, for example, a suspected 'crack house' to issue a closure notice.

The summary of CJIP, DIP and the Drugs Act 2005 alerts us to how far the systemic and strategic responses to drug use have developed in the last 10 years or so. This represents a significant development of an extensive, criminal justice based response to drug use that is extended not only through the government's current strategy and the Drugs Act 2005 but also through other recent legislative changes. For example, the Children Act 2004 and the national framework for child services detailed in *Every Child Matters: Change for Children* (HMSO 2005), have resulted in the development of a range of new and pilot drug intervention initiatives aimed at children and young people. These include arrest referral schemes for 10 to 17 year olds, drug testing for 14 to 17 year olds, the wider use of community sentences and 'child centered' case management by YOTs and multi-agency teams.

Of course, one can interpret the developments outlined above in a number of ways and government officials would suggest that DIP does strike the 'right' sort of balance between harm reduction, treatment, prevention and criminal justice approaches and provides a proactive responses to substance misuse in England and Wales. Whether or not we accept the balance as appropriate or too weighted in favour of criminal justice responses we should, I think, recognise the extent to which recent developments reflect a acceptance amongst government agencies and others that drug use is now, if not 'normalised' certainly extensive and that systematic responses to drug use are both necessary and effective.

Conclusion

It might be argued that recent criminal justice responses to illicit drug use in England and Wales do suggest a form of normalisation in the sense that detecting, responding to and controlling (or attempting to control) drug use, through multi-agency partnerships, overarching strategies and so on, has become an organising principle and driving activity of many public and statutory agencies in and on the borders of the criminal justice system. The development of DIP appears to be a key example of this. However, it is difficult for any UK government, given the history of approaches to drug control, the constraints and contexts of international treaties to which the UK is a signatory and the relationship between the US and the UK, to acknowledge formally or informally that 'normalisation' – of any form – may have or be taking place, even if they wished to. This would be a far too risky strategy. But one might argue that the current attention to policy making, the extent and systematic nature of interventions, provisions and focus, the ways in which criminal activity, drug testing and criminal justice interventions are presented as connected suggests a significant official recognition of the prevalence of illicit drug use as a everyday occurrence and social norm.

Reasonably critics of my argument here (and of the development of DIP for that matter) will point to the relatively small number of individuals in treatment or indeed the limited capacity of the proposed system of interventions to deal with the actuality of drug use. This is all true and reasonable but, I would contend, simply provides further support for my assertion that policy and policy responses can be read as cultural discourses that alert us to the ongoing social construction of drug use as a problematic and as crime and drugs locked in a direct causal relationship.

But, perhaps, it all goes further in terms of how prolific State action serves to define, redefine and then present notions of problems, their severity and actuality, to the public and society in general (as we can see historically, for example, Terry 1931; Beveridge and Edwards 1981; Beveridge 1989). Furthermore, in some senses, it might be argued, the government appears to conceptualise drug use amongst 'criminals' as 'normal' or at least the norm and the close and straightforward relationship between crime and drug use is pretty much uncontested. If, as noted earlier in this chapter, it is the case that public policies reflect varying and particular definitions or conceptualisations of social problems, it is reasonable to suggest that the current extensive and totalising response not only fits with the current trend towards the systematic extension of mechanisms of state monitoring, surveillance and control, but also reflects an implicit (if not explicit) sense of drug use as normalised. There is a sense that the policy developments reflect government concerns and perceptions amongst the public that drug use is commonplace and dangerous. But in addition the shift to such systemic responses also underlies the possible shift to normalisation and adds to the sense that normalisation has taken place.

Notes

1 See website: www.talktofrank.com/.
2 See website: www.drugs.gov.uk/drug-interventions-programme/strategy
3 The National Treatment Agency is a special health authority within the National Health Service established in 2001 to co-ordinate health responses to drug use issues and, in particular, to improve the availability, capacity and effectiveness of drug misuse treatment in the UK.
4 See for example, SMART CJS in the Thames Valley at website: www.smartcjs.org. uk
5 This might include burglary, theft and vehicle crime.

References and suggested reading

Advisory Council on the Misuse of Drugs (1988) *Aids and Drug Misuse: Part 1*. London: HMSO.

Advisory Council on the Misuse of Drugs (1994) *Drug Misusers and the Criminal Justice System, Part 2: Police, Drug Misusers and the Community*. London: HMSO.

Aldridge, J., Parker, H. and Measham, F. (1999) *Drug Trying and Drug Use Across Adolescence: A Longitudinal Study of Young People's Drug Taking in Two Regions of Northern England*. London: DPAS.

Audit Commission (2002) *Changing Habits: The Commissioning and Management of Community Drug Treatment Services for Adults*. Wetherby: Audit Commission.

Bean, P. (1994) 'Drugs and Crime: An Overview', *Drugs, Education, Prevention and Policy*, 1: 93–99.

Bean, P. (2004a) 'Linking Treatment Services to the Criminal Justice System', in P. Bean and T. Nemitz, (eds) *Drug Treatment: What Works?*, pp 219–235. London: Routledge.

Bean, P. (2004b) *Drugs and Crime* (2nd edn). Cullompton: Willan Publishing.

Bean, P. and Nemitz, T. (eds) (2004c) *Drug Treatment: What Works?* London: Routledge.

Bennett, T. (1998), *Drugs and Crime: The Results of Research on Drug Testing and Interviewing Arrestees*. London: Home Office.

Bennett, T. (2000) *Drugs and Crime: The Results of the Second Developmental Stage of the NEW-ADAM Programme*, Home Office Research Study 205. London: Home Office.

Bernhaut, J. and Peters, K. (2006) *Problem Drug Use in the South East*. Oxford: South East Public Health Observatory.

Berridge, V. (1979) 'Morality and Medical Science: Concepts of Narcotic Addiciton in Britain, 1820–1926', *Annals of Science*, 36: 67–85.

Berridge, V. (1984) 'Drugs and Social Policy: The Establishment of Drug Control in Britain 1900–1930', *British Journal of Addiction*, 79: 17–29.

Berridge, V. (1993) 'AIDS and British Drug Policy: Continuity or Change?', in V. Berridge and P. Strang (eds) *AIDS and Contemporary History*, pp 135–156. Cambridge: Cambridge University Press.

Berridge, V. (1996) 'European Drug Policy: The Need for Historical Perspectives', *European Addiction Research*, 2, (4): 219–225.

Berridge, V. (1999) *Opium and the People: Opiate Use and Drug Control Policy on Nineteenth and Early Twentieth Century England* (rev. edn). London: Free Association Books.

Berridge, V. and Edwards, G. (1981) *Opium and the People: Opiate Use and Drug Control Policy on Nineteenth and Early Twentieth Century England*. London: Allen Lane.

Beynon, C., Bellis, M., Millar, T., Meier, O,. Thomson, R. and Mackway Jones, K. (2001) 'Hidden Need for Drug Treatment Services: Measuring Levels of Problematic Drug Use in the North West of England', *Journal of Public Health Medicine*, 23 (4): 286–291.

Buchanan, J. and Young, L. (2000) 'The War on Drugs – A War On Drug Users?', *Drugs: Education, Prevention and Policy*, 7 (4): 409–422.

Carnwarth, T. and Smith, I. (2002) *Heroin Century*. London: Routledge.

Chatterton, P. and Hollands, R. (2003) *Urban Nightscapes: Youth Cultures, Pleasure Spaces and Corporate Power*. London: Routledge.

Christie, N. (2004) *A Suitable Amount of Crime:* London: Routledge.

Clark, T. (2002) 'New Labour's Big Idea: Joined-up Government', *Social Policy and Society*, 1 (2): 107–117.

Courtwright, D.T. (1982) *Dark Paradise: Opiate Addiction in America Before 1940*. Cambridge, MA: Harvard University Press.

Courtwright, D.T. (2001) *Forces of Habit: Drugs and the Making of the Modern World*. Cambridge, MA: Harvard University Press.

Davis, J. and Ditton, J. (1990) 'The 1990s: Decade of the Stimulants?', *British Journal of Addiction*, 85: 811–813.

Department for Education and Skills (2004) *Drugs: Guidance for Schools*. Nottingham: DfES.

Department of Health (1995) *Tackling Drugs Together: A Strategy for England 1995–1998*. London: HMSO.

Dorn, N. (1994) 'Three Faces of Police Referral: Welfare, Justice and Business Perspectives on Multi-Agency Work with Drug Arrestees', *Policing and Society*, 4: 13–34.

Dorn, N. and South, N. (eds) (1987) *A Land Fit for Heroin? Drug Policies, Prevention and Practice*. London: MacMillan.

DPAS (1999) *Drugs Interventions in the Criminal Justice System: Guidance Manual*. London: DPAS.

Edmunds, M., May, T., Hough, M. and Hearnden, I. (1998) *Arrest Referral: Emerging Lessons from Research*, Drugs Prevention Initiative Paper 23. London: Home Office.

Edmunds, M., Hough, M., Turnball, P.J. and May, T. (1999) *Doing Justice to Treatment: Referring Offenders to Drug Services*, DPAS, Paper 2. London: Home Office.

EMCDDA (2005) *Illicit Drug Use in the EU: Legislative Approaches*. Lisbon: EMCDDA.

Estrada, E. (2004) 'The Transformation of the Politics of Crime in High Crime Societies', *European Journal of Criminology*, 1 (4).

European Commission (2006) *Green Paper on the Role of Civil Society in Drugs Policy in the European Union*, (COM 92006), 316 Final. Brussels: Commission of the European Communities.

Ferrell, J. (1999) 'Cultural Criminology', *Annual Review of Sociology*, 25: 395–418.

Ferrell, J. and Hamm, M. (eds), (1998) *Ethnography at the Edge: Crime, Deviance and Field Research*. Boston: Northeastern University Press.

Ferrell, J. and Sanders, C. (eds) (1995) *Cultural Criminology*. Boston: Northeastern University.

Ferrell, J. and Websdale, N. (eds) (1999), *Making Trouble: Cultural Constructions of Crime, Deviance and Control*. New York: Aldine De Gruyter.

Garland, D. (1997) '"Governmentality" and the Problem of Crime', *Theoretical Criminology*, 1 (2): 173–194.

Garland, D. (2000) 'The Culture of High Crime Societies', *British Journal of Criminology*, 40: 347–375.

Garland, D. (2001) *The Culture of Control: Crime and Social Order in Contemporary Society*. Oxford: Oxford University Press.

Girling, E., Loader, I. and Sparks, R. (2000) *Crime and Social Change in Middle England: Questions of Order in an English Town.* London: Routledge.

Godfrey, C., Eaton, G., McDougall, C. and Culyer, A. (2002) *The Economic and Social Costs of Class A Drug Use in England and Wales, 2000,* Home Office Research Study 249. London: Home Office.

Gossop, M. (2000) *Living With Drugs* (5th edn). London: Ashgate.

Gourley, M. (2004) 'A Subcultural Study of Recreational Ecstasy Use', *The Australian Sociological Association,* 40 (1): 59–73.

Guilianotti, R. (1997) 'Drugs and the Media in the Era of Postmodernity: An Archaeological Analysis', *Media, Culture and Society,* 19 (3): 413–439.

Hammersley, R., Khan, F. and Ditton, J. (2002) *Ecstasy and the Rise of the Chemical Generation.* London: Routledge.

HM Government (1995) *Tackling Drugs Together: A Strategy for England 1995–1998.* London: HMSO.

HMSO (1985) *Tackling Drug Misuse.* London: HMSO.

HMSO (2005) *The Drugs Act 2005.* London: HMSO.

Holloway, K., Bennett, T. and Farrington, D. (2005) *The Effectiveness of Criminal Justice and Treatment Programmes in Reducing Drug-Related Crime: A Systematic Review.* London: Home Office.

Home Office Drugs Prevention Advisory Service (1999) *Drugs Interventions in the Criminal Justice System: A Guidance Manual.* London: Home Office.

Home Office Drugs Strategy Directorate (2002) *Updated Drug Strategy 2002.* London: Home Office.

Home Office Drugs Strategy Directorate (2004) *Tackling Drugs: Changing Lives: Keeping Communities Safe From Drugs.* London: Home Office.

Home Office (2006) *Operational Process Guidance for Implementation of Testing on Arrest, Required Assessment and Restriction on Bail, Final Guidance.* Home Office: London.

Hough, M. (1996) *Drug Users ad the Criminal Justice System: A Review of the Literature,* Drugs Prevention Initiative Paper 15. London: Home Office.

Huggins, R. (2006) 'The Addict's Body: Addiction, Embodiment and Drug Use', in D. Waskul and P. Vannini (eds) *Body/Embodiment: Symbolic Interaction and the Sociology of the Body,* pp 165–180. London: Ashgate.

Inciardi, J. and Harrison, L. (eds) (1998) *Heroin in the Age of Crack-Cocaine.* Thousand Oaks, California: Sage.

Jackson, P. (2004) *Inside Clubbing: Sensual Experiments in the Art of Being Human.* Oxford: Berg.

Kothari, G., Marsden, J. and Strang, J. (2002) 'Opportunities and Obstacles for Effective Treatment of Drug Misusers in the Criminal Justice System in England and Wales', *British Journal of Criminology,* 42: 412–432.

Lalander, P. (2003) *Hooked on Heroin: Drugs and Drifters in a Globalized World.* Oxford: Berg.

Levinthal, C.F. (1985) 'Milk of Paradise/Milk of Hell – The History of Ideas About Opium', *Perspectives in Biology and Medicine,* 28 (4): 561–577.

Lewis, R., Hartnol, R., Bryer, S., Daviaud, E. and Mitcheson, M. (1985) 'Scoring Smack: The Illicit Heroin Market in London, 1980–83', *British Journal of Addiction,* 80: 281–290.

MacDonald, Z. (1999) 'Illicit Drug Use in the UK: Evidence from the British Crime Survey', *British Journal of Criminology,* 39 (4): 585–603.

MacGregor, S. (1999) 'Medicine, Custom and Moral Fibre: Policy Responses to Drug Misuse', in N. South (ed.) *Drugs: Cultures, Controls & Everyday Life,* pp 67–85. London: Sage.

Manning, P. (2006) 'There's No Glamour in Glue: News and the Symbolic Framing of Substance Misuse', *Crime, Media, Culture,* 2 (1): 49–66.

Measham, F. (2004) 'Drug and Alcohol Research: The Case for Cultural Criminology', in J. Ferrell, K. Hayward, W. Morrison and M. Presdee (eds) *Cultural Criminology Unleashed,* pp 207–218.London: Glasshouse Press.

Measham, F, Newcombe, R. and Parker, H. (1994) 'The Normalization of Recreational Drug Use amongst Young People in North-West England', *British Journal of Sociology,* 45 (2): 287–312.

Oreton, J., Hunter, G., Hickmman, M., Morgan, D., Turnbull, P., Kothari, G. and Marsden, J. (2003) 'Arrest Referral in London Police Stations: Characteristics of the First Year. A Key Point of Intervention for Drug Users?', *Drugs: Education, Prevention and Policy,* 10 (1): 73–85.

O'Shea, J. and Powis, B. (2003) *Drug Arrest Referral Schemes: A Case Study of Good Practice.* London: Home Office.

Parker, H. (2004) 'The New Drugs Interventions Industry: What Outcomes Can Drugs/ Criminal Justice Treatment Programmes Realistically Deliver?', *Probation Journal,* 51 (4): 379–386.

Parker, H., Aldridge, J. and Measham, F. (1998) *Illegal Leisure: The Normalization of Adolescent Drug Use.* London: Routledge.

Parker, H. and Newcombe, R. (1987) 'Heroin Use and Acquisitive Crime in an English Community', *British Journal of Sociology,* 38 (3): 331–350.

Parker, H., Newcombe, R. and Bakx, K. (1988) *Living with Heroin.* Milton Keynes: Open University.

Parker, H., Bury, C. and Egginton, R. (1998) *New Heroin Outbreaks Amongst Young People in England and Wales,* Home Office, Crime Detection and Prevention Series, Paper 92. London: Home Office.

Parker, H., Williams, L. and Aldridge, J. (2002) 'The Normalization of "Sensible" Recreational Drug Use: Further Evidence from the North West England Longitudinal Study', *Sociology,* 36 (4): 941–964.

Parssinen, T. (1983) *Secret Passions, Secret Remedies: Narcotic Drugs in British Society, 1820–1830.* Manchester: Manchester University Press.

Presdee, M. (2000) *Cultural Criminology and the Carnival of Crime.* London: Routledge.

President of the Council (1998) *Tackling Drugs to Build a Better Britain: The Government's Ten-Year Strategy for Tackling Drug Misuse.* London: Home Office.

Robertson, J. (1987) *Heroin, AIDS and Society.* London: Hodder and Stoughton.

Rose, N. (2000) 'Government and Control', *British Journal of Criminology,* 40: 321–339.

Ruggiero, V. and South, N. (1995) *Eurodrugs: Drug Use, Markets and Trafficking in Europe.* London: University College Press.

Rumgay, J. (2003) 'Drug Treatment and Offender Rehabilitation: Reflections on Evidence, Effectiveness and Exclusion', *Probation Journal,* 50 (1): 41–51.

Sanders, B. (2005) 'In the Club: Ecstasy Use and Supply in a London Nightclub', *Sociology,* 39 (2): 241–258.

Seddon, T. (2000) 'Explaining the Drug-Crime Link: Theoretical, Policy and Research Issues', *Journal of Social Policy,* 29 (1): 95–107.

Shiner, M. and Newburn, T. (1997) 'Definitely, Maybe Not? The Normalization of Recreational Drug Use amongst Young People', *Sociology,* 31 (3): 511–529.

Shiner, M. and Newburn, T. (1999) 'Taking Tea with Noel: The Place and Meaning of Drug Use in Everyday Life', in N. South, N (ed) *Drugs: Cultures, Controls & Everyday Life,* pp 139–159. London: Sage.

Simpson, M. (2003) 'The Relationship Between Drug Use and Crime: A Puzzle Inside an Enigma', *International Journal of Drug Policy,* 14: 307–319.

Sondhi, A., O'Shea, J. and Williams, T. (2002) *Arrest Referral: Emerging Findings from the National Monitoring and Evaluation Programme*, DPAS Series Paper 18. London: Home Office.

Sondhi, A. and Huggins, R. (2005) 'Towards and Effective Case Management Model for Arrest Referral: Implications for Criminal Justice Interventions for Problem Drug Users', *Drugs Policy, Prevention and Education*, 12.

Sonnedeciler, G. (1962) 'Emergence of the Concept of Opium Addiction', *Journal of Mondiale Pharmacie*, 3 (11): 275–290.

South, N. (1999) 'Debating Drugs and Everyday Life: Normalisation, Prohibition and "Otherness"', in N. South, (ed) *Drugs: Cultures, Controls & Everyday Life*, pp 1–16. London: Sage.

Stimson, G.V. (2000) 'Blair Declares War: The Unhealthy State of British Drug Policy', *International Journal of Drug Policy*, 11: 259–264.

Terry, C.E. (1931) 'The Development and Causes of Opium Addiction as a Social Problem', *Journal of Educational Sociology*, 4 (6): 335–346.

Webster, R., Goodman, M. and Whalley, G. (2002) *Safer Clubbing: Guidance for Licensing Authorities, Club Managers and Promoters*. London: DPAS.

Zinberg, N.E. (1984) *Drug, Set and Setting: The Basis for Controlled Intoxicant Use*. New Haven, CT: Yale University Press.

Index

Added to a page number 'f' denotes a figure and 't' denotes a table.